Reprints of Economic Classics

THE INDUSTRIAL SYSTEM

Also published in

Reprints of Economic Classics

by John A. Hobson

International Trade [1904]
Veblen [1936]
Work and Wealth [1914]

THE

INDUSTRIAL

SYSTEM

AN INQUIRY INTO

EARNED AND UNEARNED INCOME

[1909]

BY

JOHN A. HOBSON

WITH AN INTRODUCTION BY

ARTHUR LOEB BEKENSTEIN

REPRINTS OF ECONOMIC CLASSICS

AUGUSTUS M. KELLEY · PUBLISHERS
NEW YORK 1969

First Edition 1909
New and Revised Edition 1910
(London: Longmans, Green & Co.,
39 Paternoster Row, 1910)

Reprinted 1969 by
Augustus M. Kelley • Publishers
New York New York 10010
By Arrangement with GEORGE ALLEN & UNWIN LTD.

SBN 678 00537 0

Library of Congress Catalogue Card Number
66–21676

PRINTED IN THE UNITED STATES OF AMERICA
by SENTRY PRESS, NEW YORK, N. Y. 10019

INTRODUCTION

The history of thought in any discipline is sprinkled with cases of obscure pioneers whose work was so far in advance of their time that it left little mark and was largely forgotten. Those engaged in intellectual detective work may rediscover them, but their interest is limited to an audience of specialist scholars. While it may seem fair to give these original thinkers belated recognition, still there is no gainsaying the fact that their work had little important impact on the development of the discipline. On the other hand, there are those rare pioneers whose contributions despite opposition and heavy criticism from traditionalist ranks change the thinking of their own generation and the generations which follow.

John A. Hobson (1858-1940), whose name is bound up with the underconsumption theory of business cycles, was without question the latter kind of ground-breaking thinker and certainly his insights were opposed with a bitterness similar to that aimed at the Copernican theory centuries before. He was the most important heterodox British economist of his time. His highly active and prolific career, beginning in the 1880's, spanned more than half a century. In terms of influence, his role was analogous to that of his American contemporary, Thorstein Veblen, and his basic work, also like that of Veblen, has a remarkable relevance to many of the serious problems of today.

While Hobson has been generally classified as an economist, this description insufficiently conveys the breadth of his interests. The reading of his memoir, *Confessions of an Economic Heretic*, gives the impression that in his own mind he viewed himself as primarily the dedicated reformer and exponent of a humanistic social philosophy in the tradition of John Ruskin, even before his role as economist.

Hobson's career from early youth until zenith in the Great Depression period just before his death in 1940 was marked by paradox. Nothing in his family and social background seemed to provide fertile soil for the development of an economic heretic and social reformer. In his own colorful words, he described his early years as "cast in the calmest and most self-confident years of a Mid-Victorian era, when peace, prosperity, and progress appeared to be the permanent possession of most civilized nations. Born and bred in the middle stratum of the middle class of a middle-sized industrial town of the Midlands, I was favorably situated for a complacent acceptance of the existing social order."[1]

His four years at Oxford were devoted mainly to the literary, historical and philosophical studies of Latin and Greek civilizations. Then in his mid-twenties he was drawn to the humanistic philosophy of Ruskin. This was a turning point, for it marked the beginning of his life long interest in economics as a primary instrument for reform of the social order. This direction of his career was further strengthened by a number of long and rewarding friendships with social reformers of similar leanings. Among these were the sociologist, L. T. Hobhouse, Ramsay MacDonald (who later became the first Labor Party Prime Minister) and the political scientist, Graham Wallas, one of the Fabian Society founders.

Very early in his career Hobson manifested deep concern with the problems of poverty and social justice. At first he sought for remedies in orthodox economic doctrine, but he found the search fruitless. In the late eighties, however, he came to know an imaginative businessman and famed mountain climber, A. F. Mummery, who was, in Hobson's words, a "mental climber as well, with a natural zest for a path of his own finding and a sublime disregard of intellectual authority."[2] Mummery's key argument was that over-saving creates excess productive capacity and this is the most important cause of unemployment of capital and labor. Hobson became convinced of the soundness of these ideas, and joined Mummery in preparing a volume elaborating the oversaving, under-consumption thesis: *The Physiology of Industry* (1889).

The reaction to the book amongst academic economists, almost without exception, was adverse and henceforth Hobson bore the permanent label of heretic outside the pale. The underconsumption thesis was either summarily dismissed as a long exploded fallacy, betraying an ignorance of the first principles of economic science; or ignored as unworthy of comment. An immediate result of this hostile reception was that authorities at London University who had just appointed Hobson Extension Lecturer on Literature and Economics, refused to permit him to teach political economy and confined him to instruction in literature. Hobson was never fully forgiven by the orthodox members of his profession. Despite the growing influence of his subsequent works and his association with important political and intellectual figures, no academic post in eco-

---

[1] *Confessions of an Economic Heretic* (New York: Macmillan, 1938) p. 15.
[2] *Ibid.,* p. 30.

nomics was offered to him; and when, in the 1930's, his ideas had finally achieved a degree of respectability and recognition, he was well into his seventies and close to the end of his life.

Shut off from an academic career as an economist, Hobson devoted himself to journalism as his main means of livelihood. In addition, he published a large number of books, many of which had substantial sales, and he lectured extensively both in England and the United States.

Hobson spoke of the Boer War as having been another turning point in his life. Writing at the time for the influential, liberal periodical, *The Contemporary Review,* he attacked the war severely as ruthless, economic imperialism. This association with the anti-imperialists and pacifists marked the first instance that he was active in a specific political movement. Later, during World War I, he stoutly reaffirmed his pacifist views.

From the turn of the century onward, Hobson made frequent and extended visits to the United States and Canada. While academic economics in Britain during the 1920's presented an almost unbroken neo-classical stance, nevertheless, the institutionalist views of Veblen, John R. Commons, Wesley C. Mitchell and Walton H. Hamilton were receiving respectful hearings. Also in the United States a growing and diverse group of economists now recognized the far reaching problems posed by under-consumption phenomena, and were devoting increasing efforts to the search for solutions. This group included N. A. L. J. Johannsen, J. M. Clark, the team of William T. Foster and Waddill Catchings, and Monsignor John Ryan, the latter openly proclaiming himself a follower of Hobson.[3]

There are three keystones basic to Hobson's economic thinking. The first, which has already been mentioned, was the over-saving-underconsumption theory. Briefly he held that in an advanced industrial society an essential requirement of the economy is a "right ratio" between savings-investment and demand-consumption. Such was the institution of capitalism that there was a tendency during periods of prosperity for business profits to rise much more sharply than wages. Thus extra funds were placed in the hands of the wealthy, which far exceeded their expenditures for consumption. This excess was channelled into additional investment which in turn raised productive capacity. The wage-earning classes, who spend most of their income for consumer goods, did not have sufficient

---

[3] On Hobson's role in American economic thought, see Joseph Dorfman, *The Economic Mind in American Civilization,* 5 volumes (New York: Viking, 1946-1959) III, pp. 253-254, 329, 345, 355-356, 413; IV, pp. 107, 174-175, 261, 335, 341; V, pp. 405, 440, 549, 571, 573, 641, 659.

funds to absorb the increased output made possible by increased productive capacity. The resulting glut of consumer goods led to decisions by management to shut down productive facilities until the oversupply could be absorbed. These shutdowns created unemployment and a further decline in the ability of the wage-earning groups to purchase consumer goods. The vicious cycle of oversupply triggering lay-offs, etc., snowballed downward to depression. At the bottom point of depression, profits are almost wiped out and the imbalance between investment and consumption which existed at the height of prosperity is in the reverse direction in that investment is practically at a standstill while consumption, though reduced to essentials, continues at a lower level.

Having formed his basic thinking on oversaving in his earliest work, Hobson sought an explanation of why these disproportions occur. It was in propounding an answer to this question, that he came upon the second keystone of his economic thinking: the inequalities in the distribution of income between the wealthy and the wage earners are due in large part to inequalities in bargaining, which are a normal tendency of capitalistic industrial organization. The main ways in which to redress the inequalities in bargaining power are government intervention (both by regulation and taxation), strong trade unions, or both. Here, as in so much of Hobson's analyses, there is the notion of the need for a proper balance. This applied not only to relations between employer and employees, but also between all factors of production. Such balance was necessary for progress. "[W]e see in trade unionism, as in the larger labour movement of which it forms a part, an endeavour to secure a better and more fruitful distribution of the surplus by getting a larger share for labour at the expense of the other factors. Industrial progress in any given state of civilization requires, as a first charge upon the surplus product, that it shall be so used as to evoke and nourish increased and improved powers in the several factors of production. If land takes too much, capital and labour are both starved, and progress is correspondingly retarded. If capital or ability takes too much and labour not enough, industrial progress continues to lag, for the healthy march of industry requires a proportionate advance of all the factors."[4]

The third of what Hobson called his great heresies and which, in a broader view, we characterize as a main theme was his insistence on the translation of economic goals into humanist or welfare terms. In his treatment of the two other main themes—underconsumption and inequalities in the distribution of wealth and income—his basic

[4] See below p. 215.

analysis showed little change over the five decades of his career. For example, the underconsumption theory introduced in *The Physiology of Industry* in 1889 is practically repeated in his *Confessions of an Economic Heretic* of 1938. But this was not true to the same extent of his welfare economics. In his earlier works, including the volume reprinted below, his thinking was still tied to quantitative considerations. Thus in *The Industrial System,* his theory of welfare is not very different from that found in *Wealth and Welfare* (1912) by the liberal neo-classicist A. C. Pigou of Cambridge University.[5] Following World War I, however, Hobson became increasingly impatient with the growing cults of mathematical and quantity theory monetary economics. At the same time, he insisted upon retention of the broader based conception "political economy" rather than the more restricted term "economics." Thus during the Great Depression, Hobson's interpretation of welfare had become more closely akin to that of such socialist-oriented thinkers as R. H. Tawney, Harold Laski and the younger Fabians. Recalling Hobson's grounding in the humanist philosophy of Ruskin, in some sense we see that his thinking in this area had come full circle. In his *Work and Wealth,* published in 1914, and revised in 1933, while still warmly loyal to Ruskin's main thesis that "there is no wealth but life," he restricted himself to a conception of welfare that could be quantified in monetary terms. But in his writings of the middle and late 30's, he had largely abandoned the idea that the welfare of either the individual or society could be stated in anything other than philosophical terms.

Unlike such other leading heterodox economists, as Thorstein Veblen, John R. Commons and Werner Sombart, Hobson made no effort to create a new terminology, nor for the most part did he reach far afield into other disciplines. While he recognized the interdependency of politics, law, sociology and economics, he accepted to a greater degree the validity of the traditional distinctions between the disciplines than did the aforementioned thinkers. It may be that this acceptance of the conventional framework explains in part the intensity of his rejection by the followers of the standard economics. In effect he was from their viewpoint a traitor to his own intellectual class. Perhaps his contemporaries in the academic world would have been less outraged if such heresies had come from one outside the discipline.

A further factor in his rejection by the orthodox economists was that his criticisms of the capitalist system were seized upon by doc-

---

[5] The revised version of Pigou's treatise was called *The Economics of Welfare,* (1920).

trinaire socialists and Marxist groups as proof of the self-destruction inherent in the system. This use, however, was a distortion, for Hobson was just as much a maverick toward socialist orthodoxies as he was in his attitudes toward neo-classical economic theory. To him "the dictatorship of the proletariat" was no less wrong than dictatorship by the state or dictatorship by the captains of finance. Hobson rejected all institutional arrangements which might give unequal bargaining power to any interest—political, economic, or social. As a radical reformer rather than a revolutionary, he believed that the main object of social action was to strengthen the weak and control the strong. Basically the approach was pragmatic. Moreover, to protect personal freedom, controls should be flexible and kept at a minimum.

An interesting example of Hobson's objection to rigid utopian schemes was his criticism of Henry George's famous "single tax" doctrine. George held that a tax on land to expropriate the so-called "unearned increment"—rent—would correct most of the ills of the modern industrial civilization. Hobson viewed this position as far too narrow and over-simplified. He argued that similar unearned increments (or "surpluses" in his terminology) were derived from the other factors of production as well. Therefore a tax policy to be equitable should be aimed at all such windfalls regardless of source.

This argument was especially important as it pertained to interest theory and was closely bound up with his over-investment theory of depression. If a major portion of the return on investment was, as Hobson alleged, a windfall, then both the orthodox Ricardian theory and the later dominant marginal theory of interest were invalid. In marginal analysis the rate of interest was the pecuniary expression of the marginal productivity of capital and therefore served as an automatic regulator of the flow of investment funds. Hobson contended that this thesis did not fit the facts of modern capitalist economies. For the rich there was no "pain-cost" involved in saving. Since their incomes were far in excess of their consumption expenditures, a rise in the rate of interest provided no incentive for them to increase savings, nor did a fall induce them to spend more for consumption. (This attack was strongly resented by the orthodox economists and further served to point up the gulf between them.)

The course of economic development in the half century since the original publication of *The Industrial System* (1909) has, in the main, decided the argument in Hobson's favor. No modern state would seriously consider allowing interest rates or the flow of investment funds to fluctuate without substantial intervention or controls to keep such fluctuations within reasonable limits. Of constant concern to today's policy makers is sustainable growth. This has become one of the basic measures of a nation's economic health. The key word here is "sustainable," which, after all, is what Hobson meant by balance. Thus, a sudden spurt of investment in the developed industrial nations is usually viewed with alarm; because it is feared it may not be sustainable, or, in Hobson's terminology, over-investment is occurring. On the other hand, if the growth rate is low, policy makers will normally intervene to provide stimulation.

Another strikingly modern note in Hobson's writings was his emphasis and treatment of the problem of poverty. His approach was non-Malthusian and infused with the optimistic thesis that the advances of the Industrial Revolution had placed in man's hands for the first time the means to eliminate poverty. Once again his solution was couched in terms of redressing the inequalities in bargaining power through the formation of labor unions, use of the taxing power and greater regulation of industry by the state.

Previously we touched upon the reasons why Hobson's work was for the most part rejected or ignored by the academic economists. Nevertheless by the last decade of his life this situation had been reversed and he received widespread recognition by the profession —including many of its most illustrious members. To assess his influence it is useful to explore how this came about.

The break through probably began with the publication in 1913 of Mitchell's *Business Cycles*. Here for the first time Hobson's under-consumption-overproduction theory was taken seriously by an outstanding academician. Although Mitchell (who consistently through his career held to a plural cause theory of cycles)[6] disagreed with Hobson's position as being too limited, still he accorded the thesis respectful and careful treatment.

Over the next two decades, business cycles became an increasingly important area for investigation. This area gained recognition as a separate, major specialty; it quickly attracted able people; and a substantial body of literature was produced. The various theories of the cause of depression were generally grouped under their main headings: (1) natural causes, i.e., weather, sun spots, etc.; (2) monetary, e.g., the quantity theory such as Irving Fisher's

---

[6] "You are no doubt right in seeking the cause of business cycles in a plurality of agencies—avoiding the fallacy of simplicity." (F. Y. Edgeworth to W. C. Mitchell, July 27, 1914, in Mitchell Papers in Special Collections, Columbia University Libraries).

version; (3) the various overproduction theories. Hobson's views belonged to the third group. In the textbooks of the 1920's nearly every list of the theories of depression contained Hobson's under-consumption-over-investment thesis, although in the prosperous, sanguine atmosphere of the '20's the warnings inherent in his position attracted few adherents. But then radical reforms seldom appeal except when a society is faced with crisis.

In the boom period of the 1920's economic disaster seemed increasingly remote. A cross section of bankers, businessmen, government officials, and economists would have found most in agreement that major depressions were likely a thing of the past, especially so far as the United States was concerned. Their reasoning was: the creation of the Federal Reserve System in 1913 had eliminated the threat of the money panics which had plagued the nation so often in the past; advances in science and technology were providing ways for combatting, or at least alleviating, the effects of natural disasters on agricultural production. And, as to the pessimistic views of underconsumption theory, they answered that conditions had so changed that widespread, severe, over-production was now unlikely; this latter position was particularly prevalent in the United States. The doctrine, went the argument, might have been valid under the low wage conditions which existed in the late nineteenth century (when Hobson first enunciated it); but the current high wages in America insured an adequate level of demand for goods. As a result of this thinking, business cycle theorists devoted less attention to fundamental causes, and more to such matters as technological unemployment, refinement of statistical techniques and use of monetary tools to smooth out changes in the level of prices.

Then came 1929, the stock market crash; and by the end of 1930 the United States, Britain and most of the world was plunged into the worst depression of modern times. The unbelievable had happened! The sanguine attitudes of the 20's seemed suddenly meaningless. After the first shock of realization, there followed a frantic search for explanation. At hand was a wide array of radical doctrines each of which gained small groups of adherents, but for non-Marxist thinkers the underconsumption theory of Hobson seemed to offer the most reasoned approach. By the middle of the decade, such leading business cycle theorists as J. M. Keynes in England and A. Hansen in the United States, who had strongly opposed Hobson only a few years before, had reversed their position and embraced an overproduction theory very close to Hobson's. The Full Employment Act of 1946 in the United States is an outstanding proof of how widely the underconsumption doctrine has been accepted; the wording of the first paragraph of the Act reads as if it might have been written by him.

Despite the widespread acceptance of his explanation of the cause of depression, his proposals for their prevention, because they struck at the fundamental institutions governing the distribution of income, found much harder going. Nevertheless, a comparison of the recommendations in *The Industrial System* written before World War I with the New Deal and Fair Deal legislation of the 1930's and 1940's in the United States and the post World War II welfare state measures in Great Britain strikingly reveals how much of the "mixed economy" of today he anticipated. In the 30's the fearful problem of depression pervaded almost all economic thought. Thus it was only natural that Hobson's reputation was mainly based on his underconsumption theory. While this was understandable, it unfortunately has caused other portions of Hobson's work which are most relevant today to be passed over. Yet Hobson in some sense is more of today than he was of his own time. Indeed *The Industrial System,* along with his other works, is although he did not consciously intend it as such roughly a blueprint of the present industrial systems of the English speaking nations.

ARTHUR LOEB BEKENSTEIN

New York City
November, 1968

THE   INDUSTRIAL   SYSTEM

THE

INDUSTRIAL SYSTEM

AN INQUIRY INTO

EARNED AND UNEARNED INCOME

BY

J. A. HOBSON

AUTHOR OF 'THE EVOLUTION OF MODERN CAPITALISM,' ETC.

NEW AND REVISED EDITION

LONGMANS, GREEN & CO.
39, PATERNOSTER ROW
LONDON
1910

PREFACE

IT may fairly be claimed of anyone who puts forth a volume with so comprehensive a title, that he shall present in his Preface a *prima facie* case for his claim that it shall be read. Perhaps the best way of doing this is to explain how and why it came to be written. As a student of those economic writings which professed to set forth the general principles of modern industry, I failed to find any consistent and convincing exposition of the methods by which wealth, the product of industry, was distributed among the owners of the several factors of production. After one or two unsatisfactory attempts to formulate an independent theory of distribution by correlating the accepted laws of rent, wages, and interest, I came to the conclusion that the proper way to understand how wealth was distributed was to study the various sorts of acts of distribution, i.e. the payments actually made to owners of labour, ability, land, and capital, in the different processes of industry. This involves as a preliminary the construction of an image of the actual concrete system of industry. With this object in view, in the opening chapters of this book I have endeavoured to describe, first, the structure of the various types of business; then their grouping in a trade; next, the relations of a trade to the trades which precede it or succeed it in a stream of industrial and commercial processes converting raw materials into final commodities; and finally, the contacts which these several streams of industry have with one another by drawing upon common sources of material and power and by supplying wants related by sympathy or opposition in standards of consumption. In other words, I have sought to give a true outline picture of the industrial system of the present day as a single organic whole, continuously engaged in converting raw materials into commodities, and apportioning them by a continuous series of payments as incomes to the owners of the factors of production in the different processes.

This continuous distribution of the products is achieved by a number of detailed money prices paid to workers, capitalists, landowners, *entrepreneurs*, for productive services rendered, and each payment evokes a fresh application of productive power. The primary effect of this distribution of wealth is to cause the different factors of production to dispose themselves in the appropriate forms and quantities throughout the industrial system, and to give out their full productive power in regular response to the stimuli of payments.

If we were justified in holding that the whole of the product of industry was thus regularly and automatically absorbed in the payments necessary to evoke from the owners of the factors the output of this productive energy, no problem of distribution would arise. Such has in effect been the assumption underlying the main body of authoritative economic theory in this and other countries. Competitive industry, it was held, actually apportions the product among the various classes of producers according to the respective importance of the services they render, and such portions are normally the minimum payments required to secure these services. To this ' law ' there has been one exception and one qualification. The economic rent of land, the payment made to land-owners as such, though usually justified on other grounds, political or economic, was never regarded as a payment necessary to evoke the use of land. This was the exception. The qualification consisted in recognising some ' friction ' or failure in the complete fluidity of competition in the other factors of production, causing a certain quantity of waste in the application of the stimuli to production. But normally, it was held, distribution took place by means of a number of minimum payments necessary to evoke the continued use of labour, capital, and ability, while the ' rent ' paid to land-owners was not a deduction from the proper and economically necessary share of any class of producers, but a ' surplus.' So long as no serious attempt was made to regard industry as a single living system, some plausibility attached to this view, which was enforced by the statement of separate laws regulating the payment of labour, capital, ability, and enterprise.

The criticism poured from various quarters upon this rigorous *laissez faire* theory was usually vitiated by the same ' separatist ' treatment, the same failure to realise an industrial system in which production and distribution are continuous and inseparable processes. The conception of a ' surplus,' to the recognition of which Ricardo in this country had given the sharpest emphasis, gave rise to several conflicting theories of distribution. A ' land ' school of economists arose, who argued that while competition works well enough in the relations of capital and labour, the private possession of land enables its owners to take as their surplus the whole of the growing product of industry beyond the minimum payment required to maintain labour and capital in the present state of productive efficiency. A 'socialist' school claimed that employers took this surplus as fast as it was produced by labour, keeping most of it as 'unearned' profits and interest, and handing the rest to land-owners as rent. A third variation in what is essentially the same separatist analysis, presented most effectively by General Walker, contended that after capital and ability had been paid their necessary minimum rewards the main body of the surplus passed to wages, labour being the residual claimant to the increasing product.

Now the presentation offered here destroys the fallacious simplicity of the separatist analysis of a competitive system. In the first place, it defines the problem of distribution by drawing the fundamental distinction between costs and surplus. Costs, or the payments necessary to evoke and maintain the use of the existing powers of production, represent the permanent harmony between capital, labour, and ability ; the distribution of that portion of the product required for this purpose admits of no real disturbance or evasion. Where industry creates a product larger than is needed for these costs of maintenance, the surplus is not, however, distributed by any such necessary law. It is taken by the owners of the several factors of production in accordance with the economic ' pull ' they are respectively able to exercise. The strength of this pull varies with the degree of scarcity, natural or contrived, which the owners of a factor are able to secure for the factor, and with the economic importance attaching to this scarcity. A ' monopoly ' of land, where it exists, is evidently able to take the whole of any surplus beyond necessary costs : but this is also true of a monopoly of any other special requisite of production in a particular industry. Investigation of the actual course of modern industry shows that, wherever the different factors are co-operating in the various processes of production, one or other will be relatively scarce, and will be able to take a surplus payment by refusing to co-operate unless it gets it. Sometimes it will be a particular sort of land, sometimes of capital, sometimes of ability, or even of manual labour, that will take this surplus. No single factor can be regarded as the residual claimant. The ' surplus ' passes in innumerable fragments to the owners of a scarce factor of production wherever it is found. The ' natural ' scarcity of land does not secure for its owners any power to take a larger share of surplus than the artificial scarcities which capital or specialised ability are able to enjoy in many fields of industry. Only by following closely the actual course of each stream of industry by which raw materials pass by various processes of manufacture, transport, and commerce, into the possession of consumers, can we ascertain the different forms and sizes of extra payment or surplus that emerge.

But in considering the economic nature and functions of this surplus a distinction of prime importance arises between that portion which, though not requisite to sustain the current rate of productivity in the factor that receives it, operates so as to evoke and feed an increased or an improved supply of productivity, and that which exercises no such power. Some 'surplus,' coming as a rise of interest, profit, or wages, causes growth in the industrial structure by bringing into productive use more or better capital, labour, or ability. This may be classed as 'productive surplus.' So far as the industrial system provides for the due application of this portion of the surplus to promote increased productivity, no conflict of distribution arises, and no waste. But where scarcity enables a factor to extort a price for its use which is not effective for stimulating an increased or an improved supply, such surplus is unproductive. 'Unproductive surplus' includes the whole of the economic rent of land, and such payments made to capital, ability, or labour, in the shape of high interests, profits, salaries, or wages, as do not tend to evoke a fuller or a better productivity of these factors.

This unproductive surplus is the principal source not merely of waste but of economic malady. For it represents the encroachment of a stronger factor upon a fund which is needed, partly for increasing the efficiency of other factors, labour in particular, partly as social income to be expended in enlarging and improving public life. This unproductive surplus, moreover, as 'unearned income' acts upon its recipients as a premium on idleness and inefficiency: spent capriciously on luxuries, it imparts irregularity of employment to the trades which furnish these; saved excessively, it upsets the right balance between the volume of production and consumption in the industrial system.

The 'unproductive surplus' therefore represents the failure of the competitive system to compete: it represents the powers of combination and monopoly. Our actual study of the forms and forces of combination in the various branches of the extractive industries, manufacture, commerce, transport, and finance shows 'free competition' prevailing over a very limited area of business operations, while everywhere else natural or artificial combination takes forcible toll at some point or other in the stream of industry. Instead, however, of imputing this abuse of economic power to some single class—the land-owner, the *entrepreneur*, the capitalist—we find this surplus composed of forced gains extracted in many diverse ways wherever the use of any factor of production is bought or sold.

As 'unearned income' this unproductive surplus is seen to be the only properly taxable body, for any tax which falls upon that income which is either cost of production or productive surplus encroaches on the fund of maintenance or progress, thus reducing the future efficiency of industry. It is, therefore, of paramount importance to the State to discover the forms and the magnitude of the 'unproductive surplus.' For a sound fiscal policy will be directed to secure for the State from this source such public income as it requires for the development of public services. Only in the light of this same conception can an economic justification be found for Trade Unionism and those other movements by which labour endeavours by private or political organisation to secure for wages a larger share of the industrial product.

In seeking to give more precision to the conception of a surplus fund of wealth available for industrial and social progress, I have been forced to depart from the ordinary method of measuring the productive power of land, labour, capital, and ability. To construct any consistent industrial system in which the payment for land is per acre per annum, for capital per £100 per annum, for labour per man per hour, is quite impracticable. It is, therefore, necessary to regard industrial power as issuing from the factors in standard units, good acres or men or machines giving out more of these units, bad ones less. This unitary method of measuring industrial power and of paying for it gets rid of a noxious fallacy by which 'margins' of the various factors have been supposed to exercise a regulative and a causative influence, upon expenses of production on the one hand, the course of distribution on the other. For the unitary method of measurement shows that all 'margins' are themselves determined, and that the land, capital, and labour on the 'margin' exercise no peculiar influence whatever upon costs, prices, or distribution. Only by study of the actual conditions of the markets for the sale of the uses of the several factors of production and of the various sorts of goods and services that are in process of production can we learn how far the industrial system is competitive, distributing wealth economically as necessary stimuli of industry, or how far combinative, distributing unearned incomes which depress industry and disorganise the system. In such a study one point of great significance emerges—the growing part taken by finance in the regulation and direction of modern industry, and the increasing share of the surplus which tends to pass into the hands of the *entrepreneurs* and capitalists who apply their enterprise and capital through instruments of general finance. Though no full or sufficient discussion of Socialism falls within the scope of this volume, an attempt is made to interpret the main current of modern industrial and social legislation as an endeavour to regulate the disposal of the 'surplus' for the improvement of the conditions of the labouring classes, on the one hand, and for the enlargement of the productive and regulative activities of the State, on the other. A survey of industry, indicating those processes in which combination is most successfully displacing competition, is of supreme importance for the understanding of the development of the economic functions of the modern State, alike from the standpoint of the student and from that of the statesman.

Of some of the defects of this treatment I am well aware, though others may have escaped me. Not a few important controversial issues have been ignored or slighted, such as the effect of rate of interest on saving and the intricacies of taxation of monopolies. But, in opening out an interpretation of industry which applied unusual methods and necessitated some complexity of reasoning, I have felt it essential to keep as closely as possible to my main purpose, and not to turn aside into controversial by-paths even for the purpose of meeting anticipated criticism.[1]

How far I have succeeded in presenting a coherent, intelligible account of the main operations of industry, and in particular of the origin and nature of the 'unproductive surplus,' I cannot foresee. For though I have avoided as far as possible the more abstract terminology of economic science, I have been compelled to impart either a somewhat novel or a selected meaning to a few terms often used in other or in various meanings, in order to obtain the necessary instruments for my analysis. Though I have tried to give the requisite precision to such terms as 'Cost,' 'Expenses,' 'Surplus,' 'Profit,' and the like, history has worn them into such smoothness and plasticity that there always remains a risk of their turning in one's hands or working out of line in use. This I have tried for my own benefit, as for that of readers, to guard against, by hanging in the entrance door a standard measure of the meaning of the chief of these terms, though fully aware that the logic of the social sciences is such that in so doing I am forging weapons for the use of hostile criticism.

In conclusion, I desire to express my deep sense of gratitude to several friends who have been so kind as to read the whole or portions of the manuscript of this work, and in particular to Professor E. J. Urwick and Professor L. T. Hobhouse, to whose valuable criticism I am indebted for the removal of many errors which would have otherwise escaped detection, and for many improvements in my argument.

J. A. HOBSON.

March 1909.

---

[1] The single exception to this rule is in the shape of a short formal refutation of the central fallacies of the modern 'marginal theory of distribution' as set forth by certain prominent American and English economists. This controversial argument is contained in an Appendix to Chapter V.

PREFACE TO THE SECOND EDITION

In issuing this new and revised edition, containing a few considerable alterations and additions to the argument and a good many minor corrections, I desire to express my indebtedness to many readers who have, by pointing out difficulties or obscurities in the text of the first edition, enabled me to make improvements.

The following are the most important alterations in the substance of the work:—(1) A restatement is made of the part played by minimum interest as a 'cost of production' in Chapter IV. (2) A preliminary statement of the claims of the state to a share of the 'surplus product' of industry for maintenance and grants is appended at the close of Chapter IV. (3) A new § 9, added to Chapter V., indicates the modifications in the application of the unitary method of measuring productive power required by consideration of the organic co-operation of the several factors of production in a business. (4) In § 10 of Chapter V. an explanation is given of the meaning of the term 'necessary' as applied to the various sorts of payments made to the factors of production. (5) A modification of the general law, according to which minimum interest as a necessary 'cost' has no 'ability to bear' a tax, is made to meet the case of the incidence of income taxes on high incomes, in the second part of Chapter XIV. (6) The 'ability to bear' taxation possessed by property transmitted on the death of its owner is discussed as an important factor in modern taxing policy.

J. A. H.

May 1910.

THE MEANING OF TERMS

1. COSTS are that part of the product, or its equivalent in other goods, necessary as payments to maintain the current output of productive energy in a factor of production.

2. SURPLUS is that part of the product which remains after costs are defrayed. It is divisible into productive and unproductive surplus.

3. PRODUCTIVE SURPLUS consists of such payments to owners of factors of production in excess of cost as are necessary to evoke such increase of industrial structure or power as can, by co-operation with a proportionate growth of other factors, yield an increased quantity or improved quality of product.

4. UNPRODUCTIVE SURPLUS consists of such payments (in the form of rent, excessive interest, profit, or salary) to owners of factors of production as are not necessary to secure such an increase of industrial structure or power.

5. EXPENSES OF PRODUCTION are payments which must be made to owners of the several factors of production under the actual conditions of the market for the supply of those factors. They comprise (1) costs, (2) any productive or unproductive surplus accruing to the owner of a factor of production through natural or contrived scarcity of supply.

6. SUPPLY means (1) the amount offered for sale at a given price in a given time, or (2) the rate at which goods enter a market.

7. DEMAND means (1) the amount withdrawn from supply, i.e. demanded, at a given price in a given time, or (2) the rate at which goods pass out of a market.

8. PRICE-CHANGE is the monetary register of a change in the relations between Supply and Demand.

9. PROFIT is the portion of the product left to the undertaker or controller of a business after the expenses of the factors of land, capital, and labour have been defrayed.

CONTENTS

CHAPTER I

A BUSINESS

§ 1. Businesses are units of production, extractive, manufacturing, transport, trading, financial, professional, artistic, recreative, domestic.—§ 2. Businesses differ in (*a*) size, (*b*) relative importance of their factors, (*c*) ownership and control.—§ 3. Capital comprises buildings, machines and tools, fittings, fuel or power, materials, stock, money, some of which are 'fixed,' others 'circulating.' Land, labour, and management are treated as separate factors 1–10

CHAPTER II

TRADES AND THEIR PLACE IN THE INDUSTRIAL SYSTEM

§ 1. Businesses are recognised as members of a trade, with sympathies and antagonisms arising from the fact that they are buyers and sellers in the same markets.—§ 2. Markets and trades differ widely in area and in degree of contact. Trades are found to arrange themselves in series contributing directly or indirectly to the production of classes of goods. Earlier processes are more general, later processes more special.—§ 3. The general currents of production are connected, drawing from common sources, and form a single stream of industry. Certain fundamental trades, agriculture and mining, are connecting links, and transport is a strong bond of unity.—§ 4. Numerous relations of harmony and opposition exist between the several trades, (*a*) drawing on common sources of supply, (*b*) complementary or competitive in their products or processes.—§ 5. Trades are also related through standards of consumption.—§ 6. Every force affecting one trade passes on by industrial or local contagion to others, some forces being spent locally, others spreading through the industrial system 11–38

CHAPTER III

SPENDING AND SAVING

§ 1. In any series of processes directly and indirectly producing any class of goods, a quantitative relation must subsist between the capital and labour employed in the several processes ; also between the rate of production and the rate of consumption, or withdrawal. This rule will also hold of industry as a whole.—§ 2. In a stationary society the money spent by consumers, passing up the industrial stream, stimulates the continuous processes of production and furnishes all money incomes. The real income consists of commodities and services, which are consumed as fast as they are produced.—§ 3. In a progressive

xiii

CHAPTER IV

COSTS AND SURPLUS

CHAPTER V

WAGES, INTEREST, AND RENT

CHAPTER VI

ABILITY

CHAPTER VII

DISTRIBUTION OF THE SURPLUS BY PULLS

CHAPTER VIII

PRICES AND THE RATIO OF EXCHANGE

CHAPTER IX

THE MECHANISM OF MARKETS

I

CHAPTER X

THE LAW OF SUPPLY AND DEMAND

CHAPTER XI

THE SIZE OF BUSINESSES

CHAPTER XII

TRUSTS AND MONOPOLIES

CHAPTER XIII

THE LABOUR MOVEMENT

CHAPTER XIV

SOCIALISM AND THE SOCIAL INCOME

I

CHAPTER XV

TAXATION OF IMPORTS

CHAPTER XVI

MONEY AND FINANCE

I

II

CHAPTER XVII

INSURANCE

CHAPTER XVIII

UNEMPLOYMENT

CHAPTER XIX

THE HUMAN INTERPRETATION OF INDUSTRY

THE INDUSTRIAL SYSTEM

CHAPTER I

A BUSINESS

§ 1. Businesses are units of production, extractive, manufacturing, transport, trading, financial, professional, artistic, recreative, domestic.—§ 2. Businesses differ in (*a*) size, (*b*) relative importance of their factors, (*c*) ownership and control.—§ 3. Capital comprises buildings, machines and tools, fittings, fuel or power, materials, stock, money, some of which are 'fixed,' others 'circulating.' Land, labour, and management are treated as separate factors.

§ 1.—Most men are related to the business world in two ways : as workers they are attached to some particular business engaged in producing some special sort of goods or services; as consumers they are attached to general industry by a great number of suckers. In seeking to understand the industrial system a man is thus furnished with two approaches : his narrow concentrated interest as producer, his broad diffused interest as consumer. He learns at both ends, but his curiosity is more strongly and more constantly directed by what goes on in the little corner of the industrial world in which he earns his living, the business in which he is employed.

Turning his mind from the particular process on which he is mainly occupied, as a machine tender, a clerk, a labourer, a shop assistant, to what is taking place around him, he soon comes to get a grip of the main features of the structure of the business to which he ' belongs.'

Here is an employee in a shoe factory : he sees around him a number of other wage-earners, most tending some machine, others clerks in the office ; there is the factory itself and the premises it occupies, the machinery and fittings, the stock of leather and shoes in various stages of production; lastly comes the management, summarised in the employer or ' boss.'

Such are the main ingredients of the business as he sees it encased in the four walls of the factory yard : in outline he comes to know how these ingredients are related, and he grasps the business as an organisation under the direction of the manager.

If he tried to visualise the business in this broad outline it would take some such shape as this :—

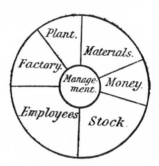

As soon as he came to realise the business as a whole, he would recognise that in the counting-house or the bank there was some money that belonged to the business.

A shop assistant or a mercantile clerk, who was not engaged in making goods but in collecting them, arranging and selling them, would find the general structure of his business similar, though the sort of work done and the instruments were different : plant would play a smaller part, there being very little machinery or tools; materials and stock would only be a different arrangement of the same goods, and would occupy a much more prominent place ; as buying and selling seemed the soul of such businesses, money would bulk larger in his conception of the business.

A farm labourer would see his business as a different sort of composition : land, which formed a small element in the factory premises, and did not bulk very large even in the city warehouse or shop, would occupy a very prominent place in the farm ; machinery might be a small factor, and the number of employees very few.

The bricklayer working for a firm of builders would, again, form a different idea of his business, which, except as regards a small yard and office, was not really contained in fixed premises, but consisted rather in a number of fluctuating contracts which affected him as ' jobs.' But though the material outlines of his business would be less fixed and less clearly defined, he would come to recognise that his employer was in control of a number of workers, business premises, a stock of building materials, and some machinery, as well as money to buy materials and pay wages.

To a keen observant worker the structure of the business in which he works would thus take shape, some of the necessary parts being clearer and better realised than others. The young business man, who enters the factory or the shop as a clerk, will see things froi a somewhat different view-point from that of the manual worker ; the employer's son, adopting from the first a managerial attitude, will more quickly get a more accurate outline of the working of the business as a whole. The worker, to whom the commercial or financial part of the factory or mine or warehouse is unexplored, often wrongly identifies his work-place as a complete business, whereas it is often only one branch or department of a larger business unit broken into a number of locally severed parts, each of which may seem to him an independent economic thing.

The intelligent observer, studying his own business from inside and others from outside, will soon see that the true size and limits of a single separate business can best be determined by watching the element of management. Is there practically independent management, and if so, what is the area of its control ? is the important question to him. If the manager of a factory or shop receives his orders from outside, or in other important ways is instructed in the uses to which he puts his employees, his machinery, &c., and in the buying and selling essential to his business life, it becomes evident that such a factory or shop is not a complete business, but only part of some larger business.

When we examine the grouping of businesses in trades and markets, we shall see many ways in which the liberty of management in businesses that seem to the ordinary employee free is curtailed ; not only in retail trade, but in manufacturing, mining, and other industrial processes, many businesses which look to the uninformed outsider free are tied by investments, contracts, mortgages, or other bonds of business life.

Here, as elsewhere, liberty is a matter of degree. But at present it must suffice to say that substantial independence of management constitutes a separate business ; where the employer or manager has substantial liberty in buying and selling and arranging his factory or shop or warehouse as he thinks best, we call his a separate business.

We must, however, if we are to carry out our intention of including in our inquiry all processes of earning incomes or livelihoods, extend the use of the term 'business' from the processes engaged in making and distributing material goods to those which make or distribute non-material goods that are bought and sold. So a lawyer's firm, a doctor's practice, an artist's studio, a 'cure of souls,' a writer's literary connexion, or any other production and sale of skill or services which are under the control of a person or set of persons and form the basis of a livelihood, must be counted as a business.

The whole of the business world must be conceived as producing quantities of material or immaterial articles, the sale of which furnishes the livelihood of the community, and the active units in these processes—extractive, manufacturing, transport, trading, financial, professional, artistic, recreative, domestic, &c.—are businesses.

§ 2.—Such businesses evidently differ from one another very widely, (a) in size, (b) in the relative importance of their constituent parts, and (c) in the ownership and control of the business.

(a) As regards size, an investigation of the industrial world shows immense variety even within the same sorts of trade. In more primitive or backward countries very few large businesses exist in which a number of workers are brought together to work under a single management with large quantities of tools and materials. In such a country as China, or even Russia, the vast majority of businesses are confined to small workshops or home industry, where the manager works alone or with a few others, with simple tools and small stock of materials. Even in the most advanced industrial countries a large proportion of the businesses remain in this small size ; the most highly developed industries in England or the United States still retain large quantities of home workers or other little business units.

In most departments of industry, even when great capitalist enterprise is prominent, great quantities of little simple businesses survive. The small peasant, working his plot of land with the labour of his own family, and living on the produce, still continues to exist in large numbers in most highly advanced nations : most of the world's food supply is still produced by these little independent farmers. Though large and expensively equipped factories have absorbed certain important branches of manufacture, and are constantly extending the reign of machinery over new fields of production, a very large proportion of the manufacturing arts still remains in small businesses, even in those textile and metal trades where large capitalism has established itself most strongly. Railroads, steamships, and carrying companies have not taken over all the transport industry; the small boatman, car driver, and carrier still keep a hold on important branches of retail local traffic. In the building trades the big contractor leaves a lot of smaller or subsidiary work for little builders. Departmental stores and branch companies hold a large share of retail distribution, but they do not prevent immense quantities of small shopkeepers from earning a precarious but independent livelihood. Even in mining and finance, two departments of activity where capitalism is supreme, there still remains an area for the ' placer ' and the small jobber or money dealer. Regarding the professions from the standpoint of business structures, we perceive the individual or the small firm still in possession of the field, except in a few branches of the recreative, educational, and publishing arts.

Whenever we look in any part of the industrial system we see businesses set out in different sizes, ranging from the single worker, who moulds some material into a useful shape by the strength of his own body and the use of some simple tool, to the huge impersonal joint-stock company employing millions of capital and thousands of employees in various parts of the habitable globe, and between these two extremes a vast variety of intermediate sizes.

(b) Certain characters in the structure of a business correspond to differences of size. A small business is usually much simpler in structure; if it is engaged in handling materials to shape them into commodities, the element of labour usually bulks more largely than the others. Done usually in the home or workshops attached to the home, it has no need of specialised buildings; tools or machinery, though essential, do not represent a large expenditure; the power used in shaping or moving the materials is mostly got from the bodies of the workers, and not from coal or other non-human source. As a rule, such little businesses can be conducted with a very little store of cash.

As we ascend towards businesses of larger size, the relative importance of these factors shifts. Separate expensive buildings are usually required; the quantity of machinery and other plant grows so large that in many a modern mill, mine, railroad, or steamship, several thousand pounds' worth of plant co-operates with each worker; fuel and the supply of power become enormously important items; the financial side of the business involves cash or credit, the use of money, as a large factor; while management, which in the small simple business was a merely incidental function of the independent worker, becomes a specialised separate department of supreme significance.

(c) The most vital of all differences between the small primitive business unit and the large capitalist unit has reference to the ownership and control of the various factors composing the business.

The factors in a business, as we have seen, are land, buildings, machinery and tools, power, raw materials and stock, money, labour, and management. Every business which handles material goods requires some of each of these factors, though in widely different proportions. In the smallest simplest business form, where a workman works alone on his own account in his own house or work-place, he commonly is himself the owner of all these factors. Such is the smallest peasant freeholder in many countries, working his own land with his own tools and cattle, sowing his own seed, and owning his house and sheds and the farm produce. The village smith or other small artisan, certain cabinet makers, and other little manufacturers in London, still represent this early type. Large numbers of little makers, e.g. tailors, cobblers, owning all the factors except the raw material, which they receive from their customers or from some merchant to whom they sell their product, everywhere survive. Here we may say that the worker is the owner of all, or nearly all, the factors, including management. As we grade the various forms of business up from this to the most developed form of modern ' capitalist ' enterprise, we see one after another of the factors removed from the ownership and control of the worker and transferred to ' management.' In the complete capitalist business, land, machinery and tools, power, raw materials and stock, money, labour-power, are owned and controlled by the management, the single check upon absolute ownership being that the management does not own the labourers themselves (as it owns the coal that furnishes machine power), but only the portions of labour-power as they are released from the persons of the workers. In certain great businesses some other factor, as, for instance, electric power or the land on which business premises stand, may be similarly hired, not owned. But, speaking generally, the management in the highly developed capitalist business owns and controls all the other factors.

Between these two types a great number of intermediate types of businesses will be found. An immense variety of small farms, workshops, shops, and other commercial or professional businesses exist where the manager begins to separate from the workers, still working himself, but hiring other workers who have no part in management, though they may still own the tools with which they work, and even, as in many farms, fishing or mining businesses, some share of the stock and product.

In some sorts of business the manager or employer owns materials, which he gives out to workers to do in their own homes, or in workshops which they provide, either letting out to them machines or tools, or leaving the provision of machinery, sometimes also of power, to the workers. In agriculture and in the textile and metal manufactures of England to-day one finds every stage of the business form represented, from the simplest type of the self-sufficient single worker to that of the joint-stock company owning and controlling every factor in production.

In agriculture the small freeholder or yeoman, the tenant farmer, the market gardener, the allotment worker, represent widely divergent types of ownership of land, fencing, tools, crops, &c. ; fishing and mining are full of anomalies in ownership of tools, product, and management ; the textile and clothing trades show every variety of business form, from the home workshop where the worker finds machinery, and, in part, raw materials, to the completely centralised factory ; the metal trades exhibit in the higher form great engineering or steel-making firms owning everything they use, even coal and iron mines, trucks and ships, but furnish a basis of survival not only for small Birmingham workshops working with hand-power on materials sometimes owned, sometimes provided for outside, but for Sheffield grinders receiving rough blades to be finished in their own workshops with hand-power, and small watchmakers in London or Coventry keeping up the earliest type of self-sufficing home workshop.

Or turning to retail trade, we find every variety still surviving in a large city : though perhaps few shopkeepers are owners of the land and shop premises, as regards stock, fittings, management, and labour, we see a gradation from the small independent shopkeeper, owning his own stock and employing only his own family, to the great store which resembles the most highly evolved capitalist manufactures in every other feature except the part played by machinery and non-human power.

When from the numerous types of business unit represented in these agricultural, manufacturing, and commercial occupations, one turns to finance, including great banking and insurance firms and small money-lending businesses, or to the professions, the fine arts, the recreative arts, and the countless businesses engaged in supplying ' personal ' services, from the Turkish bath and barber's saloon down to the individual domestic service of a household—when one takes stock of all these sizes and sorts of industry, the shapes of the business seem to defy classification. But omitting the delicate question whether certain occupations are entitled to be called separate businesses, and confining our attention to those which are commonly admitted so to rank, we find that while differing immensely in size, relative proportion of importance for several factors, and nature of ownership and control, they preserve certain common features.

In all businesses concerned with extracting, shaping, or moving matter we find the matter itself to which the work is applied, the machines or tools by which the matter is manipulated, the money required for buying what is needed, the buildings or premises where the material is stored, or the tools kept, or the work carried on, with the necessary fittings or fixtures, the land from which the matter is extracted or upon the surface of which work is done, the workers who do the work, and the employers or management. Even in businesses concerned with producing not material goods, but non-material services, such as professional advice, music, and other recreative services, &c., all these requisites, except in some cases raw materials, are needed, for the non-material services are produced under material conditions of space and shelter by workers who actually require tools or instruments and skilled direction or organisation.

In developing our picture of industry we may, however, legitimately confine our attention chiefly to those industries engaged in producing material commodities, with merely occasional references to the arts concerned with non-material services.

§ 3.—For certain useful purposes of understanding how the mechanism of industry works, it will be convenient sometimes to gather together under a single class several of the factors or requisites of business which have here been separately described So all the non-human factors in a business, except the land, may be grouped under the head of 'capital,' comprising buildings, machines and tools, fittings, fuel or power, materials, stock, money. Some would include land under capital, but for reasons which will be given later, we shall find it best to distinguish the services directly rendered to production by earth, natural forces, and space, from those rendered by the other factors. Thus distinguishing land from capital, we may also distinguish the materials which it is the object of the business to extract, shape, or move, from those material factors which are instruments for these productive processes, and which are used up with more or less rapidity as they do this work. The first, which is a continual stream of matter flowing through the business and passing out of it to customers, may be called 'circulating' capital ; the factories and other buildings where the work is done, machines, tools, railways, ships, carts, &c., may be called ' fixed ' capital, standing as it does at some fixed point in the industrial stream to forward the passage of the raw material or unfinished goods towards their final destiny as commodities. Of course every other sort of capital is used up in its work of helping to shape or move raw materials into their final form or place, and this ' wear and tear ' may be considered as passing into the goods that are produced, and so as ' circulating ' in the industrial world. But it is altogether more convenient to mark out the material whose manipulation is the direct and express object of a business, from the materials which are only means towards this process.

Certain sorts of capital it has been found difficult to classify. Fuel, if regarded as merely instrumental to the operation of a machine, may be treated as ' fixed ' ; but it is more conveniently regarded as a form of raw material worked into the main current in the form of power, and so classed as ' circulating.'

Whether the money required to run a business is to be called ' fixed ' or ' circulating ' is not certain. That money which goes in buying raw materials and comes in selling products may perhaps be considered circulating in the same sense as those raw materials and goods of which the money is the financial equivalent or shadow. But from another point of view the entire stock of money, or command of credit, which is utilised in the working of the business may be regarded as a ' fixed ' body of financial machinery. The part played by money or credit in the life of a business is, however, so peculiar that it cannot be profitably studied until a more definite meaning is given to ' circulation ' by a study of the operations of the whole industrial organisation. At present we shall name money or credit as an element in the capital of a business.

Having thus designated the non-human factors of the business under land (or Nature) and capital (fixed or circulating), we come to the human factors spoken of as labour-power and management. As in the other cases, no absolutely rigid distinction can be made. We cannot confine labour-power to the manual or physical work in a business, reserving management for the mental guidance and organisation. For all manual labour, regarded as production, contains mental and moral energy, nor is management devoid of all output of physical exertion. From the standpoint of physical and mental it would be possible to find a nice gradation in a complex modern business from the purely routine hand worker up to the general manager in his office, but nowhere could one find the point where mental exertion began or physical left off. Nor can we definitely divide them as employer and employees, though for some purposes this division will work well. For in most great modern businesses the manager is nominally, often really, an employee of the directors or the shareholders, and, so far as the practical arts of management are concerned, they are not confined to the manager, but are largely delegated to sub-managers, overseers, inspectors, and other ' officials.'

Many, bearing these difficulties in mind, wish to lump all the human exertion, physical and mental, under the general name 'labour.' But there are practical reasons for rejecting this solution. The part played by the man or men who direct the course of a business, the interest they have in the business and the gain they receive from the business, are in most instances so different from the part played by the men who merely receive and follow orders

and their interest and gain, that it is desirable to treat the two as different factors of a business.

In most businesses ' direction '[1] and ' management ' are not sufficiently distinct to warrant any further distinction. In our preliminary analyses of the business unit we shall therefore treat them as one, and regard both direction and management of the business as comprised for the most part in the manager or employer. Adopting, then, the commonly accepted distinctions, we may bring our more numerous factors of a business under the four conventional heads, land, capital, labour, and management, thus simplifying our portrait of the business as the unit of industry.

---

[1] In many 'companies' the *personnel* and the interests, as well as the work of director and manager, are of course separated.

CHAPTER II

§ 1. Businesses are recognised as members of a trade, with sympathies and antagonisms arising from the fact that they are buyers and sellers in the same markets.—§ 2. Markets and trades differ widely in area and in degree of contact. Trades are found to arrange themselves in series contributing directly or indirectly to the production of classes of goods. Earlier processes are more general, later processes more special.— § 3. The general currents of production are connected, drawing from common sources and from a single stream of industry. Certáin fundamental trades, agriculture and mining, are connecting links, and transport is a strong bond of unity.—§ 4. Numerous relations of harmony and opposition exist between the several trades, (a) drawing on common sources of supply, (b) complementary or competitive in their products or processes. —§ 5. Trades are also related through standards of consumption.— § 6. Every force affecting one trade passes on by industrial or local contagion to others, some forces being spent locally, others spreading through the industrial system.

§ 1.—THE real life of the business and the respective parts played by the several factors only become clear when we see the business in its environment, tracing its relations to other businesses, and so realising its contribution to industry as a whole.

Let us return again to the standpoint of the intelligent worker in a factory or a shop, who has got a fairly accurate understanding of the several parts of his business and wants to get a wider understanding of industry. He will come to know that his business is only one among a number of similar units, and that it makes a good deal of difference to his business what the others are doing. He may be brought into contact with workers in these other mills or shops, may join them in common action ; in many cases these other businesses, or some of them, lie in close proximity to his.

So the employee in the Northampton shoe factory finds a number of other shoe factories, the Lancashire spinner comes to know that Lancashire is full of spinning mills, the compositor in Fleet Street is powerfully impressed by the presence of other businesses. In various ways the cluster of businesses doing similar work takes definite shape in his mind as a trade, the various units of which have much in common, and also much in opposition. The extent and limits of a trade are at first dimly seen by the worker in a business.

At first the operative in the Northampton shoe factory may only recognise the shoe trade as comprised in Northampton, but he soon learns to extend his idea of the trade to Leicester, Leeds, &c., taking in all the shoe factories in the country.

But he soon hears of American competition, and that some high-grade shoes are made by skilled cobblers, and that sweating work-shops turn out cheap articles competing with the factory product, and he learns to include all these in his idea of the trade

All the businesses that make this trade, though entirely separate in their order and arrangements, and antagonistic in many of their actions, have certain sympathies arising from the fact that they are doing the same sort of work with the same sorts of instruments. Anything which checks the supply of leather—a war, or a foreign tariff which cuts off or injures a market, a concerted action of labour to raise wages—is seen to affect all or most businesses in the same way.

Other occurrences, on the other hand, bring out the separate and opposed interests of the businesses within the trade : a con-tract or order gained by one firm is lost by the others, their buyers fight for the cheapest and best supply of leather, and in securing machinery and other business requirements they may be opposed.

Of course these relations of sympathy and opposition are much closer in some trades than others, and between some parts of a trade than others.   While, theoretically, every shoe factory over the world and every cobbler or maker of anything that can be called a shoe may be members of a single world-wide trade, the connexion between some parts of this trade is so slight and indirect that it may be ignored : the shoe hand in Northampton is not in effective competition with the cobbler in some village of Central China, and though Great Britain, America, and Germany are in many places close competitors, we may still legitimately speak of the English shoe trade, the American shoe trade, as we speak of the Lancashire cotton trade, or the South Wales coal trade.

So, although a trade is sometimes used to describe the aggre-gate of businesses engaged in producing the same sort of goods or services, narrower meanings are commonly employed.   The busi-nesses comprised in a trade must employ somewhat similar pro-cesses of work, for most purposes they must be contained within the same country, for many within the same neighbourhood.

In point of fact, the limits of a trade are usually the limits of its market.   The aim or end of a business is to effect regular and profitable sales (this is the standpoint of direction or management), and the market is the area of this selling : all businesses which meet in a market are regarded as members of a trade.

Until our inquiring workman has got some notions about markets, his understanding of the businesses round him as comprising a trade does not carry him far.

The mere gathering of similar businesses into a trade may be figured thus, the connecting lines conveying some ill-conceived general community and opposition of interests :—

But even then he will not understand the meaning of the lines which form a sort of connective tissue between the businesses until he realises that the substantial unity of the trade consists in the fact that the members of it are buyers and sellers in the same market. Primarily it is the fact that the various shoe-making businesses are selling in the same market, are competing against one another for the same customers, that makes them members of one trade. Their closest community and diversity of interests lies in the market where they sell their products ; but their relations in the markets where they buy their chief raw material, their leather, are scarcely less close.

§ 2.—A market is thus defined: 'Economists understand by the term Market, not any particular market-place in which things are bought and sold, but the whole of any region in which buyers and sellers are in such free intercourse with one another that the prices of the same goods tend to equality easily and quickly.'

It is the principle, ' The same price for all articles of the same sort,' that constitutes a market.

It is, therefore, only when our workman understands the relation of the business in which he works to other similar businesses buying and selling in the same markets, that he really comprehends the nature of the group of businesses he calls a trade.[1]

[1] It may be contended that, in thus identifying the area of a trade with that of a market, we are departing somewhat from common usage, which groups businesses in a trade by virtue of employing a common process rather than as turning out products which sell in the same market. In thinking of a trade we do look directly at the process rather than the product, and for purposes of convenience we often narrow trade still further by local or other divisions. Thus we speak of the building trade, the London building trade, the plastering trade, the fruit trade, the Channel Islands fruit trade, the strawberry trade.

But, though loose and varying uses are made alike of trade and market, one grouping of businesses which make and sell the 'same' sort of product in a single trade does not involve any serious straining of the natural interpretation of facts. Businesses employing the same sort of process and materials are engaged upon products of the same sort which meet in the same market.

The exact area of a market is often as difficult to define as that of a trade. When there is close competition in buying and selling in a locality, while the businesses in these localities have very slight relations with those in other localities, we say these are separate trades and separate markets.

So for a few articles, e.g. gold, diamonds, certain classes of securities, we say there is one world-market, buyers and sellers competing over the entire industrial world. To certain sorts of cotton and woollen goods, to wheat, and some other non-perishable articles of general use, we may also ascribe a world-market, though a large part of the products of these kinds are locally produced and consumed under conditions which make their influence on the world-market very slight and indirect.

The markets for cheap perishable goods, e.g. common fruits, are very numerous and small; the same holds of some cheap durable goods, e.g. bricks; and for most articles there are many markets locally limited, not one world-market.

So, too, every market is a tolerably complex thing, for the doctrine, 'The same price for the same article,' does not carry us far. When we examine the cotton or wheat market we find many sorts of wheat and cotton not directly competing with one another, and each with its own market price : so each sort of wheat or cotton may have several definitely recognised grades or qualities, each grade forming in a way a separate market, though of course affected by the general market in which it lies. Time also enters in : for certain purposes we may say the wheat market to-day is not the same as that of yesterday, and so on. The full complexity of market and trade can, however, only be suggested here.

All the businesses in the shoe trade buy leather from tanners; they also sell shoes to retail shops : [1] in these two markets they appear respectively as buyers and sellers. In order to gain a clearer idea of the situation let us set out the shoe manufacturing trade in its relation to these two markets, thus :—

Our shoe operative, a labour unit in the business A, will see his business to be one of a cluster of businesses forming the shoe-

---

[1] Or directly to consumers through retail stores of their own, a growing custom which we may here ignore.

making trade, and this cluster he will see connected by a number of close bonds, with a similar cluster of businesses forming the tanning trade, and with a third cluster forming the mercantile or retail trade, the three trades forming part of a regular industrial series of processes with a number of continually shifting relations between the businesses in each trade.

But he will soon learn that the shoe factory in which he works, and the shoe trade to which it belongs, have relations with other sorts of businesses and trades nearly as close as those with the tanning and the shoe-selling trades. There is, for instance, the plant and machinery of the factory, which continually requires repair and improvement.

Taking the machinery and other ' fixed ' capital alone, we see that the shoe-making trade is thus dependent, not only on the tanning trade which precedes and the mercantile trade which follows in a lateral line, but that it is also connected with a vertical series of trades engaged in making machines and providing fuel, &c. So we further enlarge our picture:—

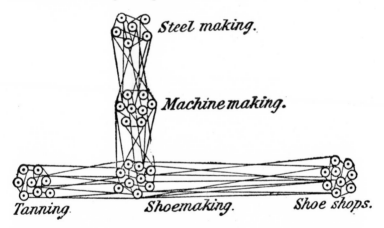

Steel making.

Machine making.

Tanning. *Shoemaking.* *Shoe shops.*

Further acquaintance with the actual conditions of his shoe-making business will show that there are other auxiliary or subsidiary trades from which the shoe-making trade buys materials or services that are of great importance, as, for instance, the coal trade, which furnishes it fuel, and the railroads, which supply carriage, to name the two most important.

Extending farther the range of his vision, he will perceive that the lateral series stretches beyond tanning to a trade of hide merchants and a trade of farmers who produce the cattle whose hides are made into shoes. So, looking farther down the vertical line

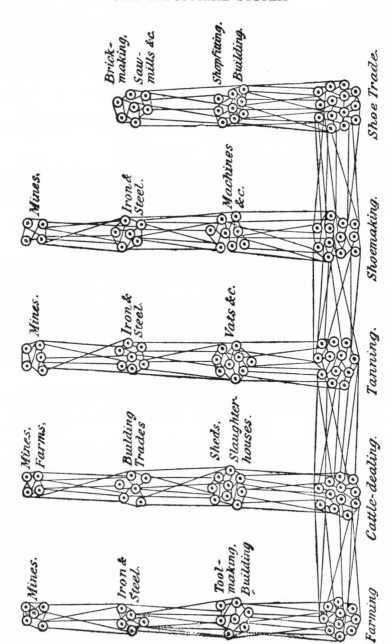

of trades needed to furnish his machines, &c., he will trace behind
the machine-making industry a steel-making industry, behind
that the foundries and iron-workers that produce pig-iron, behind
that the great industry of mining.

Finally, he will recognise that each trade in the direct lateral
series, farming, cattle-dealing, tanning, as well as the further stage
of the shoe trade, must be supplied with machinery, plant, and other
'fixed' capital by a vertical line of trades similar to those he has
already described as the machine-making trades subsidiary to his
shoe-making.

Throwing this into a simple diagrammatic form, he pictures it
as on p. 16.

Now, if instead of starting from the standpoint of a shoe operative, we took a baker's assistant or a compositor in a printing office,
we should get a similar series of lateral trades engaged in producing
loaves or books. It would run thus if confined to the main stream
of production :—

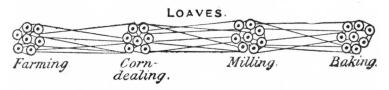

LOAVES.

Farming   *Corn-*   *Milling.*   *Baking.*
                 dealing.

Here the final process of making is commonly united with the
retail trade process. At each of the four processes machinery,
buildings, or other fixed capital is needed, and is supplied by a
number of vertical series of trades corresponding to those described
in the shoe trade.

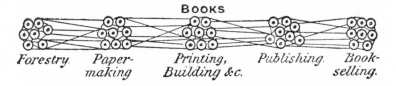

BOOKS

Forestry.   *Paper-*   *Printing,*   *Publishing.*   *Book-*
              making   *Building &c.*   *selling.*

This crude illustration, of course, regards a book as a purely
material product made by converting trees into wood-pulp, wood-
pulp into paper, paper into books.

If we inserted even the most important factors thus ignored—the
author's work of production, the trades supplying other materials
of paper and of buildings, the wholesale distributive stage in the
book trade—we should have a longer and a more complex line

of trades linked together for the direct production of books. At each stage, here also, would enter a vertical series of trades furnishing the machines, buildings, and other plant required.

So far we have taken the standpoint of an employee in a business, a shoe operative, or a clerk, or a compositor, approaching industry from a particular place inside, seeing first the make-up of the business in which he works, then pushing out to a view at once widening and clarifying until he sees his business and his trade linked with other businesses and other trades, first near, and then more distant. Note also that our employee gets a wider productive view by contact with workers in other trades.

But our employee is also a consumer, and he will bring his consumer's interest and outlook to assist his experience as producer, so as to gain for himself a fuller and more orderly conception of industry as a whole. Though his producer's knowledge is more intimate within a certain narrow area, as consumer he touches all the principal lines of industrial processes, and comes to recognise in them a great number of sets of processes related in series much resembling the set he finds in the boot-making or book-making industries.

We may then take it as admitted that the diagram representing the relation of businesses and trades in the production of shoes is in substance applicable to the relations of all other trades engaged in forwarding the production of any sort of commodity.

It will, therefore, be well to look a little more closely at that diagram and see whether we cannot represent a little more accurately the trade relations there indicated.

The first point that strikes us is that while all the trades in the direct horizontal series—farming, cattle-dealing, tanning, &c.—are separate trades, this is not the case when we look up the vertical lines. There we find much repetition, the same machine-making trades figuring in several of the series, iron- and steel-making in many, and mining in nearly all. In other words, the more fundamental trades of iron and steel and of mining evidently are connected with shoe-making through a number of various channels. But if this is so, our picture, which seems to show a number of separate iron and steel and mining trades, requires correction in order to bring it more closely in accord with the facts of the case. Instead of having two separate iron and steel trades in the series contributing to the tanning and the shoe-making, we ought clearly to have one iron and steel trade on which they are both drawing. So with the other cases: the mining trade, which figures at the base of so many of the series, must be seen as one trade through which all the trades that use iron and coal are connected.

On what principle shall we alter our picture so as to make it more closely descriptive of the facts of the industrial processes ? If in our shoe diagram we conceive that the end of the whole set of processes is to supply consumers with shoes, and taking our stand at the final stage of the retail shoe trade look down the whole series, we shall see that there is a change in the nature of the trades as they approach nearer to the goal.

Taking in order the farming, cattle-dealing, tanning, shoe-making, and shoe trade, we perceive that the earlier processes are more general, the latter more special. Though farming figures in the series of shoe-producing processes, because hides are needed, it plays a similar part in various other productive series, supplying wheat to the loaf-making series, wood to the paper-making, and so forth.

Farming and cattle-dealing are not confined to any one or two series ; even tanning has many other uses than that of furnishing leather to the shoemakers : it stands in a similar relation to the saddlery, trunk-making, and even to the bookbinding trades, amongst many others.

This process from more general to more special trades is equally obvious if we follow the tributaries which feed each stage in the main stream of production with machinery, plant, &c. Follow up these vertical lines, from the particular kinds of machines, buildings, &c., which they supply at each main process, to the machine-making and building trades, and then on to the iron and steel trades, and finally the mining industry, we clearly make the same journey from special to general trades, from trades which only make and sell one sort of machine or fitting, to those which supply a great number of different markets.

Boldly pursuing our path of inquiry, and recognising that the structure of the group of trades connected with shoe-making is typical of industry in general, let us try to convert our shoe diagram into a general outline of industrial structure, showing, (a) the business unit, (b) the trade, (c) the clusters or connected series of trades.

We shall expect them to arrange themselves so that the trades associated with the final goods or services will be the most special, while those associated with the earliest processes will be the most general.

As regards the main order we shall encounter no difficulty : the order of production in time will generally correspond with the degree of specialisation, the processes which take place first being the most general, those which take place last the most special.

First will come the trades connected with getting raw materials out of the earth, agriculture and mining being the two chief branches, with fishing as a minor branch.   These we shall class as the Extractive Trades.   They are the most general [1] in the sense that the agricultural and mining products are the raw materials of all the later processes of production.

The chief products of these extractive trades—grains, fruits, timber, textile fabrics, iron, coal, stone, clay, &c.—go to feed an immense variety of particular trades.

Next will come the early processes of shaping the raw products of the earth in order to make them into serviceable commodities or instruments of production, the manufactures of the first order.

To this order would belong the ironworks and rolling mills, &c., producing bars and sheets of iron and steel, saw mills, flour mills, sugar and oil refineries, and perhaps the textile factories producing various sorts of cloth.   To prepare raw materials by expelling foreign bodies, to sift and grade, to break up and to combine so as to produce certain combinations of stock shapes and sizes adapted for further processes of conversion—this standardisation of raw materials forms the object of our manufactures of the first order.

Manufactures of the second order will receive the standardised materials from the earlier processes, the bar and sheet iron or steel, the sawn timber, the flour or sugar, the cotton or woollen cloth, &c., and will, by a series of further manipulations, fit them to shapes and characters capable of serving human wants, or of assisting as instruments in some process of industry.   From the iron and steel trades we shall here pass to the engineering, machinery, and tool-making trades, and to the great variety of hardware, instruments, jewellery and other metal trades ; from saw mills and brick kilns we pass to the building trades ; the textile goods will carry us into the innumerable branches of the clothing trades ; while from flour, sugar, &c., we should come into the confectionery and other trades concerned with preparation of foods.

Exact limits cannot, of course, be set between the first and the second order of manufactures, but the latter will be marked by a double specialisation—one horizontal, one vertical.   The engineering and machine-making trades that take up the iron and steel from the first order of manufactures will apply them in a number of widely divergent uses, i.e. for making ships, or locomotives, or machine tools, or building apparatus, or steel rails, grates, or bedsteads ; the cotton or woollen cloths will feed a variety of different

---

[1] This is, of course, consistent with the fact that some farming may be highly specialised, e.g. producing some special fruit ; likewise some mining, e.g. diamonds.

trades which make coats, shirts, hats, carpets, upholstery, sacks, &c., and so with the other materials.

This horizontal specialisation is attended by a vertical, as where the conversion of steel into knives, cotton cloth into shirts, passes through a long series of separate sorts of business, for many of these horizontal special processes are often gathered into a single business. But so far as manufacturing processes are concerned, manufactures of the second order exhibit a greater number and a more highly specialised character than those of the first. In the 'making' industries, the farther one advances from the extractive stages of agriculture and mining, the more numerous and the more highly specialised the processes become.

Following the flow of the raw materials you will find the stream thus widening :—

Extractive	Manufacturing 1		Manufacturing 2			
	A	B	A	B	C	D
—	—	—	—	—	—	—
—	—	—	—	—	—	—
—	—	—	—	—	—	—
—	—	—	—	—	—	—
	—	—	—	—	—	—
	—	—	—	—	—	—
	—	—	—	—	—	—
	—	—	—	—	—	—
		—	—	—	—	—
		—	—	—	—	—
			—	—	—	—
			—	—	—	—
			—	—	—	—
			—	—	—	—
			—	—	—	—
			—	—	—	—
					—	—
					—	—
						—
						—

But when the manufacturing or making processes are complete, and what are called the distributive processes begin, the specialising tendency is reversed, and we pass into trades which are more general in regard to the sort of goods they handle and the work they do in moving them from the specialised factories or workshops where they are made, towards the retail counter over which they pass into the hands of the consumers.

In speaking as if 'dealing' always followed 'making,' goods being first made and then distributed, we are, of course, simplifying the actual course of industry. Between the extractive processes and the primary manufactures, or anywhere between two processes of manufacture, a mercantile or dealing trade may insert itself, or, indeed, a series of trades connected with the collection, carriage, purchase, or insurance of the material or goods in question. Between the cotton grower in Georgia and the manufacturer of yarn in Lancashire there are, of course, a number of middlemen, and there are perhaps few cases of trades where it is general for the manufacturers to buy raw materials from the farm or mine without some intermediary trade. Indeed, many of the most important classes of wholesale dealers are planted between two sorts of productive processes throughout the industrial world, in order to facilitate [1] the process by which materials or goods pass from one set of makers to another.

But for our present purpose, which is the simplest setting of the main structural outline of industry, we will ignore these classes of ' distributors,' and will confine our attention to the wholesale merchants who receive ' finished ' wares from manufacturers and other producers, and who sell them to retail shopkeepers, from whom they pass to consumers. In the history of many commodities the wholesale stage is omitted, retailers buying direct from makers, or makers supplying the consuming public through shops of their own.

But the existence of distinct classes of wholesale merchants or importers and retail shopkeepers still holds so large a proportion of modern commerce, that it is rightly acknowledged in our general scheme of industry.

Our broad picture as presented to the ordinary intelligent consumer will then show goods pouring from the final stages of manufacture or other production, into the possession of merchants whose function it is to collect them, assort them, and transmit them to retailers.

Though there is, of course, a considerable quantity of specialisation in this work, the typical mercantile firm, or firm of produce dealers, handles a far greater variety of goods than is handled by any one firm of producers. Even those importers, merchants, or brokers who confine themselves to dealing in some one commodity, such as wool, fruit, grain, timber, usually cover a far wider range of material than is covered by any of the producers from whom they buy. In a word, while a good deal of specialisation remains in the wholesale mercantile stages, not only as regards the sort of goods, but as regards market areas from which they are collected, the specialisation is far less than in the manufacturing stages.

[1] Though there may grow up in the interstices of the productive process classes of speculative middlemen who do not facilitate but impede trade, living parasitically upon it, they commonly retain some shred of an original service which consists in facilitating purchase or transfer.

When we pass from wholesale to retail trade the tendency towards the general is still more apparent, as regards the main current of ordinary commerce.

Though a large number of retail shops exist in our cities confined to the sale of some single class of food or clothing, &c., in some instances to a single narrow sort of grade of hat, tea, gloves, or tobacco, the specialisation is nowhere carried as far as in the later manufacturing processes, while as regards the general body of retail goods the opposite tendency is obviously dominant.

The universal provider, the co-operative store, the development of the grocer, the oilman, the hardware shop, into a 'general' shop, is the most salient fact in modern trade.

When we come to study the history of the structural changes in modern industry we shall recognise that everywhere the two tendencies of division of labour and of union, of differentiation and of integration of processes, have been operating both in the business and the trade, proceeding at different paces and with different forces. At every stage of industrial process we find examples of businesses which have fallen so strongly under the differentiating force that they are devoted to making a single size or grade of a single sort of cotton or iron goods, or the growth of a single sort of fruit or animal ; side by side with this we find trades of manufacture or repair which turn out a great variety of goods by hand or in part by machinery. The same is true if we turn from sorts of goods to processes : it is not possible to say whether the stronger tendency in Lancashire to-day is towards a business which unites the different processes of spinning and weaving, &c., and handles a variety of grades, or towards a single process and a single grade.

And this is typical of the whole of trade : in farming, mining, manufacture by hand, as by machines, in all the mercantile processes and in transport, we find a great variety of types of business determined by the relative strength of the specialising and the generalising forces.

But turning from these finer considerations to our rude outline of the main industrial structure, we shall find it true that the forces making for differentiation or specialisation of trades and businesses are dominant in the ' making ' processes, reaching their height in the later manufacturing trades, and that the integrating [1] or generalising forces assert themselves more prominently in the commercial processes.

---

[1] Students of evolutionary method will, of course, observe that the 'integration' of the latter processes, e.g. as illustrated in the general store, is not a mere reversal of differentiation, not a return to a merely 'general' form. The great modern store is a federal industrial state of largely self-governing departments, not a centralised unity.

§ 3.—Our shoe operative or compositor, now gathering into a more general form the knowledge of the industrial structure he has got from his related studies as producer and consumer, will try to represent industry in some single figure. Generalising what he sees in the case of shoes and loaves or books, he may picture the whole industrial movement as a stream of raw materials issuing from the earth in the extractive trades, then carried on through a series of manufactures of the first and second order, flowing next in finished shapes through wholesale and retail commerce until they are emptied out of the retail mouth into the hands of the consumer. Or he may picture the whole affair as working after the manner of a mill, some automatic flour or paper mill which sucks raw stuff into its hopper, shapes and mixes it in various processes, carries it in tubes from tank to tank, and finally deposits it sorted and packed for the market. A number of separate processes, each in due order, contribute to the transportation of the material, the several machines drawing their power originally from the same dynamos.

As he turns over these images in his mind, our practical student will recognise that this series of processes, extractive, manufacturing, wholesale and retail commerce, do not exhaust the physical requirements of the great industrial process. Everywhere some transfer of matter from place to place is involved, not only for the ' distributive ' work of commerce, but in the interstices of the ' making ' processes, goods must be conveyed from farm and mine to factory, and from one manufactory to another. In a word, the transport industry, the most general of all the subsidiary trades, must be inserted in the picture.

The general order of the processes in their relations to one another would take shape in some such image as on the following page.

Raw materials entering the stream of industry through the extractive trades are shaped and combined and carried through a series of manufacturing processes, and then are bought and sold by commercial classes of merchants and retailers who take them from the makers and bring them to consumers. Here we have the main current of industry carrying the products of the field and mine to the consumer. This work of transformation and transmission is done by the application of productive energy at a number of points along the industrial stream. At each of these points there stands a group of trades composed of businesses in which workers are operating machinery and other plant. This machinery and plant, as we saw, was itself the product of a series of processes resembling that in the main stream in which the mine and the field are once

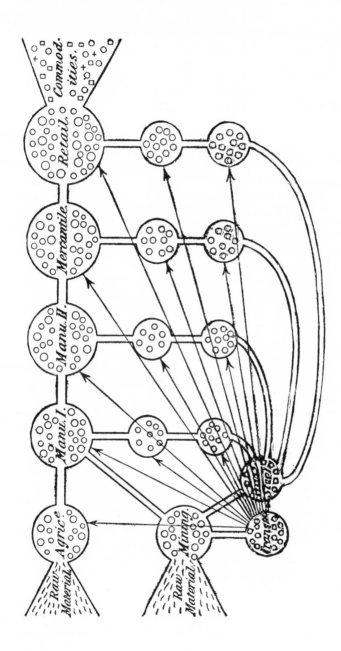

more utilised, not for the direct supply of commodities, but for the supply of instruments of production, forms of ' fixed ' capital.

The main current of industry is thus fed by the energy of tributary streams which enter it at the various productive processes.

As the main stream and the tributaries all take their rise from the earth in the extractive processes, so these agricultural and mining processes form a strong and constant bond of sympathy and unity throughout the industrial system.

But while agriculture and mining are at times to be regarded as the most fundamental processes, the unity of modern industry is even more clearly marked by the common dependence of all trades upon the transport trades. This dependence is direct : all trades require carrying processes, and most of this carrying work to-day is done by organised systems of transport involving machinery and power, and driving back by another channel to the extractive arts and their mother earth.

We have now got a general conception of the outlines of the industrial system as a material structure, marking the chief bonds of connexion between its main divisions. But in doing so we have been driven to quit the closer details which first engaged the attention of our shoe operative or compositor, and to deal with the large general conceptions of ' extractive ' industry, ' manufacture,' ' commerce,' ' transport,' and the like.

There is some danger here of stretching the analogy of the ' river ' or the ' machine ' so as to convey an exaggerated and a false notion of the amount or the sort of harmony or unity that exists in the industrial world.

As a corrective let us look a little closer at what we have called the main stream, which carries the raw materials from farm and mine to the retail counter. We illustrated this flow first through boots and loaves, and then passed to commodities in general, showing how the process was generally applicable.

But looking nearer at this main stream, we shall see that it is not a single smooth harmonious flow. Our shoe operative in his early expanding outlook of the shoe trade saw that there were both harmony and antagonism between the various businesses, both community and diversity of interests. So his wider outlook on trade as a whole will show him that this main stream of commodities is really a number of currents which flow along a course, each its own, inside the general industrial channel, and that these currents sometimes flow peacefully side by side in a broad smooth bed along an evenly graded fall, sometimes cross and conflict, struggling against one another for some easier passage as the bed narrows or curves.

In other words, he will realise that, as the several businesses in his trade have certain interests in common and others which divide them, so with the trades and with the series of trades connected with the production of different sorts of commodities. There is a great variety of co-operation and a great variety of competition or antagonism in the industrial system.

So far as it is a system, the co-operative (or harmonious) must be regarded as predominant, and competition must be regarded provisionally as a method of co-operation.

For close study let us detach from the general main stream of production the streams of processes connected with three sorts of commodities which seem not to be closely associated, viz. boots, loaves, and shirts. We soon perceive that the three sets of processes engaged in producing these commodities do not form entirely separate industrial streams, each running in its own isolated bed, but that they are at certain points connected with one another, and with various other trades.

The same farmers who raise cattle and sell the hides which go to make boots may also raise wheat, and anything which affects the relative prices of boots and loaves will evidently affect the amount of farm labour and capital which is put to arable and pasture uses.

Even the land and labour occupied in raising cotton crops, though less transferable, is not so absolutely fixed as to be un-affected by other agricultural changes. Certain farming require-ments in the shape of buildings, implements, carts, fertilisers, &c., will figure in each of the extractive processes.

So, too, the carrying trades form a common element of ever-increasing importance in all three series : the same railroads, the same ships (or ships built by the same firms or under the same con-ditions) will carry the raw materials to the manufacturer, and the finished products to the merchants or retailers in each case. Each set of processes will demand the assistance of the building trades to set up farmhouses, factories, warehouses, shops, and the mining and metal trades to supply the fuel, fittings, machines, &c., required in the different businesses.

Certain bonds of industrial sympathy and antagonism between the three streams of production are thus indicated. Anything which opens up new tracts of generally fertile or accessible land may be good for all three, reducing the cost of producing shoes, loaves, and shirts : or an opening up of new wheatlands lowering the price of bread may stimulate cattle-raising, and reduce the price of hides : a new economy in use of fuel will in different proportions affect all three commodities.

A rude diagrammatical expression of these industrial junctions may be thus given, the three main streams of industrial processes connecting with one another through common sources and common tributaries.

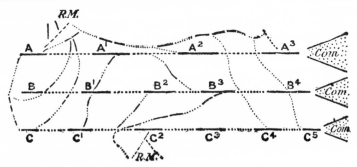

Although the three commodities, boots, loaves, shirts (here indicated by A, B, C respectively), have no specially close relations with one another, it is evident that a minute examination would show that they are economically connected with one another by many more ties of common interest than this diagram suggests.

§ 4.—Following the lines of investigation suggested by this illustration, we shall come more clearly to know the nature of the bonds of harmony and of repulsion among trades.

(a) The closest relations of common interest will evidently exist between trades which draw upon some single source of supply of raw materials or productive power.

All trades whose chief material is wool or leather, or timber or steel, pulling at some common supply, must look closely after one another ; anything which increases or reduces the common supply affects them all alike, so there is community of interest ; anything which gives one of them a better pull upon the supply than the others affects these latter injuriously, so far there is diversity of interest. The same evidently holds where a number of local manufactures are dependent for coal or other source of power upon the same supply. Dependence on some subsidiary material or other trade accessory will set up a similar relation, important or trivial, according to the part played by such material in the respective trades. The recent condition of the 'rubber' market is a striking example of the influence of an important trade accessory acting upon a large number of different trades.

(b) Trades that are complementary or subsidiary to one another in some direct way are, as we have seen, in closest harmony. The coal and iron trades are the largest, most obvious instance, but every art of production of course throws a number of trades into similar dependency on one another. Whenever a number of materials must be put together to make a commodity, such direct unity of interest is established among the trades that handle each material. Such are the relations between the fruit-growing and the sugar-refining trades, between the wine-growing and the bottle-making trades, between the numerous trades which go to feed with materials the building trade.

It is, of course, very uncommon for these complementary trades to be entirely dependent upon one another : the bottle-making trade is related also to the brewing and the fruit trades, sugar refining also to the confectionery and the mineral-water trade, and so forth. But the trades which prepare the various ingredients for any important commodity are evidently kept in close harmony with one another.

(c) Where two sorts of material or two sets of processes are alternatives for production, a keen antagonism exists between them. Here we first come across the relation known as substitution, which plays so important a part in industrial progress.

Bedsteads are made of wood or steel, so are many other articles of furniture or fittings ; sugar may be made from cane or beet ; cotton, linen, wool are alternatives for many kinds of dress or other fabrics ; electricity, gas, oil, steam are competing against one another as sources of industrial, locomotive, or domestic energy. Just here we are not concerned between different sorts of goods which satisfy the same want, bnt with the choice exercised by producers between different materials and processes which can be substituted for one another in some business process. The choice exercised by the consumer has generally some influence in the selection of material or method of production, as, for instance, in determining the alternative use of wood, vulcanite, amber in making pipe-stems, but for present purposes we may separate the interaction of producer and consumer, and distinguish substitution as a force which antagonises various trades that compete by offering some alternative material to manufacturers.

But as the law of substitution opens out, we get glimpses of a wider, more general, sympathy and opposition between trades. The productive energy of man, directly operative through labour, indirectly through capital, is within certain limits free to choose among all the various channels of industry: they are all open to him as alternative occupations. So there is a more universal sympathy and opposition between all trades than any yet named. All causes affecting the volume, fluidity, and efficiency of the capital and labour in a community will affect all trades in common. In proportion as labour and capital are free to enter several trades, and even to transfer themselves from one occupation to another, they must be regarded as forming a common fund of industrial energy which pulsates through the whole framework of industry, as the blood courses through the various organs and cells of the body, energising all alike. Though, as will appear on closer examination, the flow of labour and also of capital is far from free, and is, in fact, impeded by many economic barriers, there is enough fluidity to give a real unity to the terms ' labour market ' and ' market of loanable capital.' Capital and labour can flow into various channels of production with sufficient freedom to make every trade sensitive to the expansion and contraction, the prosperity and depression, of every other trade.

§ 5.—But trades are connected, not only through common interests in processes of production, but through changes in methods of consumption. The ' standard of comfort ' of different classes is constantly changing: every rise or fall of wages alters the proportion of working-class incomes spent on different commodities, and so directly stimulates or depresses groups of trades ; the great change from rural to city life has revolutionised the expenditure of large masses of our population ; new articles of consumption, or the cheapening of old articles which brings them in reach of poorer classes, create or stimulate new tastes which not merely absorb new increments of income, but displace older articles of consumption. Taste, fashion, and caprice constantly exert a larger influence on the expenditure of larger sections of the public. Every article of a man's consumption is in a sense competing with every other article for a larger share in his expenditure.

Any change in standards of consumption brings other changes by reason of affinity ; a man who takes to drink not only spends more on beer, but often more on tobacco, sport, and betting, while a man who gives up beer and stays at home is likely to spend more not only on tea, but on reading and quiet recreations.

The rapid spread of the taste for cycling which followed the invention of the safety bicycle, besides its direct competitive effect upon the use of riding-horses and the carriage trade, had a large number of clearly traced subsidiary effects, reducing the sale of cheap pianos and jewellery, damaging the book trade, altering the nature of the clothing trades, stimulating the sale of non-alcoholic drinks, and reviving the country inns. Nor are these influences confined to changes of material consumption. The increased demand for education in England, by its excessive strain upon the intellectual machinery of the nation, not only stimulates the teaching, the printing, and paper-making trades, it causes an immense expenditure of English money upon Swiss holidays, and helps to revolutionise the economic structure of that country. In America electric transit and the telephone not only give rise to a series of new mechanical industries, but by contributing to that widespread neurotic condition known as Americanitis, have caused on the one hand an immense expansion of the ' drug ' trade, on the other a demand for the building of innumerable temples of Christian Science as a reaction against the tyranny of the medical professions. You cannot touch the consumer at any point in his expenditure without altering in countless seen or unseen ways his whole standard of valuations, and, through alterations of this standard, affecting the entire series of industrial processes which support it.

§ 6.—Thus the growth of harmonious and conflicting desires of consumers weaves the closest and most intricate network of relations between all the various productive processes of the industrial world.

The closer we examine any section of the industrial system, the more numerous and complex the relations between the businesses, the trades, the groups of trades contained in it : the ramifications come to resemble those which the microscope displays in the section of a leaf or a bit of animal fibre.

As we recognise the fineness of these relations, we come unconsciously to shift the metaphors we use, and to regard industry less as a stream or a machine and more as a live organism with something like a common flow of blood, a common system of nerves, and an organic co-ordination of parts resting upon a complexity of business cells. None of these metaphors is strictly applicable : industry is neither river, machine, nor organism, but there are many points in which the last term gives the most correct impression. If we could follow out far enough the ties between businesses and trades and trade-groups in what we call the industrial world, we should find a sort of common connective tissue running throughout, thinner and coarser in some parts, stouter and finer in others, but binding the whole sets of industrial operations so closely together that any touch bestowed at any point may be communicated to the most distant parts.

Take any local trade : it is most closely linked with those trades which supply it with raw materials, fuel, and other important essentials of production, and with those trades or customers which buy the goods it has to sell : these trades may be widely scattered over the earth. But it is also closely linked with other trades in the same locality not engaged in producing or using the same goods. The bond of neighbourhood, though not so strong in an advanced as in a primitive industrial community, always retains considerable force. The labour market remains largely local: an increased or diminished demand for labour in one local trade affects others: in smaller industries capital is still largely drawn from the locality, so that the prosperity or adversity of one local trade affects others: most trades, though highly developed, depend for some of their materials and plant on local industries, and find for some of their products or by-products the most remunerative market close at hand. Indeed, it is only a comparatively small number of highly evolved manufactures that are substantially independent of local conditions: the transport trades usually are very sensitive to local conditions; the building trades are essentially local, both as regards materials and demand for their products; banking, brewing, and other well-developed industries are very local in their main conditions of success; the vast quantity of industry in small manufactures, in retail trade, and in personal services, is keenly sympathetic with other local industries. Thus any large sudden change causing expansion or contraction, success or injury to any trade, vibrates throughout the whole complex of industry by two wave-movements, the one conveyed through other trades belonging to the same productive series, the other operative through alien trades in the same locality. Though both waves weaken as the movement passes to trades more distant in organic or local connexion, both attest the solidarity of industry. This double bond of sympathy is, of course, marked in the organisation of capital and of labour. Capital draws together not only by amalgamation of, or stable contracts and agreements between, the various processes in the same stream of production, as where manufacturers purchase sources of raw materials and establish their own retail agencies, but also by local associations of employers for dealing with common local interests, such as transport facilities, street improvements, local taxation, and the labour market. Labour similarly combines upon the double basis: the federation of the building or the transport trades representing one mode of organisation, local trades councils the other.

The industrial atmosphere is thus kept continually vibrating with waves passing in direct currents from one trade to another distant trade, or widening from some local centre in ever larger, weaker waves over general trade until they disappear. Regarding the industrial world as a unity, consisting of all those persons who, as buyers or sellers, are in direct or indirect industrial contact with one another, one may say there is no single industrial happening which does not exercise some influence upon every person throughout the world. But we must not exaggerate the operation of these forces. The vast majority of these waves spend their force in small local areas and are negligible factors for trade in general ; nationality, race, language, distance, difference of soil, climate, and social organisation, limiting the free flow of capital, labour and trade, over wide areas, must be regarded as breaking up the industrial world into a number of subordinate industrial unities, chiefly nations, for most industrial purposes.

Thus every really large physical or political event, such as a drought in India, a new tariff in America, a war in the Far East, creates an economic shock or a series of economic shocks which are sensibly felt over large areas of the more developed countries of the West, and over contiguous countries which are less developed, while some weaker effects are traceable all over the other parts of the world ; but smaller shocks affecting less or more remote trades or areas expend their force locally, or are affected in their wider influence by counteracting forces. Indeed, the comparative stability of industry in the world is the equilibrium of myriads of minor forces of disturbance which are thus compensating and cancelling one another.

It is only when some main source of world supply in the production of a staple commodity is affected, as by a grain or cotton famine over a wide area, or some large blow is dealt to the credit of a nation by financial failure, or where some great political revolution changes the tide of immigration or opens up some large new market, that swift transformations and dislocations of industry are occasioned in nations far remote from the base of disturbance. For most purposes and on ordinary occasions there are a number of industrial worlds. Even Great Britain, which stands more exposed than any other country to foreign industrial influences, is confined within her own borders for the buying and selling of five-sixths of the goods and services she buys and sells, while the law of compensation, in its operation on the numerous foreign influences which affect her, serves so as to secure for her at least as much general stability of internal industry as those nations enjoy who are by their economic structure and policy less exposed to waves of external influence.

In this picture of the structure of industry we have confined our attention to the production of material commodities. But a scientific interpretation of industry will, of course, require us to include those processes which are concerned with producing the non-material goods commonly classed as services, the administrative services of public officials, the skilled professional advice of doctors and lawyers, the performances of actors, the personal services of domestic attendants, &c. These official, professional, recreational, domestic services, as productive processes, must be included in our wide meaning of industry : many of them are the product of a series of educative and other preparatory processes, involving the organised use of capital and labour in businesses and trades, analogous to the series which we have traced for material commodities, though not usually so elaborate. Though most of our illustrations will be drawn from the trades which produce material commodities, this will be for the greater clearness in tracing movements of materials and the activities concerned with them, not for the sake of excluding from ' industry ' the processes of producing non-material goods which engage a large and always growing proportion of productive energy in the more civilised parts of the industrial world. It would, indeed, be impossible to understand the industrial system as a progressive institution were we to confine ourselves to the production of material forms of wealth.

APPENDIX

CLASSIFICATION OF INDUSTRIES

THE object of the analysis of industry given in this chapter has been to impress upon the reader the general outlines of the structure, taking for this purpose a rude classification of industrial processes. It may be well, following in the main the classification of Jevons,[1] to append the fuller analysis of industry which a scientific census of occupations would yield :—

Proprietors of Land and natural sources of suppply.	Landowners, Quarry Owners, Mine Proprietors, Owners of Fishing Rights (Functions generally of a passive kind),
Producers of Raw Materials....	Agriculturalists, Gardeners, Woodmen, Shepherds, Herdsmen, Hunters, &c.
	Miners, Colliers, Fishermen.

---

[1] ' Principles of Economics,' p. 108, &c.

Dealers in Raw Materials (middlemen between Producers and Manufacturers).	e.g. Corn Merchants, ,, Agents, ,, Factors, ,, Chandlers, Cotton Importers, ,, Merchants, ,, Brokers, ,, Agents, ,, Salesmen.
Manufacturers (first order).	e.g. Corn Miller, Cotton Spinner, Timber Sawyer, Iron Smelter.
Dealers (between two or more manufacturing processes).	e.g. Flour Merchant (between Miller and Baker). Yarn Merchant (between Cotton Spinner and Manufacturer). Timber Merchant (between Sawyer and Carpenter, &c.)
Mauufacturers .... (second order).	Baker, Confectioner, Cotton Weaver, Dyer, Printer, Shirtmaker, &c. Cabinet Maker, Carpenter, &c. Rolling Mills, Engine Works, Cutlery, &c. (Between any two processes a class or more of dealers may intervene).
Wholesale dealers in Commodities.	Warehousemen, Produce Merchants, Exporters, &c. (Wholesale dealers in manufactured goods are often 'general stores.' In Foreign Trade, however, they specialise often (A) according to sea routes; (B) according to classes of manufacture, e.g. cotton goods, iron trade, &c.).
Retail Dealers	Shopkeepers, Hawkers, Costermongers, Licensed Victuallers, &c. (often comprising a final act of manufacture, e.g. butcher, confectioner, dressmaker, &c.).

Transport .... Carriers on
    (Distributive Industry ac-   Railways,
      cording to Jevons).   Canals,
                                Ships,
                                Docks,
                                Roads,
                                Carriages,
                                Horses
                        (carrying raw materials from farm, mine, &c., to manufacture; carrying half-made goods between different orders of manufacture; carrying commodities between factories, wholesale dealers, retailers, and consumers).

Subsidiary Trades .... e.g. Subs. to Landowner
    ('Any which merely assist   Estate Agent, Steward,
    other trades by supplying the   Solicitors, Surveyors, &c.
    minor requisites ').

                                Subs. to Farmers
                                  Agricultural Implement Makers, Seed Merchants, Manure Merchants, &c.

                                Subs. to Corn Merchant
                                  Granary Maker, Sack Maker, Corn-measure Maker, &c.

                                Subs. to Miller
                                Millwright, Machinist, Millstone cutter, &c.

                                Subs. to Baker
                                  Oven Builder, Peel Maker, Fuel Merchant, &c.

Finance .... Banking, Insurance, &c.

This classification is based upon consideration of industrial processes, and marks the standpoint of the producer.

The consumer's standpoint would yield a transverse classification on the basis of the sorts of utility or satisfaction afforded by the commodities.

Taking the chief orders of utility, we should classify along the following lines :—

Food .... Bread Stuffs,
                                Dairy Produce,
                                Meat,
                                  Groceries,
                                  Beer, Wine, &c.,
                                  (or according to materials, wheat, sugar, milk, &c.).

Clothing .... Over Wear
           (Suits, Dresses, &c.).
      Under Wear,
      Hats,
      Boots,
      Gloves, &c.
         (or according to material, Cotton,
           Wool, Flax, Silk, Leather,
           India-rubber, &c.).

Lodging .... Dwelling-houses,
      Furniture,
      Crockery, &c.
         (according to materials—Wood,
           Stone, Steel, Brick, &c.).

Refinements .... Ornaments,
      Amusements,
      Literature, &c.

Jevons, in suggesting the classification of occupations according to 'commodity,' based upon the four great classes, food, clothing, lodging, refinements, does not, however, as might have been expected, cleave to the consumer's standpoint (which I have here preferred), but divides his classes according to kinds of material used, not according to the ' wants ' satisfied.

A really scientific classification from the consumer's standpoint would be based upon a psycho-physical analysis of wants, beginning with food, shelter, clothing in their elementary uses as life preservers, and proceeding to the higher and more specialised wants (conveniences, luxuries, &c.), as they arise in natural order from the satisfaction of the primary physical wants.

Industries and occupations would then be classified in relation to these needs or wants. The term refinements cannot even be regarded as containing the germ-idea of such a classification.

The classifications of occupations adopted in the British and American censuses are monuments of illogic. They are based on a blending of three *fundamenta divisionis*, material, commodity, and process.

The first division of occupations into classes in the British census is based on a blend of commodity and process, i.e. partly on the ' nature ' of the work involved in producing them. This gives us the following classes : professional, domestic, commercial, agricultural and fishing, industrial. It is sufficient comment upon the merit of this classification to remark that mining comes under industrial, most retail dealing under industrial, while professional includes makers of dental apparatus, and photographers.

Transport is a mere branch of commercial. But it is the divisions of the industrial class that exhibits the greatest confusion.

For while the earlier divisions are based on consideration of the character of the products or the uses they serve, e.g. (1) books, prints, maps ; (2) machines ; (3) houses, furniture and decoration ; (4) carriages and harness, we soon pass into a distinction between textile fabrics and dress which is evidently based upon the time order in the processes of manufacture, and finally we are plunged into animal substances, vegetable substances, mineral substances, reverting to the basis of nature of the material.

Needless to say, this ill-constructed net fails entirely to catch certain large and important classes of workers, and ' general shop-keepers,' costermongers, contractors, manufacturers, managers (undefined), general labourers, and a considerable class of engine drivers, stokers, &c., artizans, machinists, factory labourers are thrown into a general rubbish heap at the end, under the title, ' general or unspecified commodities.'

CHAPTER III

SPENDING AND SAVING

§ 1. In any series of processes directly or indirectly producing any class of goods, a quantitative relation must subsist between the capital and labour employed in the several processes; also between the rate of production and the rate of consumption, or withdrawal. This rule will also hold of industry as a whole.—§ 2. In a stationary society the money spent by consumers, passing up the industrial stream, stimulates the continuous processes of production and furnishes all money incomes. The real income consists of commodities and services, which are consumed as fast as they are produced.—§ 3. In a progressive society some money-income must be saved, i.e. applied to buy more new capital goods. Saving is a stimulation of certain parts of the industrial system in preparation for enhanced spending and consumption. Individual saving need not cause increase of productive capital, social saving must.—§ 4. There exists at any time an economically right ratio of saving to spending, having regard to the probable growth of future consumption and the changes in industrial arts. This right adjustment may be disturbed by over-spending or over-saving.

§ 1.—Our shoe operative or shop assistant expanding his area of knowledge from his two standpoints of producer and consumer, has got a comprehensive view of the industrial system in the world as a great complex organised grouping of trades engaged in converting the raw materials and powers of Nature into commodities for the use of man. He will distinguish a main stream of processes, extractive, manufacturing, commercial, along which these raw materials constantly flow towards consumption, and the number of tributaries which continually feed the processes along the main stream, with the plant and other means which enable them to do this work of forwarding the production of commodities. At each point of production along the main stream and along the tributaries he will see a cluster of trades, each composed of a group of businesses whose structure is built of units of capital, labour, land, and management. So far as this system is working economically it seems evident that there will be a definite relation between the quantity of the capital, labour, and other factors at each of the various processes, both in the main stream and along the tributaries.

39

		Cattle	Hides	Leather	Boots	Shop Boots	
R. M.	>	A	B	C	D	E	< Com.
		a	b	c	d	e	
		a^1	b^1	c^1	d^1	e^1	

Taking the section of industry concerned with production of boots, we shall recognise that some sort of definite quantitative relations must be maintained between the trades along the main series of processes A, B, C, D, E, i.e. there must be some proportion between the rate at which cattle are converted into hides, hides into leather, leather into boots, and boots into consumers' commodities. Shop boots at E cannot be handed over the counter to consumers at a faster rate than the capital and labour at A, B, C, D respectively permits them to be forwarded ; nor can hides and leather continue to be produced at a faster pace than boot shops will receive them for supplying customers.

In fact, it is quite evident that if we have a ' system ' at all, that system must involve a definite proportion between the quantity of capital, labour, and other factors employed at the several processes of converting cattle into boots.

Confining ourselves, for convenience, to Capital and Labour, we shall say then that the quantity of employment of Capital and Labour at the points A, B, C, D, E will be mutually inter-dependent. It will be equally evident that what applies to the trades in the main current will also apply to the tributaries which supply the plant, machinery, &c., to the main processes. So the quantity of capital and labour employed at a and a1 will be directly determined by the quantity employed at A, that employed at b and b1 by the quantity employed at B, and so on, so that the quantitative relation subsisting between the main processes will apply likewise to the subsidiary processes, all the trades directly and indirectly concerned with making boots having their sizes, or their quantity of employment of capital and labour, determined by one another.

Now what holds of the series of boot-making trades will hold equally of bread-making or shirt-making, or of trades in general. Removing, then, our special application to boots, we shall assert the general truth that in the system of industry there will be at any given time a definite relation between the quantity of capital and labour employed in the various sorts of work, extractive, manufacturing, transport, mercantile, retail trade, so far as the system is operating economically. If we take either the most general or the most particular view of industry, we shall recognise that the ' system ' involves a delicate provision of adjustment between the amount of energy employed at the several points and between the quantity of the instruments of production giving out this energy.

Applying to general industry our simplified diagram—

(*Extractive*)	(*Man.* 1)	(*Man.* 2)	(*Wholes'le*)	(*Retail*)	
R. M.	A	B	C	D	E
	a	b	c	d	e
	a^1	b^1	c^1	d^1	e^1

commodities

consumption

we should first perceive that as the trade groups placed respectively at A, B, C, D, E, and at a, a1, b, b1, &c., were all engaged in carrying R. M. (materials) towards consumption, there must be a definite proportion between the work done at these several points and, therefore, between the capital and labour, &c., engaged in doing it.

We should next recognise that the amount of this productive energy given out, both as an aggregate and as apportioned between the several processes, will appear to be directly determined, on the one hand, by the rate at which raw materials (R. M.) are put in at one end of the stream ; on the other hand, by the rate at which they are taken out as commodities by consumers at the other end.

A slackening of the rate at which raw materials enter the stream at the source will appear to involve a corresponding slackening of industry (a reduction of employment of capital and labour) at each process of production, and also a corresponding reduction of the pace at which commodities flow out into consumption : a quickening of the inflow of the raw materials will appear to cause a corresponding quickening of industry, for more raw materials cannot continue to enter the stream of production than are capable of being carried forward down the stream. On the other hand, a slackening of the pace of consumption (of the rate at which commodities are withdrawn from the end of the stream) would seem equally to involve a slackening of every process of production, for any attempt to maintain at any point the former pace of production would appear to cause congestion and stoppage : a quickening of the pace of consumption (a more rapid withdrawal of commodities) must involve an increase in the rate of production, for without such increase of the rate of production no increased rate of consumption is possible.

If now we regard the entrance of raw materials into the industrial system as the first stage in production, we shall come to the conclusion that, pooling together all the productive processes, there must be a definite quantitative relation between the rate of production and the rate of consumption, or, in other words, between the quantity of employment of capital and labour and the quantity of commodities withdrawn from the productive stream within any given time.

Recognising this fixed proportion between the rate at which raw materials enter the stream and the rate at which commodities are drawn out, we need not yet concern ourselves with the question how far the one or the other determines or regulates the flow of industry. The law of gravitation, according to which water flows from the high lands towards the sea, seems to exhibit a pushing force as we watch the stream from below, a pulling force as we watch from above. So with the push and pull of the industrial process.

§ 2.—Before we consider what it is that makes the industrial system work, what that energy of push and pull is that corresponds to gravitation in a stream, we need to look a little nearer at the object which this system seems to have set before it, the result or product of all its activity.

As this object for the individual ' producer ' is said to be his ' income,' so we may say that the *prima facie* object of industry is to produce an income for the industrial society.

Now what is that income ? We are accustomed to express income in money, but we are also familiar with the notion that real income is what that money will buy, and in considering the income of industrial society we must begin with this real income. What will be the real income which the industrial system yields ? The answer to this question will depend upon our concept of the industrial society. If that society were in an absolutely stationary condition, with a fixed population, fixed wants and fixed methods of industry, the income for each year would consist in the quantity of commodities (goods and services) produced for consumption and handed over to consumers during the year. This, of course, does not mean that all the industrial energy expended that year was represented in these consumption goods, for some industrial energy must go into replacement of plant or provision against wear and tear. This provision against wear and tear does not, however, rank as income, either from the standpoint of social or of individual production. In our fixed or static society all productive energy, after provision for wear and tear fund, would be represented by consumption goods and services. The total output of commodities would be identical with the income : the new boots, loaves, shirts, doctoring, musical performances, governmental care, &c., produced during the year would constitute the real income for the year.

Although there is no real society living in a ' static ' condition, it is convenient to examine how such an industrial system would work. We should perceive a constant even flow of raw materials entering the stream of industry, passing through the various processes and emerging as commodities, and the same even flow would take place down the tributary streams engaged in maintaining the plant and other fixed capital in the several processes.

So far we have spoken of the movement of materials and goods as a ' flow,' without seeking more closely an explanation of ' how ' materials pass from one stage of production to the next stage, and finally pass from retail shopkeepers to consumers.

If we are to retain the ' flow ' metaphor, we must supplement our view of the industrial movement by introducing another ' flow ' which moves in a reverse direction to the flow of goods. This is the ' flow ' or circulation of money. What money is we need not here pause to ask : we may treat anything as money the payment of which enables him who pays to buy what he requires for consumption or for some service of production. Now if, turning to our stream of boot-producing processes, we ask *how* hides pass from the tanner's possession into that of the shoe manufacturer's, we perceive at once that it is because money passes from the shoe manufacturer to the tanner : so with the movement of shoes from the manufacturer to the shop of the merchant, it is attended by a corresponding passage of money the opposite way.

In the stable industrial society we are investigating, it is easy to see how the two streams, the goods flowing from raw materials to commodities, the money flowing from the consumers up the series of industrial processes, inter-act and correspond. The raw material gathers utility, i.e. it reaches a shape or a place where it is nearer towards satisfying some human want than in its earlier shape or place, at each stage in production by the operation of the capital and labour which act upon it, until at the end it takes the finished form of a commodity.

Now follow the course taken by the money which is paid for this commodity, boots or loaves, or other shop goods. The consumer, in buying the commodity, hands over in return a sum of money, the price. What does the shopkeeper at E do with this money? With part of it he defrays the expenses of shopkeeping, he pays his rent, expenses, the wages of his shop assistants, establishment, the interest on his borrowed capital, profits or earnings of management to himself. This disposes of a certain fraction of the money. The rest he passes on to the wholesale merchant at D, or the manufacturer at C, in payment for more goods to replace the boots or shirts he has sold, or more commonly to meet a bill in payment for goods previously received. In fact, then, the merchant who has advanced on credit the boots or flour which the retailer has sold to customers receives a part of the money paid by the customers, handed over to him by the retailer so as to maintain his stock. So a part of the money paid to the retailer at E goes to maintain in productive work the retail capital and labour, &c., the rest is passed on to the merchant at D, stimulating by its passage the flow of goods from the merchant to the retailer. Now the wholesale merchant or importer of shoes or shirts, when he has received the money from the retailer in demand for more shoes or flour, will use this money, partly to defray his current expenses, rent, wages, profit, &c., partly to replenish and maintain his stock by sending more orders to the manufacturer of shoes or shirts at C. Whether he actually pays over the money when he sends the order or receives the goods, or whether he accepts a bill, does not affect the substance of the act : part of the money which, starting from the purse of the consumer, reached him through the retailer, is used to pay the manufacturer for a fresh supply of shoes or shirts. Here, too, the flow of the money from the merchant to the maker (D to C) is the means of driving goods to pass from maker to merchant (C to D). The shoe manufacturer or shirt-maker makes a similar use of the part of the price of shoes or shirts that reaches him, in paying his various expenses and in buying a fresh stock of raw materials, leather or cotton cloth, from the manufacturer of those goods at B. These latter, in their turn, after paying their expenses of production, apply the money thus received in buying a fresh stock of hides or cotton from farmers or growers at A, which latter use the money in maintaining the productive processes by which they ‘ extract ’ their raw material (cattle or cotton) from Nature. If we looked a little closer at the payments made at each stage under the head of ‘ expenses,’ we should find that some of it went to repair and replace buildings, machinery, and other forms of ‘ capital ’ required to assist production, and involved payments to machine-makers and others, who are represented in our diagram by the letters a, b, c, d, e. These makers, as we saw, stand at the head of a series of tributary trades whose flow joins the main current at A, B, C, D, E. A fraction of the consumer's money flows into each of these tributary channels, and causes an onward flow of raw materials towards new finished plant and machinery, corresponding to the flow of goods along the main channel of industry. This illustration makes it evident that in the stationary society we are examining the money paid over the retail counter by the consumer in payment for commodities is the actual source of all money-incomes received throughout the industrial system by the owners of capital, labour, land, &c., and that its flow upward through the main and tributary channels of industry is the stimulus to each movement by which raw materials and goods are carried down the stream towards consumption.

A portion of the money paid over the retail counter is then deposited at each stage in payments to owners of labour, capital, land there employed, then the rest flows on to the next stage. These payments are the direct industrial stimuli of the continued production ; though in form they represent work already done by some factor, they are in fact material conditions and moral inducements to the owners of labour, capital, and land, to apply these factors in further industrial work. The money thus paid in wages to labour, expended in food, &c., replaces the labour-power that has been depleted, and furnishes a new supply of productive energy : though paid for work already done, this payment evokes further work by supporting the conviction that this work also will in due course receive payment. So with the owner of capital, the money paid him for the past service rendered by his capital goes partly to replace its wear and tear, partly to induce him to continue its industrial employment. The same holds likewise of the landowner's rent.[1]

The money-income received by any person engaged at any point in the industrial process as worker, capitalist, landowner is composed of these payments made to him for single uses of some factor of production, and is seen to come out of a fund which flows from the consumer. The total money-income of this industrial community would in this case be equivalent to the aggregate of money expended by consumers for commodities which would be distributed, as we see, throughout the industrial world in payments for the use of labour, capital, and land so as to maintain these factors and keep them in productive operation. The real income of the community would consist of the aggregate of commodities which passed into the hands of the consumers, or, in other words, the goods purchased for consumption by the recipients of the money-incomes.

The meaning of income is, however, somewhat confused by other circumstances which require notice. So far we have treated the industrial mechanism as engaged in producing material commodities only. But political economy is concerned with all forms of marketable wealth, services as well as material wares. Now the production and consumption of services differ in no essential point, so far as the structure and working of industry is concerned, from the production and consumption of material goods.

[1] The question of the necessity of these payments remains for later and more appropriate discussion. It is not germane to the present inquiry.

If I pay half a crown to attend a lecture or 5s. for a doctor's advice, these payments must be treated as equivalent to the payments of another half-crown for the text book I use at the lecture, and of another 5s. which I pay to a chemist for the drugs the doctor orders me to take. Just as there exists a series of industries engaged in forwarding the production of books and drugs, there exists a series of processes engaged in putting into the lecture and the doctor the serviceable information which is bought from them. Schools and colleges, laboratories, hospitals, and work of professional research are all processes which go to produce the skilled information that is sold, and though the continuity of the chain of productive processes is less visible, and in some regards less regular, it is there, and is maintained from the payments for retail services. Though the individual fee you pay a doctor or a lawyer cannot often be traced back in distribution to the earlier stages of production of medical and legal skill, it is none the less true that a demand for medical advice is a demand for medical schools, hospitals, and scientific research, and that any increase of expenditure on litigation tends to swell the profession, and to react along the paths of professional and general education. Moreover, it must be remembered that a demand for services is not only a demand for the teaching of their forms of skill, but for various material instruments subsidiary to these services : offices, books, surgical instruments, and other tools of the craft are 'demanded' by the demand for professional services. The real income of a nation will, therefore, include all professional and other personal services valued, as material commodities are valued, according to their selling prices. So, too, in reckoning the money-income of the nation we shall reckon the incomes of professional men, officials, domestic servants, &c., not as derived from or paid out of the incomes of those who employ them, but as directly representing non-material wealth produced by them which forms part of the real income of the nation.[1] It may seem a hard saying, but a gamekeeper or a secretary of state must be considered to produce real wealth in the preservation of game or of empire, which is the equivalent of the salary they respectively receive. The questions

---

[1] If I am a manufacturer receiving £5000 a year in profits from my mills, I am considered as creating, or causing to be created, a quantity of goods corresponding to that sum, the product of my skill or enterprise. If I employ a private tutor for my boys, and pay him £300 out of my £5000, his tutorial services constitute another real income, though a non-material one. Though I am said to pay him his £300 out of my £5000, the real income produced by the two of us corresponds to £5300, and the income tax commissioners rightly assess me on the whole £5000 and him on the £300. If, on the other hand, I also out of my £5000 make an allowance of £300 to my son, no real income corresponds to that £300, and my son is not assessed on it for income tax.

whether such work is socially desirable or is overpaid are entirely irrelevant in such an analysis.

A scientific theory which includes, under wealth, all marketable things, must include all paid services in this national income, and the payment for them as independent items of the money-income of the nation.

Our diagram of industry, with its main and subsidiary streams of production, its statements of the quantitative relations between the factors of production and the rate of consumption, will be just as applicable to the production and consumption of non-material as of material wealth, except that material factors of land and capital play a smaller and a less direct part in the processes of production or preparation of most saleable services, and that the series of processes of production may be shorter and less regular.

The raw material of some rude human faculty is selected from a mass of human faculties, trained, informed, and adapted to the rendering of some special service in a profession, art, or office, by the application of a carefully ordered machinery of education employing various forms of intellectual labour wielding material tools of instruction : the result of these processes is to refine a raw human capacity of small utility and value into a powerful and finely serviceable capacity with high market value. So far as the intellectual, and even the moral and spiritual, activities of man are bought and sold, the laws of their production and consumption do not differ from those of material goods as regards the application of these fundamental laws.

If we are dealing with a community fixed in its numbers and its modes, alike of production and consumption—an absolutely stable industrial society—our simple analysis of production and consumption would suffice. The whole of the money-income paid as rent, profits, wages, &c., to members of the society would be spent in demanding commodities for personal consumption.

The net real income of the community would consist of the aggregate of the finished commodities and services produced and consumed in the year, the net money-income of the money values which these commodities and services represented. The prices which described their money values would include payments made to the owners of capital and labour who replaced the waste of fixed capital and land. Thus the two currents, the stream of production from raw materials to commodities, and the reverse flow of money from the consumer down the channels of production, would maintain a regular amount of production and consumption. In such an industrial society as we have been considering, statical in population, in the arts of production and in standard of consumption, the entire real income would be consumed in material commodities and services, and the entire money-income of all its members would be spent in paying for them.   No saving would be necessary or possible.

§ 3.—But this is not the actual industrial system in which our inquiring workman will find himself living.   The industrial community, whether he regards it as a nation, or more accurately as the industrial world, must be regarded not as stationary but as changing, and the change is, on the whole, a growth.   The structure and working of the actual industrial system must take account of growth of population, a rising standard of consumption and improved economies in the arts of production.

These changes involve some important modifications in our plan of the industrial system.   If provision is to be made for commodities to meet the growing needs of an increasing population, the industrial system must be enabled to set up along all its productive channels an increased quantity of the instruments of production ; before a larger variety of shop goods can be sold at a faster pace over the retail counter to an increasing number of customers, more capital and labour must previously have been set in operation at each of the processes of production.

Now in the modern industrial world there is only one way of bringing this about.   The whole money-income of the community must not be expended in buying finished commodities at the end of the industrial process for consumption ; some of it instead must be expended in paying workers to make and set up more plant, machinery, &c., than existed before at the various points in the main stream and the tributaries of production, and to use this increased capital to work up raw materials in the different productive processes, so as to be able to put into the shops of retailers a larger flow of commodities to be sold by them to consumers.

So whereas in a stable industrial society all the money-income received for productive services by capitalists, labourers, landowners, &c., was applied at E in purchase of consumption goods, in a progressive society some of it will be applied at A, B, C, and D, and down the tributary channels a, a1, b, b1, &c., to set up new instruments of production and to work them.   In the stable society the money which circulated through the industrial system, stimulating productive activity at each point, and causing the movement of goods down the stream of industry, was inserted entirely at the end of the industrial process in purchase of retail goods.   In the actual progressive society some of this money is inserted directly at the different points of production, and serves to stimulate production at these points beyond the rate needed to maintain the former activity of production.

How it operates is quite clear. If we suppose the stable society illustrated in our diagram to become progressive, saving so as to provide for increased consumption in the future, what will happen is this. Some of the money which was regularly applied at E in bringing retail goods will no longer be applied there ; and the retailers at E, having less custom, will reduce, as far as they can, their expenses, employing less capital and labour, &c., and handing on less money to wholesale merchants in fresh orders. The merchants at D, finding their business similarly slack, will also curtail expenses and reduce their orders from makers ; and so the reduction of spending at E will cause a general slowing down of all the industrial processes, both along the main stream and down the tributaries. This is what happens as the direct effect of a reduction of spending upon commodities. But, as we have recognised, saving (as distinct from hoarding) does not mean a refusal to apply the money stimulus, but only a refusal to apply it at the retail stage in ' demand ' for commodities. The ' saving ' persons who reduce the ' demand ' for commodities apply the same quantity of ' demand ' at various interim points in the industrial process. They pay more money for developing new mines, they place contracts for putting up more mills and workshops, they give more orders for machinery. In other words, instead of applying all their money at E, they apply some of it directly at A, B, or C, so as to set up more forms of plant, &c., at these points in production.

The money thus applied at A, B, or C not only stimulates their increased activity of capital and labour, but some of it is passed on to the trades on the tributaries, a, a1, b, b1, &c., stimulating industry there. If the saving be taken as a general process, it will flow in regular proportions through the building, machinery-making, and other trades, which set up plant, and the stimulus will then pass through the early processes of the extractive and manufacturing industries, so that a fuller flow of raw materials than before will begin to pass down the main stream towards the consumer.

The first effect of saving, which alone concerns us just now, is thus seen to be a slackening of the former even circulation of money and stimulation of industrial energy, and a substitution of an enhanced circulation and stimulation in certain parts of the industrial system in preparation for a general increased flow of productive energy towards commodities.

In the stable society the only productive energy applied to making the forms of capital was confined to providing against wear and tear, so as to maintain the existing stock of capital, and this is not saving. In the progressive society productive energy is applied to making more forms of capital, setting up more mills, foundries, workshops, machines, and passing through them larger quantities of raw materials than before : this is saving.

Spending means buying commodities with income ; saving means buying productive goods or instruments with income. Spending causes more commodities to be produced ; saving causes more forms of capital to be produced.

The sort of stimulus applied by spending and by saving is the same : in each case the application of the money circulating down the series of productive processes from the point where it is applied sets up or maintains industrial activity in all the preceding processes, and causes material to flow from one stage of production to another. In spending, however, the net result is to withdraw some commodities from the industrial system for consumption, replacing what was withdrawn by another set of similar commodities, so that the general stream of industry remains as before : in saving, the net result is to add some new forms of capital (buildings, machines, material, goods), leaving the productive apparatus of the system larger than before in the various processes of industry, and so stimulating production, not from the end of the whole process, but from various interim points. Spending means buying consumption goods ; saving means buying production goods.

That all saving implies demand for creation of more forms of fixed or circulating capital is not at first obvious. From the standpoint of the individual who saves, his action consists in a refusal to demand commodities, a not-spending, or, more strictly, a postponement of spending. In primitive industrial societies, or in disturbed conditions of more advanced societies, much refusal to spend takes the form of hoarding money. Though hoarding may be fully justified as an individual precaution, its effect in industry as compared with spending is to check the flow of the industrial stream, causing a smaller employment of capital, labour, and land than would be afforded by the spending of the money that was hoarded. An increase of hoarding inevitably tends to depress trade, though the subsequent spending of hoarded treasure will ultimately redress the balance by affording a corresponding stimulus.

In modern industrial societies, however, hoarding is abnormal.[1] A person who, instead of spending, saves, invests his savings. Now there are two ways in which he may invest his savings. He may hand over the money to someone who wishes to spend it on commodities, buying property which the other sells, or loaning it on mortgage. This is the saving effected when a money-lender

[1] In a later discussion of commercial depressions, and their accompanying unemployment, we shall perceive that abnormal hoarding may sometimes play a critical part.

advances money to a spendthrift. In this case A, not wishing to
spend himself, simply transfers for a consideration the power to
spend to B, who does wish to spend. Though A saves and invests
his saving, no effect is produced upon the total volume of spending or saving : all that has happened is that B spends instead
of A, and that some ' capital ' which existed before in B's hands
now belongs to A.

(This is not quite all, for A does not hand over to B *all* his
power of spending which he saves ; he keeps back a certain share,
say five per cent., which he receives as interest. Thus A, who has
saved £100 and ' invests ' it with spendthrift B, receiving from B a
mortgage deed and £5 per annum, really hands over £95 of spending power, which B uses. If A does not save but spends his £5
interest, the total amount of spending is just as much as if A had
not ' saved,' for B spends £95 and A spends £5 instead of A
spending the whole £100.)

Neither ' hoarding ' nor this sort of saving makes provision for
expansion of production and of consumption in a progressive community. But if, instead of lending money to a spendthrift, A
invests it in his own business or in someone else's business, so as
to extend industrial operations, what becomes of the money ?
Though saved, it is nevertheless spent. But instead of being spent
in demanding commodities which, when demanded, are destroyed
in consumption, it is spent in demanding productive goods, e.g.
new mills, machines, warehouses, raw materials, &c., which, when
demanded, are not straightway destroyed, but form an addition to
the amount of material wealth in the community. Whereas spending means paying capital and labour to produce finished commodities which are immediately withdrawn from the industrial stream
and destroyed, saving means paying the same amount of capital
and labour to produce additional productive goods (i.e. forms of
capital) which are not withdrawn, but remain an addition to the
producing power of the community. Such acts of saving employ,
directly, just the same amount of capital and labour as if the money
were spent on commodities,[1] the difference being that in the former
case the capital and labour are employed in producing more productive goods, in the latter in producing more consumptive goods.

§ 4.—It is sometimes assumed that any proportion of the income
of a community can advantageously be saved. But this is not the
case. We saw how in a stable community a fixed proportion was
maintained between the amount of productive energy employed at
the various processes, and only a given aggregate of capital could

---

[1] J. S. Mill, in one of his most confused passages, argued that they
employed more.

be employed in forwarding the work of turning out the fixed output of commodities.

Of course, this limitation of useful capital no longer holds of a progressive community ; a larger amount of saving is continually wanted to supply capital to meet not only the current but the prospective increase of consumption. But, though the limits of saving are made more elastic, they are not entirely cancelled. In a primitive industrial community, however progressive in population and in needs, the quantity of ' saving ' that can usefully be done will be restricted by the simple methods of industry in vogue. Where almost all production is by hand labour with simple tools, the limit of saving as compared with spending must remain very narrow.

In the modern capitalist society there is, of course, an enormously extended possibility of socially useful saving. A large proportion of the modern social income can be saved because it is possible to put it into costly forms of capital, the services of which will fructify in the shape of consumption of goods a long time hence : railroads may be made, opening new tracts of the earth in distant lands, new harbours, mining explorations, afforestation, drainage, and other vast public or private enterprises, destined at some distant future to facilitate the production of actual commodities. Such investments may swallow up large masses of new savings. But while it thus might seem that the opportunities of useful saving were infinite, i.e. that any proportion of the current general income could serviceably be saved *provided* that at some distant time society increased correspondingly its rate of consumption, this is not truly the case. Those alterations in the arts of industry which give so much importance to capital applied in various direct and indirect processes of production, while greatly extending the limits of saving as compared with more primitive production, still leave some limits. Two important considerations maintain these limits. In the first place, most forms of new capital, even in this age of elaborated indirect production by machinery, very soon result in promoting an increased flow of finished goods, and unless the proportion of spending to saving were speedily readjusted so as to take off this increased flow by freer spending, at the same time checking the ' saving ' which sets up these sorts of capital, the machinery of industry must become congested and clogged by excessive goods and commodities unable to find an exit in consumption. Secondly, the proportion of new saving which can be so applied as to fructify at some far distant date is necessarily small, restricted principally by our inability to forecast far ahead either the needs of coming men or the most economical modes of providing for them.

Though the amount of saving that can take material shape in new railroads, harbours, and other great capitalist enterprises of a foundational character is large in itself, it constitutes a small proportion of the total saving, nor is it capable of indefinite expansion.

The very pace at which mechanical improvements are taking place, the rapidity of shifts of population and of industry, the swift transformation in methods of living, form considerable checks upon the more enduring shapes of capital. It seldom pays to put up a city building timed to last more than a few decades, the feasibility of rail-less locomotion is cutting down railroad investment, manufacturers attribute an ever-shortening life to their most expensive machinery.

The great bulk of capital fructifies in an early increase of commodities, and so the saving embodied in it is only socially useful on condition that an early increase of consumption proportionate to the increased saving takes place.

A little reflection will make it evident that this implies the maintenance of a definite proportion between the aggregate of saving and of spending over a term of years. An individual may, of course, continue to save any proportion of his income : a class of persons, or even a whole nation, may do the same provided they can find other classes or other nations ready to borrow and to spend what they are saving. But the industrial community as a whole cannot save at any given time more than a certain proportion of its income : that proportion is never accurately known, and it is always shifting with changes in the arts of production and consumption, but it imposes as real a limit on the economy of saving for the industrial community to-day as there was for Robinson Crusoe on his island or for a primitive isolated tribe of men before the era of machine production.

If this proportion is exceeded one year it must be curtailed the next, so that over a term of years a real proportion must be maintained between saving and spending. It is only by taking the partial standpoint of an individual or a group of individuals, or some other part of the industrial whole, that it seems plausible to hold that there is no limit to efficacious saving.

Though the proportion of efficacious saving to spending is always slowly changing, at any given time it must rightly be regarded as fixed in the sense that there is an exact proportion of the current income which, in accordance with existing arts of production and existing foresight, is required to set up new capital so as to make provision for the maximum consumption throughout the near future. Any miscalculation or other play of social forces which disturbs this proportion, inducing either too much saving or too much spending, causes a waste of productive power and a restriction in aggregate consumption.

In a stable society, as we saw, all the income is spent : there is no place for saving. But in a progressive society where the future rate of consumption is to exceed the present, for a larger population with a higher standard of comfort saving is essential. A little saving will only make provision for a slight rise in the volume of consumption ; more saving is needed for a larger rise. The right amount of saving out of a given income, i.e. the right proportion of saving, will be determined by the amount of new capital economically needed to furnish a given increase of consumption goods. Over a period of years there will be a rate of saving which will assist to produce the maximum quantity of consumption goods.

Any spending which reduces the rate of saving is over-spending, and involves a waste of general productive power analogous to that which was attributed to over-saving. Over-spending retards the rate of progress in production and consumption of commodities, sacrificing the future to the present. It does not, however, imply ' getting into debt ' or ' living upon capital.' These terms are only applicable to the over-spending of individuals, classes, or other parts of the industrial community. The community as a whole cannot get into debt, for there is no ' outside ' to borrow from. Nor can it ' live upon its capital,' for that, too, implies borrowing. Even if the industrial community became so reckless in its expenditure as not merely to make no ' saving,' but to refuse to provide against ' wear and tear ' of existing forms of capital, such extravagance could not be continued long ; it would soon be checked by the slackened pace at which raw materials and production goods would pass through the processes of industry into the retail shops. It is manifestly impossible for society to spend more than its actual current income, i.e. to take out at the end of the productive process more commodities than flow through the stream of industry. An individual may exceed his current income by his expenditure, a nation may do the same, but the industrial community as a whole cannot do so. Over-spending on the part of the community does not mean spending more than its income : it means a refusal to spend less now, so as to provide for an increased future rate of expenditure.

We saw, then, that just as in a stable society there was a fixed ratio between the quantity of capital and labour at the various points of production, and also between the aggregate of capital and the aggregate of consumption, so in a progressive society there is at any given time a similar ratio.

There exists at the present moment a right proportion between saving and spending in the income of the industrial community, yielding the maximum rate of consumption over such a period of time as is open by reasonable foresight to capitalist investment. Industrial progress, or the economical working of the industrial system, consists largely in the ascertainment of this proportion and the adjustment of industry to it : any disregard or disturbance of this proportion involves industrial waste.

How far these considerations of the limits of saving and spending, strictly applicable only to the industrial world as a whole, can be held to have a valid bearing upon the industrial life of Great Britain or any other single nation, is a question which may be reserved for later discussion.

Thus we recognise that the annual income of industrial society means two things. First, the net yield of goods (capital goods and commodities) and services from processes of industry during the year.

Second, the addition of the money payments made as rent, salaries, wages, and profits to owners of factors of production taking part in industry. This annual income is partly spent, partly saved. Spending signifies a removal from the industrial system of goods and services which are consumed by those who remove them. Saving signifies an increase of capital-forms which remain within the industrial system, representing an increased power of production.

While in any given year (or short period) there is no limit to the proportion of income that may be spent, and no limit to the proportion which may be saved, except as regards expenditure on necessaries of working life, over a longer period of time a quantitative relation exists between spending and saving so as to secure the maximum productivity over the whole period.

The right proportion of saving to spending at any given time depends upon the present condition of the arts of production and consumption, and the probabilities of such changes in modes of work or living as shall provide social utility for new forms of capital within the near or calculable future.

CHAPTER IV

COSTS AND SURPLUS

§ 1. Production and distribution are simultaneous and in a sense identical processes. Payments for factors of production are orders on goods. The payment of the *entrepreneurs* requires separate treatment.—§ 2. For a theory of distribution co-ordination of the factors is the first essential. Capitalisation and differential grading are both defective bases. Productive powers must be expressed in standard units.—§ 3. The first charge on the product is the subsistence wage.—§ 4. A rise in price per unit of labour stimulates an increased supply, by calling in more labourers or intensifying labour. Similarly, improved qualities of labour are evoked by the stimulus of higher pay.—§ 5. Capital has two similar costs, first of subsistence, second of growth. Minimum interest is a cost of subsistence. —§ 6. Capital may be graded like labour into different markets with different market-prices per unit. A rise of interest stimulates saving.— § 7. Land, as regards maintenance and increase, ranks as capital.—§ 8. So far as 'costs' are concerned, harmony exists in the industrial system: the 'surplus' introduces discord.—§ 9. Modern industry, enhancing the surplus, emphasises the discord.

§ 1.—AFTER the general survey of the structure and working of the industrial system, an economic student will naturally turn to a closer investigation of the movements which comprise at once the production and the distribution of wealth. These movements which he has perceived to occur continuously at each stage in every industrial series consist in the payments of sums of money which are seen to stimulate, first, the passage of goods from one stage to another along the stream of industry; secondly, the putting-out of industrial energy by all the factors of production, land, capital, labour, ability, to which the money stimulus is applied. As the money circulates up the stream, it is seen by its touch to liberate industrial energy at each point, and to cause raw materials or goods to move one step further towards the condition of shop goods and commodities.

This regular series of monetary payments has so far been regarded merely as an instrument of the productive system.

But it is now time to recognise that these same payments constitute what is called the distribution of wealth. We do not first produce a lot of wealth and then afterwards distribute it : the production and distribution not only take place simultaneously, but are in a sense identical processes.

The payments of money which constitute distribution are in effect orders upon the very goods which are being made or have just been made : the acts by which wealth is distributed are acts by which new productive energy is evoked and the general process of production is kept going.

We cannot therefore properly study the production and the distribution of wealth apart, since the actual payments, which form distribution, are the efficient causes of the several industrial activities.

We saw how all industrial incomes came from the breaking-up and distribution of prices paid for retail goods and services, or for new pieces of capital. Taking the money paid over the counter of shoe-stores for shoes, we saw how it served to pay four classes of income at each stage in production—rent, wages, interest, and profit—and how fragments of it passed down the tributaries which furnished the machinery and other ' fixed' capital required at the several stages, being distributed along these tributaries in payments for land, labour, capital, and management there employed.

This last set of payments for maintaining the buildings, plant, and other fixed capital will, of course, rank as ' wear and tear ' at the several stages, though each payment under this head is after-wards broken up into rent, wages, interest, and profits.

Taking, then, £100, received in a week over the counter in a retail shop, for shoes or for commodities in general, and tracing its movement along the main channel, we should find it broken up in some such way as the following[1] :—

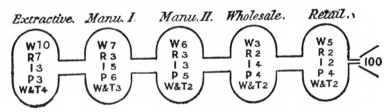

What happens at each of these stages is that a manager or *entrepreneur* hands over goods to the *entrepreneur* at the next stage (or in the case of a retailer to consumers), receives from him a sum of money, out of which he pays his rent, wages, and interest,

---

[1] This analysis omits payments made at various stages for transport and other subsidiary services, which, of course, in their turn are resolved into sets of payments of wages, rent, interest, profit, &c.

buys goods or material from the earlier stage in order to continue his productive operation, and keeps the residue for his own profit.

While for convenience we have hitherto classed profit with other payments, regarding 'management' as a factor of production equally with labour, land, and capital, it is well now to mark that it stands on a different footing from the others, and that the payment made on account of it is somewhat differently determined. Rent is the price paid to the landowner for the use of land, wages the price paid to the labourer for the use of labour-power, interest the price paid the capitalist for use of capital, but it cannot be said in the same sense that profit is the price paid to the *entrepreneur* for the use of managing ability.

The *entrepreneur* is more than a mere manager. He has an eye for a profitable project, he plans a business, buys the uses of land, labour, and capital of various sorts, embodies their productive power in materials which he likewise purchases, and markets the product. The difference between these expenses of production and the prices obtained for the product constitutes his profit. Speculation, enterprise, organisation, bargaining skill, as well as the relatively routine faculty of management, are sources of profit, helping to determine the gain which comes to him. Though all these functions may be classed together as business ability and regarded as a single factor of production, the differences between the part played by this and the other factors, and between the actual methods by which the payments for the two are respectively determined, are so great that a refusal to distinguish them in presenting the principles of distribution would be a grave source of error.

We cannot with advantage treat profits as we do rent, wages, and interest, as payment for so much quantity of productive energy utilised in the industrial processes.

Therefore, while some of the functions of the manager or *entrepreneur* may be regarded as a sort of mental labour-power, whose price is determined in something like the same way as payments for other labour, a closer investigation of profit will show that its essentially speculative nature requires it to be submitted to a separate analysis in order that we may understand the part it plays in the direction of industry.

For these reasons we shall first examine separately the payments made for use of land, labour, and capital, and the influences which determine these prices, viz. rent, wages, interest, reserving for later and special treatment the payment of profits.

§ 2.—For the maintenance and growth of industry a constant influx of new energy is required. As the human organism requires for its purposes so many units of nitrogenous, carbo-hydrate and other sorts of foods in regular proportions, so the industrial organism requires the continuous intake of new industrial energy conveyed in a duly proportioned application of the productive powers of land, labour, and capital in their several sorts.

Much of the obscurity of the ' theory of distribution ' is due to the want of a clear system of measuring industrial energy. The actual instruments of industrial energy, as we have seen, are workers commonly measured by hours' or weeks' work ; pieces of land measured in acres ; machines, factories, stock, and other forms of capital not usually measured by any reference to their concrete character, but expressed in values of so many hundred pounds.

So long as these separate conventional methods of reckoning the prices paid for the use of labour, capital, and land are retained, no intelligible and consistent statement of the distribution of wealth is possible.

Now the co-ordination of the factors of production for the application of a common mode of measurement might be compassed in several different ways. It would be possible to apply to all three the method that is applied to the forms of capital : the productive energy of acres and of labourers might be capitalised, i.e. might be expressed in terms of so many £100, and rent and wages so reduced to interest on these capital values. If, then, a superior acre of market garden land was capitalised at £200, fetching a rent of £8 per annum, while an inferior acre was capitalised at £100, fetching a rent of £4, we should have applied to land the same method of valuation that holds of buildings, machinery, and stock. Labour could be expressed similarly by capitalising the working-power of each worker on the basis of his earning-power per year.

But though this method is sometimes employed in attempts to assess the capital wealth of a nation, its effect is to fuse all distinctions between the different factors, and to bring them into a single pool of productive-power. It is therefore disqualified from serving as a mode of explaining the distribution of the product among the several factors. This purpose requires us to keep closely to the concrete nature of industry, and to express capital in terms of industrial forms rather than to reduce land and labour to financial values.

But another mode of co-ordination has been sometimes employed, by which the differential grading of acres of land is applied to labourers and to forms of capital.

As acres of wheat land differ in degrees of fertility and receive a higher or a lower rent per acre accordingly, similarly weavers or compositors may be graded according to their output with corresponding differences of weekly earnings, while machines and other pieces of concrete capital similarly graded according to their working efficiency, may be held to earn different rates of ' real ' interest.

But if this grading really has reference solely to the differences of quantity of productive-power given out by different acres, different men, different machines, &c., is it not simpler and more effective to furnish a direct measure of this quantity of productive-power, expressing acres directly in terms of units of land-power, labourers in units of labour-power, machines, &c., in units of capital-power? For this is the true attitude of the *entrepreneur* and the consumer who exercise the direction of industrial processes. What the *entrepreneur* who plans and controls industry is buying is quantities of different sorts of productive-power; *prima facie* he is not concerned with the proportions in which this power is given out by the different labourers or acres or machines. Again, what the consumer buys is quantities of the same power stored in commodities ; he, too, is not directly concerned with the varying productivity of the different acres or workers or machines. What we need, therefore, is a direct measure of units of productive-power ; for it is these units that are really bought and sold under the guise of acre productivity per annum, labourer productivity per week, machine or concrete capital productivity per annum.

Let us then firmly take the position of regarding the productive power of land, of labour, or of capital, which the *entrepreneur* buys and uses for productive purposes, as consisting of so many units of these several sorts, an acre good or bad containing so many units of land-power per annum, a labourer so many units of labour-power per week, a factory or a machine so many units of productive power of capital. Most labour-power is already reckoned and remunerated by this unitary method ; piece-wages or time-wages are payments for units of labour-power adjudged to be of standard size, the price per unit of labour-power is the direct determinant of the weekly or yearly income of each labourer. The extension of this unitary method to land will resolve differential rents per acre into differences in the number of units of land-power given out for wheat-growing or other use ; its extension to capital will require the application of differential interests per factory, machine, or other piece of concrete capital in accordance with the number of units of productivity it gives out. This last conception is not so novel as it may appear to some. Modern systems of cost-taking often employ it, records being kept of the comparative costs and outputs of the several machines, just as in a well-managed dairy farm the milk-yield of each cow is separately kept.

If we are to escape the confusion due to the attempt to build up a theory of distribution by loose correlation of separate laws of wages, rent, and interest, it is necessary to bring all the factors under some single law applicable to all buying and selling, whether of productive-powers or of commodities.

Now just as a scientific treatment of food requires that the various sorts of intake shall be reduced to some common standard and expressed in units of that standard, so with industrial energy. The flow of industrial energy through the system must be expressed in some common terms so that the contribution made by the several human or non-human instruments may be rendered comparable and capable of accurate measurement.

The labour-power given out by such and such a worker during a week or a year must be expressed in labour-units ; similarly the employment of an acre of land for agriculture or for site must be reduced to units of land use, the services of a cotton factory, a ton of coal, a locomotive, must be reduced to units of capital use. A unit of labour-power will mean a given quantity of productive-power of a certain sort, irrespective of the number of workers or the individual output of the several workers who give out the unit. So likewise a unit of capital-power will mean a given quantity of productive-power of a certain sort given out by machinery, plant, &c., irrespective of the number of such machines : a unit of land-power, e.g. for wheat-growing, will be so much productive power of land, irrespective of the number of acres employed in giving it out.

In the application of this unitary standard of productivity to individual factors, due account must, of course, be taken of the pace of productivity. A worker who can turn out twenty pieces per week is usually to be accounted as more than twice as productive as one who can only turn out ten. This is commonly recognised by a bonus upon quantity of output per week in addition to the piece-wage. There are two reasons for recognising pace of productivity as well as number of pieces. In the first place, labour-power more quickly given out means goods coming into supply at an earlier time than they would otherwise have done, and since present goods are worth more than future goods, this quickening of supply enhances wealth as measured by quantity of satisfaction. In the second place, where labour co-operates with other factors, slow labour may keep down their productivity, as is the case where a slow workman is set to feed a rapid machine or where he determines the pace for a gang of workers. Any separate reckoning of the productivity of labour must take into account such retardation of the productivity of other factors. In any really scientific cost-taking the number of units of productivity attributed to a particular workman will thus take the rate of output into account. The same qualification will, of course, be applicable to the other factors. A machine turning out 100 pieces of work a day will be worth more than twice one that turns out fifty. So, in regarding the productivity of land which is bought by rent, we must consider an acre yielding forty bushels to the crop more than twice as productive as an acre yielding twenty, land yielding two crops per annum more than twice as productive as land yielding only one.

Concerned as we are with the primary need of getting a sound co-ordination of the several factors of production, so as to apply a common rule of payment for these uses, it is of the first importance to realise that the truth underlying the law of differential rent is applicable to all the other factors. When we are measuring for purposes of payment the separate productivity[1] of an acre, or a machine, or a worker, rate of emission of productive-power as well as quantity of product must be taken into account in measuring the aggregate productivity or the number of its units.

§ 3.—Having thus built up in our minds a clear conception of the industrial system as a single whole employing various sorts of industrial energy in turning out commodities, we need to get a fuller understanding of the methods by which the inevitable waste of structure is repaired, by which new or increased structure is created, and by which fresh quantities of energy are got into the system. This repair and growth of structure, replenishment and increase of energy, are directed by the processes of distribution of income absorbing continuously the greater part of the results of production.

The industrial system will work for its keep ; each of its organs or instruments will continue to operate productively, provided it is kept constantly in repair and the energy it gives out in production is constantly replaced.

A growing industrial system requires more than its keep : it must be furnished with surplus matter and energy to make new tissue and to do more work.

In considering the distribution of the product of industry, through incomes, to the different factors of production, we may conveniently distinguish the portion which goes to maintenance from that which goes to growth.

What is the ' keep ' or ' maintenance fund ' of labour ? It is not wages but only a part of wages. Every sort of labourer giving

---

[1] Though our existing system of distribution is mainly based upon this imputation of a separable productivity, fuller analysis of the organic co-operation of factors in a business discloses the inherent defectiveness of this theory and of the practice it supports. See appendix to chap. v.

out muscular and nervous energy and consuming tissue in his labour, must receive in income the food, clothes, shelter, &c., required to maintain him in his working-power. Since he is mortal, this work of individual restoration cannot be kept up for ever; if, then, the supply of labour-power is to be maintained, the material means of bringing up children to replace aged workers must be provided.

This gives us the physical basis of the ' minimum wage ' or ' the bare subsistence wage.' This, however, will not be the same for all kinds of labour. Where greater intensity of physical energy, more skill, mental exertion, or responsibility is involved, these higher grades of productive energy usually require a higher standard of living or a larger income.

This brings us to what may be called the moral basis of the subsistence wage. Man is not a mere automaton who will work if food is put into him : he is a human being operated by ' motives.' The payment he receives for work must, therefore, suffice not only to replenish his physical output and to restore his bodily waste, it must stimulate his will. Under some conditions this ' motive ' does not involve any more payment than suffices for physical subsistence; a great deal of routine work of peasants and other labourers has always gone on upon a basis in which conscious motive involves no higher pay than a physical subsistence ; or else, as in slave and serf labour, fear of punishment or some other sort of negative payment has furnished the conscious ' stimulus.' But when we come to civilised industrial communities, where the workers have some sense of personal dignity, and perhaps some alternative to wage labour, most of them will be apt to demand a rate of pay which may be termed the moral subsistence wage, that will be somewhat above the physical subsistence level. This payment, though not necessarily identical with the whole ' standard of comfort,' approximates to it, and at any given time must be regarded as comprising part of the wear and tear or subsistence wage. This moral element plays a large part in determining class wages, and rises in importance with the skilled and highly-paid grades of workers. Thus the higher subsistence wage for an engine-driver or a compositor, as compared with a general labourer, is only explained in part by the physical necessity of maintaining a more efficient and highly organised instrument of labour, involving a larger displacement and repair. The actual subsistence wage will include the necessary stimulus of motive. This, as we shall see hereafter, does not explain fully the differences of class wages, but it is one factor.

Taking the industrial system as it is, we find a large variety of subsistence wages which are funds for replacing the wear and tear of labour.

Within each grade of labour the output of energy and the waste are greater in some workers than others, and a larger subsistence wage is required, and so far as output is a measure of waste, is obtained under a piece-wage system.

These subsistence wages, required to maintain the existing supply of labour-power, may be held to constitute a first charge upon the industrial product on behalf of labour. If there is a failure anywhere to provide this subsistence, the industrial system is weakened and diminished in productivity. A wage below this subsistence-point is a 'sweating wage.' The payment of such a wage may sometimes be profitable to an employer or even to a class of employers who have at hand a large supply of reserve labour to draw upon for the unskilled or low-skilled work which they require. Just as it was sound 'economy' for certain southern planters to work slaves to death in five or six years' labour in the rice fields, so it may 'pay' employers in some branches of the London clothing trades to give out work to women for rates of pay insufficient to maintain them in health and physical efficiency, provided that there are plenty of other women obliged for lack of any other alternative to take this work on the same terms.

All such 'sweating' is, however, a damage to the industrial system, which it underfeeds.

Or perhaps a sweating trade may rather be regarded as diseased or moribund tissue in the economic system, whose lingering process of decay involves waste of labour-power, which might otherwise be properly supported, and put to healthy employment.

§ 4.—Though this wage of subsistence suffices to maintain labour in a stable industrial system, it makes no provision for its growth. If the production of the industrial system is to increase in volume and improve in quality, provision must be made for procuring more labour-power and for raising its quality. This quantitative and qualitative growth involves an expenditure on wages beyond the subsistence fund.

An increased quantity of labour-power can be got in two ways : I., by bringing into industry an increased number of workers ; II., by inducing and enabling the existing workers to give out a larger amount of labour-power.

I. The direct influence of a rise of wages in promoting, or a fall of wages in checking, the growth of the labouring population is very difficult to assess. In Great Britain and most industrial countries until recent times a rise of real wages was normally attended by an increase in the growth of the working population, partly by promoting early and fertile marriages, partly by keeping down infant mortality, and by increasing the average length of the working life. So far as the birth-rate, however, is concerned, in most civilised countries it is clear that a rise of wages and of the standard of comfort and intelligence is at present attended by a diminution in the growth of workers, and that this tendency is not adequately offset by reduction of infant mortality and increased longevity of workers. But important as is this qualification of the former power of rising wages to evoke more labour, it must not be exaggerated in dealing with the industrial system as a whole. Most of the great populations of the world have not attained the level of subsistence or of education, which brings them under the influences which, in Western Europe and in countries colonised therefrom, are reducing the birth-rate, with a rising standard of wages. While, therefore, I am well aware that wages can be accounted only one among many social determinants of growth of population, I think it must still be admitted that a rise of wages causes some increase of working population through its effect upon birth-rate and infant survival in most parts of the industrial system.

But the effect of rising wages in increasing the number of industrial workers is not confined to its effect in stimulating the population already inside the industrial system. It may operate by bringing in supplies of labour from countries which lie outside our industrial system, or by extending the area of the system itself. The former may be illustrated by the use of wage-stimuli to bring into our industrial system Chinese, Kaffirs, Malays, and other workers who formerly were outside, the latter by the exploitation of the labour of new countries, such as the Congo or Rhodesia, by means of hitherto non-industrial populations.

II. More work may sometimes be got out of the same workers by increasing the hours of labour, or by speeding up machines and otherwise increasing the intensity of labour.

Whether we regard the industrial system as a whole or some single branch or trade, we are confronted by these two modes of increasing the quantity of the supply of labour-power, a larger number of workers, or a larger amount of work per worker.

Now both these methods operate by means of a rise of wages above the limit of the subsistence rate. If more workers are to be got into use, either by stimulating the growth of the working population in a country, or by opening up new supplies in other countries, or by bringing in these new supplies, a rise in the price per unit of labour-power is the means of doing this.

Similarly, if more work is to be got out of the existing supply of workers, the greater drain upon the muscular and nervous system involves a higher rate of pay, while the increase of painful effort reinforces the demand through the operation of the human will. Though fear of dismissal and other non-wage inducements may sometimes be efficacious in evoking more productive energy, it is normally the case that men will not work harder except for a higher rate.

Here is a shoe trade or a bicycle trade employing 300 men of different grades of efficiency. A unit of labour-power costs (let us say) 5s., and the 100 workers constituting the lowest grade give out four units each a week, earning a minimum efficiency or subsistence wage of 20s. The two other grades of men, 100 in each, produce respectively five and six units per week, earning 25s. and 30s.

This is the state in a stable condition of the industry. Now there exists a number of men in this town, either unemployed or working as unskilled labourers, capable of working in the shoe or bicycle factory, but being less efficient than the lowest of the three grades in actual use, they could give only three units of labour-power per week, thus earning only 15s., or less than is required to support them in this work.

These potential workers below the margin of employment in this trade can only be employed on condition of a rise in the price per unit of labour-power, or, as it is generally described, a rise of wages. If a growth in these trades is to occur, it can only occur through a rise in price per unit of labour-power to such a point that 6s. 8d. is the price instead of 5s., thus enabling the workers only equal to three units per week to earn the minimum subsistence wage, and adding an element of 'surplus' to the weekly wages of the workers in the higher grades.

Thus the margin of employment is lowered so as to take in out side workers and to enlarge the structure of the trade. But there is an alternative course. Instead of taking in an inferior grade of labour from outside, the existing employees may work overtime, or on a bonus system may consent to turn out 25 per cent. more output per week than before. In order to get this result, however, the employers will have to pay a rise of the general piece rate, or 'time and a half' for overtime. This is equivalent to a rise in price per unit of labour-power, required to call into use a lower or more costly grade of labour-power not outside but inside the trade.

The higher price is here economically necessary, first to provide against the greater wear and tear or waste of an intenser working week ; secondly, to induce the will of the workers to undertake a greater and more painful effort.

To get a larger supply of labour-power by either mode, a lowering of the extensive or the intensive margin of employment, more and worse men or more and worse power from the same men, an increased price per unit must be paid.

We have supposed the labour below the margin of employment to be inferior in quantity.

It may be, commonly is, inferior in quality, whether it is vested in a body of less skilful or reliable workers, or in the less effective output of the overtime of tired employees. But whether the inferiority be of quantity or quality, the enlargement of the structure of the trade can only be brought about by raising the price per unit of labour-power reckoned at the earlier standard. If the workers below the margin of employment, or the overtime work of the existing employees, are not only inferior in quantity but in quality, the price per unit will have to rise more than 25 per cent. so as to enable the producers of three units per week of a worse sort of labour-power to earn the subsistence wage of 20s.

Our example is chosen to illustrate the way in which a growth in size of a trade must be brought about, so far as the increase of its labour-power is concerned. Only by regarding labour-power as expressed in some unit of standard size and quality can we clearly present the process.

The workers, or the labour-power, give out so many units of productive energy as, reckoned at the market price per unit, afford a subsistence wage to the worst of those employed. An enlargement of output can only be got by a rise of price per unit which lets in labour-power that could not economically be sustained before.

Now take the case of a trade which needs to improve not the quantity but the skill or character of its labour-power, to add not more tissue or raw muscular energy to its system, but more accurate and complex application of existing energy. This conversion of ruder into finer service involves the direction of mental and moral power to acquiring more skill of manipulation, more resourcefulness in meeting detailed difficulties, more concentration and a higher sense of individual responsibility. A change from rough routine labour to such labour as is required in a skilled mechanic involves the acquisition and employment of these new powers. Now to evoke and maintain these finer sorts and uses of human energy will involve the existence of a higher standard of life and a higher rate of pay. For each unit of the finer sort of productive-power a higher price is necessary than sufficed for a unit of the ruder power. It is partly a question of physical, partly of moral motive. Fine and reliable work cannot be got out of workers living upon a bare subsistence wage : coarse material surroundings and the presence of poverty do not support a nervous system capable of the nicer adjustments of muscle and brain involved in fine work of any sort : there is neither the physical nor the moral stimulus to acquire and to apply such power.

If, then, a trade is to grow in quality as in size, this growth involves a rise in price per unit of human energy. As we saw that certain reserve quantities of labour-power in men already employed for an ordinary working-day could be evoked in the form of over-time, or of quicker work, by a rise in the rate of pay, so we now recognise that there are reserve qualities of labour-power which can similarly be evoked.

If a trade is to grow simultaneously both in size and in charac-ter of work, both stimuli of higher pay must be applied. This is the real significance of the rise of rate of pay which has taken place in the skilled cotton trade of Lancashire during the last half-cen-tury, as also in many other manufactures where a growth in volume of work has been accompanied by improved skill, care, regularity, and responsibility.

The rise of wages has been essential : (1) to evoke a greater supply of labour by bringing more workers into the labour market, and by getting more labour-power out of those in employment (extensive and intensive lowering of the margin of employment) ; (2) to evoke an improved character of labour-power out of the enlarged supply.

This is the so-called ' economy of high wages,' assisted, doubt-less, in its mode of operation by the organisation of the workers, but primarily based upon economic necessity, which is ultimately traceable to the play of physical and moral stimuli or motives operating upon individual workers and moulding class standards of life.

§ 5.—In regarding, then, the industrial system as a growing system, we must assign to labour two necessary payments out of the industrial income, first, a subsistence wage required to maintain the labour portion of the system unimpaired, secondly, a wage of pro-gressive efficiency required to evoke an increasing quantity of more effective labour-power. The former is a simple wear-and-tear fund, the latter an improvement fund. Both are necessary expenses of labour in a progressive industrial community.

Now when we turn to capital we find two corresponding costs : one of mere maintenance, the other of progress. By capital we here mean the concrete forms of buildings, tools, machines, stock, &c., which assist industry, not their financial equivalent or measure. This capital is continually being worn out or used up in the processes of industry, and the maintenance of

industry requires that this loss shall be continually replaced
In our analysis of the distribution of income at each stage we
described this payment under the head of ' wear and tear.'

Now in dealing with this ' wear-and-tear ' fund of capital, the
same distinction as in the case of labour, between physical and
moral stimulus, is applicable.

What payment out of the product must be made to procure
the maintenance of the existing fabric of capital, the buildings,
machinery and other plant, the raw materials, &c. ? These forms of
capital are continually being worn out or used up, and need constant
regular replenishment. What payments must be made to secure
this ? The purely physical condition of their maintenance is that
material repairs and replacement shall continually take place. In
other words, a provision corresponding to the physical subsistence
fund of labour must be made. This is furnished through what is
commonly termed a depreciation fund. Interpreted in terms of
industrial energy, this means that some energy which might otherwise
have been applied to the immediate purpose of turning out more
consumable commodities is diverted into the repair of factories,
machinery, &c.

Now this sort of ' saving ' which goes to maintain the capital
structure of a business is not commonly classed as ' saving,' for it
brings no increase of capital, nor is the payment, or book-keeping
transaction it involves, called interest.

If, in accordance with our method of procedure, we first assume
the existence of a fully equipped industrial system and consider
the costs of its upkeep, the bare provision against wear and
tear, this depreciation fund would appear to be all that is necessary to provide for the maintenance of capital. It is true that
if, refusing to accept the industrial system as a *fait accompli*, we
insist upon investigating the origins of the several factors, we may
distinguish sharply the origin of capital from that of labour. We
may, if we choose, attribute to the free bounty of Nature an original
stock of labour-power, as of land, though in both cases some
expenditure of economic effort may be required to equip them for
service in the industrial system. There is, however, no such free
original supply of capital. Whatever capital forms part of our
industrial structure must have been brought into economic existence
by the stimulus not of a depreciation fund but by another payment,
i.e. interest.

But though this question of origin has both a historical and an
ethical significance, it does not seem to justify the inclusion of
interest as a strictly economic payment for the bare upkeep of
existing capital. The premises, machinery and other plant, the raw

materials, fuel and other forms of concrete capital, are provided for not out of the portion of the product of a business which is paid away as 'dividends,' but out of the depreciation fund and the current expenses of running the business. When 'savings' have once been applied to establish the concrete capital of a business, the payment of interest to the owners of this capital cannot be regarded as a necessary 'cost' of maintenance, nor does the failure to provide this payment cause the capital to cease to function as a productive agent. So far as the 'fixed' capital is concerned, it seems evident that its continued life is secured by a wear and tear fund which closely corresponds to subsistence wages in the case of labour, and that the 'circulating' capital is similarly secured by the ordinary expenditure of a going concern.[1]

Thus, taking the existing industrial system, we are justified in assigning the depreciation fund as a sufficient economic provision for the maintenance of the concrete forms of capital contained in that system. This depreciation fund will thus rank with the subsistence wage of labour and the payment for the upkeep of land employed for agriculture. If to some readers this refusal to include a minimum interest as a necessary 'cost' of production in considering a stable system of industry seems unreasonable, we must remind them that the hypothesis of a stable or unprogressive system is set up as a convenient starting point in our analysis, and that the argument for the necessity of interest in the actual industrial system with which we are concerned is not in any degree impaired by this exclusion.

For as soon as we turn from the statical to the progressive conception of industry the economic necessity of the payment of interest becomes apparent. The growth of the industrial structure involves the creation of new forms of capital, and the 'saving' which brings into use these new forms requires 'interest' as a stimulus. No point in economics is more subject to misunderstanding or misrepresentation than that concerned with the productive service for which interest is paid.

The capital whose use is bought by interest involves as a cost of production an 'effort' sometimes described as 'abstinence,' sometimes as 'waiting.' So long as individuals are required to postpone some present satisfaction of consumption which they could obtain in order to furnish capital, the exercise of self-denial must be paid for like every other disagreeable effort that is useful for industry.

---

[1] It may indeed be urged that the shareholders in a business which paid no dividends, and showed no reasonable prospect of doing so, would refuse to provide an adequate depreciation fund, so distributing temporarily as dividends what should have gone to maintain capital.

Whether 'saving' or 'waiting' can properly be described as a 'productive process' is immaterial: if it involves some personal effort, and is necessary to the productive activity of other instruments, e.g. labour and land, it must have its price.

Nor is this consideration affected by the fact that much saving involves no appreciable effort of self-denial. Every unit of saving, like every unit of labour-power of a given sort, must be paid for at the same price. Some units of an output of labour involve no painful exertion, but since there is only one price in a market for the whole supply they are remunerated just as highly as those units which cost most painful exertion. Similarly with saving. So long as the easy automatic saving of the Duke of Westminster needs to be supplemented by the hard-felt saving of John Smith, of Oldham, the former must receive the same price per unit of saving as the latter.[1]

One other misunderstanding must be removed. The effort of saving for which payment is made does not lie in the single act of producing capital goods instead of consumption goods. The effort is not over when the factory, the machine, or the raw materials which form real capital have been brought into the field of industry.

If John Smith, though desirous to consume £100 worth of commodities, is induced instead to devote his £100 to putting up a piece of industrial machinery, he must be paid at regular intervals so long as he allows his power to consume his £100 worth of commodities to lie in abeyance. For if the original act of substituting productive capital for consumption involves a sacrifice on his part deserving payment, this sacrifice continues all the time this capital is operating in industry.

If it is worth £100 John is entitled to receive his £3 per annum, because the real payment which this £3 conveys is essential to induce John to leave his £100 machine operating instead of selling it outright and taking for consumption his £100 worth of consumables.

There is no mystery whatever attending the so-called eternity of the £100 machine. He gets £3 per annum for ever for it. He could get, say, £5 for a certain short number of years, if he were willing to accept this higher price for its use so long as it lasted in its original form, instead of a lower price which threw on the user the obligation of keeping it in complete repair and replacing any part of it which wore out. Thus capital is not merely crystallised labour.

[1] Most of the criticism of the morality or rationality of interest from Aristotle to Ruskin is based on a misconception of the nature and uses of saving. Whatever is valid in such criticism applies not to the justice or necessity of paying interest for saving, but to the processes by which much of the accumulation which enables saving to be made has been achieved.

§ 6.—Thus, whereas the material wear and tear fund suffices for the maintenance of the existing fabric of capital, varying in amount according as the actual wear and tear is light or heavy, the needs of a growing industrial system require the payment of a rate of interest sufficient to evoke the saving of the new capital. This necessary expense of industrial progress will vary with the amount required and the sacrifice involved in saving. In modern industry, wherever a free field of investment exists, the price of new saving is low and tolerably uniform. Savers can be induced to place considerable quantities of new plant and stock in the industrial field in return for a share of the industrial product which measures, say, only three per cent. of the value of the plant and stock itself. If in any section of the industrial world a sudden demand for a great application of new capital arises, the price of saving, of course, rises for a while.

So far, however, as freedom of investment (i.e. of the flow of new capital) exists throughout the industrial world, a uniform rate of payment for fresh saving exists. This uniformity is, of course, concealed by the difference of risks attached to different sorts of application of capital. The payment for incurring these risks is not, however, interest, and should be treated separately ; if differences of risk were allowed for, the rate of interest throughout the industrial world would be fairly uniform, so far as free fields of investment exist.

But though saving, or the process of applying capital for productive use, is in most parts of the industrial system far more pliable than labour, for many purposes there still remain separate markets for investment of new real capital. It is open to any saving man in England to convert his saving into a share of the steel rails and rolling stock of any railroad quoted on the Stock Exchange, or into the machinery and other goods required for manufacturing cotton cloth, beer, or bicycles. But there still remain large quantities of real capital in whole trades and countries which are the embodiment of the saving of some particular family or some small locality, or small close group of favoured investors.

Because, then, three per cent. may suffice to stimulate the normal growth of capital in fully evolved competitive joint-stock enterprises, it does not follow that such a payment will have the same stimulative effect in the detached local markets for investment or that more real capital can be got into a simple family business at such a rate of payment. Over large areas of the earth which for certain productive purposes are in touch with world markets, as in the case of Asiatic countries which furnish wheat, tea, cotton, &c.,

the real capital engaged in such production is often raised by rates of interest far higher than three per cent., determined by distinctively local conditions. Thus, taking in our view the whole amount of saving and creation of real capital required to feed the industrial system, we shall recognise a great number of separate areas of capitalisation as there are separate markets for labour, each with its own rate of interest, as each labour market has its class or specific wage. A given rise of actual interest will operate with different effect in their different markets for saving, though the *modus operandi* will be similar. Each business, moreover, within such detached area of investment, appealing for the required saving to its single owner or his family or immediate associates, will commonly have a particular rate of payment which corresponds to the individual subsistence wage in a special labour market. As in the case of labour, a rise in the price per unit of labour-power stimulates an increased supply (*a*) by bringing into use workers from outside, (*b*) by evoking increased duration or intensity of labour from existing workers; an increase in the effective supply of capital is similarly brought about by a rise in the price per unit of capital-power. A rise in the rate of real interest, i.e. in the amount of concrete goods paid to savers for bringing into use a fresh unit of capital-power, operates in two ways. First, by offering a higher reward for saving, it causes a larger quantity of new forms of capital to come into the economic field. When we are considering the structure of a business or a trade, such rise of interest evidently draws into this business or trade a larger proportion than before of the new saving that was seeking investment, i.e. a rise of interest in the cotton trade causes new cotton mills, machines, and raw cotton to be produced, instead of more steam engines, boot machines, brewing vats, &c. When we consider the industrial system as a whole, a general rise of real interest causes a larger proportion of the real income of the community than before to be saved instead of spent, i.e. to be taken in the shape of new capital-forms instead of in the shape of retail goods for consumption.[1]

[1] It is sometimes held that a fall in the rate of interest does not evoke less saving, or a rise in the rate of interest more saving, in a modern civilised nation. This contention is based on the view that some sorts of saving, e.g. saving to secure a definite income as provision for old age or as provision for a family in case of death or disability, would be stimulated and not depressed by a fall of interest, because more saving would be required to attain the desired end. But though some saving would undoubtedly take place at o per cent. interest, or even at a minus rate of objective interest (i.e. some persons would lend £100 out of a large income earned in prosperous middle-age on condition of receiving back £95 when they were old and earning nothing, provided no more advantageous terms were open to them), it cannot be deduced from this that positive interest is now an unnecessary payment. Though

Secondly, a rise of real interest will cause a fuller or intenser use than before to be made of existing forms of capital. As a rise in price of labour-power causes more to be got out of the present labour supply through overtime and intenser working, so with the machines and other forms of 'fixed capital.' Three shifts instead of two, speeding up with more risk of breakdown and more waste, the continuous operation of reserve machines, &c., will be brought into play.

These effects evidently correspond to the extensive and intensive lowering of the ' margin of employment ' in labour which we saw followed an increase of the price per unit of labour-power.

In a progressive community improved plant, machines, tools, &c., better than any or most of those at present in use, have been discovered, and are available as soon as it pays to scrap the older forms and substitute these new ones. The rate of this scrapping and substitution is directly determined by the rate of real interest. Improved plant may mean either of two things : plant capable of turning out a higher quality of work than the present plant, or plant capable of co-operating with labour so as to turn out a larger quantity of work in proportion to the cost of making it. But in either case the admission of the improved plant depends upon the economy of scrapping old plant, and a rise in the price per unit of capital-power will impart a larger gain than before to this substitution, and so will stimulate the change. This corresponds to the economy of high wages in improving the quality of the labour factor.

Thus for the use of capital in a progressive industrial system, two payments are made : a wear-and-tear fund with minimum interest for the production and maintenance of the existing fabric, and a further payment of interest to evoke new capital-forms for the quantitative and qualitative growth.

§ 7.—It is sometimes thought that land must be treated differently from labour and capital, because, while the supply of the use of the two latter depends upon the effort and will of man,

some labour would be done for pleasure, wages are necessary. So in the case of a fall of interest, though some would save as much or even more, it remains true that a rise in the price of saving will evoke a larger aggregate supply, and a fall will reduce the supply. Nor is the argument, that saving for a definite deferred income would be stimulated by a fall of interest, so strong as at first sight it seems. For among many would-be savers the difficulty of saving enough at the lower rate may approach impossibility and deter them from the attempt. This would certainly be the case if there were reason to fear that a continuous decline of rate of interest had set in. Upon the whole the weight of evidence strongly supports the application of the ordinary laws of price to the effort of saving. (The fullest account of the psychology of saving is contained in Professor Gonner's little book ' Interest and Saving.')

the former does not, Nature yielding her sources and powers of production freely.

But important though this distinction is, it is not relevant at the present stage. Our general standard of measurement for units of productive energy must be applied to land-power as to the power which emanates from workers and pieces of capital, and the payments made where land use is bought and sold must be referred to the same general law.

Is there then a payment to be made to the owner of land corresponding to the subsistence wage of labour and the wear-and-tear provision for capital ? Certainly.

Whenever anything is taken out of the land beyond what is replaced by the ordinary course of Nature, provision must be made against this loss or waste. If land has to be manured and ploughed up, irrigated and drained in order to maintain its fertility ; if it requires to be hedged, fenced, and otherwise protected, these payments for keeping up the land clearly belong to the same class as subsistence wage and the depreciation fund for capital. They are not, however, rent, and are not usually classed as such. This claim to maintenance of the land precedes rent.

If Nature, as represented by the productive powers of land, is required to contribute more to support a progressive industry, yielding more food, raw materials, fuel, &c., either more land hitherto unused must be brought into requisition, or the land already worked must be more intensely worked. In the former case, new roads must be made, virgin land broken in, and a number of expenses must be incurred for bringing into economic use the new supply of land. In the latter case, where the land is worked more intensively, it will be more quickly exhausted and the cost of restoration will be greater. Even if land remained ' free ' to every user, this further provision for maintaining land to supply natural resources to a progressive industrial system involves an expenditure beyond what is required to maintain the existing industrial fabric. This further payment is not rent any more than the earlier payment ; it is simply an expense incurred in feeding the industrial system with an increase of land-power. But it means that out of the industrial product a portion must be applied to evoke and maintain new land-power in addition to the payment made for the maintenance of existing land. Both these payments would, in our analysis of income, come under the head of wear and tear, and interest. The making of roads, irrigation, fencing, manuring, &c., which serve to repair land in use and to bring fresh land into use, differ in no wise from the expenditure in maintaining and enlarging capital, the repair work corresponding to the depreciation fund, and the expansion work corresponding to the capital growth which requires interest to evoke it.

In other words, land, so far as maintenance and improvements are concerned, is capital. The payment called rent, as we shall see, belongs to a different category.

§ 8.—Following, then, the distribution of the industrial product as it is achieved by the breaking-up of prices at the various stages of production in payment for the uses of labour, capital, and land, we perceive that definite portions are allotted for the maintenance of subsistence of the industrial system, and for the enlargement and improvement of that system in a progressive community.

So far as the distribution of the industrial product necessary for these payments is concerned, we recognise a close co-ordination of the three factors of production.

A maintenance wage or wear-and-tear fund is required in each case alike. So likewise an increase in the quantity of labour-power, capital-power, land-power, so as to provide for the growth of a business, a trade, or the industrial system, is procured by a rise of price per unit of productive-power which acts in each case.

(a) By lowering the extensive margin of employment, and so calling into economic use outside agents of production.

(b) By lowering the intensive margin of employment, and so evoking the use of lower grades of productive-power in the factors already employed.

Qualitative growth of industrial structure is similarly brought about by a rise in price per unit of productive-power, which brings into use superior sorts of power which it did not pay to substitute for the existing sorts at former prices.

In the case of each factor the lowering of the margin, extensive or intensive, is directly due to a rise in price per unit of the productive-power that factor supplies ; similarly a fall in the price per unit causes a raising of the margin.

This is the way in which the industrial system works and grows. Each one of these payments made to labour, capital, and land is a strictly necessary cost of production. These laws of the maintenance and growth of the industrial system are recognised to be analogous in their nature and operation to those relating to a biological organism which provides itself with food to repair its waste of tissue and of energy, and to provide for its growth. In neither case is the method of maintenance and growth purely physical : the psychical factor enters into both.

As the craving for the satisfaction of hunger is essential to evoke the output of organic energy in the work of acquiring food for the organism, so in the industrial system the felt pressure of demand for the satisfaction of needs constantly operates in the will of social groups, evoking fresh output of co-operative energy in the several branches of industry.

Now at first sight it does not seem inevitable that any problem of distribution, not directly and even automatically solvable, should arise. If the result of the working of the industrial system were merely to produce a fund of food and other necessaries just sufficient to replace the wear and tear, and so to maintain intact the system, no problem of distribution would come up. Capital could not, even if it would, encroach upon the maintenance wage, nor could labour deprive capital of the provision for replacing worn-out tools and material. Improper distribution, or excessive payment to any factor of production, is not possible, at any rate for long, in such a case.

But where, as is usual, the industrial system turns out a product larger than suffices for maintenance, conflicts of interest in distribution may arise. We are now confronted with the question of disposing of a ' surplus ' over and above the requirements for mere maintenance. Such 'surplus,' as we see, may be regarded in the first instance as a natural provision for organic growth, acting in the shape of minimum stimuli to evoke proportionate increases of the various sorts of labour, capital, and land-powers, for the enlargement of the industrial system and its output.

The industrial system produces more than its keep ; does the whole of the surplus flow along certain necessary channels for the stimulation of industrial growth ? It may appear that, whereas the amount required for maintenance is at any time strictly limited, progressive efficiency knows no such limits. There is, perhaps, no assignable limit to the amount of goods and services which could be consumed in such ways as to add to the productive efficiency of mental and physical workers becoming more and more skilful, intelligent, informed, and resourceful, and to evoke the increased quantity of saving and new forms of capital required to co-operate effectively with this increased and improved labour power.

That the whole of any possible increase in the product of an industrial system is capable of being distributed and consumed, so as to promote the increased efficiency of the industrial system, is a reasonable, if not an incontrovertible, assumption.

For though the rate at which a rise of wages or of profits may be assimilated in a rising standard of life, so as to promote economic efficiency, is subject to certain physical and moral limitations, if one regards a particular trade or class of producers, it is not reasonable to suppose that normally the progress of the arts of industry could exceed the pace at which the increased product, properly distributed, would serve to maintain and further to promote efficiency.[1]

We may then, accepting provisionally this view of the economy of progress, insist that every ' surplus ' can theoretically be distributed so as to figure as a necessary cost of industrial growth, feeding the industrial organism. There is, indeed, in every progressive community a successful tendency towards such a natural or productive distribution of the surplus.

But the success of this tendency is notoriously qualified : the surplus is not so distributed as to produce the maximum amount of economic progress. Portions of the ' surplus ' which might have gone as stimuli of growth are taken as unnecessary or excessive payments which, instead of stimulating, depress activity, and so the rate of growth is kept unnecessarily low. For, though it is possible and socially desirable that the whole of the surplus be distributed with the same natural equity that determines the distribution of the maintenance or wear-and-tear fund, it is not inevitable that this should happen. Nor does it happen. The abuse or uneconomical use of the surplus product is the source of every sort of trouble or malady of the industrial system, and the whole problem of industrial reform may be conceived in terms of a truly economical disposal of this surplus.

For though it is not possible for the owners of one factor of production to encroach far upon the subsistence fund of any of the others, or for the owners of one trade or province of industry to rob with impunity the owners of another trade or province of its wear-and-tear fund, it is possible for one section or interest or industry to effect a considerable separate gain by encroaching upon the portion of the surplus required to furnish growth to some other part of the industrial system. There exists no such close harmony in the system as shall furnish an automatic check upon such depredations. An industrial system may still survive and even grow, though not so freely or so rapidly, if a landlord class claims a large piece of the ' surplus,' the payment of which is not essential to evoke the use of his land, or if a class of capitalists draw an interest or a profit larger than is sufficient to induce the application of their capital or ability, or if some favoured and protected professions or

[1] Two qualifications of this doctrine are reserved for later consideration. The first has reference to the claim and the ability of the State to take its share in the surplus in order to secure the maintenance and progressive efficiency of public functions. The second arises when we endeavour to relate the specifically industrial life of society with which we are here concerned with the larger conception of a progressive society, in which allowance is made for the subordination of distinctively economic activities and wealth to a wider conception of social activity and wealth.

trades take salaries or wages which are more than sufficient to stimulate any improved efficiency they give out. In these ways 'surplus' may be diverted from its proper work of furnishing growing-power and become 'unearned income.' It is notorious that combination is primarily directed to secure some such element of superfluous gain. There is friction and antagonism between the buyers and sellers of land-power (i.e. landowners and tenants), between the buyers and sellers of labour-power (i.e. employers and employees), between the buyers and sellers of capital (i.e. investors and *entrepreneurs*), while the conflicts between buyers and sellers of various goods and services represent the struggle of trades, each seeking to get a larger share of the general product by appreciating its particular product.

So far as the wear-and-tear or maintenance fund is concerned, no real problem of distribution arises, a law of natural harmony of interests among the owners of the factors of production determines the distribution.

So far as labour is concerned, a 'subsistence' wage, as we have seen, does not necessarily provide a full living wage for workers in a trade where an ample margin of 'unemployed' or cheap immigrants is attainable. But within these limits the distribution of the portion of the product which goes for wear and tear involves no conflict of real interests among the owners of the several factors.

The importance of this harmony is often under-estimated : it furnishes a genuine and substantial basis of orderly co-operation over the whole industrial field. In most countries and at most times the great bulk of the wealth produced is normally and naturally apportioned in this way to the support of the existing industrial fabric. Until the rise of modern capitalist industry only a comparatively small proportion remained over as a surplus, either to furnish the means of industrial progress, or to pass as unearned income to enrich a class of landlords, usurers, or officials.

§ 9.—The increased prevalence and intensity of the conflicts, not only between workers, capitalists, and landlords, but between trades and groups of trades, which distribute modern industry, are primarily due to the improvement of the industrial arts, which has enhanced the relative importance of the surplus.

If there were no surplus there would be industrial peace, for necessary payments would absorb the product. If there were a surplus, the whole of which was as automatically and as naturally apportioned to feed the growth of the several parts of the industrial system as is the wear-and-tear fund, there would still be peace. But the fact that this surplus, which should be absorbed in stimuli to progress, may, instead, be forcibly diverted as excessive and ' unearned ' payment by the owners of some one or other factor of production, breaks this natural harmony and furnishes a ground for class or trade conflict.

The distinctive character of this doctrine of distribution consists in assigning the priority of significance to the division of the product into costs and surplus instead of into wages, interest, and rent. Not until the surplus has been separated from the full subsistence fund of costs does any real problem of distribution as between the several factors arise. Moreover, so far as the normal working of industry makes stable provision for allocating some of the surplus to the several factors as stimuli of growth, the economy of costs may be extended to this portion.' Both the subsistence fund and the portion of the surplus thus productively applied as food for industrial growth in a progressive society must be sharply separated from the unproductive surplus taken as economic rent, excessive interest, profits, or salaries, which furnishes no incentive to industry in its recipients.

The following rough figure expresses the threefold distinction, though the proportions assigned to the parts are purely hypothetical :—

Unproductive Surplus (unearned increments).	C.
Productive Surplus (costs of growth).	B.
Maintenance (costs of subsistence).	A.

A. Maintenance includes (1) minimum wages for various sorts of labour and ability necessary to support and evoke their continuous output at the present standard of efficiency ; (2) depreciation for wear and tear for plant and other fixed capital ; (3) a ' wear-and-tear ' provision for land.

B. The productive surplus includes (1) minimum wage of progressive efficiency in quantity and quality of labour and ability of various grades ; (2) such amount of interest as is required to evoke the saving needed to supply the requisite amount of new capital for industrial progress.

C. The unproductive surplus consists of (1) economic rent of land and other natural resources ; (2) all interest beyond the rate involved in B ; (3) all profit, salaries, or other payments for ability or labour in excess of what is economically necessary to evoke the sufficient use of such factor of production.

Modern industry tends continually to increase the size of the surplus. Part of it settles down gradually into a permanent provision for industrial growth, in accordance with the law we have already traced, raising the price for use of labour and capital above the bare subsistence point. A great deal, however, does not so settle, but forms a bone of contention. Apart from the intervention of the State, no law for its apportionment exists except the law of superior force. Landowners, capitalists, labourers, *entrepreneurs*, or combinations of these owners of the factors of production can, if they are strong enough, secure as unearned and excessive gains lumps of this surplus. Such unearned elements of income arise, as we shall recognise, in various parts of the industrial system. Where they are in the aggregate a relatively small share of the product, they cause little trouble. But when they form a large proportion of the whole, as in some developed industrial countries, they not only cause deep conflicts of industrial interest between the different classes, but are directly responsible for those great oscillations of industry and employment which involve so much waste and misery in our social system. The principal problem of modern industrial civilisation consists in devising measures to secure that the whole of the industrial surplus shall be economically applied to the purposes of industrial and social progress, instead of passing in the shape of unearned income to the owners of the factors of production, whose activities are depressed, not stimulated, by such payments.

The closer consideration of this problem must be deferred until the working of the industrial system in the production and apportionment of wealth has been more fully described. Meantime, however, it may be well to make a brief anticipatory allusion to a factor in the problem of distribution which in this preliminary setting has been purposely neglected. Building up our conception of the structure and operation of industry entirely from the standpoint of private business enterprise motived by individual interest, we have reached a preliminary explanation of the apportionment of its product as costs or surplus among the private owners of the several factors. But to the existence, operation and growth of the private industrial system, the institution of a State is necessary. It is not essential at this stage to discuss the nature or the extent of the social services which the State renders in the processes of production of wealth in the industrial system. It suffices to recognise that a strong and progressive State is essential to the stability and progress of industry, and must, therefore, rank as a co-operative agent in the production of the income which the private owners of land, capital, labour and ability seek to secure for themselves as costs and surplus.

Since the State will have certain costs of maintenance and of grants, incurred on account of the services she renders to private industry, equity and necessity alike will assign to her an income out of the product she has helped to create. Partly by the withdrawal of certain branches of profitable enterprise from private control in order to establish them as public monopolies, partly by taxation, the State will be found to assert her claim as joint-producer to a share of the industrial product. A more mature discussion of the relation between the State and the private producer in regard to the distribution of the product is reserved for a later chapter.[1] This preliminary statement is required in order to abate or remove some doubts which may arise in connection with the disposal of the 'unproductive surplus.' For so long as the product is regarded as entirely due to the private co-operative efforts of the owners of the factors of production, ignoring the assistance rendered by society through the State, it may not unreasonably appear that some unproductive or superfluous product will remain after adequate provision has been made for 'costs of growth.' Increased efficiency and enlarged quantity of labour, capital and ability may not, it may be urged, require as stimuli the whole of the 'surplus.' A rise of real wages beyond a certain moderate pace will not be assimilated so as to yield a corresponding growth of physical, moral, or technical efficiency of labour-power, nor will a rise in rate of interest beyond a certain point evoke necessarily a proportionate, or indeed any, increase of saving. So long as the claims and necessities of a progressive State are left out of account, these difficulties relating to the conversion of unproductive into productive surplus will remain unsolved. Only when the capacity of the State to utilise for maintenance and growth a share of the 'surplus' is recognised shall we be in a position to rectify the defect in the apportionment of the product which our method of exposition has involved.

[1] Chapter XIV.

CHAPTER V

WAGES, INTEREST, AND RENT

§ 1. Family maintenance is the basis of a wage system. Individual wages are adjusted to the wages obtainable by other members of the family.— § 2. Grade wages vary with the physical and moral conditions of the work: many factors, personal, adventitious, social, determine the price per unit of the different sorts of labour-power.—§ 3. The tendency of wages towards a minimum is normally true. The seller is usually weaker than the buyer in the bargain.—§ 4. Non-competitive conditions qualify this tendency. A scarcity or surplus wage sometimes is obtained.— § 5. Combinations secure similar surplus interest for capital.—§ 6. Rent of land, though not a ' cost,' is an ' expense of production,' measured in terms of the price of units of land-power. There are many supplies of land for different uses : the worst or ' marginal' land for each use pays least rent, because it yields the smallest number of units.—§ 7. Margins are directly ' determined by,' do not directly ' determine,' prices of land-use. All three factors have their margins, which similarly rise and fall with rise or fall of prices. Price changes, however, may affect supply, not at the extensive margin, but at some higher point, or at the intensive margin.—§ 8. Differential rents, then, play no real part in formulating a theory of distribution.—§ 9. Defects of the method of imputing separate productivity to units in an organic co-operation.—§ 10. Unproductive surplus, entering into prices, is a ' necessary ' payment only so long as ' monopoly ' or ' scarcity ' is maintained.

§ 1.—At every stage in the current of production we saw *entrepreneurs* buying the use of land, labour and capital, paying for it out of the prices they received for the goods they sold to the next set of *entrepreneurs* or to the consumers, and keeping the rest of the price for profit. The actual distribution takes place through these acts of sale.

If, therefore, any ' surplus ' passes as unearned income over and above necessary ' costs ' of production and progress, we shall expect to trace it in the processes which fix the prices of the uses of the several factors of production and of the goods which are bought and sold at the several stages.

In other words, such ' unproductive surplus ' will appear as excessive wages, excessive interest, rent, or excessive profit.

Let us, then, put ourselves in the position of the *entrepreneurs* who are engaged in these several classes of bargain, buying the use of land, labour, and capital and selling their product. Of course, the *entrepreneur* may be himself the owner of one or more of the other factors, using his own labour on his own land, as a small peasant, or an artisan working on his own account, perhaps with his own material and tools, or a little retailer hawking his own wares.

But these classes, important enough in many fields of industry, are not typical of modern industry, and do not serve well to illustrate the actual working of the forces which determine the flow of industry and the distribution of its product.

The typical modern business is one where the *entrepreneur* is an organiser and dealer, simply buying from three sets of persons the factors of production and selling the product to a fourth set.

Each of these markets has its special conditions.

Take first the labour market, or rather the set of labour markets, some closely connected with one another, some standing apart— exclusive repositories of particular sorts of labour-power. Everywhere throughout the industrial system the group of *entrepreneurs* whose businesses form a trade, are engaged in buying particular sorts of labour-power. How is the price they pay determined? The ordinary minimum price, as we have seen, is the sum of money sufficient to maintain the worker in the working efficiency required, and to bring up a family which will keep up the supply. The wage for a class of labour may, however, fall for a time indefinitely below this ' ordinary ' maintenance wage. Where the supply of labourers at a maintenance wage is larger than the demand, as is sometimes the case in a skilled trade which is failing or depressed, the wage may fall below the full subsistence rate, the labour-power being drained out of the workers in a short working life, and the supply being maintained out of the unemployed margin. Many parts of the unskilled or low-skilled labour market are constantly in this condition. The minimum wage here is not one of full maintenance and replacement ; it must suffice to enable the worker to keep working for some time, but it need not enable him to live out his full life or to bring up a family.

Moreover, the true maintenance wage is composed of the added wages of the wage-earners in an ordinary working family. Where economic and social conditions allow several workers in a family to contribute to the family income, the aggregate wages must usually form a full maintenance fund, but the workers need not contribute proportionately to this family wage. Where it is customary for women and children, as well as men, to work for wages, their wages usually fall considerably below the level sufficient for their full personal maintenance, the trades in which they are engaged being to this extent parasitic upon the trade of the chief wage-earner.

In towns where the chief employment is some metal trade in

which adult male labour alone is used, women's labour is usually cheap. This notorious fact has led to the introduction of textile trades into such metal towns, the payment for this textile work being lower than the necessary wage in towns which are entirely or chiefly textile towns. Where such textile employment for the women is considerable, it also exercises a depressing influence upon the wages of the male metal workers, who will not offer the same amount of resistance to reductions of wages in bad times which they would offer if the entire support of the family rested upon the metal wage.

Where there is a market for child labour, the same depressing influence is exercised upon the parents' wages. The only economically necessary wage is the family wage, and when employment is available for husband, wife, and children, there exists no security that a child, a woman, or even a man working for his own keep alone can earn a maintenance wage.

Women are, of course, impeded most. Probably most women's labour is bought at a price below the minimum of personal maintenance, partly because it is subsidised by other portions of the family wage, partly because the labour market for most women's work is permanently overstocked.

This consideration of the family maintenance as the unit of the wage-system involves some amendment of our first statement that the price of a unit of labour-power must be such as to maintain and evoke the productive effort of the worker. In saying that the price of any sort of labour-power must enable the worker to provide such a proportion of the family maintenance as the conditions of local employment impose upon him, as a member of a family, we shall approach the truer statement of the wage basis.

In a mining village or a specialised metal town the adult male worker's wage must be sufficient to support, say, four-fifths of a normal family of four or five members ; in the labouring classes of an ordinary industrial-commercial town, the adult male wage need only cover, say, three-fifths, in a Lancashire cotton town only one-half, of the family maintenance wage.

The proportion of the adult male or female wage to the aggregate family wage will vary widely according to the district and trade, and may be affected greatly by legal and customary considerations.

At any given time and place, the price an *entrepreneur* will have to pay in setting up a business will be determined by the proportion the men or women he employs have to contribute to the conventional standard of living in their class.

§ 2.—This brings us to the important distinction of grade wages

In our last chapter we recognised that there was a natural basis for the different rates of pay for different sorts of work. Work which takes more out of the worker necessitates a larger 'wear-and-tear' payment ; work which is more than usually disagreeable or dangerous usually requires the application of a stronger motive to the will of the worker, and this stronger motive usually means a higher rate of pay. These 'natural' causes explain some differences of grade or trade wages. Strength and endurance explain why British navvies, stevedores, and certain groups of workers in the metal-working and engineering trades get high rates of pay for relatively low-skilled work. Danger, however, is only a cause of higher pay where it is realised, and so acts as a deterrent to undertaking work. Some of the industrial work most dangerous to health or life is paid at the lowest rates either because when the wage-bargain is struck the danger is not recognised, or because competition for employment is so keen that it is ignored. Chemical workers and phosphorus-match workers or Belfast linen weavers get no compensation for their industrial dangers in their wages. The same applies to dirt and other disagreeable conditions. Where such work can be done by common labourers who are not squeamish or sensitive, these conditions bring no higher pay. In a refined community the assistants in a butcher's shop would earn a very high grade wage, but so long as plenty of labour which does not feel the brutalising conditions is available, there is no grade wage.

Responsibility, implying a high degree of regularity, judgment, and probity, has a market value. Work upon the due performance of which the lives of many persons, the safety of valuable machinery, money, and other property, the honour or efficiency of a business or a public office depend, is generally remunerated at a rate which implies that the workers have a 'position to keep up,' or, at any rate, that they should not be tempted by the pressure of personal needs to neglect or scamp their work. A decently high standard of comfort is recognised not merely in official but also in many departments of industrial work as a necessary factor in the wages of such men. As the technical and the financial structure of modern business becomes more complex and more delicate, this utility of high grade wages for the various classes of managers and overseers is more widely recognised. The respectability or dignity which tradition attaches to certain learned professions and officials, instead of operating to reduce their rate of pay, often serves to enhance it, because it is recognised that the physician, the lawyer, the municipal official, ought to live in a style consistent with the dignity of the post or profession he occupies. This, however, does not always hold. In America and in Germany skilled officials are commonly paid lower incomes than they would earn by private practice, regularity of employment and of income, together with the prospect of a pension, being often discounted in their present rate of pay.

But, of course, by far the most powerful determinant of grade wages is the degree of skill and knowledge required to secure regular employment in a trade or profession or, more strictly speaking, the difficulty of acquiring this skill or knowledge.

The possession and discovery of natural aptitudes, foresight, and outlay in the preparation for a trade, personal connexions and social opportunities, mobility and trade organisation, this complex of conditions, partially personal, partly adventitious, partly social, determines whether the sort of work a man does commands a high or a low rate per unit of productive energy.

We cannot, however, here closely consider how far the higher rate of piece or time work which a doctor in an ordinary practice or a foreign-office clerk receives as compared with that of a carpenter or a railway porter, is to be regarded as interest upon the capital outlay in his education and equipment, or as a prize for success in a competition in which many fail to get regular employment. There is no reason to suppose that most middle-class parents make any proportionately greater effort to equip their children for economic success than most working-class parents, or that a decline in the class wage of the professions or the public services would materially affect their outlay upon their education. Neither can it be asserted that the risks of failure are greater in these higher walks of life than in a skilled or unskilled trade, while in the latter the penalties of failure, unmitigated by ' private income ' or family supports, are incomparably heavier.

Seeing that the possession of special skill, usually combined with trade or professional organisation for the maintenance of the market value of this skill, is the main source of differences of trade wages, how far must we regard these differences as ' necessary ' expenses in production, or how far as ' surplus ' or ' excessive ' gains ?

The case of the commercial clerk is instructive upon this point. Facility in reading, writing, and arithmetic was once a rare accomplishment confined to a small section of men whose natural aptitude was assisted by special opportunity of education. The price of this sort of labour-power was then high as compared with the price of most sorts of skilled manual labour. Now that our public system of free schooling enables everyone to acquire this skill, its price has fallen below that of most branches of skilled manual labour. While it is quite likely that the special conditions of the market for this class of labour may have driven its price below the 'sweating' margin, it is also probable that in the earlier era this class wage contained an element of 'unproductive surplus,' which has been eliminated by the enlargement of competition.

Where a rapid extension of demand takes place for a class of labour which, because of the skill or experience involved, or because of the trade union limitations, cannot easily be met by an increase of supply, the grade wage, or, more strictly speaking, the price per unit of this grade of labour-power, may stand for a considerable time above the efficiency level, containing elements of 'surplus' gain which are not absorbed in stimulating industrial progress, and simply represent 'unearned income' upon the part of a class of workers. At periods of abnormal activity, large groups of miners, shipbuilders, and other workers stand in this position, sharing to some little extent the power exercised by the employers and capitalists in these trades to tax for their special benefit the general industry of the country.

§ 3.—But in applying to individual cases this conception of a grade minimum wage, an important distinction must be made. The least efficient labourer in each grade must normally earn a weekly wage sufficient for subsistence or conventional consumption of himself and such portions of a family as his wage must help to keep. If the least efficient worker can get this, more efficient workers who do more or better work in a week will get a wage exceeding this necessary minimum. In kinds of work where the difference of productivity between the best and the worst workers in actual employment is large, this differential wage, marking the superiority of workers over the marginal worker, may be considerable.

When the pace and quality of the work, or both, are levelled for the workers by machinery or other conditions of their work, or by agreement among the workers not to make full use of their individual differences of strength or skill, the weekly wage of the marginal workers may be virtually the normal wage of the grade. This is the tendency of the machine to equalise the workers.

The differences of weekly earnings between superior and inferior workers in a class of labour follow necessarily from the fact that so far as labour-power is treated as an article of commerce, to be bought and sold in a labour market, each unit of labour must be bought and sold at the same price. If, therefore, the marginal worker only gives out six units of labour per week, while the more efficient workers give out ten units, their weekly wage will contain a differential wage which measures this excess,[1] most of which may be utilised in building a higher standard of comfort within the class. I say ' most,' not all, for it may be assumed in some cases that the greater output of energy required to earn the larger wage implies a larger expenditure in personal wear and tear.

Regarding labour-power as productive energy bought in labour markets, we may say that the minimum price per unit of each kind is such that the weekly sum earned by the marginal worker just supports the conventional standard of life.   If the least effective workers in a factory trade require 20s. to support this standard and give out four units of labour-power per week, the minimum price per unit of labour-power is 5s., and any superior workers who give out six units per week (as measured by piece or otherwise) can get 30s. weekly wage.

This marginal labour, of course, must not be understood as *determining* the price of this grade of labour-power.   The assumption is simply this, ' If so much labour-power is required for this industry as to involve the employment of this four-unit labour as the low limit, the price per unit cannot be less than 5s.'

So far as there exists freedom and fluidity of labour, young labour being able to exercise choice in its application, and enjoying some liberty to pass from place to place and even from trade to trade, according as wages and other advantages are greater or less, the wages of each class of labour tends to remain at a conventional minimum for the marginal labour of each class.

This is the truth underlying the too rigorous dogma of the ' Iron Law of Wages.'   The general condition of the labourers as bargainers for the sale of labour-power is such that the price they get tends to remain at the lower level of the conventional standard of comfort of each grade, and this conventional standard approximates

[1] Though the superior amount or quality of output is the basis of this differential wage, it is by no means certain that the excess of output attending the employment of a superior worker is the measure or the separate result of his superior personal efficiency. If the ' marginal ' or worst worker in a mill produces 6 units per week and a better worker 12 units, it must not be assumed that the latter as a worker is twice as efficient as the former. For the product is due to co-operation of the worker with the machinery and other factors in the mill. When a more efficient worker is employed, more productivity is got out of the machinery and other factors in a given time than when a less efficient worker is employed. Part of the difference, then, between the 12 and 6 units is properly attributable to the more effective working of the other factors.   The differential weekly wage may, but need not, probably in most cases does not, cover payment for the whole of the 6 units which are got by employing the more efficient as compared with the marginal worker. Ultimately this criticism implies that no separate productivity as measured by product can be imputed to a particular worker, or a particular piece of capital or land, all productivity and all products being due to an organic co-operation of the several factors.

to the bare wage of efficiency. This interpretation is consistent with the fact that the actual wage of most grades of labour has risen in civilised nations during the last two generations. New methods of industry, especially under machine economy, involve a more intense industrial life, higher intelligence, and a larger nervous output, which can only be supported by a higher actual standard of expense.

While, therefore, the ' minimum ' in modern industry is not the physical subsistence minimum of the older doctrine, it none the less remains true that the conditions of the sale of labour-power are normally such as to keep the price down to the point of marginal costs of production, that is the conventional standard of comfort of the worst labour in each grade.

As soon as we realise the actual conditions of the ordinary sale of labour-power, it becomes obvious that the buyers possess such a normal superiority of bargaining power as enables them to keep the price of labour at this limit.

There is not for labourers the same liberty to refuse to sell their labour-power as there is for employers to refuse to buy. If a starving man meets a baker he will pay all the money in his purse for a loaf of bread ; the baker here exerts the maximum of economic power in bargaining for the price of his bread. Now a labourer bargaining with an employer for the sale of his labour-power is in an analogous case. He must sell, and he must sell now. The employer is not under the same compulsion to buy or to buy now. If the labourer does not sell he starves ; if the employer does not buy he loses some profit. If the labourer can find two employers and make them bid for his labour, he can sell at a price above the bare subsistence price, i.e. at a price which is measured by the minimum profit at which one of the two employers will conduct his business. If, however, the two employers can find three labourers, two of which they wish to hire, they bring down the conditions of the price of labour to the starving-man limit.

Whenever, then, the ordinary condition of a labour market is such that there are more willing sellers than willing buyers, the price is virtually dictated to the seller by the buyer at the limit which we have already defined, that of the minimum standard wage. Now the larger part of the labour market of the world remains in this condition, offering at any given moment a surplus supply of labour willing to work at the ordinary conventional subsistence wage. Such labour is virtually obliged to sell its use for the marginal cost of producton, i.e. for that share of the general product of industry just sufficient to maintain it in its accepted standard of living.

It is sometimes objected that though employers are animated by an intrinsically weaker motive, viz. profit-making, than workers, their competition to employ competent workers is as keen as that of competent workers to get employment.

This, however, is untrue unless an artificial meaning is given to the term ' competent ' as applied to workers.

The normal condition of trade is such as to make it easier for an employer to get additional workers up to the standard of the less efficient labour he already employs, than for such workers to find employers who will buy their labour.

There exists a normal excess of units of supply of labour-power over the demand at a price measuring the accepted standard of living for most working classes.

If rigorous logic of bargaining prevailed throughout the field of industry, wages could nowhere rise, except in so far as increased intensity or higher quality of working energy involved in industrial changes required the provision of a larger human wear-and-tear fund.

§ 4.—The labour market is, however, qualified in its working, more than any other sort of market, by non-competitive or only indirectly competitive conditions. Custom, personal considerations, public opinion, and legal enactments have always tempered competition, sometimes enabling the labourers to fare better than they would otherwise have fared, sometimes worse. Though law and custom are now far weaker as direct determinants of wages, considerations of humanity, sometimes of fear, have been more widely operative in establishing conventional standards of comfort above the margin of competitive wages. These standards themselves have been materially raised by legal requirements regarding safety and sanitation, and though we are far from the establishment of a legal minimum wage, the tendency of much industrial legislation, together with the adoption of non-competitive standard wages by many public and some private employers, has helped to raise many conventional standards of comfort.

But within this competitive system itself we find certain grades of labour which have raised their price above the minimum limit so as to secure by organised action a share of what we term the surplus.

There is only one way of achieving this, namely, by limiting the supply of labour in some particular field of employment so as to create a scarcity and raise ' the standard wage.'

Whenever labour can put itself in this position, it can exact a wage higher than the standard minimum : how much higher will depend upon the terms upon which employers can buy the other factors of production, and the terms on which they can sell their products in the market. Every successful enforcement of a 'standard rate' by a trade union involves some such restriction of supply. This is not, indeed, always apparent in the process of collective bargaining, which is the instrument for securing or maintaining a 'standard rate.' But collective bargaining is only efficacious where a union limits its membership by requiring evidence of efficiency, by limitation of apprentices, or by regulation of output. Where none of these conditions are available, a 'standard rate' cannot be maintained. A trade union which freely admitted everyone who said he was, or wished to be, a worker in the trade could not bargain collectively with any success.

In order that workers may raise the price of their labour above mere 'maintenance,' they must be able, by limiting the supply of labour-power below that amount which employers believe they could profitably apply to production, to throw the strain of competition upon the employers. If by organisation they can present a labour market in which every willing worker is confronted by two willing employers, it becomes more important for any given employer to secure a worker than for any given worker to secure a particular employer, and this situation is reflected in a higher price for labour.

No trade, however, can do this except by utilising some natural scarcity of skill or opportunity, or by making it difficult for outsiders to acquire or to offer for sale the particular sort of labour in which the trade deals.

Where some new rapid demand for labour arises in a new country or in some new trade, organised action, for a time at any rate, may not be needed to secure a 'surplus' wage. Examples of this are found where capital has flowed in advance of labour in the process of developing some new country. Agricultural and mechanical labour in the new Western States of America and in Canada has enjoyed this position of vantage; sheep shearers in Australia, miners in the Transvaal, artisans in Argentina, have from time to time been able to take high wages, less by reason of concerted action than because labour was short in relation to the demand for its profitable use. But in order fully to utilise and to maintain such a position of vantage, organisation is usually requisite.

In settled countries there have been conspicuous instances of this same power. The building trades in certain American cities have been able to raise their wages considerably above the normal standard where rapid expansion or reconstruction has favoured them. Among the building trades some single class of labour, e.g. plasterers or masons in certain parts of England, have been able to raise the price of their labour relative to that of the other building trades. Wherever this scarcity can be maintained, the extra price of labour which it procures ought to be clearly distinguished from the normal standard wage.

So far as this surplus or scarcity wage gradually operates through a rise in the class standard of comfort to increase the efficiency and productivity of labour, it need not cause any rise in the expenses of production in the trade, for 'the economy of high wages' may keep the price of a unit of labour-power flowing from more efficient labourers as low as before. When this directly economic gain cannot be ascribed to it, the surplus wage serving to raise the condition of the labourers in ways not directly or proportionately conducive to increased productivity, the surplus implies an enhanced price per unit of labour-power, and raises the expenses of production of the goods into which it enters. Such a 'surplus,' where it arises, must clearly be distinguished from the standard wage, in that it is not a necessary inducement to the labourers to apply their labour-power (though it may become so if it be held long enough to build a new conventional standard of comfort), but is a bonus of the nature of monopoly price. Since the most vital issue in the theory and the practice of the distribution of wealth rests upon the distinction between necessary costs of production and surplus, it is important to recognise that labour, though normally unable to obtain a wage of true efficiency, may sometimes, in certain trades, hold this position of scarcity or relative monopoly.

§ 5.—The payments made by *entrepreneurs* at various industrial points for the use of the concrete forms of capital they employ fall under the same general categories of maintenance and surplus.

The payments for maintenance, as in the case of labour, differ in the case of a stationary and a progressive industry.

Large preserves of industry are marked out in which the real capital earns a higher rate of real interest than outside. As workers can earn a scarcity wage by creating and maintaining a scarcity of labour-power in a particular trade, so can the capitalists or investors who have secured for their special advantage a particular field of investment, marking it off from the area of the free flow of new capital.

To the business man the capital upon which he pays interest is usually considered in terms of money, not of plant and stock. But if we are to place the use of capital and its price on a footing analogous to the use of labour and its price, we must consider interest as a part of the product, or real income of the community, paid to investors who supply plant and stock for the purposes of assisting production. When, therefore, we represent certain capitalists as exercising a monopoly, absolute or relative, over some trade, we mean that they enjoy some advantage which enables them to prevent outside investors from setting up plant and stock in this trade with equal opportunities of production and sale, thus securing a limited supply of plant and stock and a scarcity price for the use of the same.

If it be the case that no one but the capitalists of the Standard Oil Company can set up oil plant so as to operate successfully in most States of America, it is quite evident that they are able to get a high price for the use of this plant. If any other set of capitalists can acquire in other trades, not necessarily a monopoly so strong as this, but so strong a hold upon the whole or some part of their market as to exercise a similar sort of control, they can use this power to secure a price for the use of their capital above that which obtains in markets subject to free investment and free competition. It is a main purpose of trusts, syndicates, pools, corners, and other combinations or arrangements, local or general, temporary or permanent, to place certain trades in such a condition that the owners of the sort of plant and stock engaged in them may take a rate of real interest higher than the two and a half or three per cent. which suffices to procure the application of ' free ' capital When this end is achieved, the owners of the worst equipped mills or mines or workshops, ' the marginal ' capital, are able to obtain a surplus price for the use of their factor of production.[1]

Though the relations between the owners of the real capital and the *entrepreneurs* in most trades are much closer than those between the workers and the *entrepreneurs*, it is not necessary to identify capitalist with *entrepreneur* and to assume that their interests are the same. The control of a trade and of a market may be obtained and held by a group of capitalists in order that by limiting the entrance of capital they may earn a ' scarcity ' rate of interest on their capital. Though, as we shall see, this is not the typical modern form of industrial monopoly, it obtains in many trades and in many markets. The cases where the real capital in a trade secures a surplus interest of this kind, measuring its scarcity value, are far more frequent than the cases where labour, manual or mental, exercises this power.

. . . .

§ 6.—When we come to the case of land and the price of its use, we seem at first to require a new set of principles. Almost everywhere in the industrial system where *entrepreneurs* defray the

---

[1] Whether or to what extent this surplus should rank as the profits of *entrepreneurs* rather than as surplus-interest is a question left for later consideration.

expenses of production out of the money they get for their goods, some of it goes for rent. Is rent, then, a necessary cost of production in the same sense as the minimum wage and the minimum interest ? We have seen that the wear and tear, or other depreciation of land, is a cost that must be provided for out of current income, just as in the case of the use of machinery or other capital. In fact, so far as the payment for maintenance or improvement of land is concerned, land may be treated as a form of capital. But rent is totally distinct from such payments.

In the case both of labour-power and capital we saw that a human effort was involved in the case of the marginal workers and savers which required a payment to evoke and sustain it. No such payment seems essential to the owners of marginal land (i.e. the worst land in use for any kind of service), because the application of this factor of production involves no human effort. It would seem, therefore, that all rent of land ranks as a surplus payment, a price obtained by owners of a factor which is limited in supply and can extort from those who need its use a scarcity value. This is actually the case. The marginal land for a particular purpose, e.g. growing wheat, market gardening, city building, in developed industrial communities, almost always pays a rent which signifies that there exists a scarcity of this supply of land.

If the marginal hop land in Kent pays a rent of £2 per acre, this means that the owners of land fit for hops find themselves in bargaining with growers in a strong position, owing to the scarcity of hop land. If hops were necessaries of life, and could be procured nowhere else, their bargaining power would resemble that of the single baker bargaining with the starving man. Their power is much less than this, and is in fact limited by the fact that growers cannot raise their selling price beyond a certain point without causing a large shrinkage of demand, but it is sufficient to enable the owners of the marginal hop land to demand £2 an acre. This scarcity price for the use of hop land is determined 'n precisely similar fashion to the scarcity or surplus payment for use of some particular kind of labour-power or capital.

All kinds of land are no more ' free ' to compete for hop-growing than are all kinds of savings to enter the oil-refining business, or all kinds of labour to enter the engineering or the medical professions. Natural or organised scarcity is everywhere the origin of surplus payments, and the £2 per acre payment for the marginal hop lands stands in this respect on just the same footing as the, say, surplus 10s. per week which a plasterer gets by means of his strong trade organisation, or the surplus five per cent. which may accrue to the marginal capital in cotton thread or Englisħ banking companies. [1]

If, on a basis of scarcity in relation to the selling prices of hops, the marginal hop land can extort £2 an acre, better hop land takes a higher rent, not because its owners have a greater bargaining power than the owner of the marginal land, but simply because what is really sold is hop-growing power of land, and land which has more units of this power per acre when paid at the same rate as the worst land, naturally receives a higher actual rent. Rent is simply the price per unit for land-use reckoned per acre.

The same is true of other land employed for various purposes. Each purpose must be regarded as denoting a separate supply of land : the price or rent paid per acre for the worst land in each supply marks the scarcity or monopoly power of the owners of this sort of land, the better lands taking a differential rent; measuring the larger number of units of productive power this land yields as compared with the worst.

The old economic theory held that the marginal land paid no rent. But this is certainly untrue of most uses of land in developed countries. It may be true even in England to-day that there is rough land used for grazing which pays a merely nominal rent. This ' marginal ' grazing land is no-rent land. This means that the price per unit of grazing use is such as, spread over a large quantity of poor land, is a negligible sum. But the same is seldom true for wheat growing ; the worst wheat land usually pays some rent. The marginal land for market gardening pays a considerable rent, and, where we come to city building ground, the least eligible sites pay a rent far above the ordinary level for agricultural uses.

If, ignoring all differences of quality of soil and position, we lump all land together and regard every piece as eligible for grazing, arable, market gardening, building, and other purposes, we can find land which only secures for its owners a nominal or no rent, and measuring the value of the yield of all better lands for all sorts of purposes, we can treat the rent they afford as purely differential rent, which marks superior productivity as compared with the no-rent land on the margin.

But this treatment is too remote from industrial reality. Though in a certain sense there is one labour market, each part of which has some contact with every other, for practical purposes we have to distinguish various skilled and unskilled markets, each with its own minimum standard wage.

[1] The fact that rent of land rests on a natural scarcity which no social or industrial reforms can eliminate, while the other surplus payments usually rest on what may be termed artificial restrictions, is no reason for distinguishing the two at this stage in our analysis.

So with land. Natural conditions, habits of local industry, availability for markets, determine the use of land in particular localities much as they do the use of labour. The supply of land in a country, or throughout the industrial world, may thus be divided into a number of supplies which are tolerably distinct. Some land may be transferred from pasture to arable, or *vice versâ ;* agricultural land passes into town land, and so forth ; but at any given time there is a supply of wheat land, a supply of cotton land, a supply of fruit land, &c., for the world market or for any national or local market. The least productive land in employment for each particular purpose is the marginal land for this market, and the superiority of better land is measured from this margin. We have thus a number of margins : the land on most of these margins pays a positive rent, which denotes the scarcity of productive land for the particular supply in question.

This division and grading of land supplies may be set out by the following diagram. Take a developed self-contained industrial country with a variety of lands and industries : suppose the centre to be a populous manufacturing and residential district, while the belts of land around this centre are given to the more intensive agricultural uses, the poorer land in the remoter parts being given to ruder agriculture and pasture. The picture will take some such form as the following :—

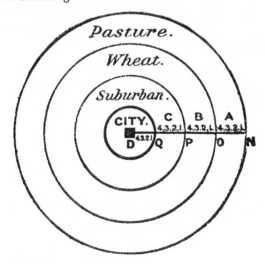

Taking first the pasture belt, we will suppose that the poorest land in use lies on the outer edge, and that as we approach the wheat belt the pasture improves.

A traveller entering this country at N, and taking a straight road to the city in the centre, will first have to traverse the rough pasture belt A, the pasture gradually improving as he approaches the inner boundary O. When he crosses this boundary into B he finds himself in a wheat belt, the poorest wheat land near the O boundary, the best near the inner boundary P. Proceeding farther and crossing at P he enters a suburban belt given up to market gardens, brickfields, &c., and gradually improving in quality as it approaches Q, the actual city boundary. Crossing at Q into the city he finds here, too, a constant rise in the value of the land until he reaches the centre where site-value is highest.

In order further to simplify our analysis, we will assume that the pasture land which we saw was improving as the inner boundary of the pasture belt was reached at O, would have gone on improving as one went farther, if the land had not been applied to wheat or other more profitable use, that is to say, that the various grades of wheat land in B would have made better pasture land than the best actual pasture in A. Similarly, let us suppose that the best actual wheat area in B, viz. the part bordering on P, is not so good for growing wheat as the worst land across the border P, now used for market gardens, would have been, or, in other words, that for wheat-growing, as for pasture, all the land improves as it gets nearer the centre. So, too, with the market garden belt C : not merely does it improve as it nears the city boundary at Q, but the actual city land itself would have made better garden land than any that is in actual use, had it not been wanted for more valuable building uses.

In a word, our assumption is that for each use the land improves in quality as it nears the centre. Now let us look more particularly at the pasture belt A. Before our traveller crosses the boundary at N he passes through some scrub land which, from soil, vegetation, and position, was not quite so good for pasture as the worst pasture land in actual use across the boundary, the pasture marked 1.

This worst pasture land in actual use can only be used if the owner will let it for a merely nominal rent per acre, for the farmer who puts cattle on it finds the feed so poor as only just to make it worth his while risking the loss of his beasts and paying the herd to look after them. Some cattle thus are raised on land which may be said to pay no rent. Farmers who prefer to put their cattle upon better grazing land farther from the outer boundary N, even on the next worst land, marked 2, must pay rent to the landowner. How much ? Evidently that sum per acre which measures the full superiority of land in A2 over land in A1 for grazing purposes. If every hundred acres in A2 furnishes so much better feed as to enable a farmer to sell a thousand pounds more meat per annum than a farmer with cattle on A1, then the price of the thousand pounds, say 250s., will be absorbed in paying rent at 2s. 6d. per acre to the landowner. He must pay this 2s. 6d. rent, for, if he objected to pay more than 2s., it is evident that our farmer who has been grazing his cattle at no-rent land in A1, will be willing to take his place, bidding for the land any sum up to 2s. 6d., for by taking A2 land at less than 2s. 6d. he will do better than on the inferior no-rent land. On the other hand, it is equally clear that the landowner of the better grazing lands cannot get more than 2s. 6d. per acre, for if he tried to insist upon 3s., or anything over 2s. 6d., it would pay the farmer to go on to the no-rent land in A1.

The rent, then, of the better grazing land in A2 is measured by the excess of the productivity of this land over the land which is only used on condition that no rent, or a nominal rent, is paid. If rent were paid in kind, the thousand pounds of meat per hundred acres would be taken : the money rent will, of course, depend upon the selling price of meat.[1]

§ 7.—But, though in measuring the rent of particular pieces of land, reference to the ' marginal ' or worst land in use is found convenient, we must carefully guard against the false notion that such marginal land in any special causative sense ' determines ' rent. The quantity and quality of the worst land in use for grazing plays exactly the same part in helping to determine rent as the quantity and quality of the better grades of grazing land. Rent is the price of a unit of grazing-power of land. Land that contains a large amount of grazing-power obtains a high rent per acre, land that contains a small amount a low rent per acre. The rise and fall of the price of grazing-power determines at a given time what shall be the marginal grazing land, this rise or fall being itself caused by the pressure of various forces affecting the demand and the supply for grazing-power. If there is some grazing land in use at a merely nominal rent, whereas the worst wheat land in use pays 10s. per acre, this merely implies that there exists a practically unlimited amount of low-grade grazing land, which has no other remunerative use, and some of which it is just worth while to employ at current prices for cattle, whereas the price of wheat is such as to impose a price per unit of wheat-growing which yields 10s. per acre of the worst

---

[1] In the long run, economic rent, if paid in money, must conform to changes of prices of produce. Where, however, no easy method of adjustment is offered by custom or law, a fall of agricultural prices has often inflicted grave injury upon tenants who are called upon to pay a larger quantity, often a larger proportion, of the product of their labour on the land in rent.

wheat land drawn away from grazing or some other use for which it could have got 9s. per acre. Though the rent, or price per acre, may be *measured* from the marginal land, the margin is directly *determined* by the price, and only in a slight and secondary sense helps to determine the price. As soon as it is clearly comprehended that rent is the price of a unit of land-use in precisely the same sense as wages are the price per unit of labour-use, and that the rent per acre depends on the number of land units it contains, just as the weekly piece wage of a labourer depends on the number of units of labour-power he gives out in a week, the notion that there is a law of rent, differing radically from the law of wages or of interest on capital, and depending in some mysterious manner upon ' marginal ' land, will entirely disappear.

The fact that rent is always a 'scarcity' price, a surplus payment, does not in the least affect the truth that rent, though not a ' cost,' is an ' expense ' which enters as an element into the price of a stock of goods just as wages and interest enter. That element which enters price is, of course, not a ' marginal ' payment for the worst worker, the worst machine, or the worst acre, but the price per unit for the use of labour-power, machine-power, land-power, of the several sorts required in the process of production. Margins, whether extensive or intensive, are derivative, not determinative.

The simplest co-ordination of the three factors of production in relation to the payment for their uses may be expressed in the following diagram :—

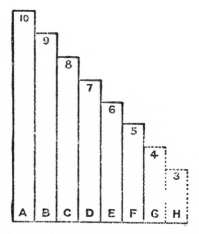

A trade requires for its operation the use of productive-power, issuing from land, capital, labour in some stable proportion, i.e. so many thousand units of land, so many thousand of labour and of capital. The supply of these units is represented by acres, men, and, for simplicity, we will say machines, taking these as representative forms of concrete capital. An acre, a man, or a machine may contain many or few units of productive-power, according to its quality. The best quality of acre, man, or machine, viz. A, gives out ten units per annum ; the next quality, B, gives out nine. The worst quality of each factor in actual use is F, giving out five units, but there are other lower qualities capable of being brought into use, if it pays to do so, viz. G, producing four units, and H, producing three. F is the ' margin ' in each case. The fact that it is the margin, and not E or G, is seen to be determined by the relation between the market price per unit and the minimum subsistence payment required by a man, a machine, or acre irrespective of its yield. The five-unit labourer at F is the worst labourer employed, because the price per unit of labour is just enough to keep him in working efficiency according to his standard of living. If the price per unit rose, some labour at G (four units) might be brought into use, i.e. the extensive margin would have fallen ; if the price per unit fell, labour at F, unable to subsist according to its accepted standard, would tend to seek other employment, and the margin would stand at E.

If instead of labourers we say machines, the same law holds good. It is the price per unit of capital-power in relation to the differential productivity of the various sorts of machine that will determine what is the worst sort in actual use. The real buying of use of capital is by units. If a machine of five-unit power is just kept in use, it is because the price per unit just furnishes a wear-and-tear payment and minimum interest ; if a great new demand, raising price per unit, makes it pay either to employ some antiquated machines worth only four units which had fallen out of use, or to incur the expense or risk of embarking in some new machines of dubious value, which likewise lie below the present margin of employment, the capital margin will fall to four. A fall in price per unit will conversely throw out of use the five-unit machines at F, raising the capital margin to E.

The case of acres of land and their payment is not different. It is true that the limitation of supply of acres at different levels of efficiency is natural, and is not directly determined by the will and needs of man, as in the case of labour and capital, but the determination of the margin is the same. It is fixed at five-unit acres or F, because the price per unit makes it just more profitable for some F acres to apply themse ves to this use than to some other use that is available : G acres are below the margin, either because they have some other use for which they are more productive, or where their units of productivity command a higher price, or else because the ' wear-and-tear ' fund would absorb the whole price of four units, i.e. because they have no true economic rent.

In each case the margin is seen to be determined by, and runs and falls according to, the price per unit of productive-power.

If a rise or fall of price per unit of productive-power must always and only operate by raising or lowering the margin of employment, in the sense of bringing in or putting out of supply acres, men, or machines at the bottom of the supply, this diagram would do all that is wanted in the way of illustration.

But the changes in supply are not solely effected at this lower margin. If the price per unit of wheat-growing power should rise, it may operate not only or not chiefly by bringing into use acres worse for wheat-growing than the worst previously in use : it may divert from some other use into wheat-growing better land, producing not four units per acre, but perhaps ten or nine units, thus adding to the supply of the most productive acres. The same holds of labour and of capital. A rise in the price of labour-power in Lancashire coal mines might bring into the supply not only remnants of the local rural population, already weakened by the migration of their most vigorous members, but new drafts of powerful Irish labourers from Connemara, feeding the supply not by lowering the margin from five units to four, but by bringing in, say, eight-unit labourers. So likewise with the machinery, which we take as representative of capital   A rise in price per unit of this industrial power may not only for a while bring back into use some old and disused machines, but will lead to the increased application of the best machines. Indeed, it is evident that this will be the more normal effect in the case of capital. Similarly, a fall in price per unit of productive-power may not operate chiefly by driving out of employment the worst portion of supply, but by driving some better portions into other uses.

Finally, a rise or fall of price per unit of land, labour, or capital may operate, not to bring into use new acres, men, or machines, or to put out of use some of those already in use, whether upon the margin or at some higher grade, but to evoke more units of productivity from existing factors. Instead of bringing in new acres, an intenser use of existing acres may be evoked ; overtime or speeding up may be applied to men and to machines, so that out of those in use a larger number of units per man or per machine may be got. This is sometimes spoken of as lowering the intensive margin of employment.

§ 8.—The advantages of adopting what we term the ' unitary ' method of measurement are now apparent. It enables us to distinguish the three several ways in which, by means of a change in the price of industrial power, the supply of factors of production is changed, and to recognise that the method of controlling the supply in the case of the three factors is identical.

It also enables us to get rid of certain misconceptions which sometimes arise as to the part played by the so-called ' marginal factors ' of supply in determining the price of the whole supply. The only sense in which the worst acres of land, or the worst workers, or the worst machines can be said to ' determine ' the price per unit of these several factors of production is that this price is, and must be, just enough to evoke their use. The same is true if we take the ' intensive margin ' : the price paid must be just enough to evoke the most intensive or expensive use of the existing acres, labourers, or machines. But this does not imply that the marginal factors exercise any special determinant influence as ' causes ' of the price. The price per unit of each sort of industrial power is ' caused ' or ' brought about ' by a variety of forces of demand and of supply, in which the marginal factors play no appreciable part. How can they ? How is it possible to say that the five-unit acres, men and machines,' determine ' in the way of *causing* the price of a unit to be so much, when we perceive that the price of the unit has directly caused these five-unit factors, and not four-unit or six-unit factors, to be marginal ? It is far more accurate to say that the price per unit causes the margin to be where it is, than to attribute any causative power to the margin, as margin, in relation to the price per unit.

It is quite true that the amount of five-unit land or five-unit labour available will have some effect in causing the price per unit to be what it is, but it will have no more effect than that which belongs to other better land or labour, its effect being only proportionate to the part it plays in the whole supply, and having no relation to its marginal character. In a word, prices determine (causatively) margins—margins do not determine prices. The fact that the price per unit must be just such as to remunerate sufficiently the worst extensive or intensive power in use, whether of land, labour, or capital, does not justify us in assigning any special place to these marginal factors in our law of distribution of the product. The grave abuses which have arisen from an attempt to erect a theory of the distribution of the product upon a basis of marginal causation are discussed in the Appendix to this chapter.

Applying, then, in conclusion, the fundamental distinction between costs and unproductive surplus to the several factors of production, we shall insist in applying it to the units of supply, and not to the particular acres or men or machines that give out these units. In other words, we neglect what are sometimes called 'differential rents' of land, or of ability or efficiency, which make and measure the superiority of the better over the worst acres, the better workers or machines over the worst, because these measurements are really irrelevant to the statement of a law of distribution. Of course an acre that gives out twice as much productive-power as another acre gets twice as much payment in rent ; of course a worker who gives out twice as much labour-power as another gets double his piece wages. This obvious consideration can throw no light upon any principle or law apportioning the product among the several members of the several factors.

The real issue with which a theory of distribution is concerned is to discover and define the forces which determine what shall be the respective payments *per unit* for the various sorts of productive-power given out by the several factors of production. It is the composition of the payment for these units that matters for purposes of industrial progress : for the analysis of these payments discloses the use or abuse of the surplus, its productive application as a food and stimulus of progress, or its unproductive application as an ' unearned ' element of income checking industry and robbing some other factor of its stimulus.

Given the payment per unit of land-power or labour-power, the difference in rent between one acre and another, one worker and another, follows from a simple 'rule of thumb,' and exercises no influences whatever upon the theory or the practice of distribution of wealth. No one would think of suggesting that the fact that twice as much money is paid for two bushels of wheat as for one has any influence in determining the price of wheat; why, then, should the fact that an acre yielding forty bushels is paid twice the rent paid for an acre yielding twenty bushels, be considered to have any ' determinant ' influence on the price of the use of land ? The fact that there are various qualities of land or labour, that some is better, some worse, some worst, and that each acre or man is remunerated according to his or its quality, is a detail of book-keeping for agriculturalists and manufacturers, not a ' law ' or ' principle ' of economic science.

§ 9.—Although convenience of exposition has led us, in the application of our unitary method, to treat the several factors as if they were separate and independent repositories of productive power, furnishing so many units of land-power, capital-power, or labour-power to the several processes of production, reflection will show that an important corrective is needed in order to bring this setting into closer conformity with facts. Acres of land, individual labourers and particular machines, to which we have accredited the possession of so many units of productive power, cannot by their separate action apply the productive power which they possess. In wheat-growing, for·instance, we have graded land, attributing to the best land in use (say) thirty bushels per acre, to the worst land ten bushels. On this hypothesis the best land would yield three times as many units of wheat-growing power as the worst, and since rent is the price per unit of this power, the rent per acre for the best land would be just three times that for the worst. But in point of fact, if the worst land in question were Essex clay, which had no other use than wheat-growing, the rent per acre for this ' marginal land' might be a merely nominal sum, far less than one-third of what was paid for the best land per acre. How is this? Clearly because, when we said that the best land yielded thirty, the worst land ten bushels, we meant that this would be the yield if the same use of capital and labour were applied in the two cases. Now if the same quantity and quality of agricultural labour and capital be applied to a bad acre as to a good, it will be the co-operative or combined action of the three factors which will produce, in the one case thirty, the other ten bushels. We may indeed take a separatist view, and say that, since the capital and labour must be considered as productive in the one case as the other, the whole difference is due to the inferior productivity of the soil. But, considering that co-operative action is essential, it would be more reasonable to say that the capital and labour, though in themselves of equal quality, functioned less productively in the one case than in the other, or, in other words, that the inferiority of the soil reacted on the efficiency of the other factors. Just as a machine is less productive if a slow or inferior operative tends it, so a labourer and a horse-plough are less productive if the time is spent in cultivating inferior land.

Now, so far as the payment for the capital and the labour is concerned, it is evident that a labourer and a plough engaged in tilling inferior land must be paid the same as if tilling superior land. If, then, ten bushels is only just enough to defray these payments, it is evident that the ten-bushel land, instead of yielding a rent equal to one-third of that paid by the thirty-bushel land, will yield no rent as compared with a rent of twenty bushels. A strict interpretation of the proceeding obliges us to admit that there is no justification for attributing the whole difference in the yield to the separate productivity of the land. For the difference in the land affects the productivity of the forms of capital and labour. In other words, there is no separate productivity of land. We have only been able to attribute the relative productivity of thirty and ten bushels by assuming that the labour and capital in the two cases have the same productivity, whereas in fact we recognise that inferior soil will infect the capital and labour with inferior productivity. Thus, though the capital and the labour employed in the bad land receive the same payment as that employed in the good land, the actual productive power they yield in co-operation with land will be less.

The real difficulty which attends this reasoning is due to the fact that our analytic method has tacitly assumed a separate productivity attributable to each part of each factor employed in a business, whereas no such separate productivity exists. Each labourer on a farm by his presence as a co-operative agent affects the amount of productive service rendered by each other labourer, and the efficacy of each labourer and of the total labour-power will be affected by the quantity and character of the machines, horses, farm-buildings, fencing and other capital, while the efficiency of each worker and of each machine, horse, &c., will depend on, and vary with, the quality of the land and the different agricultural uses made of it.

What is true in the case of a farm is equally true in any other business. The economy of division of labour, indeed, rests upon the assumption that there is no separate productivity for each labourer, but that his utility varies with the efficacy of the co-operation with other labourers. Although for practical purposes a factory manager establishes a system of piece-wages, according to which he seems to impute a separate productivity to workers, he is well aware that this is but a rough and ready mode of reckoning, and that, similarly, in measuring the productivity of different machines, a score of complicated considerations arise from the fact that a machine is only a co-operative unit in a big complex department which itself depends for its efficacy upon other departments. No system of cost-taking, however scientific, really overcomes the difficulty, which arises from an attempt to treat an organic co-operation as if it were the mere addition of a number of separate productive acts.

So intimate is the interdependence of the factors upon one another, and of the several parts of each factor upon the other parts of its own factor and upon all the parts of the other factors, that no separate productivity can rightly be attributed to any factor, still less to any part of a factor. So, when we speak of an acre yielding so many bushels, or of a worker turning out so many cwt. of coal, or of a machine with such and such an output, we are using the language of a false separatism. Though justified as a provisional approach to a theory of payment for productive power, this separatist method requires to be corrected and displaced by a distinct recognition of the organic co-operation of the factors in a business, which precludes the attribution to any factor, or part of a factor, of any particular product or any fixed proportion of the total product of the business.

No claim to an amount of remuneration can be based upon proved or measured productivity on the part of the owner of any factor.

Thus we come to the conclusion that, though what is bought and paid for in the distributive system is units of the several factors of production, this payment cannot be determined by a strict regard to the separate productivity of each portion of each factor. No worker in a factory can say : " This is my product ; I ought to have it, or its value, in wages." Nor can the owner of a patent machine say : " My machine has enabled a worker to produce double the output he produced before ; I will take in royalty this increase of output." If any such quantitative analysis of separate productivity were feasible, an accurate measurement of the separate yield of each man, each machine, each acre, &c., might yield a law for distribution of wealth which would commend itself at once as equitable and logical.

But the organic co-operation of the industrial system forbids us to entertain the notion of attaining such a law for the distribution of the product of a process or a business among the owners of the several factors, or for the distribution of the whole product of the industrial system among the owners of the factors.

The separate payments which in fact are made to the owners of particular factors in a particular business must indeed be considered to have reference to the utility imputed to the factor in question ; but that utility in its turn must be interpreted, not by any separate productivity rendered by the factor, but by its services as a member of a co-operative group, those services being enhanced or diminished by the action of other members of the group. That payment, we have seen, cannot be less than what is economically necessary to maintain the factor in its current efficiency ; how much more it may be will depend not on any separate productivity, real or imputed, but upon the degree of pressure which its scarcity relative to that of other factors of production enables it to exercise in demanding its share of the product of the business as an organic whole. In such organic co-operation, no doubt, payment will be accorded in proportion to the ' importance ' or ' value ' assigned to a unit of each factor, but that importance will no more measure the separate productivity of the factor than the relative importance which we might assign to a hand or a foot in the economy of the human body would measure its special contribution to the activity of the organism.

§ 10.—Having examined the chief conditions under which industrial power, proceeding respectively from labour, capital, and land, is sold, we are now in a position to consider the relation of the three sorts of power as expenses of production, and to state a common law of remuneration.

Every stock of commodities represents the application of a number of units of these different sorts of power working together in organised co-operation. This organised co-operation is conducted by the directive energy of a business man, an *entrepreneur*. How far this directive energy can be treated as a productive-power, reducible to the same standard as the other factors, and evoked and remunerated in accordance with the same laws, is a question which is deferred for separate and closer consideration. Here we are concerned with tracing the common part played by labour, capital, and land as concrete powers entering into a stock of commodities.

Taking any such stock of shoes, cotton cloth, or motor-cars, we find it contains the use of so many units of labour-power, capital-power, and land-power respectively, that the price of these several sorts of units enters as expenses of production into the price paid for the commodities, and is paid out to the owners of the several factors of production, according as the money which purchases the commodities passes down the ' system,' and is broken into separate payments (income) at the various stages of production.

The first set of payments consisted of those required to produce and maintain all parts of the existing fabric of industry—a maintenance fund. The product which remained after these payments were provided was termed the 'surplus.' A portion of this surplus is ' productive,' inasmuch as it is distributed so as to evoke an increased size and improved character of industry. In a progressive industrial society both of these sets of payments rank as costs of production. The rest of the surplus, economic rent of land, excessive interest, profit, salaries, or wages, is ' unproductive ' : it evokes no efficiency.

Now in dealing with the terms upon which owners of the factors sold the use of labour, capital, or land, we saw that certain payments were economically necessary in the sense that they were required to support some human effort of production, but that further payments might be obtained by the owner of any factor whose use was indispensable and short in supply.

There is a sense, however, in which these surplus payments are also 'necessary.' Those who receive them can enforce the demand for them: the payees *must* pay them. It is important, however, to realise the difference in the nature and the sanction of the necessity in the case of 'costs' upon the one hand and of 'unproductive surplus' on the other. The necessity which attaches to 'costs' is based in the nature of the physical and moral stimuli which evoke productive power. In order to secure the repeated or continued output of productive energy from each of the existing factors of production each successive output must be compensated or replaced. These costs of maintenance must be carefully distinguished. They comprise two sorts of payment, one based on physical, the other upon moral necessity. The physical wear and tear of labour is replaced or maintained by a mere subsistence wage accommodated to the amount and nature of the physical drain. Corresponding to it is the wear and tear or depreciation payment for use of concrete capital and for land. But these payments alone would not suffice to evoke continuous voluntary services from the owners of labour-power. For most sorts of labour a further payment is required, raising a bare subsistence into a standard wage for labour. These two sorts of costs of maintenance, one derived from physical, the other from moral necessity, are in practice indistinguishable: we simply recognise that they are economically necessary to support and keep in operation the existing structure of industry.

To these 'costs' of maintenance we add other payments from the product which we say are 'necessary' to evoke an increased size and better functioning of the system. In order to get more and better labour-power into the system a somewhat higher wage than 'costs of maintenance' may be required; in order to evoke a larger quantity of saving and more and better forms of capital the payment of interest may be required. The necessity upon which these payments will rest is of the same nature as that underlying costs of maintenance, partly physical, partly stimuli. They are strictly necessary costs of growth.

There is one difference, however, between costs of maintenance and costs of growth which should be recognised. It is a difference not of their nature, but of the point of view from which they are considered. When we consider the distribution of a particular product among the owners of its factors of production, no question of any 'costs' beyond costs of maintenance need arise. The question of stimulating an increase of the structure of the business or of the trade by such extra costs as we describe, does not normally arise in connection with the regular expenditure in the course of the business. Though the costs or structure of growth are in fact furnished by payments made by employers out of 'the surplus,' their full meaning and 'necessity' are only recognised from the social standpoint. For the individual is not directly concerned with the provision for the growth of the industrial system; his thoughts are usually confined to the maintenance of that little bit of the system to which he is personally attached.

Nevertheless, the operation of a progressive industrial system must be such as to provide the payment of all the 'costs' needed to stimulate a regular and proportionate growth. From the social standpoint all these are 'costs,' though part of this, viz. costs of progress, come out of that fund which from the statical point of view ranks as 'surplus.'

Now we can understand in what sense the payments by which the 'unproductive surplus' is distributed are 'necessary.' The economic rent of land, the high interest on protected capital, the high profit from a monopoly, the high fees in a 'close' profession, have no sanction of natural necessity behind them; they are not necessary to maintain or to evoke any output of energy of body or mind in those who receive them. If any legal or social forces reduced or abolished them, the reduction or abolition would in no way impair the maintenance or growth of the industrial structure. Indeed, as will appear when the depressing or inhibitive action of 'unearned income' is taken into full account, the effect of such reduction or abolition would be favourable to the growth of industry. From the social standpoint they are unnecessary payments. But from the individual standpoint they must be paid, given the existing ownership of the several factors of production. Equally with necessary costs of maintenance and growth they form 'expenses of production' to the business man: to him the legal and the economic necessity of paying them is absolute, though the necessity ultimately rests upon no other basis than that of natural or contrived scarcity.

Although the owner of land in the centre of the city would sell its use for 1s. per acre per annum if he could not get more he must be paid £100 per acre because there is a very small supply. If, owing to some great improvement of transport, a quantity of other land were made equally desirable for business and residence, the £100 might drop to £50 or £20 without causing any owner to withdraw his land for its former use; the landowner would consent to take a lower rent, and this 'expense of production' would fall, the 'surplus' or excess being squeezed out. But so long as the 'scarcity' remains, the high rent is 'necessary.'

So likewise with certain concrete forms of capital which, under special circumstances, may obtain real interest far above what is necessary to induce saving persons to create these forms of capital. The possession of a patent or a secret process, or some superior access to raw materials, or to the market, may enable the owner of such real capital, by restricting its supply, to obtain a rate of interest far above that which he would consent to take if he could not get more. This is best illustrated by the power which the Linotype Company, or the American Boot and Shoe Corporation, have been able to exert through royalties, or by the high interest secured by the Standard Oil and certain other American Trusts. Wherever limitation of output can successfully be maintained, the concrete capital in a business can obtain a 'surplus' interest. So long as the conditions supporting this scarcity hold, this surplus expense must rank as a necessary payment, and enters into the price of the commodities. But its necessity having no ' natural ' basis in human stimulus to effort, may be overthrown at any moment by some new invention, or lapse of patent, or by some other change in the shape of an enlargement of supply.

Similarly with labour-power. Whenever a professional or trade organisation can secure a close preserve for the sale of such human skill or effort, a ' scarcity ' or unearned element may be added to the efficiency wage in fees, salaries, and wages.

Apart from the causes of scarcity here named, a sudden pressure of demand for some class of commodities, or failure in some source of supply, may place the owners of some factor of production in a position to claim a scarcity price, which for the time being will rank as a necessary payment.

They are necessary payments, or expenses of production, in so much as the owners of the factors of production for whose use they are paid can extort them from those who need these factors. They are unnecessary payments in the sense that, if any change in economic circumstances caused them to be withheld, this withholding would not cause their owners to refuse the use of them.

They are also unnecessary in the sense that, after they have been paid, they can be taken in taxation without any disturbance of the industrial use of the factor of which they rank as surplus payment.[1]

---

[1] Economists have often distinguished the several payments here grouped under surplus as rents and quasi-rents, and have usually excluded them from ranking as expenses of production or as 'entering' into price. But following their actual emergence, persistence, and disappearance in industrial history, we can recognise no advantage in distinguishing rents from quasi-rents. Some of the elements of surplus are more stable and more enduring than others, being grounded upon some 'scarcity' which is more difficult to overcome; but, so long as they exist, they play the same part in distribution, enabling their owners to get a gain which furnishes no stimulus to economic activity.   Our setting of the sale of factors of production in terms of a standard unit disposes of the fallacious reasoning by which it was argued that rent does not enter into expenses of production. Of course differential rent does not ; but scarcity rents do.

APPENDIX

MARGINAL PRODUCTIVITY AS BASIS OF DISTRIBUTION

OUR analysis has shown that, in any industrial system where the total product only just sufficed to furnish wear-and-tear funds for the maintenance of the several factors of production, no problem of distribution need arise. In such a system it might be fairly held that each factor, and even each unit of each factor, received in payment the value of what it produced. Indeed, if value were measured, as it reasonably might be, by expenditure of energy, the statement that each factor, in receiving as payment its wage of maintenance, was receiving the value of its product, would be an identical proposition.

But where in an industrial system a surplus is produced over and above the necessary expenses of maintenance, can it be contended that the distribution of the entire product tends to be such that each factor receives the value of what it has produced ? Or if each factor does receive ' the value of what it has produced,' does this mean anything more than that each factor receives what it can get ?

Within the last few years American and English economists have built up among them a theory of distribution by marginal productivity according to which each unit of each factor of production tends to get, and normally does get, the value of its separate contribution to the product.

In discussing the validity of this theory it will be best first to approach it as a wage theory, because it is in that form that it has been most fully evolved and has drawn most attention.

Since this doctrine owes its fullest development to Professor J. B. Clark, of Columbia University, it may be best to set it forth as nearly as possible in the form it takes in his latest work, ' Essentials of Economic Theory ' (Macmillan and Co., 1908).

If we were to take a quantity of capital capable of effective co-operation with a number of units of labour, and were to use it all in conjunction with one unit of labour, i.e. a small group of workers, this labour would be so flushed with assistance from capital that it would turn out a very large product per man. If a second unit of labour were added to the same quantity of capital, the amount of capital would still be so ample that the product would be very large, though somewhat less than twice as large as it was before. Add a third and a fourth unit of labour, and though the capital is still abundant, the product added by the third unit is less than that

added by the second, and that added by the fourth less than that
added by the third.

'If we continue this process until we have ten units of labour,
employing the same amount of capital as was formerly used by
one, we shall find that each unit as it begins to work adds less to
the previous product than did the unit which preceded it, and that
the tenth adds the least of all ' (p. 137).

The owner of the capital will evidently go on adding units of
labour until he finds that the last unit added only just increases
the product by the amount which he must pay in wages in order to
induce this unit of labour to prefer this employment to any other
that was available.   In a word, this is marginal labour which it is
only just worth employing.   It will receive in wages just what it
is worth, the value of the product its co-operation adds.   But if
the last or marginal unit of labour receives in wages just what
it produces, so must the other nine units : for, when the ten are
together co-operating with the same lot of capital, each of the ten is
producing the same amount of the product and receiving the same
remuneration.   Therefore this labour force as a whole, and each
unit of it, receive their full product, neither more nor less.

Now the theoretical and practical validity of this theory hinges
upon the mode of measuring the productivity of the marginal or
any other single unit.   Here is Professor Clark's method :—

' How, then, do we measure the true product of a single unit of
labour ?   By withdrawing that unit, letting the industry go by the
aid of all the capital and one unit of labour the less.   Whatever
one of the ten units of labour we take away, we leave only nine
working.   If the forms of the capital change so as to allow the nine
units to use it advantageously, the product will not be reduced to
nine-tenths of its former size, but it will still be reduced : and the
amount of the diminution measures the amount of product that
can be attributed to one unit of bare labour.   Or we may add a
certain number of workmen to a social force already at work,
making no change in the amount of the capital—though changing
its forms—and see how much additional product we get.   That
also is a test of final productivity ' (p. 140).

Now is it correct to attribute as the exclusive and separate product of one unit of bare labour that diminution in the aggregate
product which follows its withdrawal, or that addition to the former
aggregate product which follows its accession ?   If the tenth unit
of ' bare labour ' is withdrawn, we are to suppose that each of the
nine units of ' bare labour ' that is left thereby becomes more productive than before.   Now we know that what really happens is
that each of these nine units is not more productive, as ' bare

labour,' but because by the removal of the tenth labour unit it gets a fuller use of capital. It is quite clear that what is added to the product by the entrance of the tenth unit of labour, and what is lost by its exit, is not the measure of the ' bare productivity ' of that unit, but of the difference in the aggregate productivity of the whole complex of units of capital and labour. In other words, the separatist treatment of productivity breaks down : even if it is possible to attribute a separate productivity to the marginal unit co-operating with the other units of labour and the units of capital, that productivity could not be measured by the difference made to the productivity of the whole complex by its withdrawal or entrance.

A very simple instance of a co-operative group of labourers, in a business where the capital element may be ignored, will serve to expose the fallacy. In a primitive fishery let us say that one man fishing alone could make a catch of ten ; a two-man group a catch of twenty-two ; a three-man group of thirty-seven ; a four-man group of sixty ; a five-man group of seventy-two. Here a four-man group is evidently the most advantageous, and that fishery would be worked upon this basis. Now in this business the fourth man ranks as the marginal worker. His presence or his withdrawal from the group makes a difference of twenty-three fish, i.e. the difference between thirty-seven and sixty. Is that to be taken as representing his separate product ? It ought, upon the lines of Professor Clark's reasoning. But it cannot be so taken. For the fourth fisher is no more productive than the other three, and if the fourth fisher's product is twenty-three, the product of all four together must be ninety-two. But, as we saw, it was sixty. His so-called separate product, therefore, must be fifteen, and not twenty-three. It is impossible to take what his presence adds, or his absence from the group removes, as measuring his individual productivity or as determining his wage.

But, though Professor Clark's tests of marginal productivity evidently break down, it may be contended that the principle still holds good. The marginal productivity of labour in the fishing, it may be said, is fifteen fish, not twenty-three. But there is evidently no ' *marginal* ' determination in the matter. The fact is that fifteen is the *average* productivity of a unit of labour where labour is arranged in this most advantageous grouping. Neither in theory nor in practice does the margin determine productivity. The fishermen say, ' A five-man group is better than a four- or six-man group,' not because of the productivity of any single man, ' marginal ' or other, but because they know that this co-operation is the most productive.

So with the case of the ' marginal shepherd,' the tenth man

whom a farmer calculates it is just worth his while to employ because he can get him for the price of twenty sheep a year, and he will just save that number by his work. Of course no farmer really plans his farm this way. If he comes to employ ten shepherds instead of nine or eleven, it is because he reckons that ten will give the best division of labour, and will, as a co-operative whole, enable him to get the most out of his farm. If the employment of a tenth shepherd means twenty more sheep per annum than the employment of nine, it cannot be maintained that twenty sheep form the separate product of the tenth shepherd, but only that a ten group is more productive by twenty sheep than a nine group.

It certainly does not follow that twenty sheep can be said to represent a single shepherd's product in a ten-man farm, and that there is any tendency in a wage law of marginal productivity to assign twenty sheep or their value as the shepherd's wage. For there may not be as many as 200 sheep to divide, without reckoning any for the interest or profit of the farmer himself. A nine-man farm may only yield 140 sheep, so that when the tenth man is added there are 160 sheep, which, equally divided as product or as wages, would give only sixteen sheep per man, not the twenty which the presence of the tenth man seemed to add. That an eleventh man is not taken on may be due to the fact that ten men form so nearly the full complement of labour required for the effective working of the farm, that an eleventh would only add five sheep, whereas every potential shepherd has an alternative employment worth a wage of twelve sheep.

It is thus quite evident that adding doses of labour and noting the increase of the aggregate product throws no serviceable light upon the determination of wages. The so-called marginal dose, with its so-called separate product, is only intelligible when regarded as an average dose in a fully equipped farm, factory, shop, or other business : no separate dose has any separate product, and the only method of assigning to it any product is to divide the whole product equally among the constituent labour units, as if it represented the mere addition of their individual productivity instead of their joint co-operative productivity.

In setting out the problem of the sheep-farm, the only valid method runs thus :—

In a farm worked by an eight group the yield is (say)
$$125, \text{ or } 15\tfrac{5}{8} \text{ per man}$$
,,   ,,   a nine group the yield is (say)
$$140, \text{ or } 15\tfrac{5}{9} \text{ per man}$$
,,   ,,   a ten group   .   160, or 16   per man
,,   ,,   an eleven group .   165, or 15   per man

In other words, the so-called final or marginal productivity turns out to be nothing other than an average productivity which varies with the efficiency of the group, and really measures that efficiency, splitting it up and imputing it in equal proportions to the constituent members. The whole notion that there is a marginal increment, or that it produces a special product, or that it plays any special part in determining wages for members of the group, is entirely fallacious.

But supposing we substitute the average productivity per unit of labour in the most effective grouping for marginal productivity, are we any nearer a law of wages? Is there any reason to hold that the ten shepherds in the fully equipped farm will get in wages (not the twenty sheep of the 'marginal' shepherd, for that is impossible!) the sixteen sheep which are said to measure their average productivity? Setting aside the question of the farmer's interest or capital, which we will suppose already accounted for in extra sheep or otherwise, is there any law which will tend to secure the wage of sixteen sheep for each shepherd? Yes, upon one supposition, viz. that there is a larger proportionate number of farmers freely competing for shepherds than there is of shepherds competing for farming jobs. If farmers can afford to pay sixteen sheep as wages (having already secured their other expenses, including normal interest and profit), they may be compelled to do so, provided that shepherds are short in supply, i.e. if there are more offers at sixteen than there are applicants at that wage. In that event the average shepherd gets as wages what has been regarded as his full productivity. If, however, there is fuller and more genuine competition among shepherds than among farmers for jobs at sixteen sheep, the actual rate of pay will be less than sixteen, say fourteen. If the alternate work open to a shepherd, e.g. as a separate squatter, is worth twelve sheep, it may take a wage of fourteen sheep to draw a requisite number of shepherds into hired service.

In other words, the so-called separate productivity of the worker furnishes the upper limit of his possible wages, as the conditions of alternative employment open to him furnish a lower limit. Whether his actual wages approaches the higher or the lower limit is a matter of the relative effectiveness of competition among employers on the one hand, and workers on the other.

It is no doubt true that, if possible shepherds had not one alternative occupation at twelve sheep value, but a great number of different alternatives, some of which were worth anything up to sixteen sheep, with no unemployed margin, they would get as wage their 'full productivity,' provided always there was such freedom and abundance of competing capital in all employments as allowed the payment of this wage. As we shall see, such absolute fluidity of competition would bring together to a single point the upper and the lower limits in a price bargain. This brings us to the real underlying assumption of the ' marginal determinants.' We have, so far, treated it as a wage theory. But its adherents claim that the remuneration of capital and of ability is equally, or at least substantially, determined in the same way by the productivity of marginal units. The same criticism we have applied to the marginal method of measuring the productivity of labour, of course applies to capital : the productivity of the last dose of capital is not a separate or separable amount, but can only be treated as a fraction of the productivity of the entire complex of co-operative units of capital. So with ability, or any other productive-power which is broken into units. It is not even true that there is any theoretical or practical method of determining the separate productivity of the whole aggregate of capital, or of labour, or of ability, in a business in which all the units of all these factors are functioning in organic co-operation. We can, and do, only determine what must under the circumstances be paid to the owners of each factor for an average unit, not what this factor, still less each separate unit, actually produces.

There is only one industrial phenomenon which appears to give importance to operations of margins. In our investigation we have seen that, so far from the supply of any marginal factor having any special determinant influence on the price of that factor, the opposite is the case : the complex of forces which, through supply and demand, determines the price per unit of each factor, determines the margin ; with a rise or fall of this price the margin (extensive or intensive) rises or falls. With each rise or fall of a margin there is an actual or potential transfer of some factor—labour, capital, land, ability—from one trade to another, from one business in a trade to another business, from one department in a business to another department, and so forth. Not only the new supply of labour and of capital seeks its employment in the most remunerative and, on the whole, the most productive occupations, but each rise or fall of price of capital or labour tempts some of these factors from one occupation to another. So as between trade and trade, business and business, the apportionment of the factors is conducted by a levelling process, which is most conveniently watched and measured from the lower limits. A rise in price of wheat brings new land into cultivation, just not worth cultivating before : here is a marginal movement which rightly draws attention. The opening of a new mine draws off spare labour from the country villages. An expansion of electrical development draws off some ability from civil or mechanical into electrical engineering, and some capital that otherwise was destined for other industrial uses. As such movements are naturally regarded as taking place at the bottom, in the sense that the new factors as they enter take the least advantageous places, so the mechanics of the procedure is visualised in margins.

But any special causative or determinative importance given to margins is quite unwarranted.

Regarded as a theory of distribution of the product, the marginal productivity theory is a misapplication of an unsound and unprofitable assumption.

The assumption is that we may profitably treat the industrial system as composed of factors of production, infinite in quantity and absolutely fluid and competitive in character, afterwards making some allowance for their not being what we have supposed them to be.

If all the labourers in a community had full knowledge of their capacities, full power to educate them, full knowledge of every labour market, full freedom to enter any, full access to the ranks of the employers in case they had ability, and to the requisite capital or credit ; if all capital were equally free to dispose itself to the best advantage, and the owners of land and ability were equally free and intelligent—in that event the whole of the industrial power would organise itself in business units of the most productive size and character in the several industries. Freedom to pass from the employed to the employing class would perfectly secure the former from exploitation by the latter, wages of ability, profits, or whatever term were used, being reduced to a common level of productivity and of payment with wages throughout the whole of industry, as they are even now approximately in an East-end sweating den. Wages would measure accurately the net cost in painful effort of an average unit of the different sorts of labour ; real interest would stand at the same level for all uses of capital. ' Rents ' of individual energy, measuring super-normal output of energy or skill, would still survive. In such an industrial society distribution might be said to be effected in strict accordance with productivity, every unit of each factor being put to its most productive purpose in co-operative action with other units. All the cotton-spinning mills would be of one or two or three approximately equally effective sizes and standards, for all the cotton capital and labour would gravitate into these moulds, and so with every other business, while the number of businesses in the several trades would be determined by equally rigorous conditions.

Any new economy of production introduced into an industry which made it advantageous to alter the structure of the business, reducing, say, the units of labour from 200 to 150, or employing a different sort of cheaper raw material, would lead to a quick automatic readjustment, workers leaving each mill and either fitting themselves into new mills of the new approved character or flowing into other industries, the value of whose goods were now appreciated in comparison with those of the trade into which a new economy had entered.

So in such a society every change in the costs of production or consumption would be attended by a shift of the less effective or 'marginal' units of the several factors from one trade to another, while the new units of each factor would fasten themselves on where their productivity was greatest.

This is the ideal of a freely competitive industrial society in which distribution will take place in accordance with productivity, though even here the particular productivity of the marginal units determines nothing. For the theoretic feasibility of the working of such a society it is, however, necessary to assume either that the several factors are 'freely' transferable in the sense in which, within narrow limits, machinery and manual labour, work of management and ordinary labour, are sometimes transferable, or else that there is an indefinite amount of each factor procurable. For unless one of these assumptions is made, there is nothing to prevent one of the factors, say land or capital, from being relatively scarce compared with the others, and upsetting the balance of distribution through productivity by drawing scarcity rents. Finally, even if we grant all the suppositions required to give plausibility to the hypothesis, it does not seem easy to conceive how a common standard measure for the different sorts of productivity will be established, so as to secure a regular and accepted distribution of the whole product. For the product, after all, will be the product of the co-operative complex of units of the several factors, and there will be no means of splitting it into separate products attributable to each. In other words, the theory of productivity, marginal or even average, as a determinant of the distribution of that part of the product which remains as 'surplus' over and above necessary expenses, has no validity.

Moreover, the assumption of an industrial system in which this general full freedom of competition and substitution prevails is not sufficiently related to the actual industrial system to make it serviceable. To treat natural and contrived scarcity and the forced gains which proceed therefrom as mere 'friction,' of which account can be taken afterwards, is an unscientific method of procedure. In the industrial system regarded as a productive and distributive instrument, combination is as much a real factor as competition, and the scarcities of various sorts and degrees which occur throughout the system are as much determinative facts, both of production and of distribution, as the free flows which they negative.

The claim of the 'marginalists' is that a natural law, the operations of which they profess to describe, tends to give to every agent of production the amount of wealth which that agent produces. 'So far as it is not obstructed, it assigns to every one what he has specifically produced.'[1] But in the first place this notion of the specific product of any agent or of any part of any agent is opposed to the co-operative working of the industrial system. In the second place, what are by marginalists regarded as obstructions are real and important parts of the industrial system. Professor Clark's 'so far as it is not obstructed' means simply 'if it were a different system from what it actually is.' If there were a free, elastic system of industry in which production was a merely mechanical instead of an organic co-operation, so that a separate product could be attributed to each factor, then each factor would get what it made, no doubt. But there is no such system.

[1] Clark, *Distribution of Wealth*, Preface I.

CHAPTER VI

ABILITY

§ 1. A modern business is an organisation. Organisation is a process enabling the various factors to function more productively. The cause or condition of an enlarged product, it requires a payment therefrom. The organiser's payment, or profit, depends on the size of this enlarged product and the amount he can hold in competition with other organisers.—§ 2. Where equal opportunities exist for 'undertaking,' profits are at a minimum. The power of the *entrepreneur* lies in areas of progressive industry. His main function is the application of profitable notions.—§ 3. Profit is, however, applied to payments for several sorts of 'creative' or 'competitive' work. Profit is less regular and less fixed than the payment for other factors.—§ 4. Profit is represented as the necessary price of progress. But it is not actually applied so as to evoke the maximum ability. Nor does competition normally serve to keep profit at the economic minimum. So ability can take a larger quantity of 'surplus,' often 'sweating' the investor as well as the labourer.—§ 5. The *entrepreneur* comes nearest to the position of residual claimant.—§ 6. But no sharp separation of profit from other payments is feasible, though certain sorts of ability obtain an increasing share of wealth in modern industry.

§ 1.—IF the units of individual power furnished by labour, capital, and land were able by some automatic process to arrange themselves so as to maintain and adjust the structure and working of industry, we should now be in possession of a complete general law of distribution.

A part of the general product of the industrial system would be carried automatically to maintain the industrial fabric through provision for repairs, or to stimulate a growth of structure and activity at various points of production : the rest would be taken as ' scarcity ' payments or ' unearned income ' by the owners of any factor which at any point was short in supply as compared with other factors.

Here in a new and rapidly growing city there might be plenty of all required sorts of labour and of concrete capital, but suitable and convenient sites might be restricted in quantity : the price per unit of building land would emerge as a scarcity payment, entering into price and assigning the various differential rents per acre.

Or, again, in a new farming country there might be plenty of fertile and equally available land and plenty of pioneer farmers, but capital might be short ; so the ' surplus ' product, after defraying minimum ' costs ' of labour and land, would go in high interest on mortgages or on bank loans.

Or where both land and credit could be got on easy terms, either from a government or from private sources of supply, as in Canada, wage labour might be relatively scarce and wages might rise so as to take a surplus.[1]

So the factors of production grouping themselves for various industrial purposes would distribute their product as costs of production, or, wherever a shortage of a factor is found or contrived, as a surplus or scarcity rent.

But the defectiveness of this account of distribution is made apparent by any close consideration of large areas of industry in which no scarcity of any of these factors is discernible, and where wages and interest are both low, while rent does not make any large claim on the product.

The old economic text-book view of the three factors of production somehow combining for productive process and dividing the product according to some ' laws ' of wages, interest, and rent, has little relation to facts. Its main defect is a failure to give adequate and separate consideration to the industrial activity of organisation. Modern industry we see as an organised co-operation of factors of production. What about the organiser, the energy he gives out and the payment he receives, and the relation of this factor to the other three ? To refuse separate consideration to these questions by classing the employer's work as a sort of mental labour, to be reckoned along with other sorts of labour and as remunerated by a ' wage of management ' determined like other wages, implies a distorted view of the industrial structure, and is utterly destructive of any clear principle of distribution

We must give separate consideration to the *entrepreneur*, regarding him as the owner of a factor of production called ability, for the use of which he receives a portion of the product known as profits. This term ' profit ' is so elusive that I must here insist upon fastening it down as payment for the activity of the *entrepreneur*, excluding from it entirely interest and payment for risks, but including what is commonly termed wages of management or superintendence, so far as these functions are performed by the

---

[1] How far wages obtained where labour is relatively scarce rank as wages of progressive efficiency or as a 'surplus' payment will depend upon the character of the labourers and the social surroundings of their life. A body of Connemara labourers suddenly transplanted to Liverpool dock work, where they can earn three times their former wage, will largely misspend the higher wage, which thus ranks as unproductive 'surplus.' A more assimilative type of worker, or a more gradual rise of wages, will imply the absorption of higher pay in improved efficiency of life, the scarcity pay thus ranking as wage of progressive efficiency.

entrepreneur. Though payments for the use of ability applied in industry go to other persons, such as inventors, who are not, strictly speaking, *entrepreneurs*, it is with the ability of this latter class we are primarily concerned here.

First let us look at the *entrepreneur* in the regular operation of what is called ' static ' industry, i.e. where fixity of industrial method is assumed.

When we consider the working of joint stock companies we shall see that a large part of this work may be detached 'from ' enterprise ' and paid for by a wage which is conveniently severed from profit, but it is best to approach the issue from the standpoint of the *entrepreneur*, who organises and works on his own account a private business.

His work falls under four heads :—

1. He plans in his mind the working of a business, selecting among existing methods, lines of goods, markets, one best adapted to his ability and his access to the other factors of production.

2. He buys the various quantities of the different factors of production required to carry out his plan.

3. He organises the factors for the various processes of production.

4. He markets the product.

Though each of these functions may be regarded as productive in as far as it is essential to the present working of industry, it is to the organising function that we must look as the chief *objective* source of profit.[1]

A single unit of labour-power left to find capital or land for fruitful action, a single unit of capital seeking profitable use in conjunction with a worker, an acre of land looking round for a farmer, can produce very little. The right number of each of these sorts of units, properly combined and directed, can produce much. The difference between the sum of the little products that would issue, if the units worked singly by and for themselves (with such assistance from a unit of another factor as it could itself acquire), and that which accrues from their co-operative working under skilled guidance, is the product of organisation and the economic fund out of which profit is paid.

Whether the *entrepreneur* as ' organiser ' can claim to be the ' creator ' or ' maker ' of this product, or whether his organising

---

[1] Profit in a particular business may arise from (1) an increase of the amount of the product due to action of the *entrepreneur*, or (2) an increase in the value of the product due to some contrived or chance rise of price in the market. In approaching the work of the *entrepreneur* as part of the machinery of industry, we first confine our attention to the former function, the socially productive one.

action is to be regarded only as a means whereby the other factors are enabled to function more productively, is not a question we need answer here. The voluntary activity of the *entrepreneur* is essential to the emergence of the increased product, and the whole or part of it is taken in actual industry as his payment.

The ideally strong *entrepreneur* would buy his labour at a price determined by what the worker could get by working for himself on such free land or cheap capital as was available, or by doing odd jobs, begging, stealing, or living on public charity. He might have to add something to this price if the separate productivity of the worker was not enough to furnish him a livelihood adequate to maintain his working-power in the efficiency required for organised industry.

The individual product of an Englishman, or even of a Kaffir, on free land would be small, perhaps too small to keep him in health and strength for digging all day.

If so, this individual production must be subsidised out of the product of organised industry.

In a word, a wage of personal efficiency may sometimes be substituted for a wage measuring the separate productivity of the worker.

So with capital. The strong *entrepreneur* planning a big business may scrape in little units of savings at a rate of interest determined by the opportunity the small savers have in their own little business, or in such small investments as lie open, or in the Post Office.

The same with land where it is wanted, e.g. the Transvaal Gold Company buys the Boer farm at a low agricultural price and a bit over.

Having thus got his units of productive-power at prices which strictly represent their separate or unorganised productivity, he organises them effectively, so as to produce a large surplus-product, which he sells so as to realise the whole difference in profit.

The theoretically maximum profit thus consists in the whole of the difference between the sum of the productivity of the separate unorganised units of the factors of production and the sum of their productivity when organised.

There is also a theoretic minimum profit, i.e. a payment necessary to evoke and to support the energy of the *entrepreneur*, determined at its lowest limit by his alternative individual productivity as a worker. Sometimes, as in the case of master sweaters in some clothing trades, the profit is forced and kept down to this minimum.

The actual profit lying between this upper and lower margin is determined chiefly by two conditions:—

First, by the capacity of the *entrepreneur* to hold the product of organisation as against the pull of one or other of the three factors which he has to buy. Where in the buying of units of producing-power for the organisation of a ' profitable ' business he finds one of them short in regular ' supply,' or possessed of some high-priced alternative employment, he is often forced to buy such factor at a ' scarcity rent,' which swallows much or most of his potential profit. High wages must be paid for some skilled labour in large demand, or in short supply. Coal must be bought at monopoly prices ; or the owner of some central site essential for business premises can make a large encroachment.

Secondly, even if he can buy all he wants of the three factors at low prices, he may be obliged to part with the bulk of the value of the technical result of organisation to the consumer, by reason of the keen competition of other *entrepreneurs* who force down the price of the product.

§ 2.—In other words, if the competing supply of business ability is as abundant as the supply of the other three factors, its price, like theirs, will be driven to the minimum. The normal price of goods thus produced would contain no surplus element, but would be composed only of minimum costs of production. The technical productivity of organisation (apart from the ' minimum profit ') would go in the processes of exchange to the owners of other goods not produced under such ' free conditions '

Wherever the competition among *entrepreneurs* is as keen as that among the owners of the other factors of production, profit falls down to a ' living wage ' of ability, through a rise in the price of the three factors on the one hand, and a fall of price of the product on the other.

To buy the other factors cheap, organise them effectively, and to market the product dear—these are the aims of the successful *entrepreneur.*

Success in doing this depends upon restricting the effective competition among *entrepreneurs.* For this restriction operates both in buying factors and in selling the product.

Wherever the structure of society is such that every man has equal access to education, business training, and other opportunities, profit in ' statical ' industry tends to stand near the minimum. Where it is easy for a man to quit wage earning and to set up ' for himself ' on borrowed capital, as in many branches of retail trade, profits sink to a bare living.

This is sometimes said to be the normal and necessary condition of stationary industries. It would be so if equality of educational and other opportunities existed. But under actual conditions ability of *entrepreneurs* is often relatively short ; it thus becomes the limiting factor : can keep down prices of the other factors by restricting demand, and keep up the prices of its product by limiting output or by partial or local monopoly.

Nevertheless, in ordinary steady industry profit is not high, for the kind and degree of skill and other powers of the *entrepreneurs* are not scarce.

Little foresight or strategy is required : even the method of organisation is stereotyped, and both buying and selling are conducted in fairly settled markets under known conditions.

The real power of the *entrepreneur* lies in areas of progressive industry.

It is here that we enter on what is perhaps the largest and most debated issue of distribution.

It is indisputably true that to the ingenuity, judgment, calculating power, and enterprise of a small number of men are directly attributable those great changes of industrial methods which have led to a vast increase of the product.

Scientists have made new discoveries, inventors have applied their principles to the technique of production, financiers and other business men have selected among the inventions those which can be ' profitably ' applied in actual industry and have applied them, while the constant reorganisation of the business structure thus required calls for fine aptitudes of judgment in the managers. These rare and conspicuous acts and qualities of mind are, it is contended, productive in another sense than the ordinary factors : the productivity of an improvement in a process or of the invention of a new machine is infinitely great, for it adds to the productivity of an infinite number of productive acts proceeding from the other factors of production. Ability is creative : labour (and the productive operations of concrete capital and nature) is imitative. Such is the radical nature of the distinction that is drawn. It virtually attributes the whole of the increased productivity of progressive industry to this small number of directing minds, and finds in the result of this increased productivity a vast fund which may be classed and claimed as profit. Now, though much of the ability which thus fructifies in industry is not that of the *entrepreneur*, and its remuneration cannot be strictly designated profit, the *entrepreneur* is the instrument through whom all such ability functions in industry, and through whom the payment which goes to the scientist, the inventor, and other outside promoters of industrial progress, is made. Through him the abilities of the others are made available. While, therefore, the particular issues relating to the nature of invention, the direction of inventing-power, and the rewards of invention, are well deserving of separate consideration, it will be better to confine our attention here to the services which more closely belong to the organisers and directors of businesses. Their most skilled and most serviceable activities distinctly belong to the ' creative ' class. As regards the new mechanical and other scientific inventions which continually present themselves for industrial use, their work is that of selection and of application. If the invention is of a new product, the business man must calculate the cost of producing it in such quantity as is likely to find a market, the competition it will meet from other products which appeal to similar tastes or fulfil similar purposes, the length of time it can be expected to hold the market, and a variety of kindred matters. His judgment will be based on a simultaneous consideration of all these relevant issues.

Hardly less critical is his judgment in the case of a new process for producing an established product. Though these acts of judgment form but a small part of the function of the ordinary *entrepreneur*, their part in determining, not merely the success of a particular business, but the progress of an industry, is of the first importance.

Detailed improvements in the organisation of a business, in economy of labour or of materials, selection among alternatives in the kinds and qualities of products, exhibit in a lower degree the same qualities of mind, and are attended by similar results in increased productivity. The other two departments of the *entrepreneur*, finance and the arts of buying and selling, though exhibiting fine qualities of mind, may be distinguished as partaking more of competitive skill, which, though promoting the success of a particular business, does not involve any corresponding progress in the productivity of industry.

If we regard the *entrepreneur* as the instrument by which new productive ideas are realised in industry, and by which the regular effective co-operation of the other factors of production is procured and maintained, we shall recognise the necessity in a progressive society of securing to the *entrepreneur* out of the total product a payment sufficient to evoke and to support these industrial activities. The profit which remains to him after paying the services of labour, capital, and land, must suffice to evoke these personal activities, and to reward the inventors and other innovating specialists whose ideas he utilises.

§ 3.—The work of the undertaking and control of industry is, however, in modern times, not confined to the persons who are strictly employers or managers of businesses, nor can the term 'profits' be properly confined to the payments made to these orders of business men.

The productive-power, here termed ability, to the payment of which profit is applied, is divided among different classes. First comes the financier. Under this head we place unspecialised 'capitalists,' promoters of companies, bankers, and other money-lenders, who deal in profitable notions, and whose productive function is to determine the application of real capital and labour to different industrial undertakings. A large part of that skill of the *entrepreneur* which consists in discussing and selecting new inventions is performed by these men, who are primarily engaged in allocating to various industrial uses the new saving of the investing classes. It must not, however, be forgotten that to the ordinary investor himself must be accredited some skill of discernment and judgment in choosing among the competing enterprises offered to him for investment. The investor who is no mere plunger, but who acts on advice and weighs this advice, must be considered to exercise a genuinely productive function in thus determining the use of capital. The gambling aspect of finance must not blind us to this genuinely productive work.

A portion of this financial work, together with part of the more general work of 'undertaking,' is performed in the joint stock company of modern times, by the board of directors, who are commonly also large shareholders and often possess personal experience in the business they control. Exercising a general supervision, and determining large matters of policy, they divide with the salaried managers the organisation of the productive forces.

The more detailed work of management, involving many acts of judgment which belong distinctively to the 'creative' function, is performed chiefly by salaried officials. It is not confined to one or two heads, but is distributed in various degrees over a large staff.

Indeed, a close analysis of business operations impairs considerably the sharpness of the distinction between ability and labour by showing that, even in what is distinctively manual and sometimes unskilled manual labour, important minute elements of judgment and responsibility enter which are creative and distinguish human labour from the purely imitative operations of machines.

But this criticism does not invalidate the importance and the convenience of placing in a separate category the work of ability as a claimant for profit.

Profit, then, must here be taken to include a variety of payments, to some of which the term is not commonly applied.

It must include (*a*) the incomes of financiers so far as these

exceed the normal interest upon the capital engaged in their profession ; (b) the royalties and other payments made to inventors
and patentees ; (c) the fees of directors and the salaries of officials
of companies, for though these can in some sort be set on a level
with other labour markets, the work done for them belongs to
the *entrepreneur ;* (d) a portion of the so-called interest paid
to shareholders who contribute ability in the selection of their
investments.

There will appear to some a certain artificiality in this analysis.
In the actual business world many of the payments here ranked as
' profit ' are set by the great financial, manufacturing, and commercial *entrepreneurs,* the great capitalist managers, on the same footing with payments for ordinary capital and labour : they buy
inventive or designing ability as they buy their various grades of
managerial skill, very much as they buy coal or machinery. These
men, great financiers, railway kings, trust-makers, mine-owners, buy
all the sorts of ability they want, and applying them to work the
ordinary factors of production, pay all these ' costs of production '
out of the proceeds of their business, and keep the residue as their
' profit.'

This view is more closely accommodated to the recent
evolution of large industry, where many sorts of ability become,
so to speak, ' standardised,' and brought, as regards use and
payment, under the ordinary economy of business administration.

But whether we take this narrower or the wider view of the
' ability ' for which profit is paid, it is equally evident that the
payment for ability stands on a somewhat different footing from
other payments, partly by reason of the peculiar position of the
entrepreneur in industry, and partly by the special character of his
motives and incentives.

So far, at any rate, as business ' profits ' are regarded as earnings
of ability, they are far more irregular in amount and far less assured
than the payment for the use of other factors. In most new or
growing trades, at any rate, and in many professions, the profits
and other payments for ability are so essentially ' speculative ' that
it seems difficult to regard them as having any strong tendency
towards any normal rate of pay such as is required to co-ordinate
this factor with the others. The motives or incentives appear
different from those which evoke the regular application of labour
or saving : the hope of large gains rather than the certain expectation of regular gains operates largely among *entrepreneurs,* and the
large proportion of failures in most sorts of business enterprise is
often adduced as evidence that the average rate of profits or wages

of enterprise is very low, since there are a few great prizes to many blanks or actual losses.

But, though both the psychology of profit-seeking and the apportionment of profits differ widely from those of the other factors of industry, they cannot be regarded as sufficient reasons for refusing to apply to ability our main principle of distribution, the distinction between necessary and superfluous payments. Certain considerable industries are highly speculative, even as regards the rewards of the ordinary labour engaged in them : gold-mining is a notorious example, but many departments of the engineering and other metal trades, where both wage-rates and employment fluctuate widely, are of the same order. But the speculative character does not prevent us from recognising that the normal law of wages is applicable to such trades. So with profits : the real chances of gain or loss are calculated and discounted according to the estimated apportionment in the several trades ; ability is distributed among the various trades according to genuine prospects of gain based on experience, though the distribution will be much less exact than in the case of other factors.

While, therefore, the peculiar structural position of the *entrepreneur* has made it desirable to give separate consideration to the payment for ability, the system of distribution brings profits under the same general laws of payment as operate among the other factors.

§ 4.—We have seen that profit consists in what remains to the *entrepreneur* after he has paid for the uses of the ordinary factors of production. Is that profit normally or naturally identical with what is required for the expense of producing ability ?

Is there any tendency for profit to become that minimum payment requisite to reward energy of management and to stimulate the arts of industrial progress ?

A new justification of the competitive system of distribution is sometimes based on the contention that profits, as they are now obtained, are a necessary payment for the contribution of ability to industrial progress. This theory gives point to the question we have put. It is contended that all profit, over and above the wages of management in a static business, is a merely temporary reward obtained by a pioneer in some new trade or process : it is a prize won by the man who is first in the field ; it helps to stimulate others to adopt the new invention and the new method ; when the adoption has become general throughout the trade, the competition of the various firms will eliminate the ' profit,' which will then pass in reduced prices to the consumer.

Now, as we have seen, there is a large variety of different

elements of ability which enter into industrial progress. Two questions of critical importance are therefore raised by the theory of profit as the price of progress. First, is there any provision that the first recipient of profit, the *entrepreneur* in the strict meaning, shall apportion the profit among the various contributors towards the arts of progress, so as to evoke their best contribution? Secondly, is there any security that the competition of other *entrepreneurs* shall be early enough or sufficiently keen to secure the gain for the consumer as soon as the stimulus has served its purpose?

Consideration of the actual circumstances which attend the payment of profit shows that no satisfactory answer can be given to either question. In actual business, as we have seen, the entire residue of the product, or of its value, after defraying the expenses of buying the other factors, falls to the *entrepreneur* as his profit. It is great or small according as, upon the one hand, he can buy the other factors cheap, and, upon the other hand, as he can sell the product dear. The check furnished by the bargaining power of the owners of some factor short in supply we have already considered; but the principal check, upon which the upholders of the current theory depend, lies in the supposed power of free competition among the other *entrepreneurs* to force down the profit by a fall of price. But the effective operation of this check assumes that competition of employers or *entrepreneurs* is normally as free and as reliable in operation as competition among owners of labour-power or of capital. If the assumption is unwarranted, there is nothing to prevent profits from remaining at a far larger sum than is required to stimulate ability to function properly in individual progress.

It can hardly be maintained by any one experienced in trade that, when a new machine or a new method is introduced into an industry, the amount of the gain which accrues to the firm which first practises this economy has any ascertainable relation to the amount necessary to induce the inventor to discover the new method, or the employer to apply it. The gain he takes, so long as he has a monopoly of the new method, may exceed by any amount the necessary stimulus to the art of progress. Neither can it be said that, when other employers in his trade are free to adopt the improvement, the profit necessarily falls either at once or in the long run to the minimum, so as to turn over the whole of the value of the improvement to the consuming public. The hypothesis that competition normally works as freely and as keenly among *entrepreneurs* as among labourers is notoriously false. It rests really upon an assumption that any worker is free to become a small employer, and any small employer to become a large employer, so that all potential employing ability can function competitively in actual industry. If this assumption were correct, it is true that the gain of each progressive step in industry would pass to society as soon as it was open to the competing businesses in a trade, though even then there is no provision for distributing the original bonus so as to reward proportionately the ability of the pioneers. But in many large fields of industry competition is not thus free or keen : either it is difficult for new *entrepreneurs* to equip themselves for successful competition, or else agreements more or less close and binding between competitors hold up prices, and with prices, profits.

Putting the same point in another way, the number of competing *entrepreneurs* buying the other factors, and selling the product of their co-operative working, is much smaller than the number of separable units of labour-power, capital and land, which are competing to find purchasers, and the competition of the former is less keen, constant, and ubiquitous than that of the latter.

This being so, by our general law of distribution, which assigns the ' surplus ' according to the relative shortness of supply of the factors, the *entrepreneurs* are able to take a profit normally in excess of their expense of production. The economy of large capitalism of course favours this power by reducing the number of competing businesses in many fields of industry, especially in those where the gain from organising many units of producing-power is greatest.

§ 5.—Upon the whole, the *entrepreneur* has the pull in modern industry : each step in improved industrial arts brings him a gain much larger than is economically necessary to evoke this step, and is held in large part by other members of the trade who are mere imitators and not innovators. To certain classes of these able men an increasing proportion of the ' surplus ' of industry has been passing in recent times. The real industrial struggle is far less keen between capital and labour than between strong groups of *entrepreneurs* on the one side and weak owners of capital and labour on the other. The small investor is as likely to be ' sweated ' in this struggle as the worker : and a living interest is almost as difficult for large classes of savers to secure as a living wage for low-skilled workers.

Though in modern industrial development the organisers of a great manufacturing trust or a transport company may sometimes be rack-rented by the owners of some natural source of supply, and in certain instances some strong union of skilled workers may encroach upon the surplus which would go as profit, the *entrepreneurs*, amongst whom are to be included the original subscribers of monetary capital, are usually able to secure in profit (inclusive of high fees, bonuses, 'free' shares, abnormal interest, and other emoluments) a growing share of the surplus. Their ability to do this rests ultimately, as we see, upon the checks they set on competition. To some workers it appears as if this relative strength of the owners of directive and organising ability were due to some natural scarcity, and that therefore their large gains might be in some sense necessary. But this is a double misconception. The sort of ability in business which gets the largest aggregate amount of the general surplus is not naturally scarce. It exists plentifully in salaried officials of companies and in high public servants, and, if education were fully and well applied, a virtually unlimited amount could be evoked. It does not imply any such high natural scarcity as limits the output of great art or literature.

Moreover, though the ability to seize and utilise inventions and other profitable notions, to organise the factors of production, to forecast or stimulate demand, to control markets, is a chief source of profit, many business gains included under profit imply no such output of ability. Only those intimately acquainted with a trade know how large a part sheer 'luck' plays in success, and, where ability does function, it is often little more than the skill to recognise and utilise a stroke of luck. No small portion of the income ranking as profits is distributed by 'luck' rather than by clear-sighted ability. Nor must the support given to the profits of an established and successful business by goodwill and mere reputation, operating as superstitious adjuncts to the real merits of a 'make,' be left out of consideration.

Thus it appears that a great deal of profit is not derived from, or attached to, any output of personal ability. But, where ability is employed, there is no reasonably accurate adjustment between its utility and the profit its owner can receive.

Even if one admits that there is scope for a few men of transcendent natural gifts, as is quite likely, the notion that the amount of 'surplus' which they can and do take is necessary to induce them to apply their rare powers of mind effectively in industry has no warrant. There is no reason to suppose that a Rothschild will give out more skill in the act of finance, if circumstances enable him to earn £1000 a day instead of £100, or that Mr. Rockefeller requires 10,000,000 dol. a year to stimulate his organising genius to function.

It has seemed desirable to discuss the ability of the *entrepreneur* separately from the other factors of production on account of the determinant part it plays in directing the working of the industrial system and in introducing changes.

This position makes the *entrepreneur* appear the residual

claimant to the product of industry after the expenses of purchasing the use of the other three factors have been defrayed. Making allowance for the power which the owners of any of the three factors short in supply can exercise to take out of the product a payment in excess of what is necessary to evoke its use, this residual claim is made valid by the normal state of restricted competition among *entrepreneurs*. After land, or capital, or labour of some sort has taken its pull out of the surplus product by exacting some surplus in the price it compels the *entrepreneur* to pay, the rest of the surplus tends to remain for long periods of time with the *entrepreneurs* as an excessive profit. Although even a close monopolist may find it pay to give the consumer some advantage out of the economy of improved production, by lowering prices and securing the largest aggregate of profit out of a greatly enhanced sale, this natural check, which enlightened self-interest imposes upon the percentage of profit that such monopolist can draw from each act of sale, does not greatly weaken the position of vantage occupied by the *entrepreneur* as the determinant of production and the recipient of the residue of the product after the owners of other factors are paid off.

Though, therefore, the growing size and importance of the work done by ability, as a factor in modern industry, would necessarily imply that a larger amount of wealth went as payment to *entrepreneurs*, there is no reason to suppose that the increased share of the product of industry, which to-day passes into their hands, is any true measure of the increased utility of this work. On the contrary, their strong strategic position in the industrial system makes it tolerably certain that a large share of their income represents, not a necessary cost, a natural stimulus to the production and display of such ability, but a scarcity rent or unearned income which they take because their superior bargaining power enables them to exact it.

§ 6.—But having thus asserted the technical difference between ability and the other factors as agents in industry and as claimants to the product, it is necessary to admit that no practical theory of economic policy can be based on an attempt closely to discriminate between profit in the sense of ' rent of ability ' and other payments which are inextricably mixed with it in the actual distribution of wealth.

The most that can be done with advantage is to note the growing strength of certain types of *entrepreneur* in important fields of industry, and to recognise the hold which they are able to maintain upon the ' surplus ' product, partly in this capacity of *entrepreneur* and partly as capitalists, landowners, and owners of legal privileges.

A general survey of modern industry in advanced countries will show that this power to secure unearned or surplus gain is shared by *entrepreneurs* with owners of other factors whose use they have to buy, unless, as is commonly the case, they have themselves become owners of the other factors which were competing with them as claimants for the surplus. If a great manufacturing trust is formed, it often obtains possession of favoured sources of raw material or fuel, or organises special facilities of transport, or obtains the protection of tariff duties, or government contracts or other public 'aid.' Such advantages often render it impossible to distinguish in 'profits' the elements which are true profit in the sense of payment for ability.

Recent tendencies show that a larger share of 'surplus' wealth has been passing into the hands of certain large interests, amongst which we may distinguish the banker and financier, the transport company, city ground owners, manufacturers of protected or patented goods in wide demand, brewers and distillers, contractors for public works.

But were it possible accurately to separate true profits from other payments, it would, I think, become evident that certain classes of ability in the direction and organisation of industry, and in the manipulation of markets, were gaining upon the owners of other factors in their power to take surplus wealth, irrespective of their economic need of it for the stimulation of industrial progress.

In England it is tolerably certain that this is the case. Setting the rise of annual land values for city sites, mines, transport and other services into which land values enter, against the decline in rural land values, it is probable that, though the aggregate of annual income constituting rent is rising, the proportion which such rent bears to the aggregate income of the country is falling. This statement is, of course, consistent with holding that rent forms a growing proportionate charge upon the surplus as distinct from the entire income.

The abundance of concrete capital at ordinary times keeps down the rate of real interest so low that it is tolerably certain that, in spite of the expanding use of capitalist methods over large fields of industry, the proportion of the national product paid in interest is declining.

Though real wages for almost all grades of regular labour have risen considerably, there is no reason for holding that the rise has kept full pace with the increased rate of productivity of industry. If these conclusions are substantially sound, an increase of the proportionate claim of profit on the aggregate product is involved.

CHAPTER VII

DISTRIBUTION OF THE SURPLUS BY PULLS

§ 1. Free competition can furnish no theory for the distribution of the surplus which, accumulating at various stages of production, is represented in the prices of commodities.—§ 2. A classification of the different sorts of surplus exhibits them as waste, impairing efficiency.—§ 3. Prices of various final commodities contain different proportions of surplus : some surpluses are permanent, others evanescent.

§ 1.—ABSOLUTELY free competition, though furnishing a consistent and thinkable system of production, furnishes no thinkable theory of distribution or exchange. Its strict condition, as we saw, was an equal abundance of all the various sorts and qualities of land, labour, capital and managing ability, for, if any one at any point is relatively short in supply, it can suspend free competition and extort a rack-rent or forced gain.

Under such free competition (assuming also full knowledge in the owners of the factors) each industry would consist of equally effective businesses, and every factor would be paid what was necessary to evoke its use, only these subsistence payments entering into price.

But we recognise that in modern industry the aggregate product of such industrial system will be far larger than is required for these payments of maintenance. If the industrial system is to grow in size and improve in quality, this actual industrial surplus must be utilised to stimulate and feed this progress. In other words, there must be some method of adding to the subsistence payments such portions of this surplus as will evoke the proper proportion of increased productive energy for future enlarged production.

Now, under the conditions of absolutely free competition, with payments of all factors at a minimum, no provision exists for securing this or, indeed, any apportionment of the surplus. There would be an annual surplus which belonged to none of the factors, and which none of them was any better able to take than the others. This unappropriated surplus would, unless it wandered ownerless and ran to waste, have to be appropriated by the State and applied by some canon of social utility to its proper purpose of stimulating industrial progress, except so far as it was needed for other public purposes.

But the actual conditions of industry, as we see, are widely different from this 'free competition.' In every process of every industry, some one or other of the factors is relatively scarce, either by nature or human contrivance, and can extort a piece of 'surplus' payment over and above that payment for which its owners would consent to apply it in production, if they could not get this surplus. This relative scarcity is everywhere assisted by lack of mobility and lack of knowledge. These pieces of surplus enter into the price of goods, thus weighting their rate of exchange, and so determining the amount of the 'pull' exerted by the industries contributing to make one sort of goods, as compared with that exercised by industries contributing to make other sorts, upon the aggregate product.

So it comes to pass that, instead of an exchange and distribution based on minimum costs of production, we have an exchange in which these costs are weighted by varying amounts of 'surplus' which express themselves in value through price.

This is not the ordinarily accepted difference between normal (natural) and market price, or even between long-time prices and short-time prices. For our investigation of the sale of the several factors indicates that many of these scarcity rents or other excessive payments are normal and enduring, though doubtless shifting in intensity. In certain industries, or professions, ability or concrete capital exercises a normal pull, in other cases certain sorts of land continue to take rent of scarcity, and even certain special labour organisations can maintain a long-time scarcity.

It matters not whether one measures the prices in which these 'pulls' find expression at the margin of production or on the average : they imply that the exchange of goods and the distribution of wealth are normally and largely directed by these pulls in which a surplus is divided according to the degree of scarcity attaching to the several factors of production.

A closer consideration of the actual mode of distribution of the surplus is, however, desirable.

For it is apparently contended by some economists that this distribution of the surplus according to relative scarcity of the factors of production is the natural, necessary and socially desirable method of overcoming this scarcity, and so promoting industrial progress. The argument runs thus. If, in a particular industry, labour or capital were relatively short, a rise of wages or of interest is the most economical method, indeed the only method, of securing industrial growth. Though this method involves an unnecessarily high payment for a time to the labour or the capital already in use, this is a necessary incident in industrial progress, and it may even be held that the occasional chance of such a rise is a wholesome stimulus to the normal flow of capital and labour into such a trade. In particular, it is urged that high profits in certain industries, which absorb so large a share of the ' surplus,' are necessary and socially desirable as a stimulus of that ability to which industrial progress is chiefly attributable.

So, it is contended, there exists a fairly satisfactory natural economy in the apportionment of the surplus for the stimulation of industrial progress, the results of which are in some measure shared by the owners of other factors of production, including labour.

§ 2.—We are thus brought to confront the question : Is the distribution of the surplus according to the relative pulls of natural and contrived scarcity of the factors an economical method of stimulating improved productivity ? Does it divide the general surplus among the different owners of the various factors of production in the various industries in the proportion which so stimulates production as to yield the maximum increase of utility to the consuming public ?

Now the payments into which this surplus falls may be thus classified :—

First. Rents for the use of land and natural powers. These rents are in substance prices for different sorts of land use. The price for a unit of grazing-power is so much, the worst acres of grazing land, producing each a small fraction of a unit, take a nominal rent, the best acres a somewhat higher rent : the prices of a unit of wheat-growing and of market-gardening or building land are on a higher scale, differential rents measuring the relative productivity of an acre within each use. All these prices of land use are obtainable on account of the scarcity of supply. So long as land is in private ownership, it is economically necessary to apply to its owners such an inducement as will cause them to apply the requisite quantity of their land to the several uses, so as to yield the maximum utility. If the utility of wheat, for example, is rising as compared with potatoes, so that it is socially desirable to put into wheat some land formerly used for potatoes, that can only be brought about by paying a slightly higher price per unit of wheat land than before, and so seducing some land from potato use. So with other land uses. Wherever there are alternative uses for land, a pecuniary inducement is necessary in order to achieve the most productive distribution of land among these uses.

But it must not be supposed that these ' rents ' originate in private ownership of land, or that with the substitution of public ownership they would disappear. These various prices of land uses are the valuations set by social needs upon natural qualities of land which are scarce. They measure the utility of these several sorts of scarcity. Neither the utility nor the scarcity arises from the fact that individuals are permitted to own land and take these prices. If all these sorts of land were nationalised, the scarcity and the utility would remain substantially the same,[1] and the State would take the rents which individual owners took before. For if the State did not take this surplus it would not disappear, but would simply pass to the occupants of the land, who would thus enjoy the ' unearned ' income which private landowners at present enjoy. Public policy might modify in certain ways the scarcity of land for some uses by improved and cheapened transport, cheap capital for scientific culture, &c. But so far as unalterable qualities of fertility, site, &c., are the bases of specific prices of land use, the surplus represented by these rents is not attributable to the oppressive action of landowners but to the natural limitations of supply.

The wide differences represented by these specific rents are not appreciably affected by the conduct of landowners. If a new discovery of wheat land or a new railway increases the supply, down goes the price per unit, and owners of wheat land get less rent : if a new population springs up in a locality, up goes the price per unit of site use, and owners get more rent ; neither rise nor fall is affected by anything they do. In a particular locality land value, reckoned by units, not acres, might run thus :—

A unit of building land costs	..	£10 per annum
,, market garden costs	..	£4 per annum
,, wheat land costs	..	£2 per annum
,, grazing land costs	..	£1 per annum

These wide divergences of price are not produced by the landowners but are imposed upon them by the presence of public needs and natural conditions of relative scarcity. They are necessary payments from the standpoint of the tenant, who must pay them to get the use of land : they are necessary in that they are based on permanent differences of nature. They are not, however, necessary payments in the sense of inducements to these recipients to perform any useful action.

Second. Dealing with the payments for the use of concrete forms of capital, real interest, we saw that in modern civilised communities a low and a diminishing rate must be paid to savers

[1] Certain artificial actions and usages of landlordism which interfere with the economical application of land for certain uses, withholding some lands from all uses, restricting other uses, and substituting non-economic for economic uses, would presumably be remedied by substituting public for private ownership.

to induce them to postpone some of their consuming power and to apply it to setting up more and better instruments of production furnished with increased quantities of materials. The amount of such saving as is socially desirable in a community at any given time depends, as we saw, upon the condition of the arts of industry in relation to the anticipated volume of consumption. This payment is a strictly necessary cost which does not rank as ' surplus.' But our analysis of the part played by actual capital shows us that, in many industries, monopoly, combination, superior access to or control of markets, protection, and other public aids, enable certain supplies of capital to take a higher rate than is economically necessary to draw free capital into the use. Such payments must be carefully distinguished from the high interest paid in certain highly speculative investments, which is not really interest at all but payment for risks, and which, if properly discounted, would leave interest at, or often even below, the normal rate. The high interest taken by artificially protected capital cannot, excepting to a minimum extent, be regarded as socially serviceable in the sense of stimulating increased productivity. If it is desirable that certain industries shall grow faster than certain others, and that an increased flow of fluid capital shall be drawn into the former, this enhanced flow can be obtained by a very trifling premium, and requires no such large surplus interest as is paid to the protected capital.

In a modern civilised community the socially profitable application of new savings can be achieved by fractional payments (not interest at all) made to financiers whose skilled business it is to distribute fluid capital according to its most productive use. At present this socially useful work is grievously impaired by the fact that this distribution of new capital is affected and often dominated by other considerations than those of its socially useful productivity. But our present point is this, that all genuine interest, over and above the minimum rate needed to evoke the new saving required to further increased production, does not stimulate industrial efficiency, and is waste in the same sense as the economic rent of land.

Third. Using the term ' labour market ' to include all sorts of human services paid by wages, fees, salaries, we have seen that, though in various grades of work payments considerably above subsistence wage are socially necessary to evoke and maintain industrial progress, the actual apportionment of such payments had little relation to the economic stimuli or to the increase of efficiency.

Monopoly of educational or other opportunities has, we saw, raised the actual prices of certain sorts of mental and even manual labour so high that much of the payment is a ' scarcity ' rent of the same kind as that obtained by naturally scarce land or protected capital, while the flooding of other labour markets, owing to the establishment of these preserves, has brought down the price of their labour so low as to deprive it of any adequate stimulus to improved efficiency. This is one important setting of the labour question, viz. that the superior pull of stronger and better organised factors of production upon the surplus robs ordinary labour of that share of the general product required to evoke the technical improvement in its efficiency which is essential to general progress. This is the true doctrine of the economy of high wages. The successful attempt of the stronger factors to exhaust the surplus by wasteful payments in rent, surplus interest and profits has continually retarded the rate of improvement in efficiency of labour, and so has sterilised much of the over-stimulation of capital and ability.

There is, however, much waste in the portion of the surplus which passes to the small grades of protected labour in high places. Our consideration of the economy of high salaries shows that, after a certain reasonable rate of progress in standard of life is provided, further payment is not merely waste but often a wage of progressive inefficiency. This is best illustrated in the highest grades of the arts, where genius is distorted to win evil popularity or enslaved to plutocratic patronage.

The ' economy ' of high wages has its limits ; when incomes rise beyond a certain pace, each increment is attended by a diminishing improvement in efficiency, and a level is reached beyond which every further increase of income involves luxurious waste and impairs industry and efficiency.

There is, as we see, no economic law relating scarcity payments for ability or labour to this economy, or preventing the payment of fees, salaries, or wages upon a scale which involves waste and stimulates inefficiency.

Fourth. Our examination of the functions of the *entrepreneur* in industry and finance, and the modes in which the payment for his services were determined, showed that our system of distribution made no adequate provision for regulating his share of wealth with regard to economy. Over large areas of industry effective competition among *entrepreneurs* does not exist, the result being that the price of their services contains a large scarcity rent which enters into price. High profits, as we saw, represent the power of the *entrepreneur* to buy units of the different factors of production at a relatively low price, so organise their co-operative use as to greatly enhance their aggregate productivity, and to secure as profit the whole or the greater part of this difference between the buying price of the factors and the selling price of their joint product.

If competition were as keen and constant among *entrepreneurs* as between the owners of the labour-power and the capital they buy and organise, their profits would be cut down to the economic minimum by the fall of prices. But over a large part of the industrial field they check this competition, and so secure rates of profit far higher than are necessary to induce them to perform their function as organisers and developers of industry. Among *entrepreneurs* the financier or manipulator of fluid capital and of credit is at present in a position of such vantage that his share of the surplus is out of all proportion to his services.

§ 3.—This analysis has shown that the present system of industry distributes the surplus wealth over and above the necessary current expenses of production by a system of ' pulls ' which have no right relation to the stimulation of economic progress throughout the system. Much of the surplus goes in overpayments which check, instead of stimulating, efficiency and progress, while other portions of the system, especially the lower grades of labour, are deprived of the share needed to evoke, educate and support the growing efficiency requisite for participation in the more rapid march of modern industry.

This unequal distribution of the ' surplus ' of current industry is reflected in the normal prices, and so in the rates of exchanges between the various classes of goods. For if we were to trace the different processes of industry by which goods of different sorts passed from raw materials to commodities in the possession of consumers, analysing closely the sale of the units of the factors of production in the agricultural and mining processes, the manufacturing, wholesale and retail distributive processes, in the various transport and financial processes connected with the moving of goods and of the instruments of capital and labour ; if, further, we scrutinised the various professions, such as engineering, architecture and the like, subsidiary to the production of material commodities, we should find that, at each stage in this long process, some owner of a factor of production was, by reason of a natural or contrived shortness of supply, able to extract a ' forced gain ' or surplus price which entered into and enhanced the price of this particular process, and so was passed on until it was reflected in the retail price of the commodity. Sometimes it would be a mining *entrepreneur*, as in the case of diamonds, who would get the chief pull, sometimes a landowner extorting high ground rents, sometimes a railway company charging ' all the traffic will bear,' sometimes a financier effecting a ' combine,' sometimes a manufacturer thriving on sweated labour, a banker thriving on high discount for loans and overdrafts, contractors securing tenders by agreement at profitable rates, coal merchants cornering supplies and holding up prices, or rings of local tradesmen raising the margin between wholesale and retail prices for milk and bread. Every retail price of commodities contains some of these surplus elements which have entered in at different points in the series of productive and distributive processes : in most cases there will be a large number of these additions to the strictly necessary expenses of production. In many cases the large addition will take place at some one point where a powerful monopoly, or a close scarcity, gives a particularly powerful ' pull ' to some protected interest, some combine or some owner of a natural source of supply. But the proportion in which these surplus payments enter into the retail prices of various commodities will be widely different : in some cases price will be mostly surplus, in other cases keen competition down a whole line of processes will keep down the price near to the strictly necessary expenses of production.

These differences will all be reflected in normal prices, expressing the values of different commodities.

If the analogy of ' rent ' be applied to these various sorts of surplus payment, it must always be insisted that these rents are specific rents paid for all portions of a supply, not differential rents measuring the superior qualities or opportunities of some particular portion of a supply. These differential rents, which disappear under the application of our unitary method, are, of course, not represented in price. The specific rents are so represented, for they imply that the price per unit of supply of land, capital, labour, ability is increased by the presence of these several sorts of surplus.

These rents or ' forced gains ' or ' excessive payments ' have, for convenience, been treated as permanent or normal elements in price, to be distinguished from merely temporary rises of price due to some new swelling of demand or some casual shortage of supply. But this distinction between normal and market prices has, of course, no clear logical validity. Some of our ' rents ' or ' forced gains ' are based upon fairly permanent restrictions of supply or competition, others upon less reliable restrictions. Many of these ' rents,' though based on permanent conditions, yet fluctuate in amount. Some of them are short-time rents, casual or recurrent, and are, in fact, indistinguishable from the short movements of market prices. In fact, every change of industrial methods, or of size and character of consumption, affects these ' rents ' so that, as regards many of them, the particular points of their emergence and their size are constantly shifting. Closer study, however, shows that some of them possess a high degree of strength and permanency, especially those related to the main processes in the production of some necessary or prime convenience of life strongly fixed in the standard of consumption of a people.

The unsubstantial and fluctuating character of many of these rents, reflected, of course, in price changes, is a source of great inconvenience and loss in the working of our industrial system, quite apart from the main waste which the uneconomical distribution of the surplus represents. If all goods exchanged according to their strictly necessary expenses of production, or according to these expenses increased by a regular proportion of the surplus applied by some law for the encouragement of industrial growth, a high degree of stability of prices would give security to commerce, and would enable producers and consumers to exercise more intelligent foresight in the use of their resources. In a word, it would eliminate a large element of hazard involving waste of mental energy and of material wealth.

From whatever point of view we regard the distribution of this surplus of ' unearned ' and forced gains we shall see in it the prime cause of almost all the maladies of our industrial system.

CHAPTER VIII

PRICES AND THE RATIO OF EXCHANGE

§ 1. Neither marginal costs nor marginal expenses can afford an explanation of rates of exchange for goods.—§ 2. The ' marginal ' determination is based on a false imputation of separate costs to different parts of a supply. Neither theory nor business practice supports this separation. Normal, not marginal, expenses determine supply prices. Productive power tends to flow into the most efficient business type, and the expenses of this normal business regulate prices. This holds both of manufacture and of agriculture.—§ 3. In any given market mean expenses govern prices. The same analysis applies to demand prices : mean, not marginal, utility determines them. Selling prices are the equilibrium of mean expenses and mean utility, as expressed through demand.

§ 1.—OUR analysis of prices has shown that the price of any supply of goods consists of and breaks up into a number of payments made in the different stages of production to the owners of labour, capital, land and ability, for units of these factors of production bought at varying prices. These payments are all expenses of production, which, under the social circumstances of supply in each case, must be paid ; but the expenses are not all necessary in the same sense. For while some parts of the expenses are physically and morally necessary to support and to evoke the power of production given out, other portions are only necessary in the sense that they can be got by use of an economic pressure resting upon a natural or contrived scarcity of a factor.

But so far as the composition of prices is concerned, no distinction can be made between the necessary costs in the narrower sense and the surplus elements. As we have seen, the latter enter into price equally with the former, the price of units of land use equally with the price of units of unskilled labour, though the latter contains no ' surplus,' while the former is entirely surplus. The fact that in the one case painful human effort is involved, while in the other Nature gives out her free energy, makes no difference as regards the constitution of the price of the goods into which these payments enter.

We are now in a position to understand why different sorts of goods exchange with one another at the rate they do ; why, for example, a top hat of a particular make exchanges on equal terms with a ton of coal, but will take two pairs of low-grade boots to purchase it. In other words, the ratio of exchange, the respective values set on different sorts of articles expressed in their prices, will become manifest.

The top hat and the ton of coal exchange on equal terms, each with a price of £1, because analysis of the price in each case shows that the sums of the price of the different units of factors of production happen to come to the same figure, whereas the sum of the price of the productive units in a pair of boots only comes to half that figure.

This, of course, only amounts to saying that supplies of goods exchange according to their expenses of production, their prices being composed of these expenses.

It is commonly held by those economists who look at prices, or exchange ratio, from the side of production, that the expenses which determine (or measure) the normal selling price of a supply of goods are the marginal expenses, i.e. the expenses of producing that portion of the supply produced by the worst-equipped mill or least efficient labour, or the least fertile land, or the least efficient combination of factors. Now it is obviously true that some of the material or mental factors contributing to the production of a supply are inferior to others, and that the selling price for the whole supply must be sufficient to furnish to the worst combination of factors an inducement to contribute towards the supply. If there were an equal abundance of all the factors of production (the quantity of each grade being, however, limited) and perfect freedom to enter the industry, and contribute to supply, the selling price would evidently be just sufficient to remunerate the worst combination of factors. It might then be correctly said not only that the marginal costs of production measured the selling price, but even that they ' determined ' it, in the sense that any increased demand for goods at this price would be checked by the limitation of the supply of these least efficient factors, and by the necessity of having recourse to still less efficient ones. The selling price in such a case would just cover wear and tear and minimum wages, interest and profit at this margin : owners of more efficient factors would, of course, receive payments measuring the superiority of this efficiency over that of the factors at the margin. If industry in general conformed to this idea, the selling prices of all goods and services would be exactly measured, and in this sense determined, by these marginal costs of production ; and since selling prices are only the instruments for exchanging goods against goods, we should have a quite simple and satisfactory law of exchange based on the relative costs of producing marginal supplies of the several sorts of products.

Now, as we have seen, industry does not in general conform to this idea so far as to secure that the least efficient combination of factors in a trade must receive or does receive nothing but these bare minimum costs. There is not normally an equal abundance of all the factors, but a relative scarcity of one or another : there is not perfect freedom of the owners of all factors to apply their factor in any trade. This normal and general interference with free fluidity of productive powers is such that the ' expenses ' of production by the least efficient businesses in most trades contains elements of ' surplus ' which also enter into the selling price as measured from the margin.

But, though admitting that the marginal expenses of production may often, or even usually, be weighted with some of these ' surplus ' elements, it may still be contended that the most serviceable law of exchange is one which compares them at the margin, and holds that goods tend to exchange in the ratio of their marginal expenses of production.

Now the practical utility of such a law of exchange has never been apparent, and our analysis of the actual co-operation of factors in production has partially exposed the nature of its inutility. For it has shown that in a business or trade the question where the margin shall lie, i.e. what particular acres, machines, men shall be the worst in use, is itself directly determined by the price of the goods ; while the part played by the marginal supply in helping to determine the price of the goods is neither greater than, nor different from, that played by any other portion of the supply.

It is absolutely true that the worst factors of production contributing to a given supply must receive a price just adequate to evoke their productive power, and ean only receive more where monopoly conditions, restriction of supply of some factor, exist. If, as the result of a growth of demand, there is a lowering of the margin, worse factors being taken on, the price per unit of productive power must rise so as to remunerate these worse factors which would not have been adequately remunerated at the former price per unit. But it is not true that the factors, i.e. men or acres, at the former margin must be getting at the new supply prices a rise of price measuring the *separate* superiority of their productivity over that of the men or acres at the new margin. The enhanced price they will get will be determined by the enhancement of the mean expense of the new complex of factors as compared with the old complex, and, though this new complex will imply a larger expense per unit, the amount of this increase is not determined by comparing the old margin with the new.

The whole idea of attributing a *separate* productivity to men or

acres or machines at a margin of employment, and of regarding
expenses for the whole supply as determined or even measured by
this separate productivity, is inconsistent with the rationale of
business structure.

§ 2.—A somewhat more formal refutation of the validity of the
' marginal expense ' theory of exchange is, however, here necessary.
Let us restate our question thus : How far is it true that within
a business or within a trade the separate expenses of production of
the ' marginal ' portion of supply can be ascertained, and if they can
be ascertained, does this portion of supply exercise any greater
influence in determining the price of the whole product than any
other portion ?

So far as a single business is concerned, it cannot be shown that
any separate expense of production exists for a particular portion
of the output.

The true theory, agreeing substantially with the business
practice, denies the existence of a number of separate expenses of
production applied to different portions of an aggregate supply.

The true formula runs thus : If 1000 tons be produced, each
ton costs 10s. ; if 2000 tons be produced each ton costs 8s. ; if
5000 tons 7s., and so on.   But if the cost [1] of a ton always depends
upon the number of other tons produced along with it, a ton can
never be rightly regarded as a separate economic unit with a
separate cost.   It is only the whole output that has a true cost.

This is the view taken by a business man, a manufacturer who
contemplates laying down a new plant.   He calculates that by
laying down such and such a plant, he can turn out so many
thousand tons and can sell them at such a price, earning such a
margin of profit.

He treats the process of production as a whole, recognising the
fallacy of regarding any particular quantity of capital and labour
as allocated to the production of a particular part of the output.
He compares in his mind the differences in net gain from producing
on various scales, but it is always one aggregate product he sets
against another, not the different increments of the same product.

Even when he considers whether a particular order, involving
overtime, is worth taking, he does not in fact treat this order as an
entirely separate thing, asking whether on this order he is earning
a living profit on his capital invested.   He sometimes treats it
separately as regards ' prime cost,' asking whether it yields any
margin ; but usually he has regard to the general effect upon his
future trade of accepting or refusing the order.   If he sees his way

---

[1] Here we use the term in its ordinary business signification as equivalent
to ' expenses.'

to cover prime costs, he is usually contented, though aware that certain other fixed expenses are involved. He is aware that he cannot justifiably reckon a separate total expense of production for this order, because of the inability to make a true allowance for fixed expenses and for the general effects of this order on the organisation of his business and upon his market.

In planning a business, it may be urged, he surely considers whether he shall put down a plant worth £10,000 or £12,000 or £15,000. If he selects the second it is because the difference of output between that of a £10,000 and a £12,000 plant is just worth while producing. But in operating the £12,000 plant, upon which he decides, it cannot be pretended that any part of the output is produced at a different cost from any other, and this is the assumption required for the marginal cost theory.

What he calculates is the normal ' cost ' of producing a ton upon a larger or a smaller scale, and he selects that scale upon which any ton can be produced so as to yield a margin of profit which, taking the whole trade, will yield a maximum net profit.

Now, so far as clear knowledge of industrial conditions and free access of capital and labour into the industry exists, it seems manifest that the productive power within the trade will tend to throw itself into businesses whose shape and size will depend upon those technical conditions which determine the cheapest rate at which a ton can be turned out. If the price of a ton of steel rails in England or America is 30s., does that mean the price is determined by the condition of the worst equipped mill or the least efficient labour employed in the trade ? No, it means that the normal type of the most efficient mill, to which all businesses in the industry tend to conform, turns out goods which, at that price, pay the ' cost ' of producing a ton, together with any margin of surplus due to combination or lack of free competition.

But even if we suppose free competition, the same is true : the expense of producing not the ' last ' but a unit of the product by a normal type of efficient business must be said to be the direct determinant of the normal supply price.

The superior ability, or other special technical economies inaccessible to the body of the trade, may enable a few businesses to produce a ton more cheaply than the typical business : if so, the supply price yields them a differential rent : a few others may survive for a time with old-fashioned machinery or antiquated methods, barely paying their way. The abnormally high profits of the former, the abnormally low profits of the latter, are evidently determined by prices dependent on the expenses of production of the normal mill.

In an industry where perfect freedom of competition exists, including equal access to materials, equal knowledge of methods of production and of business organisation, equal access to markets, it is clear that all businesses would closely conform to one type, or at least to two or three equally effective types. In such an industry any aberrations of expenses of production above or below the normal would evidently be temporary and in no sense real determinants of price. Though such degree of freedom of competition is seldom attained, the law still holds good, at any rate, so far as the businesses below the normal in efficiency are concerned : [1] they cannot long survive, for the dominant part played by the competition of normally equipped and ordered businesses in determining expenses and price, by denying them a living profit, must gradually starve them out. It is, therefore, not to the least efficient, but to the normal business, that we must look for the expenses of production that determine and measure normal prices.

In a freely competitive industry the vast majority of the ' supply ' will be produced by businesses of ' normal ' efficiency. It may be said that in this case the normal is the marginal. But this is not actually true. We should do better to keep to the actual facts of industry, which show that at any given time in such an industry, a few super-normal and a few sub-normal mills are contributing to supply. If so, the sub-normal will inevitably appear to be ' marginal,' though their continued operation is not assured. So long as they operate their output has some slight effect in determining supply price, but the operation of the normal makes it the main determinant.

The same will hold of agricultural production so far as it is regarded as subject to free flows of industrial power. A farmer settling in Canada will calculate how much capital and land he shall put into wheat, working it with ordinary machinery and ordinary labour, knowing how much he must pay for his land and his labour, and reckoning whether current or expected prices will yield a margin. It is more speculative than in manufacture, but essentially the same method : he reckons a normal cost of production for a given output to be sold at a given price. This type of farmer may be said to fix the normal expenses of production per quarter, and the supply price conforms to it ; lucky or superior farmers get more profit, unlucky or inferior farmers get less : this divergence ranks as a surplus or a deficit.

On a particular farm no part of the wheat can be said to be

---

[1] In chap. xii. we shall see that certain special forces tend in some trades to raise the business to a size exceeding the true ' economic unit of efficient prcduction.'

more expensive to produce than any other part. The ' marginal labourer ' working with the ' marginal use of machines,' ploughing, fencing, &c., is a fictitious creature, the product of an illicit separation of the farm which is an organic whole for production. There may be a field just worth sowing, a hand just worth hire, but this is because such enlargement of the business so affects the arrangement of the factors of production as a whole, as to make it hardly more productive than before, not because the particular wheat due to this last field or last hand, determines the supply price. What our farmer would ask is : ' How would the employment of this new field, or this new hand, affect the general expense of production of a bushel on my farm, through altering the disposition of the capital and labour in use, and how far will the estimated increase of supply, at perhaps a slightly enhanced expense per unit, yield a larger aggregate profit ? '

§ 3.—There is, however, some danger in laying too great stress upon the statement that the expenses of production of a unit of supply by a normal business determines the supply price for the whole supply.

The number, relative importance, and endurance of abnormal types of business, above and below the normal, will evidently exercise some modifying influence on the supply price. Indeed, strictly speaking, every unit of supply exercises an equal influence with every other upon supply price, and the conditions affecting any of these units affect price equally. Contributing to the supply of a given class of shoes there may be some factories with the best up-to-date machinery, others with old-fashioned machines, and some hand-made work just managing to pay a declining wage in competition with machinery. Though the latter evidently exercises no special determinant influence on prices, yet so long as it furnishes part of the supply, it may be held to have a proportionate influence ; if it were suddenly withdrawn, prices would rise until machine production was increased to take its place. But in looking at price change through supply, we should not look at this least remunerative, or marginal, section of the trade. Price change may equally occur, and far more commonly does occur, as we have seen, through some cause affecting, not the margin, but other parts of the supply, e.g., the introduction of an improved clicking machine into the best-equipped factories, or some rise of wages among the well-organised section of the trade, directly affecting, not the margin, but perhaps only the middle section of the trade located in some centre which has not kept pace with the latest labour-saving improvements.

The same holds of the wheat supply. It is not true either

that the wheat grown on the worst English soil, or with some
' final ' dose of capital and labour on ordinary soil, or the wheat
grown on the recently opened free lands in Canada, ever exerts
any peculiar force in determining wheat prices in England. The
conditions under which all these different crops are raised affect
price in proportion to the size of the several crops, and, if we are
studying the reasons for some normal rise or fall in wheat prices,
we should not look to what happens to marginal wheat so-called,
more than to wheat grown under more advantageous conditions.
Of course, it is true that the worst shoe factory which keeps on
turning out shoes, and the least productive farm that continues
growing wheat, must cover their ' expenses,' and cannot do more,
but it is not true that they determine in any special way the supply
prices for shoes or wheat. Moreover, a type widely diverging
from the normal cannot long survive. Neither, on the contrary,
is it strictly true that they exercise no influence on prices. Their
influence is simply commensurate with the proportion of their
contribution to supply.

If this is correct, it is the mean expenses of production that
directly determine supply price, and what we called the normal
type of business only determines it so far as it represents this mean.
Whenever, in any industry, the play of industrial forces is free, and
one type of business efficiency prevails, this normal type so far
absorbs the whole of the production that it is seen to dominate
the supply price. So in America one may reasonably recognise
that the price of steel rails is determined by the well-equipped
Pittsburg mill. Given free fluidity of capital and labour, with
equal access to technical and business information and to markets,
the whole of a manufacturing industry tends to crystallise in one
or two types of business of the same size and structure, and the
supply price measures the expenses of production (with or without
a ' surplus ' representing restriction of supply).

In a word, the poorest farm, the worst field, the last ploughing,
exerts no special determinant influence on the supply price of
wheat. The worst steel plant, the last hour's work of the least
efficient shift of labour, exerts no special determinant influence
on the supply price of steel rails.

Mean expenses of production determine the supply price of
wheat, and this supply price determines what shall be the poorest
land in use and how many ploughings are worth while. Similarly
with steel rails and with all other products. Mean expenses of
production, not marginal, determine supply prices.

A corresponding analysis is applicable on the demand side.
The normal or mean, not the marginal, utility to consumers

determines demand prices, i.e. determines the amount of money (ultimately of other goods) which will be paid for a given quantity of supply at a given price.   The schedule of demand prices for a ton of steam coal is chiefly determined by the normally well-equipped modern steamer, and an ill-equipped steamer has to pay this price ; a new steamer with a new superior boiler need pay no more. Similarly, it will be recognised that the demand price for a gallon of whisky is fixed by the place whisky occupies in the normal standard of consumption of regular drinkers, not by the marginal utility as represented by the demand of occasional drinkers (the extensive margin) or as represented by the utility of the last glass of topers (the intensive margin).   Where these margins fall is itself determined by the demand prices which the normal or mean utility has fixed.

The amount of demand at these margins only operates upon demand prices in proportion to its extent, as in the case of margins of supply.

Given our scales of normal supply and demand prices thus determined by mean ' cost ' and mean utility, the equilibrium of a normal selling price is reached.

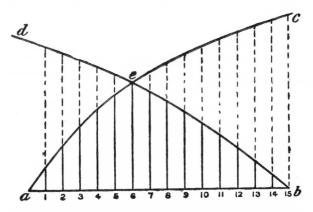

a b is a line of ascending prices rising from zero at *a* to 15s. at *b*.   *a c* is the supply curve expressing the relation between rise of price and increase of supply, the increase of supply at each point being measured by the perpendicular rising from the base and intersecting the supply curve.   *b d* is the demand curve representing the increase of demand as the price falls from the maximum 15s. towards zero.   The supply and demand curves intersect at *e*, the perpendicular from 6, thus giving 6s. as the normal selling point, that where the supply equilibrates the demand.

The selling price may be considered to measure either the mean expenses of production or the mean utility of consumption, and the ratio of exchange thus attained between various classes of goods and services may be regarded from either point of view.

From the business standpoint the ratio of exchange will be reckoned according to the respective expenses of production; from the sociological standpoint the standard will be mean utility.[1]

Since we are here primarily engaged in analysis of industrial operations, we shall prefer in the present stage of our investigation the former standpoint, taking for our standard of exchange the mean expenses of production of the various goods.

In setting out the respective ' values ' of various sorts of goods, as represented in their normal selling price, we shall then be simply measuring their relative mean expenses of production. But in these expenses, it must be borne in mind, we reckon all the elements which a business man would reckon, including elements of surplus gain, or scarcity rents, which are extorted in some of the processes of production contained in the history of the goods in question.

Round the normal price thus interpreted the market, or short-range, prices will fluctuate. The difference between long-time, or normal, and short-time, or market, prices has of course no logical basis, it is a matter merely of convenience.

Changes in the relative expenses of production, and utility of consumption, of different sorts of goods are continually going on ; some are slow and regular, others quick and irregular.

If we turn to the distribution of the surplus, it is not vitally affected by the difference between normal and market prices, though in certain markets, as for instance the money market, considerable changes in the distribution of surplus gains are due to contrived short-time scarcities. The fluctuations of a market round normal prices cannot cancel, as is sometimes supposed, the major gains derived from the strong positions held by owners of factors which are scarce by nature or by durable contrivances. For if we examine the various classes of markets in which the uses of the several factors of production, or the various classes of material or immaterial goods, from raw materials to finished commodities, are sold, we shall find that in these markets sellers or buyers, as a body, are unequally matched, in some markets the sellers, in others the buyers, being the stronger, and able to impose their strength in the process of fixing a market price.

[1] This does not, however, signify that sociology is indifferent to the ' cost side of the problem. This will clearly come into it in terms of the ' disutility ' of production.

CHAPTER IX

THE MECHANISM OF MARKETS

I

§ 1. Economic bargaining approaches but does not usually reach a definite market price.—§ 2. An equilibrium of supply and demand prices involves infinite divisibility of the supply.—§ 3. Various restrictions impair the 'freedom' of a market.

II

§ 1. Analysis of the different markets for the sale of factors of production and of goods and commodities shows that free bargaining only operates over a small portion of the industrial field.—§ 2. Most final commodities contain elements of surplus which pass into their price by 'pulls' or 'scarcity rents' at various stages of production.

I

§ 1.—COMMERCE, or the art of exchange, enables any person with a claim upon some particular product to convert it into a claim upon any other sort of product. A person thus exchanging anything for something else is actuated by one of two motives : either he desires to exchange his superfluous product in order to get some other articles which he wishes to consume, or else he desires to get some materials, tools, or other concrete capital to use in some process of production.

All buying and selling has one of these two ends in view, to assist production or to assist consumption, by enabling persons to convert the ownership of some particular goods into the ownership of some other goods.

In other words, it enables every person receiving his income in the shape of a claim upon particular goods, which by the use of his labour-power, ability, land or capital he has helped to produce, to realise that claim in any other sort of goods which he prefers.

The general economic functions of exchange are two : first, to increase the utility of an income for purpose of consumption ; secondly, to increase the utility of the factors of production. In a primitive society where there is no exchange, but where every family is a self-sufficing economic system, the productive power is wasted because it will be necessary for all land, labour and tools to be employed in some few processes without much division of labour or other effective co-operation, while the consumption of the results of labour will be correspondingly restricted.   Where exchange is confined within a small local area, thinly peopled, the economy of production and of consumption remain similarly restricted.   Every expansion of the area, every improvement of the mechanism of exchange, increases the wealth of each member of the economic society, by enhancing the productive efficiency of his particular factor of production, and by making his command over commodities more general, so enlarging the variety and amount of satisfaction he can get by spending his income.

Regarded from the standpoint of modern industry, the prime function of exchange is as the instrument which apportions the proper quantities of the several factors of production at each point in the industrial system.   This is accomplished by the buying and selling of the various factors of production, until they are disposed in places, in quantities, and in combinations, which render their use most productive or, at any rate, most profitable to the *entrepreneur* whose work it is to plan the organisation of the several businesses.

Though the various markets have each its own peculiar conditions, which deserve separate consideration, certain common characters are seen in every market, whether for the sale of factors of production or of consumable commodities or services.

A market, as has been pointed out in an earlier chapter, consists of a certain restricted area of place and time in which there is effective bargaining between buyers and sellers.   Remembering that what takes place immediately in every modern market is an exchange of specific against general wealth by means of a monetary transaction, we shall do well to try to ascertain how this transaction takes place, or, in other words, how a market price is actually attained.

A fisherman, with one fish in his basket, who met a shipwrecked sailor, starving, with £20 in his pocket, could, if he knew the circumstances, get the whole sum of money as the price of his fish.

If, on the other hand, there were two fishermen each with a fish and no other possibility of selling it before it went bad, the sailor could get either of the fishes for a penny, though the mean expenses of catching a fish might be 4*d.*

Here is the force of monopoly in the determination of a market price.

Now let us approach a little nearer to an actual market.   A has a horse which he will sell at £30, or as much more as he can get.   *a* and *b* are two men willing to buy this horse, and having no other horse in view ; *a* would go as high as £36, *b* as high as £40.

If all the parties knew the circumstances, it is evident that bidding between a and b will go on until the price is driven up to £36, and at any point just above that sum the horse will be knocked down to b. Both parties to the sale, A and b, will get a substantial gain, but an unequal one, A making £6 more than he would consent to take, b nearly £4 less than he would consent to give.

Now let us set the market differently by putting in a second seller with a different minimum price.

A, a seller with a minimum price of £30
B, „ „ „ „ £34
a, a buyer with a maximum price of £36
b, „ „ „ „ £40

B, by refusing to come into the market at less than £34, makes that the minimum market price, for a and b will run the price up to that point at once in competing to buy A's horse. a, dropping out of the bidding at £36, makes that the maximum market price, for above that point b is confronted by two willing sellers and can fix his terms. Between £34 and £36 there are two willing sellers and two willing buyers : all would take part in an act of sale at any point between £34 and £36 indifferently. No bargaining can take place between these points. If we isolate the market, and assume full knowledge on both sides, competition or higgling cannot fix a price.

Let us now add a third party to each side with a separate reserve price. The market will then be thus set out :—

A, seller with minimum price £30
B, „ „ „ „ £34
C, „ „ „ „ £35
a, buyer with maximum price £36
b, „ „ „ „ £40
c, „ „ „ „ £42

If the bidding began at £30, there is only one willing seller and three willing buyers; the latter will raise the price by their bidding, and at £34 another seller, B, enters the market. But, as there will still be three buyers to two sellers, the price will rise higher until at £35 C enters in, and there are three sellers and three buyers. £35 is thus fixed as the minimum market price, for all are willing to buy and to sell at that price. Similarly, it can be shown that £36 is the maximum price, for at any point above there are more willing sellers than buyers, and the odd seller, afraid of being left out, will keep the price from rising above £36. The market price must stand between £35 and £36, but may stand anywhere between, and there is nothing in the process of bargaining to determine where.

In either of these two markets the price-point between the minimum and maximum must be reached by extra-economic means : the parties must toss up. This is on the assumption that all the parties have full knowledge of the respective valuation of all the buyers and sellers. In a point of fact bluff, based on ignorance, and not chance, would usually fix the price-point. It is evident that we may add a fourth, a fifth, or any limited number of competitors to the supply or the demand side of this market without affecting, save in degree, this method of determining price. The larger the number of competing buyers and sellers, or the nearer their respective valuations to one another, the closer will be the upper and lower price limits within which the price-point, the actual market price, should fall. But unless there is an infinite number of units of supply and units of demand, or unless the valuations of the determinant buyers and sellers should happen to coincide, the process of bargaining by itself could never reach a price-point. Now, in the application of economic theory to economic price, the recognition of this fact is of great importance. Let us formulate it thus : ' So long as the number of willing buyers is equal to the number of willing sellers no movement of price can occur, and within the limits of this equality of supply and demand no price-point can be reached.'

' Increase the numbers of buyers and sellers, approximate their expenses of production and their purchasing power, reduce the size of the units of supply, the competition becomes closer, and the upper and the lower margins nearer together. But except in an ideal market they do not touch. There remains an unearned gain distributed by chance or force.'

And yet in practice we constantly see market prices reached and changed by means of bargaining.

§ 2.—The theory of the determination of a market price, as commonly set out in economic text-books, starts with an assumption of an infinite divisibility of supply. It is evident that, if instead of our market for live horses, we put a market for dead horse-flesh selling by the pound, the bargaining, even in so small a market as we provided, would bring the upper and the lower margins of price so close together that the difference might be negligible, and so what was to all intents a price-point might be got by mere bargaining. For A could not then be accredited with one fixed minimum price for his single unit of supply. We should have to set out a much more elaborate valuation for A as the owner of 1000 lbs. of horse-flesh, unless we assume the conditions of a forced sale, which we did not before. We shall suppose that the number of pounds A will sell will vary with the price he can get :

A will sell 1000 lbs. at 6d. per lb.

,, ,, ,, 900 ,, ,, 5d. ,,

,, ,, ,, 800 ,, ,, 4$\frac{1}{2}d$. ,,

and so forth.

Similarly with B and his 1000 lbs. of horse-flesh, except that his supply-schedule will vary indefinitely from that of A. B's schedule might run thus :

B will sell 1000 lbs. at 7d. per lb.

,, ,, ,, 900 ,, ,, 6$\frac{1}{2}d$. ,,

,, ,, ,, 800 ,, ,, 5d. ,,

So C's scale will also vary from that of A and B, not merely as to the price at which he would sell his entire stock of 1000 lbs., but as to the amount of reductions at which he would sell various smaller quantities.

But in the market, A and B and C do not separately offer their different sections of supply. For purposes of the market it is a matter of indifference whether a buys from A or from B or C, or how much from each : he only looks to see how many pounds he can buy at such a price. We must therefore set the supply in terms of so many pounds offered at such a price, so many more pounds at such a lower price. In order to get this setting we must ' pool ' the special valuations of the separate owners of supply. The supply schedule might then run thus :

3000 lbs. supplied at 6$\frac{1}{2}d$. per lb.

2900 ,, ,, ,, 6$\frac{1}{4}d$. ,,

2800 ,, ,, ,, 6d. ,,

2700 ,, ,: ,, 5$\frac{7}{8}d$. ,,

2600 ,, ,, ,, 5$\frac{6}{8}d$. ,,

2500 ,, ,, ,, 5$\frac{1}{2}d$. ,,

and so forth.

Similarly we must handle the demand schedule of the buyers. a and b and c will be willing to buy different quantities at various prices : these variations will differ for the three buyers respectively, according to the urgency which drives them to buy much or little. So we should get one generalised demand schedule corresponding with the supply schedule but reversed in form.

3000 lbs. demanded at 4d. per lb.

2900 ,, ,, ,, 4$\frac{1}{2}d$. ,,

2800 ,, ,, ,, 4$\frac{3}{4}d$. ,,

2700 ,, ,, ,, 5d. ,,

2600 ,, ,, ,, 5$\frac{1}{2}d$. ,,

2500 ,, ,, ,, 6d. ,,

Here, if no smaller units than 100 lbs. were saleable, it is evident that no exact equilibrium would be reached where supply would equal demand at a price-point. The price ultimately reached would be at any point between 5½d. and 6d. for 2500 lbs. But if, as is reasonable to suppose, after the preliminary bargaining had brought the two parties nearly to a price, by bids for not less than 100 lbs., they began to make interim bids between 2600 and 2500, bidding by tens and finally by single pounds, they might be able to reach what would be virtually a price-point which would effect an aggregate sale of (say) 2540 lbs. at 5⅝d.

Thus the ability of the bargaining process to reach a price-point varies with the area of the market, and with the divisibility of the commodity for purposes of sale. Even in a small market where wheat or cotton is sold, bargaining between a small number of buyers and sellers can reach a price-point.

§ 3.—A good deal of practical importance in the determination of the distribution of wealth depends upon the question of the proportion of markets which are approximately free, in that the bargaining is ordinarily such as to reach a price-point without the intervention of force or bluff.

The following are the chief conditions which determine how far a class of goods is suitable for a ' free ' market.

(1) Quantity of supply here and now. Where (a) nature, or (b) the circumstances of production, or (c) artificial limitation, reduces the supply to a small number of indivisible objects, competition of buyers and sellers is seldom such as to reach a true price-point. An instance of (a) would be the building sites in a particular locality ; of (b), the pictures of a particular master ; (c), the fifty copies of an *edition de luxe*.

(2) The time limit. Perishable goods or services have a narrow time-market. The fact that they must be sold now confines the effective demand to those accessible persons who want to buy now and have the wherewithal to pay.

Examples are the fruit market for cheap fruits, and in general the labour market.

(3) The place limit. This area of an effective market will differ for different commodities. Bulk in relation to value is the principal determinant here, though much depends upon the means of transport. Where a class of goods is not portable, the conditions of their use for production or consumption often limits the number of units of supply. Ordinary building stone will have a small local market ; so will houses, means of transit, &c.

(4) Even where the quantity of supply is small, as we have seen, divisibility may be such as to secure ' free ' competition in a market. But where the organic principle of life determines the size, as in the horse market or in the case of valuable shrubs ; or

where a certain size and structure are essential, as in the case of a house, or a workshop, or a machine, the local available supply may often be such as to restrict greatly the power of ' free ' bargaining.

(5) Even in the case of goods which are divisible and in large supply, competition, as a determinant of price, is not fully effective unless there is a guarantee of the quality, size, &c., of the parts of the supply.

A fully effective market involves methods of production which afford reliable standards of goods and full confidence on the part of buyers in the reliability of these standards. Without this standardisation each fraction of a supply stands more or less on its own known or imputed merits, and the market lacks the unity required for effective competition ; each portion of the supply forms a separate centre for bargaining, which is thereby reduced in freedom and efficacy for the attainment of a price-point. In a horse market, however large, the facts that (1) no two horses have the same combination of qualities, (2) that no two sellers and no two buyers set the same value on any two horses, cause the elements of chance or bluff to reach a maximum.

Where a supply is minutely graded, as in the sale of many raw materials of manufacture, such as grains, cotton, wool, though the grading implies a corresponding specialisation of markets and a reduction of the number of buyers and sellers within these limits, there is sufficient play for substitution of neighbouring qualities and grades to secure the conditions of a set of price-points obtained by bargaining.

(6) Closely related to the first condition, quantity of supply, is a corresponding condition of wide and regular demand on the part of buyers. A small, fluctuating and capricious demand obviously disorganises a market, reacting upon production and supply. Special grades of luxury goods, dependent on the taste and fashion of small classes of rich or peculiar persons, do not lend themselves to ' free ' bargaining. The prices of early fruits, a new fashionable hat, diamonds, or high-priced opera seats are determined as much by caprices of consumers as by restrictions of producers.

II

§ 1.—The various restraints upon freedom of bargaining in markets affect vitally the problem of the distribution of wealth. A slightly more detailed survey of the chief classes of markets for the sale of goods and services will help us to understand the extent to which other practices qualify or supplant bargaining and free competition in the fixing of prices.

Let us turn first to the bargains for the price of factors of production, and inquire how far such prices are reached in open markets with freely competing buyers and sellers.

LAND.—Prices for the sale of land or its use are notoriously subject in most countries to a variety of special conditions which are not those of a free market. Land is seldom put up for sale or rental in any form of market which permits close, thoroughly informed bargaining between groups of sellers and buyers. Even in new countries, where land can be bought from Government, from railroads or lands companies, the sellers are few, and often fix supply-prices by agreement ; the expense and difficulty of inspection, the lack of adequate standardisation of land values, and the practical limitation of divisibility to a quarter section, the needs of housing, of capital, the means of transport, constitute great interferences with bargaining. Neither the articles themselves nor reliable samples can be assembled under conditions that favour free, genuinely informed bargains.

In old countries various other barriers intervene. Free supply is impeded by legal conditions, such as laws of entail and primogeniture, expenses of conveyance, or by custom or class feeling, which limit sale or impose hampering conditions. Similar restrictions are operative in the renting of most land for agricultural or other uses. Attachment to particular localities, limitations of quantity and the immobility of land inevitably break up the market for land into a large number of semi-independent markets ; feelings relating to tenancy upon the side of landlords and of tenants play so large a part in determining to whom and on what terms land shall be let or sold, and the possibilities of bluff and squeeze are so numerous, that most land-prices for sale or hire cannot be regarded as reached by bargaining in a free market. Sometimes class sentiment, personal fancy, pride, or obstinacy enormously affects the supply and the supply prices, while land-hunger, only in part economic, similarly affects demand prices, often leading to prices which are in no true sense market prices.

Only in the sale or hire of real estate in or near a large city can it be said that the conditions approximate to those of a ' free ' market, and even then, especially when the land is bought or hired for housing purposes, the differences of position and other detailed distinctions in the several ' lots ' generally allow some margin for bluff or chance.

LABOUR.—Seldom are the conditions of the sale of labour-power those of a large free market. In countries where labourers were sold as slaves or serfs, sometimes an actual market was set forth with competing buyers and sellers, though even then the personality and individual qualities and the indivisibility of the articles of sale precluded competition from reaching an exact price. Slave-dealing as a rule was not a fine economic art ; deceit played an even larger part than in a horse market.

Turning to what is termed to-day the labour market, we see it break up into a great number of trade and local sections, independent for purposes of market prices. Though employers undoubtedly compete among themselves for the most efficient labour, and occasionally for the largest share of a limited supply, it cannot be said that the setting of the labour market from the side of the buyers favours close bargaining. Where large organised trades are concerned, the bargaining is usually conducted by a trade union and a large employer or federation of employers. Though non-union firms and non-union workers may temper, by actual or potential competition, the arrangements made by these collective processes of bargaining, they do not so compete as to fix a price. Nor can it be said that collective bargaining fixes a price by the higgling of the market ; a standard wage built up, partly on competition, partly on custom, partly on economic force, is raised or lowered by bluff or force, with some reference to supposed profits and the conditions of trade ; a price thus fixed for the bulk of a trade becomes more or less a customary wage for the rest of the trade, with variations in the shape of bonuses or sweating. It cannot be maintained that in such industries as mining, railways, docks, the main branches of metal and textile trades, printing, building, shoemaking, or in public employments, wages are market prices closely reached by competitive bargaining.

Where labour is little organised, as in most low-skilled manual trades, in nearly all women's trades, and in most distributive industries, there exists keen indirect competition on the sellers' side, but the method of securing employment affords the sellers no opportunity of making the buyers compete, and the latter generally impose a customary price, which is in no adequate degree a market price.

In agriculture and most country employments, as well as in town workshops and other smaller businesses, it cannot be said that competition fixes prices, though it affects them, altering more or less the local customary prices for labour. In most instances, unskilled or low-skilled workers are powerless to make the few employers accessible to them compete, the surplusage of the labour supply being normally such as to render this competition unnecessary. In any case, the setting of the market is such as to make the competition one-sided. The nearest approach to a true labour market in form, though hardly in substance, is the statutory fair where farm labourers and other servants present themselves for hire, employers inspecting them and making open offers.

Labour exchanges, as established in certain cities of Germany, where employers can apply and arrange terms with individual workers, furnish some of the conditions of a true market.

But the general habit by which a worker out of employment hawks his labour round to employers, offering it to them one by one, does not secure a wage-point by competitive bargaining.

ABILITY.—Though there is often keen competition to secure managerial, official, and other professional posts in private or public services, this competition is but slightly and seldom directed to the determination of a price. That there exists a sort of market price for the manager of a cotton mill, for the town clerk of a city of 100,000 inhabitants, for a first-grade civil servant, is in a very rough sense true ; but these prices are seldom such as would obtain if the competitors were allowed to bid against each other for salaries. In most of such instances the price of ability is not closely fixed by competition, even in indirect ways, but is determined by a combination of customary, personal, and competitive considerations.

CAPITAL.—In its concrete form, as we use it, capital consists in the machinery and other plant, materials and goodwill, &c., of a business. All these things, save the last, are separately saleable as goods, and fall within the ordinary conditions of such sales.

But when the ownership of a business, as a whole or in shares, is bought and sold, we have to deal with a special sort of market, the market for investments.

The ordinary way in which such ownership is conveyed is in the money market, where it is sold as stocks and shares. These are so abstract and intangible in form that it is seldom adequately realised that when a man buys for £140 a share of railroad stock nominally worth £100, he is buying a certain quantity of rails, engines, &c., becoming part owner of the whole concrete capital.

This sort of buying and selling is in general the nearest approach to an absolutely free market, for it enables the most indivisible objects, such as a railway station or a steam engine, to become infinitely divisible, the most perishable things to become permanent, the most various objects to be standardised, the most distant objects to be grouped together. Moreover, the structure of the money market enables the freest and most constant competition to take place between vast numbers of actual and potential buyers, in a market whose area, usually large, may become world-wide.

By a similar financial machinery concrete forms of capital are loaned or rented to *entrepreneurs* or employers, who pay the price for their use, which we call interest. The terms upon which these loans are effected are determined in large modern businesses by the processes of company promotion with its flotation of shares. In smaller or less organised businesses, capital can be borrowed from banks or other professional money-lenders, or from private friends : in almost all cases this capital is loaned in the shape of money, but since the money is converted into plant, machinery, &c., for business use, the substance of the proceeding is the hiring of this concrete capital, and the interest is the rent for its use. Such loans of capital for the establishment or enlargement of a business are usually the subject of close competitive bargaining on the part of the investors, so far as the conditions of the business enable them to understand the risks and chances of gain that are involved. Indeed, with this proviso it may be urged that for large bodies of investors there exists a single investment market, the price of such use of capital being fixed by freest conditions of competition. But by no means all advances of capital for interest are of this character. Not only in agriculture the world over, but in many departments of small business, capital is loaned by banks, usurers, manufacturers or wholesale merchants, upon terms virtually dictated by the lender, and accepted by the necessity rather than the free will of the borrower. The price or interest for such loans is in no sense a market price.

GOODS.—If we follow the series of acts of sale which material forms of wealth undergo in their passage from raw materials to shop goods, we shall recognise that competitive bargaining differs very widely in form and in degree. The producers of raw materials, farmers, hunters, fishers, are usually in a weak position as sellers— much of their product is perishable, and must be sold in distant markets by agents whose negotiations they cannot check ; even lumbermen, stockraisers, and large growers of cotton, tobacco, and other valuable crops, are liable to meet serious obstacles to free bargaining in the shape of combines and corners. Producers of coal, metals, and other non-perishable products of the soil are usually in a better position as sellers, and the markets in which they sell are normally free, while the nature of the goods permits close higgling for a market price.

Where materials or semi-manufactured or wholly manufactured goods of staple kinds are sold in advanced industrial communities, the competitive bargaining is usually close. It is in fact the prominence assigned to these classes of markets that chiefly supports the belief that a market price is reached entirely by the higgling among buyers and sellers acquainted with the goods and the circumstances of the market.

The prices paid by millers for grain, by weaving mills for cotton or woollen yarn, by shoemakers for leather, or machine makers for steel bars, are rigorously determined by competition of buyers and sellers, except so far as trade agreements among sellers, or more rarely temporary corners of supply, upset the nicer mechanism of the market. Attempts by organisations of sellers to hold up prices by fixing minimum selling prices are, however, playing a part of growing importance in the iron and steel and in some other markets for staple manufactures.

COMMODITIES.—In retail trade, bargaining, though very keen, is for the most part one-sided. The seller appears at first sight to have two advantages : in the first place, he is a specialist as regards the goods he sells, while the buyer is usually an amateur ; in the second place, the seller usually fixes a price and the buyer accepts it without higgling. But these apparent advantages of the seller are in large measure affected by the close and often cut-throat competition of other sellers, which forces him to fix a price that cancels his technical advantage in dealing with customers. So far, at any rate, as prices are concerned, this keenness of competition among sellers enables consumers to do almost as well as if they were close bargainers themselves. In this condition of trade the retailer is driven more and more to take his advantage indirectly in passing off adulterated or inferior goods for accepted brands. Where goods, by reason of their perishable or bulky nature, must usually be bought near at hand, trade agreements may often operate on local prices, as in milk, bread, or coal. Moreover, retail prices have for most buyers a customary support which enables retailers to obtain higher prices for some time after a fall of wholesale prices would enable keen consumers to claim a corresponding reduction.

It must not be forgotten that a considerable and a growing proportion of the income of most consumers is spent upon buying from public or semi-public bodies commodities and services the price of which is not determined appreciably by bargaining. The water, gas, and tramway transport, street accommodation, lighting, police, use of parks, libraries, &c., which he buys with rates, or at tariffs fixed by the corporation or some non-competing local company, the various state services in the form of military and judicial support, public health, education, &c., are not bought at market prices. The bargaining factor in the determination of transport rates for his person or his property, by rail or water, or by other local services, is slight : professional fees, subscriptions to clubs, societies, tickets for concerts, theatres and other entertainments, retail prices for books, newspapers, &c., and a large variety of other large and small prices are not directly or immediately susceptible to the higgling of the market. Considerations of public utility, private monopoly more or less restrained by legal and other conditions, trade or professional agreement, custom and sheet inertia on the part of buyers, keep large provinces of retail price outside close competition.

§ 2.—This short survey suffices to show that the theory of markets in which freely competing buyers and sellers reach the equilibrium of a market price, by elaborate schedules of supply and demand prices, is only applicable to a small fraction of actual sales.

Though the competition of buyers or of sellers, or of both, is usually present in some measure, its operation is seldom such as to determine a market price.

This means, of course, that in most market prices as well as in most ' normal prices ' there is an element of unearned and unnecessary payment, which represents not a genuine cost of production, but a superior power of bargaining.

Though for convenience we have accepted the common distinction between normal and market prices, and have made a separate analysis of the modes of their determination, it is well once more to emphasise the artificial nature of the distinction. The natural or contrived scarcities, which are found to be the sources of the various surplus or unearned elements in normal prices, likewise express themselves in the limitations of freedom of bargaining which most markets exhibit. Since market prices, so called, are the actual prices which are paid and received, in them we must expect to find the elements of surplus expenses which have gathered in the various direct and indirect processes of production that go to the making of every class of commodities. If we could take the retail price of a loaf of bread in London, we should find it to consist not only of a number of necessary costs of production incurred by farmers, carriers, merchants, millers and bakers, re-solvable into a great variety of payments for the factors of production employed at these several stages, but of other surplus expenses which might imply ' squeezes ' of the Elevator Company, the Shipping Combine, the Harvester Trust, the English Railway, the Miller, a local Bakers' Combine, each or all of these, with various minor squeezes of landlords in rent, coal owners, makers of milling machinery, &c. The price of 5d. a loaf might contain fractions of such squeezes amounting to, say, twopence. added to the 3d. which represented the necessary payments to evoke productive energy in the various processes. There are probably few, if any, final commodities where a shortage of some factor has not occurred in some necessary process, stamping its impress upon the price in the shape of such a ' surplus.'

CHAPTER X

THE LAW OF SUPPLY AND DEMAND

§ 1. Supply and demand must be treated as 'flows,' not fixed 'funds.' Price-change is then seen as shifting with the rate of flow : its cause will be an increase or decrease of demand in relation to supply.—§ 2. Industrial causes affecting supply relate to (a) changes in economy of industrial arts; (b) changes in supply of the several factors.—§ 3. On the demand side (1) changes in the art of consumption, (2) changes in the number of consumers or their aggregate income, are disturbing influences on prices.—§ 4. A fall in expenses of production will affect price according to 'elasticity of demand.' There may be several possible new price levels. —§ 5. Elasticity of demand varies with (1) the degree of importance attaching to the article, (2) the effect of a price-change upon the other elements in a standard of consumption.—§ 6. Elasticity of supply is quicker and less calculable in its working, for the arts of production are less conservative than the arts of consumption.

§ 1.—WE have seen how the expenses of production are composed that constitute and determine the normal prices which express the rates of exchange between various classes of commodities ; we have also seen how market or short-time and short-place deviations from normal prices are determined. It remains for us to get a closer and clearer understanding of the mechanism of price-changes, the direct instrument of alterations in the rate of exchange for goods and services, and so of the distribution of wealth, among various classes of producers.

This mechanism is commonly spoken of as ' the law of supply and demand.' But what is meant by the law ? First of all we must define the terms.

The supply which thus operates in price-change evidently does not mean the total stock of goods in existence, but the quantity which sellers are willing and able to sell at the current price. Similarly with demand. If we are to place it in true relation with this supply, demand must mean either the quantity of goods which buyers are willing and able to buy at the current price, or the quantity of money buyers are able and willing to pay for goods at the current price. If, however, taking these meanings of the terms, we turn to the mechanism of the market, we find them defective in that they furnish a merely statical setting to a dynamic problem. Supply and demand, thus conceived, are stationary amounts.

Now price-change is a process, and in order to understand this process, what we have to estimate is the rate at which the stock of goods is increased and depleted—a flow and not a fund. But if we conceive supply and demand as quantities of goods (or money) regarded at a particular time, we conceive them as funds. In order to study price-change properly, we must express supply and demand as flows, i.e. measure them as processes taking place in time. Consistently with this purpose, supply may mean the total stock offered for sale at a price during any given time, and demand may mean quantity of purchases at a price within a given time, or quantity of money expended at a price within a given time. But it will be more convenient to define the terms more narrowly, confining supply to the rate of increase of stock : demand to the rate of withdrawal from stock (or the rate of payment of money withdrawing from stock). Thus alone do we rightly come to regard supply and demand as processes or ' flows,' and the supply and demand with which we concern ourselves will be equivalent to the rate of production and of consumption.[1]   Where goods flow out of a stock at the same rate as they flow in, the price remains firm, and demand and supply will be said to be equilibrated ; where the inflow is faster than the outflow, prices fall, and supply will be said to exceed demand ; where the outflow is faster, prices rise and demand exceeds supply. This setting regards demand primarily as a rate of outflow of goods. But if we regard demand as a power exercised by the purchaser, it signifies and is measured by an inflow of money. The quantitative relation of supply and demand may be expressed in either measure of demand. But in dealing with the mechanism of exchange. it is best to regard demand as an action proceeding from the buyer and to measure it in the terms of purchasing power.

Any increase or decrease of money, expended upon goods at a given price within a given time, implies a corresponding increase or decrease in quantity of goods bought, so that no error will arise from substituting the money measure for the goods measure of demand, and regarding it as an inflow of money from the purchaser instead of an outflow of goods from the seller.

Keeping clearly in mind this conception of supply and demand as a rate of flow, it is hardly possible to misstate the law of price change.

---

[1] The term 'consumption' is here used in the loose business sense, in which, for instance, it is said cotton yarn or iron is consumed when it is utilised in manufacturing processes. In strict statements of economic theory it is desirable to confine consumption to the use of retail goods by so-called consumers.

So long as a body of sellers in a market, maintaining the same stock of goods, can sell those goods at the same pace at which they have sold them hitherto, they will not lower and cannot raise the price. If they lower the price, this act means either a fall off in the pace at which buyers ask for goods, or it means that they have increased their stock, and in order to make sales correspond with this increased rate of supply, they must stimulate demand by lowering prices ; if they raise their price, it means either a reduction of supply in face of a constant or an increasing demand, or a growth of the rate at which purchases are made from a constant or decreasing supply.

Thus the immediate cause of a rise of price is always a decrease of supply or an increase of demand ; the cause of a fall of a price, an increase of supply or a decrease of demand.

Here we have the general law of price-change so far as it relates to the play of economic forces and not to the arbitrary will of a government or a private monopolist or combine.[1]

So self-evident is the logic of this ' law ' that it would appear impossible for economic reasoning upon prices to evade it. Yet there has been no more frequent source of error than such evasion. Though the direct, immediate, efficient causes of price-change are always shifts in the relation between supply and demand, there are diverse causes, near or remote, of these shifts ; and nothing is more common than for business men, or economists, to leap from some industrial or financial fact to its assumed effect on prices without taking the trouble to show how the fact in question operates upon supply or demand for commodities.

A bad harvest, a large new discovery of gold, heavy taxation for war expenditure, a rapid growth of population, a cheaper generation of industrial energy, an extension of bank facilities, these and many other changes affect prices ; but unless the mode of their operation upon the supply and the demand for commodities and services is clearly traced, the nature and importance of their effect on prices is likely to be gravely misunderstood. When we treat of money we shall see how persistently the upholders of the strict ' quantity of money ' doctrine have erred by their habitual refusal to trace how an increase or decrease of gold, or other money, operates upon the supply or demand for commodities.

§ 2.—Let us now classify the chief industrial causes which,

---

[1] It may be observed from history that attempts on the part of government or of monopolists to fix or change prices, for commodities, for land, for capital, for labour, in defiance of the law of supply and demand are usually frustrated or set at naught.

increasing or diminishing the supply or the demand of goods at existing prices, alter these prices.

First turn to supply. An increased rate of supply of freely produced goods at a given price can only occur through a reduction in mean expenses of production.

This reduction of mean expenses of production may be due (1) to improved economy in the arts or methods of production, or (2) to an increase in supply of one or more of the factors of production reducing its surplus value and its price.

I. Under the head of improved economy of production we may place—

(a) Improved appliance of mechanical, chemical and other scientific knowledge to industry. To this class belong the main economies of the substitution of machinery for hand labour, as well as the substitution of new, cheaper forms of raw materials and power.

(b) Improvements in business organisation, either on its productive side, through better division of labour and specialisation of productive power, or on its commercial side through better modes of buying and of selling, or on its financial side through better methods of cost-taking, credit, and book-keeping.

(c) Improvements in the quality of labour-power.

II. Under increase of supply of factors of production we may distinguish—

(d) New discoveries of natural sources of materials, or the greater development of sources already existing. Enlarged, improved and cheapened transport by land and sea, leading to increased knowledge and availability of the resources of the earth for foods, raw materials of manufacture, fuel and other power, has been the chief instrument of such increase of supply.

(e) More capital flowing into industry, as the result of enlarged productivity and saving reduces the surplus elements of 'interest,' by abating the 'scarcity' of capital, thus diminishing expenses of production. The fall of prices of cotton in Lancashire after the 'fifties' was due primarily to a reduction of rate of 'profit' on capital.

(f) Increased supplies of labour, by immigration or by planting out industries in new areas of large populations, may cheapen expenses by removing any surplus wage in a protected labour-market, or even by introducing a sweating economy, as for instance where large drafts of cheap European labour have been drawn into the anthracite mines of Pennsylvania.

(g) Extended education, increasing the available supply of ability, may reduce the surplus element in profit, and so lower expenses. All these industrial and social movements, making for an increase of supply at former prices, tend to reduce prices. Similarly, a reversal of any of these movements, reducing supply, will tend to raise prices. Although, under modern conditions of education and communication of knowledge, it will be rare for any positive decline in the arts of industry to occur, a shrinkage in supply of some factor of production, or a failure to respond to the normal requirements of growing industries, often raises the expense of production by enabling the short factor to take a surplus. A depletion of the best sources of raw materials, animal, vegetable or mineral, is, of course, the most frequent cause of such a rise of supply price, and is so common as to have a special niche accorded to it in the temple of economic science as the ' law of diminishing returns.' To this so-called law we shall return later in considering the size of maximum efficiency for a business. At present, it is enough to mark the important part it plays in creating a surplus price which, entering into expenses of production, diminishes supply at existing prices.

A shortage of capital, due perhaps to destruction of property by war or some natural convulsion, or to political insecurity, a shortage of labour due to migration, plague, famine or reduced birth-rate, will operate similarly to check or reduce supply by raising normal expenses of production.

§ 3.—Turning to the demand side of the equation, we shall recognise that an increase or decrease of the rate of demand for any class of goods at existing prices is attributable to one of two sets of causes.

I. A change in the art of consumption. Any improvement in the economy of consumption of commodities, such as a better method of combustion, more temperance in the use of food or alcohol, or any other change in the standard of consumption of a people or a class of consumers, reducing the importance of a particular commodity, must of course react in reduced demand at a given price. Conversely, any change of method of consumption which gives increased importance to some commodity in a standard of consumption, as for instance sugar as an article of diet, wool for clothing, will operate in enhanced demand.

The law of substitution is constantly operating on the side of consumption, displacing one article by another. Sometimes the stimulus to substitution proceeds directly from the changed taste, or convenience, or knowledge of the consumer ; sometimes it is suggested to him or imposed upon him by some class of producers : sometimes it is permanent, sometimes temporary. So intimately and intricately related, both physiologically and psychologically, are various elements in any standard of consumption that any change in taste or habit directly affecting one class of commodities must have countless reactions upon the positive or relative demand for other classes. So, for example, the abandonment of alcohol may operate upon other food factors by reducing the consumption of meats, and increasing that of vegetable and dairy products; while the change of companionship it causes may displace expenditure on betting and on music-halls by expenditure on literature or on home comforts of various sorts.

II. Apart from all changes in the art of consumption, demand at a given price may be increased or decreased by any change in the aggregate money income of the former body of consumers, or by an expansion or contraction of the number of consumers. Any rise in the money income of a body of consumers tends, apart from all changes in the nature of their consumption, to induce an enlargement of demand of all those elements which have not reached satiety. The study of the effects of rises or falls of income in the various classes of consumers upon the class standard of consumption and so upon the demand, is one of the most delicately complex and least explored provinces of political economy.

The relative increase or decline of various classes of population by natural causes, or by migration, also plays an important part in their influence on demand for various sorts of commodities.

When we turn to what is often called 'productive consumption,' in which the supply and demand relate, not to commodities for human uses, but to goods used up in processes of production, we perceive that any economy in use of such goods operates directly as a reduction of demand in one industry, and as increase of supply in another.

A discovery of a furnace which shall save 10 per cent. of the waste energy from burning coal will act as a reduction of demand for coal, or as an increase of supply of steel at former prices. Moreover, these two opposed effects will go on propagating themselves throughout the whole industrial system, altering the relative and positive demands and supplies of all the different markets. This necessarily follows from the organic interaction which we have traced throughout the industrial system.

So, any change which takes place in any of the arts of production or consumption, or in any mere expansion in the quantity of production in some class of industry, or of consumption in some class of consumer, alters the whole system. An Eight Hours Act for Miners, raising by 5 per cent. the price of coal in England, a Hudson's Bay railway for carrying Canadian wheat more cheaply to the European market, a new storage economy for electric motor traffic, the growing use of cereals or of cocoa as articles of diet, a thousand great or little economic incidents, affecting directly some specific industry, are seen to produce innumerable and sometimes immense changes of industry at points in the industrial system very distant from the initial change.

To the modern business man nothing that affects any other business in the world can be a matter of indifference.

But with the important social implications of such a doctrine we are not here concerned. Our object here is simply to establish a firm recognition of the *modus operandi* of price-change through the agency of demand and of supply, and to distinguish the general nature and mode of the forces which act respectively upon the two sides of the equation of price.

§ 4.—Recognising that the sole efficient cause of every change of market price is a prior change in the relation between the rate of supply and the rate of demand, and that every change in supply or demand prices, affecting the rate of one of these processes, affects the other, we have to inquire a little closer into the interaction of changes of supply prices and changes of demand prices. If the introduction of clicking machines into a branch of the shoe trade reduces the expenses of producing a 10s. pair of boots by 10 per cent., the supply of this class of shoes selling at 10s. will be increased, manufacturers and dealers lowering their price to dispose of this increasing supply at the same rate as they disposed of their earlier supply. How much must they lower the price to reach a new level at which supply keeps pace with demand, and what will be the increase in the aggregate of sales ?

If any number of 10s. shoes can now be produced at 9s., it is evident that the new selling price must fall to 9s., for, until that point in the drop of prices is reached, the profits upon the trade will be such as to turn out more shoes than can find a market, and the keener competition of sellers, thus stimulated, will cause them to undersell one another. But when this struggle to sell the largest quantity of shoes at a profitable rate has brought the price down to 9s., it will not bring it lower, for a lower price would make the margin of profit less than it was before, and would check any further increase of supply.

The quantity of increased sales of shoes effected by this fall of price will depend on what is called ' elasticity of demand.' This will differ in different markets and different parts of the same market. If everybody has already reached a standard of comfort which involves the wearing of sound shoes, the reduction of price from 10s. to 9s. will not be attended by any large increase of sales : a few consumers will discard old shoes earlier than before, but the larger effect may be an increased sale of a higher grade of shoe, if the economy applies to higher grades as well. If, however, there are unshod or ill-shod people, or if some new outside market can be tapped, the fall of price to 9s. may be followed by a large extension of sales. More complicated will be the problem if, as is more usual, the reduction of supply prices is not the same for all qualities supplied. If the new machinery is worked more economically by turning out a larger supply of shoes than could be sold before, the determination of the new price level and of the quantity of sales at this level will not be so simple.

Formerly 1000 pairs of shoes per week were sold at 10s. a pair. Now the normal rate of profits can be earned in this trade by any one of the following conditions of the market :

1000 pairs selling at	9s.	0d.
1500 ,, ,,	8s.	6d.
1800 ,, ,,	8s.	0d.
2500 ,, ,,	7s.	6d.

We may suppose that the full economy of the new machinery is exhausted when the output has risen to 2500 per week, and that a larger number could not be turned out at less than 7s. 6d.

If everybody has as many shoes as he wants, the new condition of the market would be one which sold 1000 pairs at 9s. But this absolute rigidity never exists. A fall of price always stimulates demand : the only question is ' how much ? ' If the elasticity of demand for shoes is such that 1500 pairs can be sold for 8s. 6d., whereas another drop of 6d. will not lead to an increased sale of 300 more pairs, the new price level will stand at 8s. 6d. But if, on the other hand, though 8s. is not a possible price, a still further reduction to 7s. 6d. might bring into the market a new class of hitherto shoeless persons, or induce a poor stratum of consumers to buy a reserve pair, or open up some foreign market, the new price level might fall to 7s. 6d., with a sale of 2500. It is also clear that, though only one new price level can be reached, it may consist in a choice between two possible and equally profitable new conditions of the market. It might be that, either 1500 pairs could be sold at 8s. 6d., or 2500 at 7s. 6d., with the same net aggregate profit.

If so, no theoretical reasoning can determine which of the two equally desirable alternatives would be selected. Practically, the former would probably at first be chosen, for following the gradual fall of price and increase of sales from the former level, manufacturers would find that, after a market of 1500 at 8s. 6d. had been reached, a further lowering of price to 8s. was followed by diminished profits with no stability of demand, and they would not further increase their output so as to reach the figure 2500, which, at 7s. 6d., would liberate a fresh volume of demand and so secure an aggregate profit equal to that obtainable at 8s. 6d.

It is, of course, unlikely that an exact equilibrium between rate of supply and rate of demand would be reached at any of the new prices here named. The actual new market would, in its preliminary state, stand somewhat as follows :—

1000 pairs supply at	9s. 0d.	1150 pairs demand	
1500 ,, ,,	8s. 6d.	1470 ,,	,,
1800 ,, ,,	8s. 0d.	1650 ,,	,,
2500 ,, ,,	7s. 6d.	2300 ,,	,,

A curve treatment of the problem, based on an ideal divisibility of supply and of prices, would yield a new market price of equilibrium between supply and demand at a precise point, say 1483 pairs at 8s. $4\frac{1}{10}d$.

But though makers and dealers, in quotations of prices and in bidding, would make a nicer discrimination of quantities and prices than we have here represented, the treatment indicated above is much nearer to the actual facts of industry than a curve treatment implying infinite divisibility. In cost-taking, actual makers always proceed by round numbers at fairly large intervals, so that the probability of an exact price being reached by pure bargaining is very slight.

§ 5.—Though, therefore, it may be said that a reduction in expenses of production, through its effect in increasing supply at former prices, always lowers selling prices, it has no tendency to cause a fall proportionate to the fall in expenses. The frequent assumption in popular economics that the displacement of labour by the introduction of some machine which reduces the expenses of production for a commodity will tend to be compensated by the increased demand for the commodity, following a fall of prices, has no validity whatever. A reduction of 10 per cent. in price, thus caused in one trade, may stimulate so large an increase of demand as to lead to 20 per cent. more workers being employed than before the labour-saving machinery was introduced. In another trade a similar reduction of price may be followed by a very slight increase of sales, and a considerable net displacement of labour. A comparison of the recent history of employment in the cotton and the printing trades will serve to illustrate this truth. Recent improvements in cotton spinning and weaving processes have been accompanied, during the last three decades, by a reduction in the aggregate employment in the trade, in spite of increased supply at lowered prices : on the other hand, the introduction of type-setting and other mechanical improvements in printing has so stimulated demand through reduction of supply prices as to lead to a large increase of employment in the trade.

The elasticity of demand for a commodity, i.e. the effects of a fall in supply prices upon the rate of sales, depends upon a variety of conditions, the principal of which are as follows :—

First. The degree of necessity or actual desirability attached to a commodity. An absolute necessary of life, such as bread, will have very little elasticity for the well-to-do classes, who will not buy any more however much the price fell, or any less however much it rose. Even for the regular skilled working classes in this country a moderate rise or fall of prices will have little effect if the former price is a moderate one. Only among the positively poor will a rise in bread appreciably reduce demand, or a fall in bread appreciably enlarge it.[1] Much, even in the case of bread, will depend upon the possibility of substituting other foods, i.e. upon the degree of absolute necessity attaching to this single article.

In the case of what may be called necessaries of the second degree, such as fuel in an ordinary English winter, the elasticity will be tolerably great, both among the poor and among the thrifty portion of the ordinary working classes, but very little for the well-to-do classes.

As we rise through the various grades of conveniences, comforts and luxuries which satisfy a diminishing urgency of need, the elasticity of demand becomes greater over a larger proportion of the entire market.

A moderate fall in price of expensive luxuries, such as furs or diamonds, will often, by the imitative force of fashion, cause a large extension of the market, though it will have little or no effect in increasing the demand among the rich former customers. When such an extension has once fastened a new commodity in the standard of consumption of a class, the elasticity of its demand in such a class is greatly diminished, but while it is fresh a rise in price may easily expel it. So strong, however, are pride and custom, that there is much more elasticity in the direction of the extension of demand than in the direction of abandonment or even of reduction : *caeteris paribus*, the effect of a 10 per cent. fall of price in increasing demand is larger than the effect of a 10 per cent. rise in diminishing demand. The amount of this difference will, however, vary with the nature of the consumption : where

---

[1] Even there the law of substitution must be taken into account. There is some reason to hold that a rise in price of bread has very little effect upon the purchase of bread even by the workers, but will act rather to reduce their demand for other forms of food, &c.

consumption belongs to display, and touches pride, a rise of price but slightly checks consumption, whereas a fall of price may greatly extend it. In such luxuries, however, a fall of price, so large as to admit new social strata to a common use of what were formerly exclusive goods, may lead to a diminished use or even a disuse among the rich, for their utility as instruments of display may be greatly damaged by their spread. Where, however, a luxury appeals primarily to some special physical taste, it will not be easily discarded.

There is only one class of goods of which it can be said that the normal action of elasticity of demand is reversed, i.e. those goods the main attraction of which consists in their rarity. The elasticity of demand for a rare *edition de luxe* will, as a rule, be very slight, and may be less than zero ; that is to say, it might be possible to sell 100 copies at five guineas each, but only fifty if 500 were offered at two guineas.

Articles which are put to several uses have generally more elasticity of demand than others, unless, indeed, an equal degree of necessity happens to attend to each use. Water is the commonest instance where it is an article of sale. Drinking, cooking, washing the person and clothing, cleaning in general, watering the garden : these uses lie in a descending scale of urgency, so that a comparatively small rise in the water rate may cause a large disuse for irrigation, and a more economical use for general purposes of cleaning, though no reduction of its use for drinking or for cooking.

There will be considerable differences in the time taken for a given rise or fall of price to work out its full effect upon demand. Much will depend upon the inherent conservatism of classes so far as an extension of demand is operative, and here again the question how far the new commodity conforms to or harmonises with accepted habits of consumption is of importance. It took a very long time for cocoa, oatmeal and bananas to secure the place their cheapness and intrinsic attractions have enabled them to win in the ordinary English standard of consumption. There have been, on the other hand, two or three epochs in the short history of bicycles when a moderate fall of price has brought a rapid, large extension of demand.

The primary habits of consumption are the most conservative : the later and less firmly established items of expenditure are naturally more subject to change. Food consumption stands at one end of the scale ; amusements at the other.

Secondly. The effect of any given rise or fall of price must also depend upon the price changes that are going on in every other class of commodities, as well as upon the growth or decrease of the aggregate income and its distribution among the various classes of consumers.

Every rise of price, not attended by an exactly corresponding shrinkage of demand, affects the demand for various other classes of commodities which have not changed price, and the effect upon the demand and the selling prices of these other commodities is communicated to others more remote, so that a rise or fall of prices in any market commonly affects prices in every other market. Some of the largest and most direct effects may be produced at a long distance from the original seat of disturbance. When a fall in the selling prices of bicycles first brought them within the reach of the lower-middle and upper working classes, one of the most direct and large effects was a reduction in demand for cheap pianos and for certain classes of books.

Every growth of the income of the community or of any class will evidently affect the elasticity of demand attaching respectively to each element in the standard of consumption, and also to each organic group of commodities. For anything which causes an increase or decrease of demand for a certain class of goods may closely affect other goods which ' go with it ' either in final consumption or in some process of production, or which, competing with it either in production or consumption, rise with its fall and fall with its rise. So the growth of motor cars not merely brought a stimulus to the oil trade, but affected beneficially or detrimentally the market for several sorts of house property, improved certain branches of upholstering, damaged the harness trade and the higher grades of the cycle trade, altered the market for male and female head-gear, and exerted an enormous variety of considerable influences upon the entire expenditure of large groups of the well-to-do, creating almost a revolution in many of the luxury trades.

Corresponding to these subtleties of the influence of changes of supply price through the varying elasticity of demand for different articles, at different times, in different places, among different sorts of consumers, will be the reactions which changes of demand price exert upon the various expenses of production and so upon supply prices.

Every rise or fall in the scale of demand prices, i.e. in the amount of money consumers are willing and able to pay for a supply of goods at the current price, will, through causing a larger or a smaller supply to be produced, alter the methods of production, the positive and relative amounts of the various factors of production, and the prices that are paid per unit for their use, so raising and lowering the margins of employment, extensive and intensive, of each factor.

Still more important are the influences which the rise or fall of demand prices for staple materials of manufacture exert upon the structure of whole groups of trades, and so upon the supply prices of the goods they make. The rise of demand prices for such articles as copper, rubber, oil, paper, leather, due to new or increased demands for electric apparatus, motors, cheap literature, &c., have altered the economic and even the political administration of whole provinces.

§ 6.—The elasticity of supply, i.e. the response which expenses of production make to a rise or a fall of demand at previous prices, is much less calculable than the elasticity of demand. For, whereas the latter commonly depends upon the gradual action of large bodies of consumers altering their habits of consumption, the former is usually achieved by quick changes in methods of production spreading rapidly over whole trades of producers. Production is normally less conservative than consumption, and is more alert to seize and adopt new economies. For though habits of industry make for themselves deep grooves, and labour, capital, and ability, being specialised in certain methods, resist innovations which, however beneficial in the long run, involve present trouble and loss, competition forces reforms. Whereas a new habit of consumption propagates itself among consumers by voluntary imitation which may be very slow where it takes place, like most consumption, within the privacy of the home, a new method of production proceeds by forced imitation, for, if a manufacturer refuses to adapt himself to new and better methods, he goes under. But though a rise or fall of demand at previous prices must always produce some effect upon methods of production, the size of the effect will have even less direct relation to the size of the price-change than in the case of demand. A rise of 20 per cent. in the demand for wheat at current prices, due to increasing European population with rising wages, may cause poorer wheat-land to be brought under cultivation, so that the normal supply price of wheat per quarter for the enlarged demand is raised by 30 per cent., or it may stimulate new railway enterprise which shall open up some vast new granary like Assiniboia, or bring some new method of fertilisation into vogue which may in a short time equate the enlarged supply to the enlarged demand at a price even lower than that which formerly obtained.

The normal influence of rising prices due to enhanced demand is twofold : first, a considerable rise in supply prices takes place, due to the necessity of recourse to less efficient factors of production and higher prices for factors previously in use ; next, stringency of supply at these higher expenses furnishes a strong incentive to economies of invention and administration, with the subsequent result that the increased supply can be turned out at a rate as low or lower than before. The nature and the magnitude of these economies, which form the real measure of elasticity of supply, belong, however, to those wider considerations related to the economic size of a business.

CHAPTER XI

THE SIZE OF BUSINESSES

§ 1. There is no universal tendency for businesses to grow in size. The extractive industries show large numbers of small business forms.—§ 2. Transport in all advanced countries tends towards large capitalistic forms. So does manufacture in its chief staple branches.—§ 3. Wholesale trade is in big and growing forms: retail trade shows opposite tendencies, though the small surviving businesses have only a semi-independence. Finance is a domain of large businesses: the arts and professions of small businesses.

§ 1.—THE question of the size to which different sorts of businesses tend to grow is of great importance in considering both the production and the distribution of wealth. Modern conditions of capitalist industry have in many prominent trades led to so large and so continuous an increase in size of successful businesses as to have given rise to a loose popular notion that a general, if not universal, tendency exists for successful businesses to grow bigger and bigger without assignable limit and for small businesses to disappear.

So far as present-day tendencies are concerned, our brief preliminary survey of the industrial system will have served to indicate that, in many fields of industry, small and middling businesses appear to hold their own, and that, even in trades where monster businesses occupy a prominent position, businesses of moderate or small size sometimes survive.

A general survey of the facts does not support any sweeping generalisation about the economy of concentration of capital and the general movement towards great trusts or monopolies by the progressive elimination of smaller businesses.

The question, to what size does a business under favourable or under normal conditions tend to grow, can only be answered by a separate scrutiny of each branch of industry.

AGRICULTURE.—Turning first to agriculture, we find the most diverse types prevailing in different countries and for different purposes. Most of the staple work of agriculture for growth of grain and fruits, and even for stock-raising and dairy produce, is done by small holders conducting more or less independent businesses. Save, perhaps, for stock-raising, and in certain countries for some sorts of fruit-growing, there is no admitted economy in large farming and no widespread tendency towards the substitution of large for small holdings.

The typical business or economic unit for agriculture in its main branches shows no general tendency to grow, so far, at any rate, as the land and labour factors are concerned. But in every civilised country the capital factor in a farm tends to grow: tools and machinery, artificial manures, &c., play a larger part than formerly. Improved scientific agriculture, indeed, often makes in favour of small land units by substituting intensive for extensive cultivation. There is a type of agricultural business where land becomes a factor of diminishing importance, the cultivation being conducted in glass houses with imported and manufactured soils, and with artificial power. Even in such businesses, however, so important are the elements of personal care, local knowledge, and in some instances purely local markets, that the small local business is able to hold its own and survive, even in this the most capitalised sort of agriculture.

The stock-breeding, grazing, lumber, and certain fruit-growing businesses in new countries show the greatest tendency towards large units. But even in such countries as the United States and Canada, the normal limit of a farm does not often exceed what can be worked by a single family, with a little regular or seasonal help.

Special climatic and geographical conditions sometimes favour large farms devoted to some single crop, but even the bonanza farm does not exceed a certain size.

Where great modern capitalism presses upon agriculture is through the use of hired machinery and through control of transport and of markets. These powers, exercised by railroads and elevator companies, and sometimes by companies owning threshing and other machinery, may be regarded in some instances as serious infringements upon the independence of farmers as the owners or controllers of a business.

The mere survival of large numbers of small tenants or even freeholders cannot be understood to imply a survival of small businesses in agriculture, if an increasing share in the ownership of the factors of production, and an increasing share in the product, are possessed by large businesses related to finance, machinery, transport, or markets. The question of the relative independence of the farmer must enter as a factor into the interpretation of the size of the agricultural business.

In outward form, however, it is clear that the greater part of agriculture does not tend towards large business units.

MINING.—So far as more valuable metals are concerned, the tendency towards large capitalistic businesses is strong and rapid, though each new discovery of such metals is liable to pass through an experimental era of small businesses. The application of scientific methods, involving expensive machinery and treatment, as in modern gold or diamond mines, has been a principal cause of this concentration, assisted in some instances by advantages of market control. Deep-level mining involves such large preliminary outlay, such large organisation, and so heavy a speculative character, as to necessitate a great joint stock enterprise.

Small businesses may survive where cheap products are got out for local markets, as in the case of brick and stone.

FISHING.—This, the third branch of the ' extractive ' industries, is difficult to assess. In developed industrial countries steam trawlers owned by large companies displace the small businesses worked by individual fishermen or small co-operative groups, over a large and growing portion of the trade. But in certain branches the small fisher holds his own, partly because fishing is a seasonal trade and so irregular as to require great detailed care and an adaptability to time and place, conditions which are better suited to the simple fishing business.

§ 2.—TRANSPORT.—The businesses which carry raw materials from the farm, the mine, the seaport, to the factory, the commercial centre, or the consumer, and convey the goods from one centre of production to another, tend strongly towards large capitalist structure. This holds, indeed, of every sort of carriage, of goods, persons, or information, or for the direct distribution from a centre of such utilities as gas or water. Not merely the great bulk of the business on the main highways of land and water is conducted by huge companies, but local carriage and communications are passing more and more into large public or private businesses.

The private cab driver or small livery stable is disappearing, and with the growing elimination of the horse such transport business as survives will yield to the competition of mechanical traction.

MANUFACTURES.—If we use this term to cover all the processes by which raw materials are transformed into finished commodities, we shall perceive that most of the manufactures engaged in the main processes of making food, clothing, houses, and other material necessaries and conveniences of life, have passed or are passing into large businesses. The railroad, economies of machinery and of division of labour are chiefly responsible for this growth of the business unit, and the largest businesses are generally in those productive processes which best lend themselves to these economies. Wherever the raw materials are sufficiently uniform to admit of purely mechanical treatment without damage and waste, where this treatment can conveniently be broken up into a number of separate processes, where there exists a widespread regular and accessible market for the product, the large capitalist business form prevails. Such businesses as milling, and the principal textile and metal manufactures, conforming closely to these conditions, tend towards a large size. Even industries dealing with less tractable material, such as leather, or involving some processes where individual human skill or care is required, as in watch-making or clothes-making, pass into large businesses, provided some one or more necessary process requires expensive machinery, or minute organisation, supported by a large regular demand.

But while a large number of the staple trades settle down into big businesses of various sizes under the pressure of these concentrative forces, other trades tend to remain in small businesses. A small, fluctuating, and incalculable market does not permit the use of expensive plant or large business organisation : hence many luxury or fashion trades remain in small businesses. Even in the principal textile and metal trades small factories and workshops survive for special orders. Every staple trade contains several subsidiary trades engaged in supplying minor needs, or in executing some special process which cannot conveniently be done in the factory, or some work of repair. Such a town as Birmingham is still full of such small subsidiary businesses in the metal trades.

Attached more or less closely to large manufacturing or distributive trades are quantities of small workshops or home industries, receiving their materials from a large firm, but executing the work upon their own premises, sometimes with their own machines and power, under a variety of conditions of semi-independence.

How far the Sheffield grinder, the jewel cutter, the matchbox maker, the shirtmaker, is entitled to be regarded as a genuine business unit is a difficult question. There is any number of degrees of dependence in modern industry. The number of manufacturing businesses where a genuinely independent craftsman or other maker buys his materials where he likes, makes what he likes, and sells either directly to consumers or to competing firms, is probably small. There still survive, however, in country and even in towns, considerable numbers of small builders or independent craftsmen in some building trade, smiths, shoemakers, and other small ' tradesmen,' executing special jobs for local customers, though most of the work, especially such as is connected with clothing, furniture, and foods, has been taken over by large organised firms. The small businesses which survive belong for the most part to two classes. First come those connected with the execution of small irregular orders for consumers or for large firms, businesses for local supply of perishable goods, e.g. bakers, confectioners, &c., or, in rare cases, small businesses making skilled high-grade commodities for rich persons of taste or caprice, as in the dressmaking trades, cabinet making and other trades of an artistic character. To these must be added a great number of small businesses engaged in supplying new articles not yet so firmly planted in class standards of comfort as to furnish large regular markets. All these may be considered genuine survivals of small businesses. From them we may distinguish the small sweating business, the servile workshop of the middleman, or the small tied workshop whose survival is due to low wages, long hours, saving of business rent, and to other well-known economies of the sweating system.

Speaking generally, we may say that the typical size of a business in the manufacturing processes varies with the relative importance of the factor of capital and with the proportion of capital laid down in machinery.

§ 3.—COMMERCE AND RETAIL TRADE.—Wholesale commerce is essentially a province of large businesses. The big capitalist business has its chief origin in commerce, and until recent times was virtually confined to commerce and finance. But the older mercantile firm was often engaged in transport or in some process of manufacture which has now usually passed into a separate business. The work of buying and of selling, sorting, grading, and storing, which belongs to the wholesale merchant, is work which, to be done effectively, economically, and securely, requires a large capital. For the merchant is constantly confronted with changes of markets, he must be prepared to buy and sell large quantities of goods and to hold them when necessary, and at certain times he must be prepared to undergo heavy losses. Though there will be in some wholesale businesses a large element of regular routine, and care and foresight may greatly mitigate the risks, such businesses are essentially speculative in their single transactions, and for success require a large capital.

The growth of large departmental stores, of company enterprise in drapery, grocery, tobacco, jewellery, &c., and the establishment of large numbers of local distributing centres by great manufacturing firms, especially in the clothing trades, sufficiently illustrate the tendency of retail trade to take on large capitalist shapes. At the same time many small shops survive. Highly specialised luxury goods, sometimes involving skilled selection on the vendor's part, are still sold in Bond Street and other fashionable shopping quarters : perishable foods such as fish, fruit, vegetables, are often bought, by preference or by necessity, in neighbouring shops, and though improved facilities of communication and of distribution in large towns have taken much of this custom away from the small local shop, or have converted the latter into a mere branch store, the old condition of independence still survives for many purposes, especially in new suburbs and in slum districts. Though the spread of packet and patent goods, and in general of sales on commission, has eaten largely into the economic independence of the small shop, the full economy of capitalistic concentration is not applicable to retail trade.

ARTS AND PROFESSIONS.—Where production is required to furnish goods or services not of standard sorts, but adjusted to the particular needs or tastes of the individual consumer, machine methods and minute division of labour are not available. Even in the ordinary course of manufactures we see that small businesses survive where special orders are in question. Wherever a high degree of individual skill is imposed on the product by the demand of the consumer, an ' art ' economy is substituted for a mechanical or ' routine ' economy. This makes for the independence of the producer, involves study of individual needs and of the modes of satisfying them, inhibits the profitable use of machines whose economy consists of exact multiplication of the same productive action, involves the confinement of the worker to a small number of orders, and commonly compels him to do the whole of the productive process himself, or in case he co-operates with others, to supervise the whole and secure its unity of effect. These are the main differences between art and manufacture, and the skilful handling of any material for the satisfaction of a particular individual taste makes a fine art. Though the term ' artist ' is perhaps usually confined to those arts where the producer consults directly his own taste rather than that of the customer, or buyer, this condition is not essential to the distinction here made. The artist who works to earn a livelihood, thus falling under our broader meaning of industry, must with more or less of conscious purpose aim to satisfy the need or taste of a known or hypothetical buyer.

An artist, or in some arts a small voluntary group, always tends to be a complete business unit : the economies of large capitalism have very little direct hold upon his industry. Where the market is tolerably large and some considerable elements of routine are conveniently attached to the definitely artistic work, as, for instance, in artistic bookbinding, or lace making, or other trades where the designer requires sympathetic intelligence and manual skill of a tolerably common order to ' execute ' his creative plan, a fairly large business unit is feasible. But, the finer the art, the greater the tendency to a one-man business

The organisation of certain branches of the dramatic, musical, and literary arts into large profit-making businesses, sometimes of a highly monopolistic order, appears to infringe this law. But though a theatrical syndicate or a publishing house may be a large capitalistic operation, with subdivided labour and more or less ' tied ' artists, the latter generally retain some degree of economic liberty, their name, reputation, or talent constituting each of them a more or less separate ' business.' Though a newspaper belongs to capitalism, many of the contributors are business units, making separate sales of their output to several firms, and the same holds of painters, musicians, &c. So in the learned professions, though large capitalism or co-operative business sometimes arise, especially in the teaching and medical professions, they do not cover any large proportion of the whole, and such businesses seldom attain large proportions.

FINANCE.—Banking, broking and the whole machinery of credit, investment, and insurance, constituting the financial side of industry, has generally assumed very large business forms. The earliest forms of co-operative capitalism are found in these departments, and though for money lending, and even for insurance, small local businesses still widely survive, there is no other economic field which has fallen so largely under the control of the great capitalistic business as banking, insurance, and general finance. The rapid consolidation of banking business in Great Britain during the last two decades is a most striking exhibition of the centralising tendency in finance. Probably, for reasons which are very obvious, the staple branches of the insurance industry, life, fire, and marine, have reached the highest measure of centralised control, being vested in a small number of great businesses closely related by binding agreements regulating competition.

Summarising, then, the extent and the force of the several tendencies making respectively for large and small businesses, we perceive that in finance, transport, mining, the major branches of staple manufactures (especially those connected with textiles, metals, and buildings), and in the distribution of necessary goods and services in large towns, the economy of large businesses prevails, and the general drift has been towards an ever-increasing size. On the other hand, in agriculture, the more irregular and subsidiary branches of manufacture, over a large part of retail trade, and especially in the arts, professions, and other personal services, small business forms tend to survive in varying degrees of independence, by reason of the personal factors of individual skill, care, judgment, and character, which the nature of their material or their processes involve. But in a large proportion of the small surviving businesses, especially in those engaged in the making or the distribution of material goods, dependence upon some large, and often non-competing, business for some necessary material, for carriage or marketing of goods, or for financial assistance, tends to encroach upon the real autonomy of the small producer or employer.

CHAPTER XII

TRUSTS AND MONOPOLIES

§ 1. The size of 'the cheapest unit of production' is determined by the relative importance of (1) cost of raw materials, (2) wages, (3) standing expenses, in the several sorts of industry.—§ 2. The cheapest business unit may exceed the cheapest establishment unit. Businesses may grow beyond the unit of cheap production, seeking the largest aggregate profit. —§ 3. Trusts or combinations, largely exceeding the 'cheapest unit,' may arise, provided they have superior access to materials or power or transport, tariff supports or other legal privileges.—§ 4. The United States Steel Corporation illustrates the growth of a trust by lateral and vertical expansion. But the chief experiments of capitalism are in forms of federal business structure.—§ 5. The power of a trust or other monopoly over prices is always limited, by elasticity of demand and by substitution. Its control over labour, though great, is seldom absolute.

§ 1.—The analysis of the industrial system into industries and trades, and of these into businesses, involves, as we recognise, a good many arbitrary and somewhat artificial lines of distinction. In reality one trade often shades off gradually into another, as furnishing into building, engineering into ship building and machine-making; or trades overlap at certain places, especially those contributing to produce a single class of commodities by different processes, as in many branches of the wood and metal trades; or a number of trades are separate in some places and grouped together in other places, as in the case of spinning, weaving, dyeing, and other textile processes. In looking at the business unit we see that the criterion of independent single control is very difficult of application. The tenant-farmer on a large estate, the ' tied ' shopkeeper, the insurance agent, the workshop taking orders for repair, or making up materials given out, the Sheffield grinder hiring a room with power, the artist working for an illustrated paper, enjoy as business units varying degrees of independence. Then again, for certain purposes, a factory, a local gas or tram service, a mine or group of mines, will rank as separate businesses so far as actual industrial operations are concerned; but from the standpoint of financial and wider business control they may form parts of a bigger capitalist unit. The investors in a financial company are owners of shares in several railways, mining and land development companies; these again may not only work other businesses subsidiary to their main employment, but they may invest their reserves in various outside industries. Even where the whole of the factors directly employed in the processes of a business are owned and controlled by the persons co-operating in that business, the actual or con-tractual dependence of the ' firm ' upon some producer of raw material, or some merchant, or some machine-makers exacting royalties, or upon other firms with which it has made agreements regarding output and prices, may restrict to an indefinite extent its real economic independence as a separate industrial unit. This reticulation of business interests and overlapping ownership of one or other of the factors of production in a business render it impossible to mark out a clear logical distinction of the term ' business,' though it is impossible to dispense with the term in any industrial analysis. This caution is particularly needed in the task to which I now address myself, viz. the consideration of the factors which determine the normal size of business tending to prevail in various industries.

Let us approach the problem first in relation to the ex-penses of production in an ordinary manufacturing business, i.e. a business comprising a single plant and competing freely with others to turn out some standard order of commodities for common use.

The factors in ' expenses ' or ' costs ' [1] of production may be placed under three heads :—

(1) Cost of raw materials.

(2) Productive wages, i.e. wages of persons directly employed by the business firm in handling the materials used in the manu-facture.

(3) Standing expenses, virtually inclusive of all other expenses incidental to manufacture and to buying and selling. This will usually include rent of premises, upkeep of machinery and other plant, motor power, lighting and heating, general care of premises, superintendence, office expenses, travellers, advertisement, in a word all expenses which are not appreciably affected by the gain or loss of any particular order, but are involved in the general process of keeping the business going.[2]

---

[1] Here once more business usage requires us, for immediate analysis, to identify ' costs ' and ' expenses.'

[2] (1) and (2) are commonly taken as ' prime cost.' As regards individual orders, the manufacturer looks to the difference between ' prime cost ' and selling price to see whether the order is worth acceptance, and not to the ' net profit,' which would require him to take into account standing expenses, though of course some dim reference to the latter will be present. In other

With regard to (1) cost of raw materials, though a small business may often be at a disadvantage, both in knowledge of markets and in the financial ability to use it, a medium-sized business can usually buy as cheaply and as well as a large one.

' If a manufacturer is purchasing raw material, there is generally a market price for it which all must pay, and which any one can obtain it for, so long as he buys the customary minimum quantity ; while, if what he requires is a partly manufactured article, purchases amounting in value to hundreds of pounds per annum, accompanied by prompt payment, can generally be made at the cheapest possible rate. The sole advantage enjoyed by the largest concerns in the purchase of raw materials seems to me to lie in the possibility of occasionally clearing the market of raw materials or of a surplus output of partly manufactured stuff, by some purchase quite out of the power of a smaller concern to compass. Such an operation, however, partakes of the nature of a speculation, and the profit, when gained, is hardly to be called a cheapening of the cost of production, if only for the reason that the opportunity for such a special purchase cannot be relied upon to occur very often, and when it does occur is perhaps as likely to result in a loss as in a gain.' [1]

(2) In regard to productive wages as an expense of production the question is, of course, of the limits of economy of division of labour. In most manufacturing industries there is a size of factory large enough to admit full differentiation, and so to enable every worker to confine himself to the work he can do best. In cotton spinning or weaving this may be attained in a factory employing some 200 or 300 persons. In a great engineering firm 1000 men or more may be required to secure the full economy of sub-divided labour in a more or less elastic business.

Every sort of business will have its own special limit : any increase in number of employees beyond that limit will not be advantageous, for, although some further gains may accrue from finer division of labour, they will be relatively small and progressively smaller, and will be more than balanced by waste in supervision and management, and in enforced idleness during slack times.

words, while net profit is his general motive in business, his specific calculation for each job is upon a basis of gross profit, i.e. margin between prime cost and selling price. (The analysis of manufacturing economy here adopted is largely taken from or founded on the able pamphlets and articles of Mr. W. R. Hamilton, F.C.A., to whom I am also indebted for valuable private information.)
[1] W. R. Hamilton, *The Cost of Production in Relation to an Increasing Output* (p. 3).

(3) The chief economy of large-scale production is often found in 'standing expenses.' Many elements in this outlay, superintendence, office expenses, advertising, travelling, expenses of plant, seem nearly as great for a small as for a large business, and a further enlargement does not appear to involve a proportionate addition to those charges.

But this notion is largely false, attributable to the customary point of view from which the manager regards a single new order or contract. This he commonly considers can be carried out without any appreciable addition to his 'standing expenses,' and he will undertake it, if it leaves a margin over 'prime cost' in materials and wages. But this disregard of 'standing expenses,' legitimate in a single concrete instance, is quite inapplicable to a general business economy. If one new order after another be added to the output of any plant, the time will come when new, sudden, large alterations or additions to plant, buildings, staff and other standing expenses must be made.

'If the items which make up the standing expenses be looked at in detail, it will be seen that in each case there comes a point at which the utmost efficiency is gained, and that this point often comes at a very early stage. A certain size is necessary that there may be due sub-division compatible with superintendence, and that the general factory staff—engine drivers, time-keepers, store-keepers, and the like—may be fully employed.

'As for the plant, the essential point is that the number of machines of each description be such that each is fully employed. When this is achieved, no further reduction in that item is possible. As for the factory building—or shops or sheds, whichever it may be—there is a size which is convenient and workable, and to increase this size is only to build another factory. Capital invested in stock and book debts bears a fixed relation to his turnover, and a large business, contrasted with a small one, neither gains nor loses.' [1]

In regarding the economy of production in a single factory or other plant, it appears that each of the three elements in 'cost' favours a different maximum size. A business with an output of twenty units may have virtually attained the full economy in prices of raw materials ; but it may require an output of thirty to reach the full economy of division of productive labour, an output of forty for best economy of superintendence, of fifty for the cheapest advertising and marketing.

If this is so, a pooling of these several economies, in accordance with the relative importance attaching to them in each particular

---

[1] *The Cost of Production* (pp. 8 and 9).

sort of business, will determine the most economical size of business
—the ' Unit of Cheap Production '—where ' operatives, foremen,
management, office staff, selling agents, all co-operate to the best
of their ability with each other, and with capital in the shape of
factory, plant and credit to one end.'

§ 2.—In thus recognising, however, the natural limits of this
economy of the ' cheapest unit of production,' we have not found
the maximum size to which a business tends to grow.

For a single plant or establishment is not necessarily co-extensive
with a business. A capital of £30,000 with a staff of 300 operatives
may be the ' cheapest unit ' in a textile trade. This may limit the
size of a single plant, but certain special economies may make for
the growth of joint-stock businesses possessing and operating a
number of such plants. The business unit may be indefinitely
larger than the establishment unit.

In trades where large changes of business policy are essential to
success, where the rapid execution of large sudden orders, the supply
of a great variety of goods produced by different processes, large
credit, great proportionate expenditure on advertising and on
marketing are necessary, the most economical size of a business
may enormously exceed that of a single productive plant. It is,
in fact, these and similar considerations which make for the growth
and survival of gigantic businesses in many staple manufacturing
industries. Wherever credit and other financial operations become
of the first importance in business success, the economical business
unit tends to great magnitude.

It is the economy of finance, and of industrial policy closely
associated with finance, that makes for those largest modern
businesses which express the full tendency to concentration of
capital.

But before considering more fully this tendency, we must carry
a step further our analysis of the maximum unit of business efficiency
As there is in a trade some fairly fixed limit to the size of a plant,
say £30,000. so it would seem there must be some limit to the size
of a business operating a number of such plants. Beyond a certain
point, say ten plants, no further large economy of credit, advertising, marketing, &c., is available, while central management would
grow weaker and the essential irregularity of demand would cause
a larger waste from slackness of employment : £300,000 would in
such cases appear to constitute the business unit of maximum
efficiency. This would be the size that would yield the largest
margin or rate of profit on its invested capital.

But does it follow that a business which has grown to this size
will not tend to grow any further, and that in this industry the

evolution of the business is towards a number of competing units of £300,000 each ? Given full freedom of competition, it would appear that no business either smaller or larger than this size could survive, and that all the productive-power in the industry must come to group itself in businesses of £300,000.

But no such freedom of competition is anywhere operative, and both larger and smaller business units can survive. The case of survivors of smaller businesses need not detain us long : it is due to the fact that they do not come into really close competition with the large business, but make use of special advantages of a more or less adventitious kind. A small high-grade business, in a trade mainly occupied by large businesses, may hold its own by some speciality, or by looking out for small profitable jobs and ' picking its market.' Some buyers prefer to deal with a small concern over which they can exercise special influence, getting extra quick delivery and particular variations in design or make-up, or something else which it would not be possible to procure from a large house.   In this way a good deal of the very best and most profitable work may remain in the hands of small businesses competently managed.

So in a fairly conservative industry a few small businesses may survive, their owners preferring a safe, good business of moderate size with a high rate of profit to a larger, more speculative business with a bigger aggregate profit earned on a narrower margin between ' costs ' and selling prices. In point of fact, however, it is rare and difficult for any sound business in a progressive industry to refuse orders, and to resist the temptation to expand and to extend, even though such increase means more risk and a lower average rate of profit on the larger business.

In strict economic theory it is no doubt impossible to extend the size of a business beyond the unit of cheap production, the £300,000 of our manufacturing company ; for a number of businesses which have reached that size will, by competing, bring prices down so that the profits are at a minimum.   But in point of fact this theoretic condition is seldom attained in a progressive industry. Where modern mechanical and business improvements are continually occurring, the best-equipped businesses, which have reached the unit, will not be cutting prices so as to earn a mere minimum of profits: each of them will, for a time at any rate, be earning a surplus rate of gain, and will be driven into expanding and undertaking further orders, even though this course involves enlargement beyond the unit of cheap production. Nor, in point of fact, is such enlargement necessarily foolish from the profit-making standpoint. For we must distinguish the unit of cheap production where the highest *rate of profit* is got from the unit which, with a lower rate, yields a *larger aggregate profit*.

A business which has been earning 12 per cent. on its invested capital of £300,000 may grow to £500,000, if it can earn 9 per cent. on this large capital.

Since it is aggregate profit, at any rate above the minimum, rather than the highest rate of profit in itself, that furnishes the business motive to business men, it is evident that economic forces may thus drive businesses into sizes larger than the cheapest unit of production.

This growth of uneconomically large businesses will normally occur in an industry where such growth may itself become an instrument for repressing competition, and so for preventing such a fall of prices as will lower profits to a minimum. In other words, if a manufacturing business, which in its ' cheapest unit of production' size, at £300,000, is subject to keen competition (because at such a size it cannot command the market), finds that, by doubling its size, or by combining with a competitor of the same size, it can absolutely or partially control the market, it will be profitable to make this enlargement, because, by holding up prices, it can thus secure a larger aggregate profit than by remaining at the ' cheapest unit of production ' size.

If it were impossible for a business to grow beyond the ' cheapest unit of production ' without suffering loss, our industrial system would possess an automatic check against monopolies, at any rate in most industries in large states. For unless this ' cheapest unit ' was so large as to enable one such business to supply the whole market, competition must occur. If, for instance, the ' cheapest unit ' in all the textile industries did not exceed £300,000, or in the metal industries £500,000, the competition of businesses endowed with this maximum efficiency would prevent the growth of any ' trust ' or unified business which could monopolise any market in these industries. There might be trades of secondary or tertiary rank where the ' cheapest unit ' was large enough to secure a monopoly, at any rate in a ' protected ' country, though the tenure even of such monopolies would be precarious. But in the markets for staple commodities it would be very unlikely that the ' cheapest unit ' would be large enough to hold the market.

§ 3.—How then, it may be asked, does it arise that large national, or in a few instances, world markets fall under the control of a single business corporation ? How is the actual size and power of the great manufacturing ' trust ' consistent with the doctrine of ' cheapest unit of production ' ? The answer is twofold. In the first place, by confining our analysis hitherto to units of manufacturing production we have ignored certain factors which, combined with manufacturing economies, tend often to enlarge the ' cheapest unit of production.'

Everyone knows that it is not the economy of large production in manufacture that accounts for the power and magnitude of the Standard Oil Company, or the Sugar Trust, or the United States Steel Corporation. Inquiry into the history of these or any other ' monopolies ' indicates that their profitable growth, extending far beyond the ' cheapest unit ' for manufacture, rests upon superior access to raw materials, or power, superior facilities of transport, tariffs, bounties or other legal privileges, patents or special secret processes.

Of these supports the transport industry is the most important. It is in this branch of industry that the economic conditions favour so large a type of business as to make normally for monopoly. There is only one shortest road between any two points. From this indisputable fact proceeds the chief economy of the large over the small transport business by land. The railroad, or the pipe line, which is best laid, has a natural advantage, enabling it to undersell would-be competitors and to increase its size of business until it has a monopoly. Even sea-transport is in part subjected to similar restrictions, favouring the growth of shipping companies which have secured the best terminal connexions with railroads, preferential dock and coal accommodation, &c.

These advantages are, in the case of railroads and sometimes of shipping companies, secured and enhanced by charters or governmental subsidies, which, assisting them to keep out competitors, enable them to grow until they have more or less absorbed entire markets for carriage of goods and passengers. When it is considered that in these great transport industries the genuine economies of large capitalist enterprise would in themselves tend towards a very big type of profitable business, we perceive how the natural and legal supports enable great transport companies to wield large monopoly powers over great areas of land and sea.

Whenever, then, a manufacturing business can either procure such transport-power as an appendage to its productive processes, or can make agreements with carrying companies which give it an advantage, the profitable size of such a business may be raised so as to enable it to control the market for its products. Most very large manufacturing businesses, which transcend the mere economy of large-scale production, derive part, if not most, of their strength from their superior control of transport facilities, either for raw materials and fuel, or for their product.

Most of the greatest manufacturing businesses are seen stretching out to strengthen themselves by owning their own railway cars and other transport facilities, sometimes their own coal mines and natural supplies of other raw materials, or securing contracts for the carriage of their goods which give them an advantage over actual or possible competitors.

But while some classes of business in the transport industries, in mining, manufacture, and finance, which are enabled in some measure to control a market, may thus largely outgrow the ' unit of cheapest production,' the main tendency at the present time is towards a federal type of business organisation which, without departing widely from the ' economic unit,' so far as its individual members are concerned, shall by regulation of output and of selling prices, and by such control of the market for materials, labour, and transport as its new condition enables it to secure, maintain monopoly rates of profit for large masses of capital grouped in businesses of an economical size.

In a few instances, relying upon one or more of the external supports I have named, a single business will bloat itself out, absorbing other businesses, until it controls a market, and maintaining a size, as a single unit, which, so far as efficiency of production goes, is excessive.   But in most branches of industry, especially in staple manufactures, where no business enjoys any marked superiority of external support, businesses tend towards federal union rather than towards a single centralised government.   The typical product of modern capitalism is a ' combine ' between businesses of efficient size, which retain a large measure of independence in management and methods of production, but present a common front to the consumer and to sellers of materials and labour-power, as well as to the political government.

This is no proper place to enter on a close investigation into the various forms of ' combine,' from the strong federation or ' trust ' to the cartel, ring, pool, alliance, conference, association, and agreement, which are operative in so many of the great manufacturing, transport, mercantile, and financial industries in every advanced nation.   All these may be regarded as experiments in a federal type of business, based on a desire to combine the efficiency of the ' cheapest unit of production ' with certain managerial, financial, and political advantages accruing from federal unity, so securing regulation of competition and a corresponding control of markets.   In different trades, in different countries, and at different times, different types of federal union emerge ; in some there is no stability of structure, and they soon disappear, as in the case of the Birmingham alliance ; in others, weak agreements on price lists give place to closer and more enduring associations, such as the steel rail association and the conferences in the railroad, shipping, and insurance trades. The coal and iron cartels of Germany and Austria, with their selling syndicates, their elaborate regulations of output and prices, accompanied by regular inspection of accounts, and fines for breaches of agreements, are important experiments in a new business structure, especially accommodated to trades whose local conditions differ very widely. In manufactures of standard articles by routine methods the tendency is towards closer union ; and bodies like the United States Steel Corporation are seeking after new methods of combining local independence and stimulus, for individual establishments in a variety of related trades, with a general trade policy and a strong central finance.

§ 4.—If, then, we so modify the popular conception of a business as to make it cover every arrangement of economic forces which operates as a single unit in a market, we perceive that the limits which appeared to be set by economy of production on a single factory, farm, mine, shop, or other plant may be enormously exceeded by various systems of federating such productive units under a single commercial and financial control.

The growing size and complexity of the business structure thus evolving is based upon the following considerations :—

(1) The unit of cheapest production in a single productive process ;

(2) The group of units of cheapest production under a single 'company' ;

(3) The linkage of several such groups or companies in a single trade or process, either by amalgamation or by agreements of various degrees of stringency ;

(4) The inclusion in a single commercial and financial control of groups of productive units in the related processes of production and of distribution of a class of commodities.

The double process of expansion here indicated may be illustrated best in actual industry by the United States Steel Corporation, in the class of strong 'federal' business. Here are groupings of (1) plants in the extractive processes engaged in producing raw materials and power; (2) plants in the several transport industries with subsidiary processes; (3) plants in the several processes of manufacture, showing widening diversity as they approach the final stage of manufacture.

UNITED STATES STEEL CORPORATION.

Iron Ore Coal Mines Coke Natural Gas	Railroads Ships Docks, &c.	Blast Furnaces	Rolling Mills Furnaces, &c.	Steel { Hoops Rails Wire Tubes Tinplate Bridges Cars Elevators Electric works, &c.

The properties owned were described (1905) officially as follows : ' seventy-eight blast furnaces, with a capacity of upwards of 6,500,000 tons of pig iron yearly, or half that of the United States in 1900 ; 149 steel works and 6 finishing plants, including bar mills, standard steel and plate mills, with an annual capacity of about 9,000,000 tons of finished material ; 18,300 coke ovens ; about 70 per cent. of the ore mines of the Lake Superior region, producing, in 1900, 12,724,900 tons ; 70,830 acres of coal land, about 30,000 acres of surface lands in the coke region, and 125 lake vessels, &c.'

In Great Britain and in Germany there are several instances of great engineering companies which upon a smaller scale have attained a similar structure ; and such railroad companies as the L. & N. W. and the Midland have absorbed a long continuous series of productive processes, which furnish the greater part of their larger material requirements.

It is not possible to determine the limits of the centralising tendency, how far in the several departments of large capitalist industry it is driving towards such complete financial and commercial unity of control as is illustrated in the United States Steel Corporation, or in any of the genuine trusts, or how far it will reach its limits of economy in some such looser form of federation as is represented in a ' cartel,' a ' conference,' or other agreement, with some machinery for securing community of interest and unity of policy in markets.

In Great Britain the present stage is one of experimentation in trade agreements allowing a maximum of independence in the businesses. But in most cases the need of a stronger federal control to prevent under-cutting, secret rebates, and other breaches of the spirit, or even the letter of the agreement, is becoming evident. The regulation of output and of selling prices is, of course, the direct aim of all such agreements ; though the federal machinery may also be used for controlling markets for raw materials, for bargaining with labour and with carrying companies, and for securing legal and other governmental assistance.

It is difficult to say what, if any, economic limit can be assigned to the size of such ' federal businesses.' Yet from the standpoint of the practical problem of distribution this is a most momentous question. For if, when there is a natural limit to the size of a single productive plant, or even of a single business in the old sense of that term, there is no such practical limit to the growth of a federation of businesses, it seems more and more certain that this large federal structure of capitalist forces will be utilised to secure control of markets and that possession of the ' surplus product ' which such control entails. The survivals of the competitive system will be more and more devoted to a struggle for the evolution, in the several departments of industry, of that special type of federation which is best adapted to the conditions of the trade and country. In some trades a close amalgamation of capital and business control may prevail, in others a simple federal instrument for enforcing a profitable scale of selling prices.

The general law will be that the processes, where mechanical routine methods can be best applied to the supply of standard articles for large regular consumption, will fall under a closer federal unity, while those processes where irregularity of materials or of working interfere with ' standardisation,' and require more elasticity of local management, will remain under a looser federal government.

But while an important limit seems thus set upon the federal tendency, it must be borne in mind that, when any instrument has been evolved for a particular use; there is a disposition to apply it to other uses, and to strengthen it so as to make it thus available. So here, though the *raison d'être* of a business federation is control of selling prices, the advantages of common action in dealing with markets for raw materials, for power, for machinery, and above all for resisting the demands of organised labour using trade unionism and politics to gain their ends, will certainly dispose the federal businesses to assume larger functions and to require larger powers for exercising them.

The naïve economic theory, therefore, which, based upon the operation of a so-called law of diminishing returns, adduced the limits to the profitable growth of a single business as a sufficient preventive of monopolies, at any rate in a nation allowing free imports, must be set aside. We cannot, of course, assert that there is no limit whatever to the economic size even of a federal business. It might be the case that the growing size of a federation of diverse businesses in a long and complicated series of related processes would reach a point when federal control became so difficult and so inefficient as to invite the competition of some smaller and more efficient capitalist structure. At any given time it cannot be denied that there must be some theoretic limit to the economy of such federal control. But from the standpoint of protection against monopoly, the question is whether this theoretic limit stands upon one side of ' monopoly ' or upon the other.

Now upon this point the weight of evidence afforded by recent experience in the most developed industrial countries of Europe and America seems to support the following judgment. Where a large amalgamation or federation of businesses attempts to secure so strong a control of markets as to raise or maintain a rate of profits higher than commonly obtains, without the support of any monopoly of natural resources, or preferential facilities of transport or protection or other State aid in its markets, it generally fails. There are, indeed, a few instances of trades of secondary and tertiary importance where a control of the market appears to have been maintained by pure force of business organisation in manufacturing processes, without any large assistance from any of the above-named sources. Perhaps the International Sewing Thread Trust is the most conspicuous instance of a ' monopoly ' which appears to rest upon the economy of concentrated capital and centralised control. But all the great American trusts or ' combines ' which have shown a marked ability to retain a control of markets and prices are known to owe their origin or their maintenance of power to superiority of natural resources, railroad aid, or tariffs, bounties or other governmental assistance. Most of them enjoy more than one of these external aids. When a number of related processes of manufacture or of transport are involved, the control of, or preference in, any single indispensable process is, of course, sufficient to yield a power of monopoly. It is this consideration which plays so prominent a part in building up the strength of such a powerful trust as the Standard Oil Company and of the Carnegie Steel and Iron Company, out of which the later Steel Trust grew. Preferential rates and facilities of railroad transport were the instruments by which these trusts gained a position which afterwards they were enabled to secure and strengthen by tariff supports and control of raw materials.

A tariff is more rightly regarded as the foster-mother than the mother of trusts, unless, indeed, as in the Steel Trade of Canada, a bounty accompanies the tariff. But in not a few instances it is likely that, growing by normal processes up to its limit of efficiency in size, it is enabled by a tariff which excludes foreign competition to obtain so effective a control of the home market that it can profitably exceed the unit of efficiency which would be its limit under the pressure of competition. The high prices secured by a sufficient control of the home market raise the unit of maximum aggregate profits above the unit of maximum profits under competition.

§ 5.—This brief sketch of the natural history of trusts, combines, and federal businesses suffices to explain the origin and nature of those great business units or combinations which, in many fields of manufacture, transport, commerce, and finance are seen exercising a control over prices that enables them to take large surplus gains over and above the normal interest and profit.

The so-called law of diminishing returns, which simply means the fact that there is some limit to the economical development of every business structure, is not in effect operative in this class of businesses, which by skilled decentralisation of administration on the one hand, and by monopoly of market on the other, can continue to grow, earning an increasing aggregate of profits.

So far as monopoly of market and consequent enhancement of prices is concerned, there are, of course, limits to the use of such a power.

There is no such thing as complete monopoly, and if there were, except in the case of an absolute necessary of life, such monopoly would not mean an unlimited power over selling prices.

For a substantial control of market and of prices it is often sufficient for a business to be by far the largest single seller. In England it has commonly been held that a minimum of 70 per cent. of the trade is indispensable to the success of a combination or amalgamation ; but this is evidently a question of the sort of trade, the relative strength of the remaining outside firms, and the distribution of the control over the several local or industrial sections of the market. It would probably be unsafe for a trust commanding even three-quarters of the entire market to leave another free business in undisputed control of a local market covering 20 per cent. of the whole and able to make encroachments beyond its borders. But even the strongest trusts have their market limits. The Standard Oil Company, for instance, upon its reconstruction in 1899 claimed only to produce about 65 per cent. of the country's total output of refined oil, though its proportionate hold over the Eastern and middle Western States was far larger than this percentage.

But apart from the check through the survival of free businesses (which is often weakened by the fact that the latter may, and often do, prefer to let the trust fix profitable prices, which they adopt, and upon which they thrive), there are two other checks on the power of a ' monopoly ' over prices. One is contained in the elasticity of demand, which in every case affords a natural limitation on the power of raising prices. A monopolist must be careful not to spoil his market by excessive prices, and to calculate carefully what price will give him the largest aggregate profits.

The other check is afforded by the possibilities of substitution. In each of its main uses as illuminant, motor, lubricant, &c., oil competes with other articles, and the possibility of recourse to some alternative article qualifies every monopoly.

The profitable nature of a monopoly, however, depends not merely on the strength of its control over selling prices, but upon its power to keep down expenses of production. If it is strong enough, or sufficiently well placed, to control the market for raw materials and fuel, to get cheap freight, to dispense with competitive expenses, and to dictate its own terms for the hire of labour, the margin between expenses and selling prices will be larger and aggregate profits will rise correspondingly. The power of a trust or other 'combine' over the market for raw materials and for labour will correspond in general with its control of selling prices, though the existence of alternative uses will qualify this power.

The history of the dealings of the Standard Oil Company with the owners of oil lands in Ohio and elsewhere, of the Sugar Trust with the sugar growers, and the acquisition of ore mines by the Steel Trust, illustrate the economy of trust administration through control of raw materials.

The power over the labour market possessed by a trust will, of course, depend, not merely upon the degree of the monopoly it wields, but upon the amount of specialised skill and other particular conditions which are attached to the labour.

In a skilled trade where there is only one employer, a trust or combination, the workman must accept any terms of labour which are preferable to seeking employment in the unskilled labour market. The ordinary routine worker in a highly elaborated modern works is upon the whole less competent than any other class to transfer his labour-power without loss to another trade. Now it is in such trades that trusts and combinations most flourish, and the fact gives them a power in bargaining with labour far greater than is possessed in a competitive trade, where rival firms are apt to be confronted by a single trade union or federation of trade unions.

Various considerations, however, may temper the use of the superior power of bargaining with labour. Trusts and combines have in some instances recognised the advantage of a liberal treatment of employees by introducing an element of 'profit-sharing,' or other preferential payment, which shall have the effect of detaching their employees from the general labour market and of securing industrial peace. It is also claimed, apparently with good reasons, that some trusts, notoriously the Standard Oil Company and the Steel Trust, recognise more fully than other firms the economy of high wages for their more skilled and responsible employees. But the conditions recently prevailing among large bodies of less skilled employees, in so strong a monopoly as the anthracite coal trade, indicate that the workers in general have no security of any share in the economy of industrial monopoly.

In rare instances, where the specialised skill in a monopolised trade is powerfully organised, it may pay the employer to purchase industrial peace by giving the employees a share of the monopoly profits, or even to organise a joint-trust of capital and labour, as was tried in the Birmingham alliances, and as has been more than once proposed in the South Wales coal trade. The recent development of a policy of fiscal protection in Australia and elsewhere, designed to secure preferential conditions for the workers in protected trades, points to the possibility of substituting inter-trade antagonisms for the conflict between capital and labour in the several trades. This consideration belongs, however, to the future rather than the present.

CHAPTER XIII

THE LABOUR MOVEMENT

§ 1. Inadequate defences for trade unionism are found in 'the economy of high wages' and the alleged power to give labour a share in 'booms.' —§ 2. So far as minimum costs are concerned, there is harmony of capital and labour, though labour is not necessarily precluded from pressing for rises of wages.—§ 3. The surplus forms the economic objective of the labour movement. Where it arises labour can get some of it, if strongly organised. Such surplus, got by labour, will usually be productive of efficiency.—§ 4. The endeavour to get surplus is the main motive of labour-politics, and social reforms are chiefly valued as strengthening the power of collective bargaining.

§ 1.—THE commonly accepted interpretation of the working of the industrial system under competition furnishes no adequate or even intelligible theory of the labour movement. If the normal working of the system is such as to keep interest, profits, and all payments for ability at a minimum, any temporary rise acting as a bare incentive to evoke an increased application of ability and capital so as to secure industrial progress, while rent consists entirely of differential payments which do not affect price, then the labour movement, so far as it aims at the improvement of the economic condition of labour as a whole, has no real validity. If no general fund exists which can be diverted from some other form of surplus income into wages, trade unionism becomes a mere device for adding to certain well-organised groups of workers a scarcity wage paid by less favourably placed workers. For if the higher wages which organisation seems able to secure do not come out of rents or other 'surplus' otherwise taken by other factors than labour, they must come out of enhanced prices for the goods which they assist to produce, and these higher prices will hit hardest the weakest and worst-paid workers. Again, effective organisation implies a policy of exclusiveness achieved by apprentice rules, entrance fees, and other regulations, all of which help to keep the labour markets for less organised trades in a chronic state of over supply and so keep wages at a bare subsistence point. If, then, no surplus exists which labour can secure by organisation, trade unionism inflicts a twofold damage on the unorganised workers, keeping down their wages and raising the prices they must pay for goods produced under trade union conditions.

There are two ways by which advocates of trade unionism have sometimes sought to extricate themselves from this dilemma. One is the assertion that trade unionism and the higher wages and other more expensive conditions it extorts so increase the efficiency of labour as to furnish an extra-product. In other words, the trade union helps to induce employers to adopt the enlightened economy of high wages. But we have already seen that this doctrine cannot be promiscuously applied, so as to support the view that every improvement in pay and other conditions of labour will be attended by a corresponding rise in efficiency and output. Even in public employments, where the full efficiency of the worker and his family falls within the business outlook, some limits are prescribed by considerations of the public purse and the class standard of comfort. In private competitive industry closer limits must be assigned to the practice of the economy of high wages. It is not to be argued seriously that trade unionism is merely engaged in levelling up the efficiency of labour, and in taking, by higher wages, shorter hours and other improvements of working life, the product of this higher level of efficiency. The enemies of trade unionism indeed contend that by restricting employers in selection of operatives, number of apprentices, the introduction and working of machinery, and in particular by agreements to limit the output of labour-power, the trade union makes not for enhanced but for reduced efficiency. But while the exact measure of truth contained in this view need not be discussed here, it may, I think, be confidently asserted that neither the theory nor the practice of trade unionism can be or is in fact defensible as a policy merely based on the application of the economy of high wages, or any other doctrine which implies that the gain a trade union can secure for its members is measured by and is contingent upon the increased productivity of the labour-power which they give out.

The other widely prevalent ' compromise ' view limits the efficacy of trade unionism to its ability to accelerate the pace of a natural economic movement which would secure to labour its share in a spell of prosperous trade. A new invention or other industrial improvement, coming into general use and lowering the expenses of production, may for a time increase the margin between ' costs ' and ' selling prices ' ; or a large expansion of demand, raising market prices, may create a highly profitable state of trade. Though competition of employers, stimulated by the rise of profits, would in the ordinary course of things cause wages to rise in such a trade, each employer seeking to increase his business and his output, and new capital flowing in to share the abnormal gains, this rise of wages may be delayed if no organisation of the workers exists to take advantage of the situation. Where a strong union exists, it will be harder to resist a demand for higher wages when the profitable condition of the trade enables them to be paid, and the higher wages will become operative at once over the entire trade instead of being secured in driblets. To this it is sometimes added that trade unionism can delay a reduction of wages when a trade becomes depressed, by deterring firms from accepting contracts at prices which can only pay on condition that wages are already lowered.

This defence of the use of trade unionism, so far as it is valid, implies the existence of short-time surpluses which, passing in the first instance to ' capital,' can be secured by labour where it is strong enough. But it can hardly be put forward as a sufficient economic basis of trade unionism that it exists to enable certain groups of workers to get their share of a boom a little earlier than they would otherwise have done. It does not, moreover, enable them to hold it, for, according to this theory of distribution, competition of employers will soon bring about a fall of selling prices which will hand over the ' surplus' to the consumer. In this event, though the worker may continue to get some gain in his capacity of consumer, since it is spread over the whole consuming public, it will be much smaller than when it was held in higher money wages, and, moreover, his trade unionism is in no sense the instrument which has secured for him this permanent benefit.

Finally, if the only effective function of trade unionism is to force the pace by which the gains of industrial improvements thus pass to the consumer, or to interpose a period during which they are held by the employees as high wages, there is some weight in the objection that trade unionism, by curtailing the time during which progressive employers reap the reward of their superior efficiency, may damage industrial progress. If the high rates of profit which accrue to ably-conducted businesses, either through the adoption of improved methods of production, or through occasional ' booms ' of trade, are in reality necessary inducements to evoke the output of ability and enterprise, considerable danger may attach to a labour movement which seeks continually to raid this fund of progress, in the interests of a particular body of labourers, who cannot claim it on the ground that they have created it, or that they need it more than the labourers in other trades.

§ 2.—Our fundamental distinction between necessary costs and unproductive surplus affords to the labour movement an economic basis which it otherwise lacks, furnishing an intelligible and consistent theory alike of the harmony and the antagonism of capital and labour.

We have recognised that in any trade at any time there is a minimum rate of interest and of profit necessary to maintain its capital and managing ability, and that similarly there is a wage of minimum efficiency which any intelligent employer will pay to the various grades of labour he requires. If, in a trade, the competition between businesses is such as to enable them to pay these minimum expenses of capital and labour, leaving no surplus, it would appear as if the harmony between employer and employee were complete. Any attempt of a trade union in such a trade to extort a higher rate of wages, involving a reduction of interest or profit below the necessary margin of subsistence, would react detrimentally upon wages by starving the trade in capital and ability. Similarly an attempt of the employers to reduce wages would, by impairing efficiency of labour, prove suicidal. So far as these minimum costs are concerned, the interests of employer and employed are identical.

Those to whom this condition appears the normal one conclude that the conflicts between capital and labour are due, either to ignorance, or to perversity of temper on the part of one or both of the combatants. But this is not necessarily true. Even in the case of a trade where prices only suffice to pay a minimum wage and a minimum interest and profit, a forward labour policy may be economically justifiable. For it may be feasible and advantageous to labour, by securing a rise of wages, to force a rise of selling prices. The power of organised labour to prevent a fall of wages, contemplated as a result of acceptance of contracts to deliver goods at lower prices, has often been tested, and is admitted. It is evident that, where a labour organisation is strong enough, it can in a particular trade exercise a similar power to compel a rise of prices adequate to allow a higher rate of wages, provided that its power extends to all or ' nearly all ' businesses contributing to the supply. A trade union of local bakers can often enforce their demand for higher wages through a rise of prices. The South Wales miners exercise a similar though a more restricted power. An important check upon the use of such a power, of course, exists in the effect of the rise of prices upon demand. Where demand is so elastic that even a small rise of price diminishes appreciably the sale, this economic weapon of trade unionism may be of very slight avail. In any event its use must be sparing, and it cannot apply where foreign or other non-union competition enters in.

But there remains another mode of pressure. A trade paying

a minimum rate of profit and interest may be paying a scarcity price for one of its factors of production, some raw materials, or patent, fuel, transport, or other service, the sellers of which are monopolists in the sense in which we use that term. In other words, there may be some expense of production which contains, in the price paid for it by the trade in question, an element of unproductive ' surplus.' Mining rents and royalties form such surplus elements in the expenses of collieries ; a rise of miners' wages, obtained at a time when mining profits could not bear the advance, and when it would not be advantageous to raise the price of coal, would tend to bring about a reduction of such rents and royalties and would actually do so whenever renewals of mining leases occurred. In manufactures, where power was bought from a company or a public body at monopoly prices, or where expensive machinery was subject to royalties, or where some trust or combination made high profits by controlling the supply of raw materials, the surplus element in any of these ' expenses of production ' would be exposed to attack where labour was strong enough to extort a rise of wages in the trade into which they entered as factors. The force would operate in this wise. A railroad company having a monopoly of the carriage of goods in a manufacturing trade, or the machine company which rents to the trade some necessary machines, has been charging rates calculated on ' what the trade will bear.' Now a strong trade union has raised wages so that the trade can no longer bear the former rates or royalties. Unless concessions are made by the railroad or the machine-makers, the manufacturers cannot pay a living profit and must decline and gradually perish. Such concessions can and will be made, for it will not pay to charge the manufacture ' more than it can bear.' Hence it is sometimes possible for a labour movement to force a rise of wages, or to resist a fall, even though the existing rate of profits in the trade is standing at a minimum, provided that there is some factor in the expenses of production of the trade that is weighted with an unproductive surplus.

But, of course, the main economic justification of the labour movement, in its efforts to secure higher wages, shorter hours, improved hygienic and other conditions, all of which raise the wages bill, consists in the fact that, in many trades at all times and in most trades at certain times, the margin between necessary expenses of production and selling prices affords a net interest or profit higher than is needed to remunerate capital and management. Our analysis of the industrial system has led us to the conclusion that the employing and organising classes, by command of natural resources or by contrivance, are normally in a state of scarcity or restricted competition over large sections of the field of industry, and that this position of vantage enables them to buy the labour, frequently the capital, and sometimes the natural agents they require so cheaply, and to regulate the prices of the goods they make and sell so successfully, that they can maintain a margin of profit containing a considerable unproductive surplus.

This surplus element is frequently concealed in watered capital or in high directors' or managers' fees or bonuses, and sometimes it is frittered away by the loose management which is liable to occur in protected businesses : much of it may not be represented in the actual interest received annually by shareholders, but may have been extracted beforehand by the promoters of a business, or by sales at a premium by original shareholders. In these and other ways ' surplus ' is concealed. But wherever such surpluses exist they form an object of attack for the labour movement, for, since they are *ex hypothesi* unnecessary or excessive payments, taken by capital because they can be got, they can be secured by labour in higher wages or other improvements of conditions, if labour is strong enough. Wherever a trade is, by its possession of some permanent source of strength, such as monopoly of natural resources, legal monopoly, transport preference, in a position to earn continuously a surplus rate of profit, this surplus is a standing challenge to labour.

Whenever a trade, normally subject to such competition as keeps down profits near the minimum, is lifted for a while into the possession of such a surplus by a temporary boom, labour is often able to share the gain by organised pressure. Here, however, an objection is raised which deserves recognition. In an essentially speculative or a fluctuating trade, where periods of boom and depression are normal features of the trade, it might be an unsound policy for a trade union to endeavour to secure in high wages a surplus which was economically needed to set off a previous or a subsequent deficit. For, unless the average earnings of capital and ability exceed the required minimum, the temporary surplus is no real surplus and cannot be taken without discouraging the application of capital and ability to the trade.

So large a proportion of industry is subject to considerable fluctuations of profit that it is frequently suggested that the apparent surplus is entirely of this spurious order. But this suggestion needs no refutation for those who have followed our analysis of normal prices, and accept the general judgment upon the relative strength of the organisers of industry as buyers of the factors of production and as sellers of the product.

The economics of the labour movement hinge mainly upon the

existence of this 'surplus' held by the employing class and distributed as rent, extra profits, or interest, fees or salaries. The whole or any part of it can theoretically and in practice be diverted into real wages, if labour is strong enough to take it.

§ 3.—If no such surplus exists, the validity of the labour movement, both in its trade union and its political policy, as an instrument for the general economic improvement of the wage-earners, is limited to the economy of high wages; that is to say, no rise of wages, reduction of hours, or other advantage, can be got, unless it is accompanied by a corresponding increase in the efficiency of labour. Particular groups of workers may evade this limit, by forcing up prices in trades exempt from outside competition; but such gains are acquired mainly at the expense of other workers who pay the higher prices, and moreover have no permanency.

The proposals to put down sweating by using the state to improve standard wages and other elements of 'a common rule' must, on the supposition that there is no unproductive surplus, be subject to great perils. For in most sweating trades, especially among women, there seems no reason to suppose that a rise of piece-wages, imposed by a wage-board, will be attended by any corresponding improvement in the pace or quality of the work. If, as is often admitted, the first effect of such regulation of sweating workshops is to drive the work into factories, the normal immediate result must be an increased cost of production there, for it is foolish to contend that the givers out of work are so unintelligent that they give out material which they could make up just as cheaply on their own premises.

In the absence of a surplus, sweating can only be overcome by measures which destroy some trades and dislocate others, forcing increases in expenses of production and in selling prices which must, by reaction on demand, reduce the size of many trades and re-organise the scale of exchange-values. This course would involve large shifts of employment for labour and capital, and much waste and loss while the readjustment was taking place.

Finally, since there is no reason to suppose that the general efficiency of labour would respond at once to the new wage policy imposed on industry, the higher wages of the sweated trades would be paid at the expense of the better-paid grades of labour, tending to diminish their efficiency.

In other words, unless a surplus exists which can be diverted into wages, the labour movement, alike on its economic and its political side, is restricted to such improvements of the conditions of labour as are immediately reflected in improved productivity. But, since employers, as a class, would undoubtedly prefer to employ more efficient workers at high wages than less efficient ones at low wages, the only defence of the labour movement would be that it was necessary in order by compulsion to induce employers to recognise their own true interest. In such a case the efforts and sacrifices involved in the labour movement would seem to be a very extravagant price to pay for this educational work.

If, however, we admit the existence of a large and varied surplus widely diffused over the field of industry, an intelligible basis is given to the labour movement. Trade unionism will rank as an organised attempt to divert rents, excessive interests and profit, and other ' unearned ' income, into wages. In thus interpreting the main function of trade unionism, it is not necessary to assume that the miners, who by collective power of bargaining extort a share of what would otherwise be surplus mining dividends, have any natural or inherent right to this surplus, on the ground that they made it, or that they need it more than other workers. This would be trade-individualism based on a defective grasp of the organic character of industry. The miners have no special claim in nature or in social justice upon the surplus that emerges in the mining industry, nor have the cotton spinners upon the high profits of a cotton boom. This sectional action of trade unions ranks as a make-shift method of redressing the balance of power between the factors of production which we see everywhere struggling each to get for itself as much as possible of the surplus product. In certain industrial conditions the landowner, in others the capitalist, is the strongest, and takes most of the available surplus in rent or high dividends : normally in developed industrial nations the owners of organising and managing ability hold the balance of power. The history of successful trade unions, in such trades as the cotton, iron, mining, printing trades of Great Britain, has consisted in raids upon surpluses which from time to time swell up in these trades, followed by prolonged struggles to retain the whole or part of the proceeds of such raids.

This interpretation, however, does not imply that it is a matter of social indifference whether the employers or the workers in a trade get such surplus. On the contrary, if our general analysis of the situation is correct, the normal working of distribution by ' pulls ' is to deprive labour of its fair share of wages of progressive efficiency, allotting an excessive amount to other factors. Where this is the case, trade union action, which secures for the workers in a trade a portion of the surplus emerging in that trade, has some justification in social utility. For though the workers in a particular trade have no absolute or separate claim upon the surplus in that trade, this piece-meal method of redress has not been wholly ineffective, and the larger use of federated action among trade unions may go far towards enhancing its efficiency.

Reverting to our earlier analysis, which identified the surplus with the fund of economic progress, we see in trade unionism, as in the larger labour movement of which it forms a part, an endeavour to secure a better and more fruitful distribution of the surplus by getting a larger share for labour at the expense of the other factors. Industrial progress in any given state of civilisation requires, as a first charge upon the surplus product, that it shall be so used as to evoke and nourish increased and improved powers in the several factors of production. If land takes too much, capital and labour are both starved, and progress is correspondingly retarded. If capital or ability takes too much and labour not enough, industrial progress continues to lag, for the healthy march of industry requires a proportionate advance of all the factors.

§ 4.—If, as we have shown, labour is normally the weakest claimant for the surplus, the labour movement in its largest aspect must be regarded as an attempt to equalise opportunities among the factors, so as to produce a more socially profitable circulation of wealth.

It is an endeavour on the part of workers by group action to obtain for themselves as individuals an increased share of wealth and leisure, by seizing and utilising such portion of the surplus as emerges in their trade or business. Collective bargaining is the chief instrument they employ, and the history of trade unionism has been mainly a series of experiments in the methods of using it. The general result of these experiments has been to show that modern organisation of capital, by its abler direction and its longer purse, is able to offer successful resistance in most industrial fields to the more important demands of labour. This discovery has driven the labour movement into politics, workmen seeking to use legislative instruments to strengthen their power of bargaining.

This change does not, so far at any rate as Great Britain and America are concerned, consist in the substitution of political for private co-operative methods. The attitude of steadfast opposition maintained by working men towards compulsory arbitration shows a firm resolve to make their own bargains with employers, at any rate so far as wages are concerned. But there is a growing disposition to use the state as an adjunct to trade union effort.

This labour politics is not socialism, in the sense of an attempt to substitute social for individual or free co-operative effort in industry. Though state machinery is employed, in the shape of Employers' Liability, Factory and Eight Hours Day Acts, such provisions are regarded primarily as strengthening the power of the workers through their unions to bargain for wages, by relieving them from certain frictions and weaknesses which experience has shown to be detrimental to the main purpose. The growing disposition of trade unions to favour drastic land legislation, unemployed relief works, old age pensions, wage-boards in sweating trades, as well as to promote large schemes of public education and public credit, is not attributable to any distinct theory of state functions or any preference of public to private enterprise. These projects are primarily viewed in their bearing upon the bargaining power of the workers. Land reform will help to relieve congestion of the labour market ; unemployed relief and old age pensions will economise the financial resources of the workers and their unions ; education, poor law reforms, the repression of sweating conditions, will help to build up a more solid basis of working-class organisation. The entire body of what has been called anti-destitutionalism falls in this category. Adequate public provision against destitution will enable trade unionists to struggle for the ' surplus ' with better chances of success than they would otherwise possess. For the ultimate weapon of capitalism has always been and still is starvation. Just in proportion as economic security of life and of efficiency is secured by means of public support, the liberty of bargaining with employers for the sale of labour-power is enhanced.

The labour movement doubtless means much more than this mere concentration on the sale of labour-power. It takes other forms besides trade unionism and serves many other purposes —economic, educative, recreative. But it is engaged primarily and fundamentally in endeavouring to secure for labour an increased share of the surplus product of industry, which remains after all minimum costs are defrayed, and which is distributed according to the respective powers of bargain possessed by the owners of the several factors of production. Normally weaker because he sells a perishable article under conditions of a forced sale, the labourer seeks to strengthen his position by combining with his fellows. The strength thus gained is measured by the material and moral damage sustained by an employer in dismissing all his men at once and replacing them by others instead of dismissing and replacing them one by one. For though this does not appear upon the surface as the distinctive feature of the collective bargain, it furnishes the ultimate test, and the knowledge of employers that, in the event of a strike or lock-out, they must deal with the men collectively, and not as units, is the main force of trade unionism. This force, however, is relative to the force of the employer, and the growth of organisation among employers weakens the efficacy of trade unionism when a critical issue arises. The recognition of this weakness explains the growing tendency of trade unions to fortify themselves by public supports, the moral and material support of the unorganised public, and the more regular and reliable supports of organised state aids.

The labour movement uses these public supports to enable it more effectively to press the claims of labour upon the surplus product, and these claims continue to be pressed in a separatist spirit by the special group action of workers in a trade seeking to obtain the particular fragments of surplus which emerge in the industrial processes of that trade.

The federation of trade unions, and the community of spirit and of purpose which inspires in an increasing degree their joint operations in many fields of industry and politics, important though they may be as educative influences, must not be allowed to obscure this central fact which distinguishes trade unionism from socialism, the struggle of separate groups of workers to obtain for their separate advantage portions of what socialism regards as the social income.

CHAPTER XIV

SOCIALISM AND THE SOCIAL INCOME

I

§ 1. State ' interference ' with industry takes three chief forms : (1) State regulation, (2) State operation, (3) Taxation. The main object and result of (1) and (2) are the diversion of some ' unearned ' income, actual or potential, to social use, either for the workers in a trade, the consumers, or the general public.—§ 2. The doctrine of a surplus affords a new interpretation to ' ability to bear ' as a canon of taxation. For surplus alone has such ability.—§ 3. The single-tax interpretation of ' surplus ' has barred the acceptance of this theory of taxation. Marxian Socialism fails to distinguish costs from surplus by its exclusive stress upon labour as basis of value.—§ 4. The supreme issue of public finance is the determination of the proportion of the surplus which can be profitably applied to public work. The solution depends upon the relative power of individuals and states to apply incomes for progress.

II

§ 1. Taxing policy demands close consideration of incidence. Every tax on a cost tends to be shifted on to a surplus. All taxes are borne by producers.—§ 2. But taxes on costs tend also to remain where they are put, and their shifting is a slow and wasteful process. This applies especially to taxes on wages or working-class expenditure.—§ 3. Some surpluses can be measured and taxed separately, but most cannot. Hence a graduated income tax, based on the hypothesis that surplus varies directly with income, is the best instrument.—§ 4. Death duties are an important adjunct to income tax.—§ 5. These may be supplemented by indirect taxes imposed in the interest of social order, or falling upon specific luxuries. —§ 6. Our industrial treatment of the use of wealth requires correction when a wider view of individual and social life is taken.

I

§ 1.—So far we have treated the distribution of wealth throughout the industrial system entirely from the standpoint of individual incomes, the whole of the product of industry passing to the several owners of the factors of production in payment for the use of their factors. The actual methods of distribution, according to our analysis, apportion that part of the product which remains over after provision has been made for the maintenance of the factors, according to economic force operating through natural or contrived scarcity ; the result being that a large part of this surplus, instead of serving to stimulate and feed increased industrial efficiency, becomes unproductive unearned income. The labour movement we have interpreted as an endeavour to adjust the balance of economic forces in the factors pulling upon the surplus so as to procure a better distribution, by enabling labour to get a larger share which would serve to raise the general efficiency of this factor of production without reducing the efficiency of the others.

But historically the labour movement has been at best a clumsy and an unreliable instrument of such redress; the force it applies is irregular, and the re-distribution of wealth it procures is both inadequate in amount and ill-proportioned in its application to the various grades of workers. Those whose low condition is most detrimental to efficiency, and who, therefore, need most their ' fair ' share of the surplus, are least able to obtain it, while the aristocracy of labour who need least get most. Moreover, the friction of such a method of redressing the balance is fraught with enormous industrial waste.

Is it possible that some method of assigning the surplus product more equitable, regular, and conducive to industrial progress than the method of force can be devised ?

Modern states are coming more and more in various ways to interfere with industrial operations or their products, with the result, and sometimes the intention, of effecting a more equitable and more socially advantageous distribution of wealth.

We may distinguish three chief modes of such public intervention :—

(1) State regulation of industry.

(2) State operation of industry.

(3) Taxation in order to raise revenue for public consumption.

Each of these public activities has other aims besides that of affecting the course of distribution ; but here it is this aspect and effect that engage our attention.

(1) Under state regulation we include all legal powers wielded by public bodies, in control of the conditions of private industry, which have the effect of diverting what would otherwise figure as interest, profit, or other emoluments of the stronger factors of production, into wages or other expenses connected with improved conditions of the workers.

The simplest illustration of such method is the State Wage Board or State Arbitration Board with powers to determine wages, hours, or other conditions of labour. When wage boards are empowered to deal with sweated trades, securing a minimum time or piece-wage, part, at any rate, of the rise of wage, or other increased cost of working over the purely competitive rate, must be regarded as a diversion of ' surplus ' profit into wages, leisure, or other benefit of the employees. Even if the condition of the trade from the employers' point of view obliges or enables them to throw the increased cost upon the consumer in a rise of prices, or upon some other productive process, analysis of the incidence of such a 'tax' will lead us to conclude that it settles mostly upon elements of income which can bear it, and implies some conversion of unearned income into efficiency wages. But whether this be provable or not, it seems certain that the net effect of such public intervention on behalf of a minimum wage tends to increase the proportion of the aggregate product which is taken by the workers in pay or other advantages.

The same general conclusion is applicable to other industrial legislation, such as Employers' Liability Acts, public limitation of hours of labour, improved sanitation, and other measures imposed by law upon trades for the benefit of employees. All such public regulation, except so far as it is directly productive of improved efficiency of labour commensurate with the expense, must be regarded as having the result, though not usually the direct intention, of shifting the balance of distribution in favour of labour. The chief conscious motive in the adoption of such regulative measures is sometimes humanitarian sentiment, concerned with the health or general well-being of workers, sometimes considerations of public order, sometimes protection of the consumer as regards quantity, quality, or price of goods. But the general effect of such interference is to convert certain elements of otherwise possible profits into wages, leisure, safety, sanitation, or other ingredients of well-being in the workers, the consumers, or the public at large.

(2) The object of the operation of an industry by the state or the municipality is generally to divert to public use monopoly profits which were left in private hands. Public industry, it is true, is not confined to such cases.: public order, safety, or other convenience induces states to participate in or to monopolise various industries, such as the manufacture and trade in weapons and explosives, alcohol, and processes connected with the preparation of meat, milk, and other foods. Part of the motive of the public ownership of roads, railroads, and local means of transport, of postal and other communications, and of many other public services, must be imputed to considerations of public order rather than of public income. In certain other cases a state monopoly is established not as a substitute for private monopoly, but as an instrument for raising revenue, as in the state assumption of the tobacco and match trades in several continental countries.

But the great majority of business operations undertaken by states and municipalities are such as, left to private enterprise, would not be carried on under conditions of free competition and would enable profit-making firms to make surplus profits from monopoly prices. Where such industries are engaged in supplying goods or services the use of which forms part of the standard of consumption of a people, the power vested in a private monopoly is recognised as intolerable. Hence in civilised nations there is a growing tendency for the public to assume ownership and control of services of transport and communication affecting the mobility of persons, goods, and information, city lands and houses, mining resources and sources of industrial power, banking and insurance, water, gas, and other routine local services, and such other industries connected with necessaries or conveniences as, owing to dependence on land or other natural factors, or through artificial restriction of competition, tend to become monopolies.

These, as we have seen, are the types of industry in which large surplus profits are obtainable. The chief economic motive of state or municipal socialism is to socialise these profits. This may be done in any or all of three ways. The state may continue to charge monopoly prices and may use part of the surplus to pay high wages of efficiency, or otherwise to improve the conditions of the employees in the industry. Or it may lower prices, and so let the 'surplus' pass to the consumers. Or it may retain the surplus as a public income for general public purposes. All these methods of dealing with the surplus may be regarded as making for a better distribution of wealth. To divert surplus profit into wages of efficiency for the workers in the trade, though a sectional benefit, may be regarded as a sound social policy, inasmuch as a reasonable wage of efficiency, in making for the progress of a trade, reacts advantageously upon the whole industrial system through processes of ordinary exchange. But there must be a clear limit to this policy of using the 'surplus' : to divert the entire extra profits of a strong monopoly into the wages of the workers in that trade, so as to raise their wages above the ordinary level of efficiency for the class of work, would not be a social policy but one of trade preference.

Where the goods or services produced by the industry are generally consumed, and in tolerably equal quantities, by the wider public, the 'surplus' may be disposed of by lowering prices or by improving the quality of the goods or services. This also may be regarded as a socially beneficial distribution. Part of the large potential surplus profits of state postal or railway systems is frequently applied in thus lowering prices or improving facilities of carriage.

Or, finally, the state or municipality may charge monopoly prices, and after paying the standard wages to its employees, may retain the ordinary and the surplus profits as public revenue to be applied to general public purposes.

No general theory regarding the disposal of the actual or potential ' profits ' of a state monopoly as between these several methods can be laid down.   Many politicians and economists will hold that, after standard wages are provided, the rest of the ' surplus ' profits should be remitted in prices to the consumers, the ordinary profits, if any, which remain, ranking as public income.   But few would be prepared to apply this principle to the case of a state trade in alcohol, and it cannot be accorded any general validity.

When public ownership enables a state or a city to take economic rent or other ' unearned ' income by retaining such prices as a private business would charge, there is no *prima facie* presumption against this policy.   It cannot be said that individual consumers have any inherent right to obtain the goods or services at a bare cost of production.   Sometimes it may be a sound public policy to charge a price which shall contain a ' surplus ' element ; sometimes, upon the contrary, it may be wise to subsidise from other public sources a particular public service so as to sell its product below ' cost ' price, or even to supply it free.   So state-owned alcohol may reasonably be sold at a price which contains a ' surplus ' ; workmen's fares may be subsidised out of the other fares on trams and trains ; a telegraph service as a whole may be subsidised from other proceeds of the Post Office ; public baths may be supplied below cost price, and public libraries and music in the parks may be ' free.'

Now in many of these public enterprises it is not held that the state or the city can or does conduct the business upon the whole more economically or more efficiently than private enterprises. But it is held to be a public duty to intercept and to divert into public income what would otherwise be the surplus profits of a private monopoly.   If the public administration of the industry is so much inferior to private administration that the whole surplus profits of the latter are likely to be absorbed in the increased expenses of the former (apart from provision for efficiency wages), the socialisation of such an industry is *prima facie* inadvisable.   But if the public administration can be conducted so as to yield some surplus profit, it is *prima facie* a sound step in socialism.

For the underlying assumption, upon which depends the political economy of the whole process, is that this ' surplus,' representing a product beyond what is needed to remunerate adequately the owners of the factors of production in the industry, belongs to society, forming part of a social income, and that the state takes this income, as representing the rights and interests of society.

Whenever private enterprise tends to evade competition and to set up monopolies or trade restrictions in the supply of primary necessaries or conveniences of life, society through its public institutions defends itself against this dangerous power, and working the monopoly itself uses the surplus profits as a social income. Some portions of the rents of land and other natural resources, and of the gains arising from concentrated capitalism applied to routine industries, thus pass into the public purse.

§ 2.—(3) But the essential nature and significance of social income are best recognised in dealing with the third mode of state interference by taxation. To regard taxation as a process by which society acting through the state takes income which it has earned by social work, and which it needs for social life, is not an entirely novel conception, though widely divergent from the commonly accepted view. This latter view may be stated thus :

All property is due to the efforts of individuals, and belongs by right to them. But the state, organised by individuals for their joint protection, must have such income as is required to perform this service. For this purpose, and this alone, it must be empowered to invade the property and incomes of individuals, and take by taxation what is necessary.

Such taxation, it is held, inflicts an injury on the rights of individual property, involving a ' sacrifice ' on the part of those who pay.

Two chief principles for the apportionment of taxation have been laid down, one that taxation should be imposed in proportion to ' ability ' to bear it, the other that it should be imposed in proportion to ' benefits received ' by its expenditure. According to the latter doctrine the state produces and sells protection of army, police, &c., to those who need it : the price of this protection is paid in taxes, and those who, having most to lose, gain most by such protection, pay most in taxation.

Historically, the origin of many taxes is directly traceable to this view of the state as a purveyor of special sorts of services : stamps, tolls and other contributions to our national revenue still rank as specific payments proportioned to specific benefits, while our system of rating for local taxation carries many signs of the same interpretation. But the enlarged modern conception of the duties of the state and the complexity of its functions have involved of necessity a growing disuse of the measurement of specific benefits as a taxing principle : to collect a number of separately estimated and earmarked taxes is no longer feasible. The tendency, therefore, has been to substitute, as a substantially equitable principle of taxation, ' ability to bear,' as indicated by rental, income, property or other measure of financial strength.[1] Though the idea of a tax as an interference with private property only justified by public necessity, a burden or sacrifice imposed upon the individual, with its implication that sound public finance requires that taxation be kept down to the minimum requisite to carry on the barely necessary work of government, is still generally prevalent, certain speculations and theories regarding ' ability to bear ' have long begun to sap the old conception.

The first and most fruitful of these speculations relates to the doctrine of economic rent of land. It has long been recognised that the differential rents of land, and the scarcity rents attaching to lands limited in quantity for certain uses, are incomes which have a special ability to bear a tax. This ' ability ' to bear is of a two-fold nature. In the first place it is recognised that a tax either directly placed or settling upon such land values lies there and cannot be transferred. In the second place it is recognised that, since these rents are not ' earned ' by efforts or skill of the landowner who receives them, the tax is borne without disturbing his incentive to apply his land as a factor in production.

Out of this attention to the nature and taxable capacity of economic rents of land has grown the doctrine that such income ' unearned ' by the individual landowner is ' earned ' by society, and that, in taking rents by process of taxation, society, through its instrument the state, is taking an income which belongs to it in the same sense as wages belong to the labourer, interest to the capitalist, and profit to the employer, viz. because its efforts have made the income.

In what sense is it true that these rents are made by society and therefore belong to society as social income ? So far as the productive powers of Nature are concerned, they are evidently not made by man, individual or social, and the ' scarcity ' of these powers, which is a condition of their value, is a natural scarcity. But society operates in two ways, so as to give positive value to this scarcity of natural powers. In the first place, the work and wants of the multitude of men, constituting society, make as a necessary incident of their economic life the demand for the various uses of land which, acting on its scarcity, make it valuable. The growth of a population on a piece of land, discovering and developing various arts for dealing with land as a fund of raw materials and of power, or as surface, gives values to various sorts of natural properties. The creation of this value can seldom be traced to individuals ; it is distinctively social. Again, in all civilised

---

[1] J. S. Mill's substitution of ' equality of sacrifice ' for ' ability to bear ' is an unfortunate instance of ' *obscurum per obscurius.*'

communities the state, as the direct instrument of society, expends public effort in making roads and other means of communication, in preserving peace and order, in furnishing important and expensive services for the protection and advancement of industrial and other operations which develop the uses of surface, soil and position, and is thus directly instrumental in creating land values.

Thus, though the physical properties of the land which become valuable are not socially created, the value which attaches to them is so created. Individuals, it is true, by putting their energy and skill into land, improve it, but in any close consideration of the matter, theoretical or practical, the value of such individual improvements must be separated from land values and rank as capital. Land values proper, whether attaching to land in virtue of fertility and other contents or of site, are directly due to social action operating in one of the two ways above described. The annual yield of these land values, thus socially earned, is claimed as a social income.

§ 3.—If.this important implication of the doctrine of taxation of ' unearned increments ' is not yet adequately realised, the lack is due to two causes. One is that to no appreciable extent has the taxing doctrine yet been applied to land values. The other is that the defective analysis of distribution adopted by single taxers on the one hand, and of vaguely extravagant socialists upon the other, has prevented a clear recognition of the nature and dimensions of the social income thus available for the enlargement of public life.

Those who persist in confining the productive efficacy of social forces to the creation of land values are defeated in their efforts to convince and to apply their policy of taxation by the patent fact that, in this country at any rate, most large and evidently unearned incomes are not derived directly or indirectly from the monopoly of land but from other economic advantages. Moreover, the logic of the single taxer is bent before the difficulty of distinguishing land values from capital values in many instances, while the feasibility of the single tax policy is damaged by the obvious injustice of imposing special taxes upon what has been regarded so long and so generally as ' one form of investment.' The mere fact that taxation placed upon existing economic rent cannot be resisted, and will cause no shrinkage in supply of land, does not seem an equitable ground for distinguishing for purposes of taxation such an element of income from the ' interest ' with which it has become merged in the ordinary processes of exchange by which the ownership of land, along with that of various forms of capital, has continually been changing hands. If I have recently invested

£1000 in a trust company which pays me £50 per annum in dividends based upon rents, while you receive the same sum in dividends upon bank shares in which you have invested £1000, the fact that rent is an 'unearned increment' does not seem a sufficient reason for placing upon my £50 a tax from which yours is exempt. So far as you and I are concerned, our incomes from the two sources are 'earned' or 'unearned' precisely to the same extent ; when I invested in a trust company's shares, I was not even aware that rents would be the real source of the dividends, nor were you aware, when investing in bank shares, that the dividends would not be derived from mortgages on land or other rental sources.

The fact that common modes of reckoning and general industrial practice have inextricably and immeasurably confused land values with capital values, not merely in agriculture, housing, mines, railroads, and all forms of organised businesses in which land is ' capitalised ' along with buildings, machinery, stock, goodwill, &c., but especially in the general investments of banks, insurance, development and trust companies, which play so large a part in the financial direction of modern businesses, renders it as impracticable as it would be inequitable to make existing land values the single separate basis of taxation. This view, however, need not preclude the special or separate taxation of future increments of land values or rents. For if it be contended that part or the whole of such future rises of value has already been anticipated in the past contracts for the sale or rental of land, and that it would be unjust to take from existing owners or lessees any part of the prospective values they have paid for in the terms of their contract, we can only reply that this cannot be held to be a proper interpretation of the conditions under which reasonable men have recently made contracts for the sale or annual leasing of land. The proposal in this and other countries to raise an increasing proportion of the public revenue from increments of land value has figured so prominently in the practical politics of all progressive parties that it may fairly be presumed that the probability of such special taxation has been taken into account in recent negotiations for sale or leasing. This being so, the objection to such a tax on the ground of inequitable discrimination against a special form of income collapses. If I have really paid £900 for a piece of land for which I must have paid £1000 but for the probability that special taxation would shortly be placed upon it, I can have no ground for complaint if this probability is converted into actuality.

If, therefore, it be admitted that, on grounds of equity, existing incomes from land values cannot be subjected to special taxation from which other incomes from investments are immune, it is quite legitimate for the state to take by taxation as much of the future increments of land values as she can detect and separate from other values and can apply to the performance of public services.

Moreover, a special case for taxing existing values may be urged, if it can be shown that such taxation will promote a more socially productive use of land.

But while the difficulty of the single tax policy of public finance is due to a too narrow interpretation of the unproductive ' surplus ' available for public income, socialism has done as much to blur a clear conception by a doctrine of surplus value which includes not merely all rent but all interest and profit as well. Confusing the economies of a hypothetical society, in which the state, owning all the instruments of industry, need no longer take into account the categories of rent, interest, or profit, with the economic analysis of current industry, Karl Marx regarded payments for mental and manual labour as the only legitimate expenses, pooling rent, interest, profit and a large part of salaries as surplus wrung by the exploiting classes from the workers who were the sole producers of income. The rejection of this interpretation of distribution by most reasonable persons, and the resentment felt at the refusal of socialists to recognise the actual industrial services rendered by saving and the direction of industry, and the validity of some interest and profit in payment for these services, has discredited the conception of a ' surplus ' as much in one way as the narrow single tax doctrine in another.

For purposes of a taxing policy, the surplus value of ' orthodox ' socialism is invalid, because it refuses to recognise a minimum rate of interest and of profit as economically necessary payments in a society which needs to evoke the voluntary individual efforts of saving and of direction of industry. It would defy the facts of existing society in the name of its vision of a future society. When society does all the saving, it will be unnecessary to designate as ' interest ' any separate part of the increased social income of the future : in similar fashion, both rent and profit will disappear when the practical utility of these distinctions is gone. But for our existing society these distinctions remain valid in the theory and the practice of the distribution of wealth. What we have to do is to distinguish, as completely as we can, the portion of these payments that is socially necessary under existing industry from that which is socially unnecessary.

The doctrine of unproductive ' surplus ' or ' unearned increment,' in the meaning here given to it, including all sorts of scarcity gains, is of supreme significance in public finance. For this

' surplus,' as we have already asserted, is the sole source of public revenue : it alone can ' bear ' a tax, and its ability to bear it is absolute. Just as economic rent cannot shift a tax once placed or settled on it, so with every other unearned element of income. The tax cannot be shifted, because the existence of the unearned income not being an incentive to the application of the land, capital, or ability from which it is derived, the imposition of the tax will cause no withdrawal of the supply, and therefore no raising of the price. A tax placed on economic rent cannot be shifted because, so long as it leaves any rent untaken, it will still pay the landowner to keep his land in use, and so long as he does so, the total supply of available land remaining as before, the landowners cannot by raising rents shift the tax on the lessee. Similarly with a tax placed upon high interest or profits. A tax upon banking dividends in this country would not cause any shrinkage of banking business, for the paid-up capital in the industry is remunerated at a far higher rate than is needed to evoke its use. Mr. Rockefeller could not advantageously resist a tax upon his income by raising the price of oil, nor can De Beers raise the price of diamonds as a means of meeting the new taxation put upon the profits of their monopoly.

In tracing the elaborate and multifarious ways in which such ' surplus ' is super-imposed upon necessary expenses, wherever a factor of production is in a position of natural or contrived scarcity, we have indicated a ' fund ' of a complex nature which is, in principle at any rate, amenable to the taxing process on the same terms as economic rent.

§ 4.—In this assertion of the doctrine that the surplus, or complex of ' unearned incomes,' is the sole legitimate source of public revenue, it is not implied that the state is entitled to absorb by taxation, or otherwise, the whole of this surplus, on the ground that society has created it, needs it, and intends to utilise it for social expenditure.

We recognised distinctly, in dealing with the claims of individual owners of the factors of production, that whereas their wear and tear or sustenance funds were, in theory at any rate, a fixed ascertainable first charge upon the product, their further claims for an income of progressive efficiency were more elastic. With rising wages is usually associated an increased quantity or improved quality, or both, of labour-power ; higher interest and profits, though with less certainty, evoke a larger application of capital and ability. If, then, the term ' surplus ' be applied, as we do apply it, to the whole of the product over and above the wear and tear fund, regarded as the progress fund, it is evident that we are called upon to adjust the respective claims of the progress in efficiency of the individual producers and of society. To this same surplus the individual must look for his wage of progress, and the state for its entire income, including both its wear and tear fund and its wage of progress.

This way of setting the problem makes it evident that the wear and tear or sustenance fund for the state should form a first charge upon the general surplus. In fact, if we had been able to begin with a clear assertion of the co-operation of society with the individual in all productive work, we should in the first analysis have put the public wear and tear fund on the same level with that of the individual producer, and have reduced the surplus accordingly. This, however, would have imposed undue complexity upon our earlier analysis. But now that we are confronted with the task of harmonising the individual and social claims upon the surplus, we must make the necessary preliminary readjustment, admitting that the working expenses or upkeep of the existing fabric of the state must rank, like those of the individual producers, as claims on the product prior to the emergence of a surplus.

Thus the surplus is reduced to its true dimensions as a fund of economic progress whose proper disposition is determined by the respective powers of individual and social factors of production to utilise surplus for purposes of improved efficiency. In our earlier survey we admitted that there were natural limits imposed upon the capacity of individual producers to assimilate and utilise for progress surplus income. The economy of high wages, however liberally interpreted, has limits. Though the wholesome wants of man may be considered infinite, the pace of their evolution, and of their assimilation in his standard of life, depends on a great variety of physical, psychical and social considerations. The same applies to the stimulation of the increased growth and efficiency of capital and ability in our industrial system. There are, in the case of all the factors, limits to the assimilation of surplus for the promotion of economic efficiency.

Then arises the question: 'Must we not apply to society, and in particular to its instrument the state, a similar restrictive principle?' The answer must clearly be in the affirmative. Just as an evident waste of surplus is occasioned when a Connemara agricultural labourer arriving at Liverpool is put suddenly in possession of a weekly income four times larger than he has ever had before ; just as every other sort of *nouveau riche* is apt to consume his excessive income in ways which, so far from advancing, degrade his personal efficiency, so with a city or a state. The organic conception of these social institutions obliges us to admit that their laws of growth impose certain limits upon their rate of taking on new functions and enlarging the activities of old functions, and therefore of applying public income in serviceable progress. A city or a state might easily become a reckless spendthrift if it took more 'surplus' than it could digest, as many a parasitic instance testifies in history.

The claims of the individual producers and of society, in the form of the state, upon the true surplus, must then be set upon a level, to be adjusted in accordance with a wise interpretation of their respective capacities of growth, and of the needs implied in these capacities.

Here is exposed what is, from the economic standpoint, the most important duty of statecraft—that, on the one hand, of creating the conditions most favourable to the absorption of 'surplus' by individual producers in proportion to their capacity to use it; on the other hand, the application of the remainder of the surplus to the direct use of the state for public services.

These tasks, as we have already recognised, are by no means mutually exclusive. For the modern state uses its power and its financial resources largely to secure what is termed 'equality of economic opportunity' for its individual members, which really means that it assists them to absorb from the 'surplus' increments of income what they can apply to the promotion of personal efficiency.

But the performance of this work, as well as the expenditure upon directly public services, involves on the part of the state a careful calculus of the respective requirements of the state and of the individual for purposes of progressive efficiency.

This is the supreme issue of public finance, to determine what proportion of the surplus can be advantageously taken as public income to be applied to the growth of state functions. This proportion will evidently vary, not merely with the nature of the political economic civilisation, but with the actual conditions of the distribution of the surplus. Where the 'surplus' is small, and upon the whole is apportioned in accordance with the 'needs' of the several factors of production, the state would make a moderate use of its taxing power, having in mind the nice adjustment of the use of surplus for individual and social growth. But where a large surplus was quite evidently absorbed by the economic force of some factor whose efficiency it hindered rather than helped, the state would apply its taxing powers rigorously so as to absorb this wasted surplus.

Our analysis of the actual working of the industrial system has shown the emergence of large quantities of waste surplus. It is to the social utilisation of this waste surplus that the taxing power of the state is rightly directed. For the economic rents, the extra profits, interest, salaries, &c., which are got by the use of economic force in creating monopolies or artificial scarcities, are not merely failing to perform the true functions of a surplus, as the fund of progress, in stimulating the efficiency of factors of production, they are damaging efficiency, by enabling whole classes of persons to be consumers without producing. Such injurious consumption of the surplus in destroying efficiency it is the evident duty of the state to stop; and a taxing policy which transfers such private destruction of efficiency into the means of a public increase of efficiency is doubly productive.

Thus the true policy of public revenue is based upon the duty of the state to take as public income whatever portion of the surplus is not already allocated to the stimulation of efficiency of the individual factors of production, but is taken in rents, extra profits, or other ' unearned ' income.

The two methods by which the state endeavours to secure its income are, as we have seen, public operation of industry and taxation. The former is usually confined to the case of large industries, engaged in the supply of goods or services for the satisfaction of urgent common needs, which, left to private enterprise, become strong monopolies. The state, assuming these monopolies, either takes the monopoly profit for general purposes of revenue, or assigns portions of it to the employees in higher wages and improved conditions of employment, or to the consumers in lower prices or better services. If the state decides to raise the wages of public employees or to lower prices, thus foregoing the actual collection of the monopoly profit, it must nevertheless be considered to have disposed of this ' surplus ' by a socially advantageous expenditure. How much of the profits of public monopolies shall be utilised in such specific subsidies and how much gathered into general revenue, is a question to be answered from detailed consideration of each case. Where the state or municipality takes over a private monopoly on terms enabling it to secure the surplus profit, it will commonly dispose of a portion of this surplus in converting subsistence wages into wages of progressive efficiency ; another portion it may apply to such lowering of rates or extension of services as may be socially remunerative from the standpoint of net profits : the remainder of the surplus, if any, or of the ordinary profit, may be applied to general purposes of public revenue. Some states, however, using public monopolies primarily as a means of general revenue, concern themselves little with the progressive efficiency of employees, and charge the highest prices or rates which they can profitably extract from the consumers. Such use of public monopolies as an indirect method of general taxation will, however, be less likely to occur in states which have developed an enlightened system of direct taxation. While public operation of industry will generally be applied to intercept the large regular surpluses which accrue from monopolies in the prime necessaries or conveniences of life, taxation will be applied to secure as much as possible of the surplus which is taken in the operation of industry by the owners of strongly placed factors of production, but which does not issue through the forms of definte monopoly in routine industry.

Surplus obtained by one of these two methods is the sole legitimate source of public revenue, it is the only sort of income available for public use. States dominated by shortsighted avarice may sometimes attempt to encroach by taxes upon the subsistence fund of labour or capital, or at least to annex that additional payment required to evoke and to support progressive efficiency in the industrial system. This 'sweating' policy has frequently been practised by despotic rulers or classes, utilising the powers of the state to make forced levies on the resources of the people.

Such an abuse of taxing power in its operation upon agriculture has probably been the greatest single influence throughout history in the retardation of industry ; and many modern civilised states, by excessive or inclusive taxation which assails costs of production and diverts the factors of production from more productive into less productive channels, inflict upon single trades or upon the national industry injuries which weaken its present and its future yield of surplus, so diminishing the fund of public revenue.

II

§1.—Accepting as our basis of taxation the principle that all taxes should be so laid as to lie upon unproductive surplus, we have to consider what taxing policy is best adapted in a modern industrial state to secure this result, and to obtain for the public revenue the largest quantity of this fund without undue risk of encroaching anywhere upon expenses of production.

If unproductive surplus alone has ability to bear a tax, it might seem at first sight a matter of indifference where a tax was laid, because, if laid upon any necessary expense of production, it would be shifted until its ultimate incidence was upon some portion of the surplus. Reasoning along this line we might hold, with Ricardo, that no tax could lie on ordinary wages of labour, because a tax thereupon imposed would, by reducing real wages below the necessary minimum, diminish the supply of labour and so raise its price until the tax fell upon the profits of the employer. Similarly, it might well appear that any tax imposed on interest or profit must, so far as minimum interest and profit are affected, be shifted either upon rent, in the case of agriculture and other industries into which land enters as a considerable factor, or upon the consumer through a rise in prices.

It is so important to realise clearly both the validity of this reason in and its limitations that it will be well to test it by a concrete instance. Advocates of state pensions upon a basis of compulsory contribution have sometimes urged that employers should be required to stop a certain sum from the wages of their employees for this purpose, in other words, to levy a direct tax on money wages to furnish a state revenue for pensions. Let us suppose that 6d. per week were stopped by every employer of unskilled town labour out of the 18s. which may be taken as the normal weekly wage.

If, as we may assume for the purpose of this argument, 18s. is a minimum wage of efficiency for the average unskilled workman and his family, the stoppage of the 6d. will have a first effect in reducing the efficiency of labour, which in unskilled labour is equivalent to a reduction in the supply of labour. To this effect, which may at first be small, will be added the withdrawal from the regular labour market of what we may term the ' marginal labour ' at the earlier wage, that is to say, those who were just induced to keep in regular work for the food, housing, and bed, which 18s. would buy but which 17s. 6d. will not. In these two ways the tax of 6d. per week will reduce the supply of unskilled labour. As the demand may be assumed to remain as before, the price must rise until part or the whole of the 6d. is paid out of the pocket of the employers. So far as our assumption that the wage is a bare subsistence wage is correct, the effect would be to throw the whole tax on the employer, even if somewhat less labour was employed than before. The first shift of the tax thus seems to be from wages on to profits. But will it necessarily settle there ? In prosperous trades, where profits are higher than they need be to remunerate employers, the tax will lie upon these surplus-profits, for employers, though they might like to shift them on to the buyers of the goods they have to sell, will not be able to do so. Why not ? Because, if they are competing, one employer dare not raise his price for fear of being undersold by another, who can afford to do so because he would still be earning a sufficient profit by keeping to his former price. If, on the other hand, the surplus profit of the trade was due to combination in holding up prices above the competitive level, the imposition of this pension's tax would confer upon them no new power to raise still higher their monopoly price. It is therefore clear that, if the tax falls upon surplus-profit, it stays there. But the case of employers in trades where keen competition keeps profits at a minimum is different. Minimum profits and interest have the same power to throw off a tax as minimum wages, for even if the existing material capital will continue functioning at a rate below the minimum, no fresh capital or ability will enter such a trade, and this starvation will issue in dwindling output, and, demand remaining as before, in rising prices. Rising prices seem, then, to throw the tax on to the consumer. But prices cannot always be raised. Where home producers are in close competition with foreigners whose ' expenses ' have not been burdened with the tax, there is no power to raise prices. The effect of a tax on such a trade would be to destroy a large part of it, knocking out all the weaker businesses until the reduction of output was such as to raise the price for the reduced supply (the aggregate foreign and domestic supply) to a point which would enable the tax to be borne by the surviving businesses. If all the businesses in such a trade were equally equipped, and all earning minimum profits, the logically necessary effect of such a tax would be to kill the trade.

Where, as in the case of many large industries, e.g. transport, building, shopkeeping, no direct effective foreign competition is practicable, the pension would, it appears, be successfully shifted on to the consumer. This to some appears the end. There is, however, a false air of finality about the statement 'the consumer pays' which is most injurious to an understanding of the incidence of taxation. It is clear that the tax cannot lie on all classes of consumers alike. For instance, our unskilled labourers who first began to shift the pension's tax imposed on them by law are consumers, and will be called upon to pay the higher prices. But they can no more pay the tax in this shape of higher prices than in that of lower money wages. If the shifting of the tax has caused a rise in the price of any elements of food, shelter, &c., which enter their standard of life, the same economic necessity which enabled them before to shift the tax on to their employer will operate again. And what applies to them will apply to every other class of consumer whose real income only covers expenses and leaves no surplus. If his income at previous prices only just suffices to induce him to give out his labour-power or his ability, or to apply his capital, he cannot and will not bear the tax which seems to fall upon him as consumer through rise of prices, but will shift it as before. If any class of consumers possess an income which is not a wage of bare efficiency or a minimum interest or profit, but which is composed wholly or in part of rents, extra profits, or other surplus, such consumers can and will pay the higher prices, without power to shift the tax contained in them. But it is clear by this instance that such consumers bear the tax, not as consumers, but as owners of incomes which contain a ' surplus ' element.

From this reasoning, if it be correct, there issue two conclusions. First, that a tax imposed in the first instance upon an income which is a subsistence wage, or any minimum cost of production, tends to be moved on until it finds, in the course of its shifting, elements of ' surplus ' income on which to settle. Second, that no consumer, as consumer, can be considered to have any ability to bear a tax : taxes must ultimately be held to be paid out of such incomes as can bear them.

In any scientific analysis of incidence of taxes we must trace the incidence to incomes derived from ownership of some factor of production, or to property accumulated from such ownership. In a word, all taxes are ultimately borne by owners of productive agents.

§ 2.—So important is this doctrine of the implied inability of minimum wages of efficiency to bear a tax, that some closer discussion of it is advisable. For simplicity we have stated it in a hard dogmatic form which requires some qualification. If it were true that all taxes imposed upon any element of income which was a cost of production were instantly, automatically, and easily shifted on to the unearned surplus, methods of taxation might appear to be a matter of no great importance. But, in fact, the shifting is often a slow and wasteful process, accompanied by much disturbance to industrial processes. For there is also a tendency for a tax to lie where it is put, even when it is put upon a person or an income which has no real ability to bear it. Our example of the pension tax correctly assumed that the first effect would be to break down a wage of minimum efficiency. Our implication that this effect would be avoided by shifting the tax in the first instance on to the employer, though substantially correct, evidently needs qualification. If the unskilled wage were an absolutely fixed sum, expended entirely in ways which made for efficiency, no portion of the tax could lie for any time at all. But even the fixed standard of consumption of unskilled labour usually contains some elements which are not contributory to efficiency. It is suggested that the 6d. per week might easily be paid by reducing expenditure on beer. Here is a way in which the tax might be borne without causing any diminution of efficiency of labour. Would it so be borne ? Probably to some small extent it would. For though the drink habit will be too firmly fixed in habits of consumption to bear the whole or even the chief brunt of the attack upon the workers' budget, it would bear some of it : to some slight extent the tax might nibble at the standard of comfort, and to that extent it would lie where it was first put. Again, where unskilled wages were for other reasons rising, and new unsettled elements were emerging in the class standard of consumption, the tax might lie, though at the expense of checking a rise of efficiency accompanying the rise of wages. In other words, the state, by imposing the weekly tax, might earmark 6*d*. in the rising wages for its pension scheme, diverting it from some other more or less desirable object of expenditure to which it would have been put.

The issue is obviously a delicate one. The general effect would be to resist the tax, in so far as it implies an attack on the established class standard of comfort, even though that standard contains some elements that could be abandoned without loss of efficiency, and to shift it on to the employer. But where the tax was put upon rising wages, some of it would probably stay, though the social effect, in preventing a rise of current consumption, and so current efficiency, might be injurious.

The same reasoning will apply to the class wages of higher grades of labour. If these wages are strictly wages of the higher efficiency involved in skilled labour, they have no real ability to bear a tax which, if imposed, must either break down efficiency or be shifted on to the employer. But so far as they contain elements of merely conventional value, capable of being abandoned without reducing efficiency, they can bear some portion of the tax, if the workers consent to forego their use. The issue becomes largely one of class psychology. If the unnecessaries are firmly fixed in the class standard of comfort, there will be no willingness to reduce their consumption in order to pay the tax, but a strong disposition to shift the tax by a refusal to work for wages involving a reduced standard of comfort.

But though the physical and moral necessities that underlie subsistence and efficiency wages for the various grades of labour have a great power of resistance to taxation, this resistance is often a process entailing great misery to the working classes and great waste to the industrial system. A tax on the food or other necessaries of unskilled labourers may drive large numbers of the weaker members of this class into casual employment, a tramp life, or the workhouse, while its effect upon the nurture of the rising generation may inflict grave injury upon its industrial efficiency. Similarly, the operation of taxation upon skilled workers and their families may be such as to drive them or their children to a lower level of work and life. In other words, the state, by an unwise and oppressive measure of taxation, may injure the workers in the same way as a sweating employer or a grasping landlord. The actual condition even of the unskilled labourers in such a country as England or America is not one of such close subjection to ' an iron law of wages ' as to cause every encroachment on a standard of living to be at once reflected in a corresponding shrinkage of supply of labour. The injurious effects of a tax imposed on a standard wage may often be slow in their operation, and so the food taxes, by which the efficiency of labour is crippled, may be permitted to remain even in nations where a democratic franchise exists. But the grave injury done by taxation of the labouring classes consists in the direct absorption by the state of new increments of real wages which, though on their way to build up a higher standard of life for the workers, with a corresponding rise of industrial efficiency, have not yet been firmly embedded in that higher standard

What applies to wages clearly applies to any tax imposed directly or indirectly on minimum interest or profit or payment of ability ; the process by which such a tax is shifted involves not only unmerited injury to the owner of some capital or ability who is deprived of his normal anticipated income, but a temporary check upon the activity of the industries in which these factors are employed, with a consequent waste of productivity and a disturbance to other businesses related to them.

In fine, any tax imposed upon elements of income which are economically necessary costs of production is directly evil, endangering the efficiency of the owners of the incomes, and involving industrial waste by the process of shifting which commonly ensues. This applies with peculiar force to taxes placed, either on the money wages of the working classes, or on the prices of commodities consumed by them.

This treatment of the incidence and shifting of taxation, based upon a distinction between expenses of production and surplus, requires one important qualification. A tax imposed upon the minimum interest or profit necessary to evoke the due flow of capital and ability into a trade would be shifted, as we see, by a rise of prices in the product of this trade ensuant upon the stoppage or check in the growth of the trade-structure. Capital and ability will flow by preference into other trades where the minimum remuneration remains untaxed. If, moreover, minimum interest, profits and salaries were subjected to a general taxation throughout the national area, new capital and ability would tend towards foreign investment. In so far as this alternative was not available, the tax would reduce saving and the flow of new capital into industry, causing a corresponding slackness in the application of ability. This, of course, follows from the simple fact that the so-called 'minimum' interest, profit, or salary only just suffices to evoke the existence and use of certain portions of the capital and ability which flow into a trade.

But though taxation levied indiscriminately upon these 'minimum' rates of payment would not lie, this is not the case with taxation imposed upon these payments when they form parts of high incomes. To revert to an earlier comparison, John Smith of Oldham will not save and apply his savings unless 3 per cent. is secured to him; the Duke of Westminster, who gets the same price for saving, would save for 1 per cent., or even at zero. If this be so, it follows that though the 3 per cent. investments of John Smith will not bear a tax, those of the Duke of Westminster will, and a system of direct discriminative income tax could secure a contribution to the revenue from the so-called 'minimum interest' paid to the Duke. In other words, our 'minimum' payments, though able to resist taxation when figuring as 'expenses of production' in a trade, are often taxable when, passing into income, they admit of reference to individual forms of economic motive. Regarding such payments as elements of income, we find no fixed 'minimum,' or rather, we find a number of different minimums varying with the motives of different classes and individual savers.

The general result of such analysis is to enlarge the taxable 'surplus' by adding to the 'unproductive surplus,' which analysis of processes of production discloses as the taxable body, a number of personal elements of 'unproductive surplus' only discernible by consideration of motives disclosed in analysis of incomes. In other words, not only rates of interest or profit, but amounts of interest or profit, affect ability to pay. If, as is not unreasonable, we may assume that the subjectively necessary rate of interest, profit, salary, tends to vary inversely with the amount of the income which it helps to form, we have a strong additional support for the feasibility and productivity of a progressive income tax. Not only will high incomes be taxable on the hypothesis that they contain larger quantities of unproductive surplus in the sense of excessive rents, and excessive rates and payment for capital and ability, but in that the minimum inducements to save and apply capital and ability are lower in their case than in the case of recipients of smaller incomes.

The total *corpus* of taxation theoretically available for public revenue is extended by this consideration beyond that portion of the product which in our objective analysis of distribution ranked as unproductive surplus. For this objectively conceived surplus is supplemented by a subjective 'surplus' consisting of the differential 'surpluses' of certain owners of producing power who do not require the payment of the normal minimum price as an inducement to evoke the industrial use of the particular power which they own.

§ 3.—Since all taxes ultimately settle and are borne by the income of producers or by property accumulated therefrom, which thus constitute the only sound source of taxation, it might appear that the only sound method would be to measure the various forms of unearned income and property and take them by direct taxation. This would be both simple and expedient if such surpluses were always ascertainable and measurable. If it were possible to secure returns of all incomes in which expenses of production were separated from unearned income, the whole of the latter or such portion as seemed desirable could be taken by direct taxation. In so far as it is possible, or can become possible, by accurate valuation, to distinguish such unearned incomes as rents, values of liquor licences, or even the surplus profits of such highly organised and generally profitable industries as banking and insurance, it might be advisable to place specific taxes on such forms of surplus, either taxing them as they emerge in the net profits of some company or other business form, or in the incomes or inheritances of the personal recipients.

But it is evident that the greater part of the surplus is not thus clearly traceable and measurable, emerging as it does in a large and changing variety of forms amid the intricacies of industrial life. Wherever there accrues a permanent or temporary scarcity of some factor of production, a corresponding surplus income is created which passes to owners of this factor. But no particular register of these elements of surplus is possible ; though most large incomes contain many of them, they are often indistinguishable even by their owners from the elements which are earned.

It is tolerably clear that no taxing instrument for measuring directly these fluctuating ' surpluses ' can be devised. Indeed, even the rough distinction at present drawn in the income tax of Great Britain between earned and unearned incomes, from £700 to £2000 per annum, is open to serious criticism on the ground that it implies all ' interest ' to be unearned without distinguishing between minimum and surplus rates. To some extent it thus certainly operates as a deterrent of saving and investment. There is no reason to assume that high salaries or profits of business or professional men do not contain ' unearned ' elements, and no reason to treat low dividends upon invested capital as ' unearned ' by their recipients. A main instrument of rational taxation is a graduated income tax, without any further discrimination of sources than is conveyed in such specific taxes on rent, &c., as may seem expedient and feasible. The validity of this method is based on the assumption that unproductive ' surplus ' varies directly with the size of incomes. All modern states to some extent have accepted this assumption as a basis for their taxing policy. No one will dispute the fact that an increasing proportion of high incomes can be taken by taxation, without impairing the incentives of the owners of the land, capital, or ability, from which these incomes are derived, from applying them as they apply them now to production. When it is clearly and generally recognised that this is equivalent to an admission that these elements of income, thus taken in taxation, are not earned by their recipients, but are attributable to social causes of scarcity value, it will be understood that no injurious burden or sacrifice is imposed, no confiscatory policy pursued, but that the state is simply seeking to collect a portion of the social income. A portion only, evidently not the whole! No policy of graduated taxation, applied to general aggregates of income, can collect more than a certain proportion of the social income. For the hypothesis that unearned surplus varies directly and closely with the size of income is probably not accurate, and is certainly incapable of verification. Considerable caution must therefore be practised in graduating the tax so as to avoid any risk of trenching upon earned elements of income. Especially in its earlier years, such taxation must be largely experimental, so as to find the curve of graduation which is most productive of revenue. Even were it possible to measure experimentally the proportion of each size of income which is 'unearned' and therefore taxable, it would not be feasible to take more than a proportion by process of national or local taxation. In the United States high local taxation is frequently evaded by a change of legal settlement, and even in such a nation as England no small proportion of the largest incomes belong to financiers and other persons who would escape the excessive rigour of taxation by change of domicile or by concealment of investments.

But when due account is taken of theoretical and practical difficulties, it remains true that a careful system of direct graduation could secure a large increase of public revenue. Income tax and inheritance duties scientifically treated are supplementary instruments for this purpose. But for their proper working two reforms in fiscal procedure are urgently required. The first is a compulsory return of income from all sources imposed on all persons liable to income tax and enforced by adequate penalties. This return must be checked by empowering the Inland Revenue to demand a return from all companies, giving particulars of all dividends, bonuses, and salaries. If, as may be convenient, incomes derived from companies are taxed 'at the source,' such tax should be graduated, not, as at present, on the sum of the net profits, but on the rate of interest earned on the paid-up capital. The present method would be indefensible, because, by taxing large businesses at a higher rate than small ones, it would interfere injuriously with the grouping of productive power in its most efficient forms. The other reform consists in the substitution of true graduation for graduation by sudden leaps at arbitrarily determined points in the scale of incomes and properties. These sudden advances are inequitable and obviously wasteful. The taxing system should be measured in percentages, carefully considered curves taking the place of the awkward irregular stairs which constitute the present rude notion of graduation.

But probably a government bent upon a scientific and productive application of the graduation policy would decide, in spite of authoritative warnings of conservative officials, to abandon 'collection at the source' and to substitute throughout a personal collection enforced by compulsory declaration of all incomes, and adequate penalties for failure to comply. Until compulsory declaration is enacted it is impossible for the state to possess the knowledge which will enable it to estimate the incidence and yield of any graduated income tax which shall aim to obtain for the revenue a considerable share of the unearned surplus in the higher grades of income.

§ 4.—The practical difficulties of obtaining any large amount of public revenue by taxing elements of surplus as they emerge in annual income has in most modern states led public financiers to pay more and more attention to accumulated wealth as an object of taxation, and in particular to those accumulations which are transmitted by inheritance. More 'surplus,' it is urged, can be safely intercepted in this way than by any attempts to perform the delicate and difficult work of distinguishing 'unproductive' and 'unearned' from 'productive' and 'earned' income. Hence most modern Governments are looking to 'death duties' as a principal source of growing income for the state. The taxable 'corpus' is better ascertained and far more accurately measurable than in the case of income, and, more important still, a larger share can usually be taken without danger of disturbing or weakening any stimuli to production. The whole of an inheritance is unearned by its recipient, and if it is a large estate it generally operates to diminish instead of stimulating the productivity of its recipient. Speaking broadly, one might say that the whole of the income it affords to the heir is 'unproductive surplus.' But the proportion of such inheritance that can be taken advantageously by the state depends, of course, upon the feelings or the actions, not of the legatees, but of the legator. An excessive rate of duty upon property transmitted at death might cause certain types of business men to give forth less productive energy (thus producing lower incomes) to save a smaller proportion of these lower incomes, and to dispose of a larger proportion of their smaller accumulations during their lifetime. Such effects would be regarded as upon the whole injurious to the cause of industry, and would *ex hypothesi* reduce the public revenue derived from inheritance duties. But the experience of many modern states tends to show that, while avoiding such excess, it is possible to secure, especially from large inheritances, a great and increasing revenue. Graduating in two ways, according to the size of the estate and the distance of relationship to the testator, the state is able to secure a large share of accumulated surplus.

Regarded as instruments for securing revenue, graduated income tax and graduated death duties are partly alternative, partly complementary. Since large accumulated properties are mostly derived from the higher grades of unearned income, a highly graduated income tax will reduce accumulation, so reducing the yield of death duties upon inherited wealth. High death duties, again, will check the growth of large incomes; the diminution in the net property received by legatees will *ipso facto* reduce the income which these properties will yield to their new possessors, and will limit the further increase of income from investment of the unused portion of the inherited income. On the other hand, the two processes of taxation are complementary in that they are both endeavours to secure for the state, by different methods and at different times, a share of 'surplus' wealth. A large portion of that which escapes the income tax collector is taken in its capitalised form through estate duties, while the net estates which pass by inheritance become further instruments of public revenue in respect of the incomes which they subsequently yield.

One issue of great practical importance arises in relation to the assertion by the state of its claim to a share of the 'surplus' by income tax and death duties. By treating the annual receipts from death duties as income available to defray the current public expenditure of the year, the state undoubtedly encroaches upon the *corpus* of industrial capital. While the yield of the income tax can fairly be transferred to the account of current expenditure in the state book-keeping, it is contended that the slice of capital which passes to the state in death duties should become public capital whose income alone should be available for current expenditure.

But this charge of dissipating capital by converting private property into public expenditure is less serious than at first appears, for a large proportion of expenditure in a progressive state is of such a character that it would be considered capital expenditure in ordinary accountancy. Such, for instance, is the annual expenditure upon public buildings and equipments, roads, harbours, and other more or less permanent works, together with a considerable portion of the expenditure on war-ships. It is, indeed, probable that the net result of the taxing system in a progressive state is to increase rather than diminish the amount of capital.

But it is evident that the whole question demands fuller treatment in regard to the wider policy of public finance. Many of those who approve a larger public ownership and control over property and industry look to the taxation of inheritances as the chief instrument for effecting their purpose. If the state could intercept, hold, and maintain a fifth of the larger properties which pass at death, treating it as public capital, it would at no distant time be the owner of a substantial share of the land and the industrial capital of the nation, without any of the inconvenience, expense and irritation ensuant upon more violent methods of expropriation with or without compensation.

The Budget of 1909, by its provisions enabling death duties to be paid in kind, gave clearer significance to this proposal. If the state, receiving payment in land or in shares, kept possession of these instruments, it would soon find itself partner, sometimes controlling partner, in many of the large businesses of the country. In this capacity it could draw public income for current expenditure, while exercising, as shareholder, a growing control over industry, which would thus, as far and as rapidly as might seem advisable, pass from private into public enterprise. By changing the nature of the investments which come into public ownership by death duties thus paid in kind, it would be feasible for the state to select those industries which by peaceful penetration it would 'socialise.'

§ 5.—When a state recognises as its first duty that of collecting from the industrial system the social income which at present passes wastefully to individuals who have not earned it, it will apply experimental science to the ascertainment and the taking of the income. With this end in view it will discard all forms of indirect taxation except such as may be defended on other than purely fiscal grounds.

There are, however, two not unimportant grounds for maintaining certain forms of indirect taxation. Duties and excise upon such articles as alcohol, and perhaps tobacco, are defensible, not merely on the ground that their contribution to the revenue of most modern states is so considerable as to render their withdrawal obviously impracticable, but because the regulation of the consumption of alcohol (and possibly of certain other articles) may be deemed expedient in the interests of social order, and taxation may legitimately be utilised in such cases as a means of maintaining social order.

The other use to which indirect taxation may be applied is to redress a certain inequality of incidence in the application of our main instrument of taxing policy, the graduated income tax. Our broad taxing principle rested on the assumption that 'unearned' elements varied directly and proportionately with the size of income, and that these unearned elements could equitably be taken because they represent income which would not be expended in ways conducng to the increased efficiency and productivity of their owners But, since in most cases direct evidence of the unearned character of such elements of income is not forthcoming, we have seen that the taxing policy based upon this assumption of the origin of income may be usefully qualified by taking into account considerations relating to the actual use of individual incomes. Mere size of income is not in itself conclusive as to the amount or the proportion of unproductive surplus it contains. If of two incomes of £1000 a year one is owned by a man with no dependants, while the other goes to support a wife and six children, it is evident that the amount of 'unproductive surplus' differs widely in the two cases But the size of a family is only one factor in the problem, so far as utilisaton of income for purposes of efficiency is concerned. The age, sex, and health of the family, the nature of the career of its rising members, the question whether the mother is alive or her place taken by a paid housekeeper : these and other relevant matters might be taken into account. Again, the nature of the income has an important influence upon its use : a large proportion of a precarious income can be invested so as to maintain in the future the efficiency of the family, while a safe income drawn from gilt-edged securities admits no such 'productive' use of its surplus.

If the taxable 'surplus' inferred from size of income were to be subjected to such direct tests of use, a close impartial scrutiny of the special circumstances of each family would be necessary. This method is applied in Prussia, where the local assessors take into consideration for purposes of abatement not only the size and age of the family, but various illnesses or other accidents affecting the expenditure of the family.

If the difficulties of entrusting to local assessors a task of so much delicacy and discretion seemed to render this method inapplicable in Great Britain, the same end might be attained by a lower scale of graduation in the income tax fortified by duties upon luxuries. In other words 'unproductive surplus' might be partly taxed through its expenditure. Motor cars, carriages, yachts, and other pleasure vehicles, race horses and other gambling implements, sporting and park lands, jewellery and other articles of personal display might be subjected to special taxes as indications of super-fluity of income.   In one or other of these two methods, by abate-ments based on evidence of productive expenditure or by taxes upon luxuries, the graduated income tax should be supported in order to give adequate validity to its main assumption that unearned surplus varies directly with the size of incomes.

§ 6.—One question relating to the principles and policy of public expenditure, the utilisation of the social income, demands recognition here.   How far can public expenditure be rightly dominated by con-siderations of mere industrial efficiency ?   In our treatment of the industrial system we have regarded it as engaged in producing goods and services which, rightly distributed, might be entirely devoted to promoting industrial advancement.   Our discussion of the part played by the state in determining distribution has also assumed a distinctively industrial end, the state, by regulation of industry, by public operation, and by taxation, intervening to secure a distri-bution favourable to industrial prosperity.   Whether state activity was directed to protect labour or the consumer, to work certain public industries, or to utilise the income obtainable from these latter and from taxation, the assumption has been that this state activity was devoted to securing such improvements in society as would be reflected in enhanced industrial productiveness.

It is, however, evident that this assumption, arising naturally enough in a treatment of society entirely as producer and distributor of economic goods, is quite unwarrantable.   An individual in making a good use of his income is clearly entitled to promote other ends than that of mere industrial efficiency.   A portion of his income earned by industry is rightly devoted to non-industrial purposes, to satisfaction of tastes and desires which, though contributing indirectly to his economic efficiency by promoting his wider personal development and well-being, cannot be valued upon this economic basis.   An individual is entitled to spend some of his income for purposes which have no direct or measured reference to his present or future economic productivity.   The same truth evidently applies to the state's use of the public income.   Industrial efficiency and progress must be regarded as only one factor in that social efficiency and progress for the furtherance of which the state must use its financial as its other resources.   In our final chapter, where we endeavour to indicate the place of industry in social life and the principles of the relation between industrial and social values, we shall perceive more clearly the need of rectifying the dislocation in the social system involved in any sort of treatment of industry separately from other human activities. Such dislocation and readjustment are, however, essential to the separatist treatment which science for purposes of economy must adopt. Attention is here directed to them in order to provide against a grave misapprehension of the principles and policy of public expenditure which might arise from the special attention devoted here to the industrial functions of a state. The question of the right adjustment of economic and non-economic claims upon the individual and the social income is one of great delicacy and moment, as also is the nature of the reactions between these economic and non-economic uses of income. But the solution of these problems clearly belongs to a wider economy, individual and political, than lies within the compass of our study of the industrial system.

CHAPTER XV

§ 1. There is no ground for a separate law of exchange for international trade, or for a special law of incidence of taxes upon imports. Political areas are not economic areas.—§ 2. Even were two nations isolated so far as direct flow of capital and labour is concerned, an import tax will lie upon surplus incomes in the exporting or the importing nations, irrespective of political area. It cannot normally be used merely to tax the foreigner. —§ 3. Only where rent of land or other surplus is a normal expense of production can any part of an import duty fall on the foreigner. The proportion of a wheat tax borne by the producer will be very small. —§ 4. Such slight contribution by the foreigner is more than offset, where the duty is protective, by the injury done to the taxing country by protection. It can only take foreign surplus which foreign governments have failed to take.—§ 5. Protective duties reduce the aggregate wealth not merely of the world but of the protecting country. They also reduce the share of this reduced aggregate taken by the workers in wages, enhancing the proportion of 'surplus.'

§ 1.—THE widespread belief that a government can profitably supplement the income derived from imposing taxes on the unproductive surplus of its citizens by import duties, which foreigners shall bear, requires some separate consideration. Such taxes are believed to produce two separate gains to the nation imposing them: an addition to the national income by making the foreigner contribute, and a protection and encouragement to home industries competing with foreigners, which makes them more productive.

Now since we have not directly discussed the effect of putting taxes on commodities, we will approach the issue first by asking what, in conformity with our general distinction between costs and unproductive surplus, must be the operation of such a tax imposed within this country, and then proceed to inquire what difference, if any, occurs when the tax is an import duty instead of a domestic tax.

If you put an *ad valorem* tax upon every article in a given supply the tendency of that tax will be to settle on the ' surplus ' profit or interest of the normal business, if the latter is in the possession of any such surplus ; if there is no such surplus profit or interest, but the normal expense of production includes some economic rent of land or some surplus in the price paid for any other factor of production, the tax, in part at any rate, will fall and lie on that. If, for instance, a tax were put on each ton of coal produced in this country, at a time when profits of the mining industry were at a minimum necessary to remunerate capital invested in it, the tax would fall in large part on royalties, for it would no longer pay to work the thinner or more difficult seams unless the royalties were reduced, and the actual or threatened stoppage of such working would bring about a reduction of royalties whenever new contracts with coal owners were being made.

Similarly, if a small tax were put on shoes or newspapers, some of it would probably be shifted on to royalties paid to patentees of machinery used in making shoes or in printing newspapers.

But if a tax were put on articles produced under conditions yielding no one any ' surplus,' the tax must cause a corresponding rise of price and so fall on the ' consumer.' As we saw, however, the ' consumer ' as such is not a taxable person, and a tax on him shifts restlessly until it settles upon the incomes of those classes of consumers which contain some elements of surplus upon which the tax ultimately rests. This process, as we perceived, was slow, wasteful, and imperfect in its working, but it followed this general law.

It is sometimes supposed that a tax will operate differently if it is imposed on goods produced abroad and imported into a country, and an elaborate theory of incidence of taxation is built upon this view. It is urged that whereas capital and labour flow pretty freely between trades within the same country, keeping values of different goods produced by these trades fairly proportionate to their normal expenses of production, there is very little free flow of capital and labour between different countries, so that goods exchanging between these countries do not necessarily tend to exchange according to what would be their normal expenses if they were produced in the same country. Exchange between two sorts of goods produced by isolated economic groups will, it is said, be different from exchange where groups are not so isolated.

But this argument for a special law of taxation as applied to imports is doubly defective.

In the first place, it is not true that there is such free fluidity of capital and labour as between trade and trade within any country on the one hand, or such lack of fluidity as between one country and another on the other hand, as to justify setting up a different law of exchange and of incidence of taxation in dealing with foreign trade.

There are plenty of trades and professions in this country into which the flow of capital, ability, and labour is so greatly restricted as to make them almost isolated economic groups But this fact only affects the rates of exchange between the goods of such trades and those of other less restricted trades, in so far as the isolation precludes effective competition among the members of such groups and so gives a monopoly or surplus element to the price of the goods.

If the same degree of effectve internal competition exists in two trades the fact that no direct transfer of capital and labour is possible from one of these trades to the other does not affect the operation of the ordinary law of exchange.

Apply this reasoning to the exchange of goods between groups of producers living in two different countries. Why should the existence of political barriers be assumed to make the ordinary law of exchange inapplicable ? In the first place we are not entitled to regard political areas as isolated economic areas. The modern internationalisation of capital, and to a less degree of labour and ability, has gone far to break down the isolation between most civilised political areas. A common world investment market has been set up which distributes capital for many productive purposes all over the world, making for a common level of real interest, while whole races like the Jews, Italians, Swiss, Chinese, Malays, form an international fund of labour with a similar levelling influence. It is not necessary that there should be close direct connexions between all or even most countries and trades, in order to secure such a degree of equilibrium as to destroy the validity of the argument for isolated groups. A small constantly open conduit between two pools of water suffices to keep them at one level, and a small constant flow of capital and labour as between the industry of one country and another operates similarly.

§ 2.—But even were this not the case—were we justified in regarding England, France, Germany, and America as isolated self-sufficing units, in a sense in which the several trades within each country are not—there would still be no justification for applying a different law of exchange in the two cases and basing on it a different law of incidence of taxation.

If England and Germany are exchanging with one another two sorts of articles, A and B, A produced in Germany only, B in England, under terms of such free competition as prevail in the respective countries, we may fairly assume that their selling prices correspond to normal necessary expenses of production in the two countries, though these may differ, for instance, as regard rates of wages or of interest. If they do so correspond, the mere fact that normal wages or interest differ in the two countries does not warrant the application of a theory of exchange different from that applied to commodities exchanging within one of the countries, in trades where wages and interest are the same; still less does it warrant the supposition that a tax will operate differently in the two cases.

If there is absolutely free competition in the production alike of A and B in their respective countries, the expenses and the normal selling price of each will be at a minimum, and if England put a tax on A entering England, or Germany on B entering Germany, no portion of such tax could lie upon the foreigner : if no portion of the foreign producers were making more than a minimum profit, the importation could only continue at a price which virtually made the importing nation bear the tax.

If, on the other hand, the foreign goods were produced under conditions of monopoly or restricted competition, so yielding a surplus profit, to that extent an import tax would tend to settle on the foreigner and to be paid out of his surplus. We could possibly make the Standard Oil Trust pay an import duty, or the bulk of it, on oil, or De Beers an import duty upon diamonds (were it not for facility of smuggling).

But in neither event, whether the industry producing the articles taxed is earning a surplus or not, does the incidence depend on whether it is an import duty on foreign goods or an excise on home produce. If there is a surplus it bears it, if not, the tax is shifted.

Let us, however, suppose that the foreign industry, upon whose imports a tax was levied, was partly subject to free competition, partly not, some better placed or equipped businesses earning surplus, others only covering expenses—a common case.

The foreigner here may seem to pay some part of the tax. But even here it can only be borne by such businesses as were earning some surplus, or only for a short period, for no trade can long survive at below a living profit. In any case the foreign industry would be damaged, and the new capital and labour which had hitherto flowed into it would go into other trades C and D, which must be considered slightly less productive. These latter trades would seem to grow and to turn out an increased output, while the trade hit by our import duty would decline in size and output. It seems at first sight that, if these other German trades can also export their surplus to England, they would now have a larger surplus to dispose of and would sell it to us, if we did not tax it also, at a lower price than formerly. So the result of our taxing one German commodity A would be that, though we took a smaller quantity of it at a higher price, we made it up by getting a larger quantity of C and D at a lower price. If we take account also of the contribution made to our national exchequer by the import duties paid in some part by Germany on A still entering our country, it seems to some that we may have shifted the balance of exchange in our favour, and may get a larger aggregate of goods from Germany in proportion to what we send her than before.   If this were so, it might justify a policy of import duties.   But if we look closer at the effect upon C and D of the flow of capital and labour liberated from A, we shall see that the reasoning just stated is fallacious.   In the first case, unless C and D were previously earning surplus profits by holding up prices above the competitive level, or were so inadequately supplied with capital and labour that their businesses were not properly equipped, it is not possible to admit that any new influx of capital and labour could enable them to lower prices either for domestic or for foreign markets, except as a temporary expedient.   If C and D, or any considerable section of these trades, are working at a minimum profit, we are not entitled to assume that more capital can advantageously flow into them, so as to lower prices in the English market.

But even if capital and labour, expelled from A by the English import duty, could flow into C and D, stimulating these trades, and causing them to put larger quantities at lower prices in the English markets, we cannot deduce from this proceeding any net gain for England.

For the capital and labour now flowing into C and D, instead of into A as formerly, is less productively employed, and the new product in goods of C and D available for exportation is a smaller one than that formerly produced in A.   Though, therefore, there will be an increase in the supply of C and D entering England as imports, which will bring down the price, that increase will be smaller than the decrease in the importation of A, and the rise in price of A will be greater than the fall of price in C and D.   By forcing some German capital and labour from a naturally more productive to a less productive employment, we cannot bring about a change in exchange, as between England and Germany, which will benefit the former by getting a larger quantity of German produce than before for the same quantity of English produce.   On the contrary, a unit of our export B which formerly went out to Germany in exchange for A will now buy a smaller unit of C and D than formerly of A, for C and D are more expensive to produce than A, and there will be less of them available for exchange.

Even if we added to the English account the proceeds of the tax paid on the portion of A, if any, which still came in, setting it off against the rise of price, there would still be a net loss to England, as also to Germany ; for instead of the portion of A, which has been prevented from being produced and exported by the tax, a smaller product of C and D is produced and exported. There is no reason to expect that a policy which should thus lower the average efficiency of capital and labour in Germany could produce a balance of trade favourable to us in the sense that it enabled a unit of British produce to buy a larger German product than before. It is evident, upon the contrary, that the purchasing power of a unit of British product over German goods must be reduced.

So far, we have taken the case of a tax on German products not produced in this country, the tax being imposed primarily for revenue, not for protection.

If the effect of putting an import duty on A, when A is only produced in Germany, is to divert some German capital and labour into less productive industries, and so to reduce the average and aggregate productivity of German industry, what will be the effect when A is also produced in England? The same tax which drives capital and labour out of A in Germany will operate, reversely, in England to call in capital and labour from other trades into A. Since it must have been more productively employed in these other trades before it was artificially diverted into A, there is evidently caused a damage to the average and aggregate productivity of English capital and labour corresponding to that caused in Germany, the injury being shared by the two countries. The only way by which supporters of protective tariff can evade this conclusion is by questioning one of the premises, viz. the assumption that there is a natural tendency for all the capital and labour in a country to flow into its most productive employment. Protectionism lives as a creed by the implicit or explicit denial of the validity of this assumption. If the effect of England taxing imports of A from Germany were to drive some German capital and labour from A into equally productive employment in C and D, then England, by substituting cheaper imports of C and D for dearer imports of A, would sustain no loss in exchange, while our national exchequer would gain the import duties paid on A.

If, again, the effect of protecting by tariff an English production of A were to draw into this trade some capital and labour from trades where it was no more productively employed, or even to give employment to capital and labour which otherwise could find no employment, then there could be no damage to our national productivity and might be some gain.

Indeed, so far as the beneficial influence of a tariff is concerned, the entire claim of the protectionist is seen to rest on one of two contentions.

The first is that, for some reason which is not explained, there tends to exist a superfluous amount of capital and labour which can by protection be brought into employment in protected trades without diversion from any other occupation. The second is that the natural distribution of capital and labour, directed purely by considerations of immediate individual profit, affords no sufficient guarantee for the proportionate development of a far-sighted national industry, which should be prepared to undergo certain immediate sacrifices for distant gains, and to substitute some fuller and more balanced standard of public welfare for the present profits of individual traders.

The 'infant industry' is one case of this second contention, which is at once a criticism of the *laissez faire* assumption that it is socially serviceable for the course of trade to be determined by the enlightened self-interest of tradesmen, and an assertion that the state can and will make a better disposition of the productive resources of the nation by using the tariff as an instrument.

§ 3.—The only valid case for import duties designed to tax the foreigner is where the duty is imposed on goods produced under conditions of monopoly or restricted competition and therefore carrying in their price a surplus element upon which the tax will lie. In other words, it is a method by which the national exchequer of one nation can tax indirectly certain unearned income made in foreign industries and enjoyed by foreigners. If the British Government chose to put a moderate tax upon paraffin oil coming from America, it is likely that the Standard Oil Company would not find it profitable to restrict its importation of oil into this country, so as to enable it to shift the tax on to the British consumer by means of an enhanced price.[1]

When, as is the case in agricultural produce and in certain kinds of manufactured goods, rent of land or other payment for natural advantages enters into normal expenses of production, and thence into price, an *ad valorem* duty imposed upon such goods when imported will fall in some degree upon the producer. This is the slight element of truth in the contention that a tax upon foreign wheat will be borne by the foreigner.

First take the hypothesis that a country entirely dependent upon foreign wheat imposed an import duty. The shifting of the import duty which the importer would be called upon to pay would be in this wise. Suppose the price of wheat paid by the importer prior to the imposition of the tax were

[1] It is not strictly true that the imposition of an import duty could have no effect on the selling prices of a monopoly. Operating, as it would, directly to reduce the margin of net profit on a certain part of the sales, it might cause the producer either to increase his output and so to reduce his prices, or to diminish his output and raise his prices. But there will be no normal tendency to increase selling prices and so to shift the tax.

25s. per quarter, the miller buying this same wheat at 27s. 6d. and leaving to the importer 2s. 6d. margin, which we will suppose to be the minimum necessary to pay him his wage of ability and interest on his capital. A 5s. import duty is now imposed on wheat which the importer is called upon to pay. He cannot, on our hypothesis, bear any of this tax himself, and must either throw it forward on to the miller, who, if he has no surplus profit, must pass it on to the consumer in raised prices, or he must throw it back upon the foreign farmer in the reduced prices he pays for this imported wheat. So long as the wheat continues to come in as fast as before it is not possible for him to raise the price to the miller. The first effect, therefore, must be to cause importers to stop buying wheat from foreign producers at the pace they bought before ; indeed, they will obviously refuse to enter any new contract to pay 25s. for more foreign wheat. The demand for foreign wheat at 25s. stopping, while the supply at that price remains as before, the buying price must fall. But must the price fall from 25s. to 20s., so that the price to the miller is 27s. 6d. as before, and the same margin, 2s. 6d., remains to the importer ? Not so, for as soon as the price paid by the importer to the foreign producer begins to fall below 25s. some foreign wheat will seek other markets, some foreign wheat lands will be diverted into other uses, and some poor wheat land will cease to be used at all ; thus the supply of foreign wheat for the importers to buy will begin to shrink. As the supply of foreign wheat shrinks, owing to importers offering lower prices, importers will find themselves able to raise their prices to the miller, who will have to replenish his stock from a reduced supply ; the miller having to pay a higher price must buy less, unless he can get bakers and consumers to pay a higher price and buy the same amount as before. This he cannot do, for if he raises his prices to consumers they will buy somewhat less. So he, the miller, must buy a smaller quantity at a higher price from the importer. Our importer thus recoups himself for his 5s. duty, partly out of higher prices paid on a smaller quantity of sales by the miller, partly by a lower price he pays for a smaller quantity of wheat to the foreign farmer. It is quite evident that some of the tax must be shifted each way, for to suppose that the foreigner pays nothing implies that the same amount of foreign wheat flows in as before, and this implies that the consumer will buy the same quantity as before, though he has to pay the extra price of 5s., a denial that there is any elasticity in the demand for wheat. It is equally evident that the foreigner cannot be made to bear all the tax, for this would imply that all the foreign producers were growing wheat on such favourable terms as to obtain a surplus of not less than 5s. per quarter on which a tax would lie.

The apportionment of the 5s. tax between consumer and producer would evidently depend upon the relative elasticity of demand in the consumer and of supply in the producer. The fact that bread is the prime essential in the standard of consumption of all classes in the nation will mean that the elasticity of demand is very slight, while the existence of a world market for wheat and the adaptability of most wheat land for other agricultural purposes will mean that the elasticity of supply is very great. In such circumstances, nearly all the tax will be forced on to the consumer, the producer paying comparatively little.

Of course, the distribution of such a tax would be affected by the question whether the taxing nation were entirely dependent upon the foreign supply. If it were not so dependent, and home-grown and colonial wheat were left untaxed, the 5s. duty being confined to foreign wheat, the effect would be slightly to increase the proportion of the tax borne by the foreigner. For while the fall in price paid by importers of foreign wheat as the first effect of the duty was operating in driving foreign wheat into other markets, and foreign wheat land into other uses, some compensation for this result would be obtained from the effect of higher selling prices in this country in putting more home and colonial land into wheat growing. This increase of the proportion of the aggregate supply of wheat exempt from the tax must evidently moderate the influence of the tax to raise prices to the consumer, and to that extent increase the proportion borne by the foreigner.

But just in proportion as this substitute of non-taxed home and colonial for taxed foreign wheat actually took place, the yield of the tax would be diminished, so that, though the foreigner might have to bear a slightly larger proportion of the tax than if he were the sole source of supply, the actual amount of taxation got from him will be even less.

The possibility of getting anything out of the foreign producer by import duties is thus seen to be confined to cases where an import duty finds some monopoly or other surplus in the foreign price which is not already taken in taxation by the foreign state, and which it can tax as such without appreciably affecting the supply. If there were foreign wheat lands which had no other positive use except to supply wheat for the English market, a special duty on this wheat might be made to some considerable extent to be paid by the foreign farmers. For some of the tax would settle upon rent and lie there. But the existence of a world market for wheat precludes this operation.

In the case of foreign manufactured goods imported into a country, there is no reason to believe that any appreciable part of an import duty can be shifted on to the foreign producers, except in the case of goods made by trusts or other monopolies, earning an excessive rate of profit by charging non-competitive prices. Under normal competitive conditions of manufacturing industry, the capital and labour in the trade will be disposed in businesses which are earning minimum rates of interest and profit : they cannot bear a tax, and they cannot raise their prices, for higher prices would mean reduced output, and they cannot reduce their output without increasing their normal expenses of production and so probably reducing their margin of profit or, if not the margin, their aggregate net profit.

§ 4.—This somewhat elaborate argument has been necessary in order to enforce the simple lesson that the power to tax the foreigner is strictly limited by the ability to shift a duty, first paid at our ports by our importers, on to surplus elements in foreign incomes.

Where an import duty can be got on to such foreign surpluses it will lie. But, of course, a tax on the price of commodities is a far clumsier and less effective way of taking a surplus than the direct income tax imposed on surpluses within our national area, and always involves some repercussion that is damaging to the people of the taxing country.

Moreover, it can only be got at all upon the supposition that foreign governments do not understand, or at any rate do not exercise, their own taxing powers in their own interests.

If Germany, America, or any other nation from which we receive imports, leaves untaxed surplus incomes derived from industries engaged in producing those goods, it is possible for our government by means of import duties to attach some small portion of this foreign surplus. But if we suppose, as is in fact the case, that most foreign governments are moving in the same direction as ourselves, and are trying, either by public operation of monopolies, or by taxation, to secure for their use the unearned elements of income within their nation, the futility of using import duties as a source of revenue becomes apparent. For direct taxation of net unearned income by the government of the country within which these incomes emerge is of necessity a far more potent method of attaining its end than import duties laid by a foreign government upon a portion of the goods which yield this income.

But though it is thus in theory, and sometimes in practice, possible for a nation by means of import duties to get hold of some elements of surplus income in a foreign nation, it would be profitable to use this power only in cases where the import duties were not protective. For if, as in the case of a tax on foreign wheat, the tax were designed chiefly to stimulate the production of domestic or colonial wheat, whatever income could be got by taxing the foreigner must be more than counterbalanced by the damage inflicted on the aggregate real income of the taxing nation. For this damage is not, as seems at first, confined to the rise of wheat prices paid by the consumer upon the whole of his wheat supply, a rise which it is the first object of a protective or a preferential tax to bring about. The damage inflicted through the effect of this protection upon other trades may be even more serious. For if a tax on foreign wheat, raising prices, makes wheat growing more profitable in the taxing country, capital and labour will be diverted from other industries into agriculture, the output of these other industries will be diminished, prices of their products will rise in the home market, and their export trade will also suffer. All these consequences are necessarily involved in a fiscal interference with the course of industry which has the effect of causing capital and labour to be engaged in intrinsically less productive channels than they would naturally have taken. These injuries would be ill compensated by any precarious income obtained by a protective duty from such foreign producers as were in enjoyment of a 'surplus' income which their own government had failed to tax.

The broader injuries inflicted by import duties are measured by their effect in impairing division of labour and local specialisation of industry throughout the industrial system of the world. Except in the rare case when an import duty falls upon a producer's surplus produced under monopoly, it must always damage the aggregate productivity of the nation imposing it, by diverting productive power from a naturally more productive into a naturally less productive industry, an effect which again reacts detrimentally, through exchange, upon the aggregate wealth of the foreign country, as indeed of all other foreign countries with which the taxing country is in commercial intercourse.

It is thus manifest that not merely do protective duties act so as to reduce the aggregate of world wealth, by impairing the co-operative action of the whole industrial system, but they operate so as to reduce the aggregate real income of the taxing country. For the reasoning which is adduced to show that, though the aggregate of world wealth is lessened by a protective tariff, the protective country itself may be a gainer, is quite invalid. The protecting country must always suffer in two ways; first, by impairing the aggregate productivity of its internal resources through employing some of them less productively than it would otherwise have done;

secondly, by reducing the amount of foreign goods it will get by process of exchange. The nearest the protectionist ever comes to making a case is where he can show, as he sometimes can, that the injury his tariff inflicts upon some foreign nation is greater than that which it inflicts upon his own.

But there remains another way in which a protective tariff affects injuriously the industrial system. Not merely does it cause a reduction in the aggregate product, both of the system as a whole and of the nation imposing the tariff, it damages the distribution of wealth within the nation, and so the efficiency of national production, by increasing the proportion of the reduced total product which goes as ' surplus ' to the owners of scarce factors of production. The practical politician surmises this to be the case by the energy and persistence with which rent and profit receivers advocate protection : though the nation loses, they may stand to gain. Import duties upon foreign agricultural produce raising the price of domestic produce, raise rent, the price of the scarce factor of production, land.

Similarly, manufacturers who, by a tariff upon imports which compete with their goods in the home market, can secure the market for themselves, and by means of syndicates or trade agreements can muzzle competition, will be able to sell their goods at prices which give them an excessive margin of profit.

The prime object of protection is to raise prices, and the benefit of the rise of prices is distributed among the owners of the factors of production in proportion to their economic strength, which normally means that it passes as ' surplus ' to the owners of land, or capital, or ability. Labour is certainly the loser, obtaining a smaller proportion of a reduced national product. If in some instances the workers in highly protected trades appear to benefit in higher money wages, most or all of this benefit is lost in higher prices paid on other goods in a protected country, while the workers in unprotected or less protected trades are unqualified sufferers from the tariff. This damage to the real wages of the workers, by reducing the proportion of the reduced national dividend which goes as payment for labour, is probably the most serious single injury wrought by a protective system, because it reacts by impairing the progressive efficiency of labour, and thus retards the growth of the productive power of the industrial system.

CHAPTER XVI

MONEY AND FINANCE

I

§ 1. All other uses of money are subsidiary to its use as medium of exchange. Everything with currency is money. Government usually maintains a standard unit of money.—§ 2. Most currency is paper, made by Government, as notes, or by private enterprise, as cheques and bills. A cheque is the joint product of an individual and a bank.—§ 3. Credit in the shape of bill-discounts and bank loans is based upon vendible property of all sorts with a gold guarantee against undue shrinkage or collapse of the property basis.—§ 4. The tendency of modern industry is to use all assets, material and immaterial, as a basis of credit-money. Money based on fictitious capital thus becomes a dangerous element of currency.

II

§ 1. Governments, banks, and money-lenders are the only considerable 'owners' of money: others 'hire' its use from them, paying interest or discount, directly or indirectly.—§ 2. An increase or decrease of gold supply has no regular or proportionate effect on volume of currency or on prices. Such effect as gold exercises is confined to the stimulation of demand for commodities.—§ 3. Quantity of currency varies with the work of conveyance of property to be done. Currency rests ultimately not on gold but on general wealth realisable by taxation, though some gold is, under existing circumstances, essential to maintain confidence.

I

§ 1.—IN tracing the operation of the industrial system we saw how money circulated through this system as a common universal fluid, acting at each point in the processes of production as a measured stimulus to the owner of each factor of production to apply his labour, capital, ability, or land in special productive arts. All income, as we saw, consisted of these payments, and by their means the distribution of the industrial product is effected. Attendant upon each industrial act is a financial or monetary act, payment which is at once a register and a motive to the industrial act. So we find in finance, or monetary activity, a complete replica of the productive industry which shapes and moves all forms of saleable commodities.

Whereas each industrial action differs in some regard from every other, being applied to different materials, in a different way, or in different circumstances by different persons, the action of money is almost absolutely uniform, it is the same sort of oil flowing to lubricate and stimulate all parts of the machine.

This fluid is, however, itself a part of the industrial system ; it is produced by various business processes which employ capital, labour, and ability, and it is bought and sold like other goods and services. But its nature, the methods of its production, and the terms for the sale of its use are unique, and require separate consideration.

What property or quality is it that enables money to evoke industrial energy wherever it is applied, constituting it a universal motive ? Industrial man is willing to give out industrial energy for money, because money is the most convenient instrument by which he can convert this energy, or the single sort of product that it yields, into the various other sorts of products that he wants.

Money acts primarily as a medium of exchange.

Money is not essential to all industry. In a self-sufficing communist family or group there would be no machinery of exchange required. Even where there is exchange, it can be carried on by barter, for after all every man who has superfluous goods of some particular kind desires to exchange them eventually for other particular goods of other kinds, and if he can find a man who has these spare goods and who wants the sort of spare goods he possesses at the same time, they can do business.

It is consideration of the defects of barter that brings out the virtues of money. In barter you may have to go far to seek your man who has what you want and wants what you have : you may want nothing now but something in the future, in which case simple barter fails ; if you meet your man there is no easy, peaceful way of settling how much of your superfluous goods should go against a given quantity of his.

If, therefore, anything can be found which everybody wants for his personal use all the time, or which many people want, which will keep, and which is fairly uniform and divisible, it will evidently save trouble for any one who has superfluous goods of any sort to let them go in exchange for this, and to use this to get the several sorts of other goods he wants. So in tea, tobacco, corn, or iron bars he can find a money which acts as an effective medium of exchange. If it satisfies a general want of an equable and lasting character, and is enduring, portable, divisible, and easily recognisable, it will serve for money, and the best money is that which has the best assemblage of these qualities. All of what are called the other uses of money (1) as a standard of value, (2) as a store of value, (3) as a security for future payment, are subsidiary and supplementary to the service of money as a medium of exchange. The owner of superfluous goods.

will take money for them because he is convinced that he can get, now or in the future, an approximately known quantity of any other sort of goods he wants. Anything that will give him this assurance or faith will act as currency, and is rightly classed as money.

Though intrinsic utility, widely recognised, is in most primitive societies an indispensable property of money, this is by no means always the case, and in modern civilised communities a large part of the medium often consists of inconvertible notes or tokens, or of coins whose intrinsic utility is below their purchasing power.

The part which government plays in creating, regulating, and maintaining currency is peculiar. The practice of taxation and of tribute by rulers of large domains first gave vogue to coined money. Coinage was designed as a certificate of weight and fineness of the metals to which it was applied : the stamp operated ' to save every man the trouble of carrying about with him a bottle of acid and a pair of scales.' Government has now come in most countries to claim a monopoly of the issue of coinage, fixing a standard unit of value—a certain quantity of gold or silver or other substance—and issuing coins which are a fixed fraction or multiple of the standard. In England the sovereign, containing 123·27447 grains of gold, is the standard. A shilling gives the right (up to 40s.) to demand gold to the extent of one-twentieth of the gold in a sovereign, though the actual exchange value of the silver in a shilling, as against the gold in a sovereign, is about 30 per cent. below one-twentieth. A shilling is thus, to the extent of 30 per cent., a token coin : a penny is the same to the extent of about 75 per cent. Tokens hold value and operate in currency because law or custom, or both, enable them to exchange freely for standard coins. Government not only standardises and issues these forms of money, but compels individual sellers to accept them, gold without limit, silver up to 40s., copper up to 12d. So it creates and puts in currency money which is legal tender. This legality or government authority has power to support the token value of the shilling and the penny. But if silver were made legal tender up to any sum equally with gold this inflated value of silver could not be retained. One of two things must happen. If any holder of silver can demand that it be coined into shillings and that shillings be legal tender to an unlimited extent at the ratio of 20 to 1 in sovereigns, a boom in silver mining would occur, and silver miners would bring great quantities of silver to be minted ; a corresponding slump would take place in gold mining. Every bullion dealer, money changer, &c., would cause gold coins to be melted down and to be exchanged as a commodity against silver which he would take to the mint and get coined, for he could get more shillings for his sovereigns in this indirect manner than by passing sovereigns directly against shillings. No one, in fact, would pay gold for any debt when, by exchanging his gold into silver, he could pay more easily. So it would appear that gold would pass out of circulation, the cheaper driving out the dearer sort of money in accordance with what is known as Gresham's Law.

Whether this would actually happen would depend upon the condition of the art of mining in gold and silver respectively. If the government said that a sovereign should exchange against twenty shillings, though the cost of producing the gold of one sovereign was equal to that of producing twenty-seven shillings, it is evident that the process of expulsion of gold from use would begin. Supposing that the increasing output of silver which now took place involved no increased expense of production, improved machinery and treatment compensating the cost of recourse to worse mines or worse seams, while, on the other hand, the net expense of producing the smaller output of gold by using only richer mines was not smaller than before, the full, continued operation of Gresham's Law would take place. But if the so-called law of diminishing returns were operative in the mining industry in such wise that the increased output of silver brought into use mines or seams which were more expensive to work, while the reduced output of gold correspondingly diminished the normal expense of producing gold, the expulsion of gold by silver for money might be checked by altering the ratio of industrial production so as to coincide with the legal ratio, at which point no further disturbance would take place. Gold mining would shrink, silver mining expand, until the expense of producing a gold sovereign was equal to that of producing twenty-seven shillings instead of twenty as before.

§ 2.—But most of the buying and selling is done by money which is not itself legal tender, and is not even issued or authorised by government.

Among the various forms of paper or representative money in this country only Bank of England notes are legal tender ; but all alike purport to entitle their holders to demand payment in some legal tender. The great majority of the payments made in the operation of the industrial system are made in paper not in coin. Only two large departments of payments are made chiefly by coin, the payment of wages of labour and retail purchases, though an increasing proportion of the latter are now paid by cheques or money orders. Probably 80 per cent. of the work of money in this country is done by paper ; in the greater part of the United States none but small coins are used at all.

When Bank of England notes, however, are used, or other notes against which an equivalent amount of standard money must be kept, the work of currency done by this paper may be attributed to the metal money.

The total work of finance, however, done by all sorts of governmental or publicly made money is much smaller than that done by the different forms of private-adventure currency. Though all cheques, bills, and other paper with which most of our buying and selling is conducted purport to enable the holder to get legal tender, the difference between the two is vital. For in the one case the guarantee is that of government, in the other case that of some private person or company of persons.

The difference in the degree of certainty, confidence, or credit attaching respectively to public and private forms of money, and to various forms of private money, is reflected in the area and duration of their currency. Whereas public money, whether coins or notes, in civilised countries under normal conditions, is current throughout the whole political area at its legal value and remains in currency until its material form is seriously impaired by use, private money is more restricted in its circulation.

Though the cheques and bills by which most large purchases are made are often called money substitutes, as distinct from money, no advantage is derived from this distinction. The essence of money is that it forms a medium of exchange, and anything that does this work should rank as money. The relation of cheques and bills to the legal tender money which is held to support them and to enable them to circulate is an important question, but it does not affect the fact that these instruments perform the function of money. They differ in efficacy from legal tender money in the fact that they have a shorter and a more restricted currency ; after serving as a medium of exchange once or a small number of times they are withdrawn and disappear. This restricted currency is a register of the fact that such money conveys no general confidence that its holder will be able to convert it into legal tender when he wants, or to use it freely for acts of purchase. Public money has free currency, because law makes its acceptance obligatory in all purchases or payments of debts where no special mode of payment is contracted for, and usage has made unquestioned acceptance universal. Private money carries no guarantee of continued purchasing power other than the promise of some private person or company of unknown solvency to convert it, on demand or at some stated time, into legal tender. This is made clear by consideration of the origin of all forms of private money.

A cheque is a form of money made by a private individual who has deposited gold (or an order on gold) in a bank, or who has been granted by the bank a right to demand a certain quantity of gold on account of a deposit of securities. The bank has undertaken to pay gold up to the amount of the individual deposit to any one to whom the depositor gives an order. Now, if everybody knew three things for certain, first, that the person whose name signed or endorsed a cheque had an account at the bank on which the cheque was drawn, secondly, that the account would not be overdrawn when the cheque was presented, thirdly, that the bank itself would be able and willing to pay legal tender, such a cheque would command the same confidence as legal tender itself, and if drawn for a round sum would circulate with the same freedom. But none of these conditions attaches to a cheque ; the person whose signature appears on the cheque may not in fact have any account at the bank ; if he has, that account may be overdrawn, and there remains the chance that the bank itself may not have the money wherewith to pay. It is evident that no one will take such ' money ' for goods unless he thinks he has some special knowledge of the character and financial circumstances of the drawer and of the bank, or that he can recover the goods or compel valid payment in case the cheque is not cashed.

The cheque, then, as an instrument of currency, is the joint production of an individual and a bank. Though the drawer is formally the person who brings into existence the particular cheque, the cheque system must be regarded as a product of the banking industry. In effect, a cheque is an undertaking of a bank to pay gold on demand up to the amount of a deposit. Since no bank keeps more than a small proportion of the legal tender deposited with it, to pay cheques presented at the counter or to meet its balance at the Clearing House, it is evident that if all persons entitled to demand repayments presented their claims simultaneously, they could not get gold. Banks do not keep this money in safes to meet cheques that might be drawn upon it.

The depositors who own this money do not want to draw any of it out in gold except for smaller domestic and personal uses. They want to draw cheques to make trade payments, but the business men who sell them goods and receive those cheques do not want to draw in gold, they want in their turn to make business payments and so on. For the larger movements along the industrial system little gold is used. What becomes then of cheques ?

From branch banks they pass to the head office, thence to London agents, thence to Clearing House to be sorted, set-off, and cancelled with small differences paid by cheque.

Very little gold or notes need be kept to meet the vast sum of indebtedness which at any given time the banks have incurred.

Most banks only keep gold sufficient for the till; this reserve (some 25 per cent.) is deposited with a London bank, probably the bank of which they are branches, and the London bank deposits a similar proportion of reserve with the Bank of England. Thus the only gold kept by the banking system (apart from till money) to meet its obligations to depositors is the ten or fifteen millions reserve in the Bank of England. Certain other money of depositors is put out in such ways as to be easily recalled. About 30 per cent. of deposits is thus kept in hand or at call. The other 70 per cent. the banks can lend on bills or loans at interest.

§ 3.—The origin and nature of the bank money which goes into currency through loans on securities or discounting bills are not mysterious.

A person holding shares in a substantial business or any other claims upon realisable property may be able, by depositing such securities with a bank, to get bank money as a loan. Here a bank enables an individual who has some special sort of property to exchange it for a time for money or general purchasing power. This money must be held to be the joint product of the borrower and the bank; the former by his security furnishes a basis or natural support, the bank undertakes the risk of transforming the security into bank money on which it undertakes to pay legal tender, holding a certain sum derived from its paid-up capital and its deposits to guard against this risk.

In essence, bill discounting, whether undertaken by bankers or brokers, amounts to the same thing, except that here the substantial basis of the credit or bank money is not ' securities ' but goods. A manufacturer supplies goods to a merchant who is not able or does not choose to pay cash for them. The seller draws a bill at three months, the buyer accepts by appending his signature, undertaking to ' meet ' the bill with cash when it matures. The seller endorses the bill. If the seller wants money for his goods which the buyer could not give, he takes the bill to a bill discounter accustomed to deal with this class of paper, who discounts it, giving him the discounted value in money which he generally borrows from a bank on his own security; in other cases the bank discounts the bills. So the manufacturer gets during the three months a sum of ready money which he would not otherwise possess, and which is created by bankers and brokers undertaking to provide out of their resources against the risk of the goods not being sold by the merchant before three months elapse at a profitable price, and the further risk of dishonesty or misfortune disabling the merchant from applying the proceeds of their sale to meet the bill when it is due. When, then, it is said that some 70 per cent.

of the money deposited with banks is used for loan or discount purposes, this does not mean that it is used to create advances to an extent merely equivalent to the amount of the deposits so used. It means that on the strength of these deposits the bank creates a much larger volume of ' credit ' which it uses for loan and discount purposes, the deposits helping to sustain the larger fund of ' money ' which it has set afloat in the commercial world.

The essence of this credit system is that it enables purchasing power or medium of exchange to be created on the basis of a claim to any sort of saleable property, by any substantial person or group of persons able to furnish an adequate guarantee to safeguard the holder of the claim against the risk of being unable to convert his claim into ready money when he wants it.

A bill discount means a bet on the part of banker or broker that the goods in respect of which a bill is drawn and discounted will sell, and the bill be met at maturity. He creates money on this belief, keeping a small reserve to meet the contingency of a failure of this expectation.

Since by far the greater part of buying and selling is transacted by means of these forms of credit or bank money, based on claims to vendible property, it is evident that the sense in which the whole money system is said to stand on the basis of the gold held by the Bank of England and other banks and private persons is a very restricted one. The gold reserve is a safeguard against the possible collapse of credit money based on specific forms of property which may shrink in value or prove non-vendible when it is required to realise on them. The fact that every form of privately created money purports to be, and legally is, a claim on gold or legal tender, tends to over-emphasise and even to falsify the part played by gold in the money system. In the working of the private monetary system of banking a margin of gold is essential, but no definite relation exists between this quantity of gold and the quantity of money and monetary work said to be based upon it.

It is far sounder to say that the quantity of money and monetary work is based upon the quantity of valid claims to vendible property that exist, and upon the conditions of commerce which afford security to these claims. For by means of the joint action of owners of property and bankers we perceive that all sorts of property can become the basis of credit, performing within a limited range of currency the function of money as a medium of exchange.

This capacity of all vendible property to become a basis of credit currency is a fact of immense significance in modern industry. For, since there is a business advantage in a firm using to the full its credit, there will be a tendency for every business to secure for its use bank credit corresponding to its full assets which can form collateral security. There will also be a tendency driving business into joint stock forms in which such use of assets to form security for credit is most available. This superior facility for utilising credit is one of the admitted advantages of large corporations. As more and more industry takes these forms the quantity of such credit currency is enlarged. The movement is towards a state of industry in which there will be credit currency corresponding to every sort of asset.

§ 4.—Thus we are brought to approach the question: 'How much money does there tend to exist?' with the answer that every piece of vendible wealth has potentially, and tends to have actually, its monetary or credit shadow, for any owner of such wealth can, under a fully developed system of banking and broking, get a constant use of bank money corresponding to that wealth.

Such a system does not indeed to-day exist, even in the most highly evolved financial communities. But if we include pawn-broking and other money-lending agencies, we shall find that there are comparatively few sorts of vendible goods of a material order which cannot, under stress, be converted into money, and that in larger organised businesses it is a point of ordinary financial economy to use the whole available assets when required as means of credit. The amount of credit money raised thus, and acting as purchasing-power at any given time, will of course vary very widely with the requirements of particular businesses and the general condition of trade, and advances upon any given piece of vendible property will not intentionally be made to cover more than such percentage of the whole value as leaves a sufficient margin for market fluctuations. For such loans and discounts and other forms of short currency must normally be cancelled by the sale of the goods upon whose value they are based, the money to cancel them coming from the proceeds of the sale.

Now, if all property upon which credit could be based were tangible assets, the quantity of such 'money' which would be available would fluctuate with the increase or decrease of the production of such tangible goods and with their market price. But a more complex consideration enters here. When, as is common, the whole capital value of a business becomes 'security' for credit or bank money, this capital value includes not only tangible but intangible assets, under which come 'goodwill' and other values expressed in share capital. Now the valuation of these intangible assets is very delicate ; the usually accepted basis of the valuation is the calculated or imputed earning capacity of the business, i.e. the rate and amount of future dividends. That the goodwill of a business is a genuine asset, and that, as such, when properly valued, it may form as sound a basis of loan credit as the material assets themselves, is true. But the valuation of such a property is essentially precarious and lends itself to the creation of excessive speculative values, i.e. to over-capitalisation. When the goodwill is estimated not upon the actual earning-power of the business in the past but upon the speculative or imputed earning capacity in the future, we perceive that credit based on such values may be entirely illusory or gravely excessive. For such a calculation deals with several ' unknowns,' the amount of future demand operative at various prices, the amount of future supply operative at these same prices, and the proportion of the total demand that will be supplied by this particular business. It is clear that in the fluctuations of modern industry credit founded on such calculations must be exceedingly precarious. Yet skilled company promoters and dealers in shares are largely engaged in capitalising businesses upon this basis, creating as much fictitious share value or ' water ' as they can.

This fictitious capital, so long as confidence supports it, can be utilised along with tangible assets and genuine ' goodwill ' as a means of loan credit. Thus at certain seasons large quantities of this bubble money may be endowed with an actual purchasing-power, though it must eventually collapse ; meanwhile it helps to swell the total mass of purchasing-power, and to operate upon prices of actual commodities.

Even honestly computed assets based on estimated earning capacity are subject to rapid changes from fluctuations of demand and changes of the margin of profit. That the monetary system should become more and more dependent upon the values imputed to these intangible assets is one of the great dangers of our time, illustrated most dramatically in the recent American crisis, due primarily to a rapid shrinkage in value of collateral securities based on over-estimated earning-power. With this disturbing effect of the wide and ill-controlled use of credit money we are not at present concerned. This brief exposition of credit is designed to show that the greater part of the actual purchasing instruments to-day is formed by converting all sorts of property into currency of limited but real circulation.

Money, or purchasing-power, we now perceive to be of two orders, differing in origin and nature. First, there is legal tender, consisting in this country of gold and other coins and notes convertible into gold on the guarantee of the government which issues such legal tender. Secondly, there is a variety of different sorts of so-called representative money, created by bankers, brokers, and other financiers, based primarily upon different species of valuable properties, tangible and intangible, the value of which they transmute from fixed to fluid assets, and the fluidity of which they purport to guarantee by keeping a reserve of legal tender.

Side by side in the actual operations of transferring property these two mediums of exchange work, the small mass of solid coins and notes constituting legal tender, and the large mass of privately issued paper resting on present and anticipated goods, and requiring the withdrawal from actual currency of a certain portion of legal tender held as bank reserves.

II

§ 1.—We have seen what money is and what it does. It is now important to ask how far the ordinary law of regulation of prices of commodities is applicable to the use of money. Does the supply and the demand for ' money ' differ from the supply and demand of commodities ?

We have first to distinguish the part played by government and banks from that played by the rest of the community regarding money.

The only persons who require to own and to hold permanently any quantity of money are governments, banks, and other money-lending businesses. To these certain coins and other forms of money are capital, and they require to own them as instruments enabling them to produce certain financial services. This arises from the fact that governments and banks are engaged in the currency business. Governments manufacture the portion of currency called legal tender, using expensive materials and making comparatively little out of it in the shape of margin of profit between expenses of production and the payment in terms of goods and services for which they supply the currency for general use. Persons who supply goods or services to government buy these forms of government money which are thus put into circulation, and having bought them own them for the time being. Being their owners they could consume them by boring holes in them and wearing them as necklaces, or melting down the gold into ornaments or otherwise. But they do not want to consume them in these or any other ways. Neither do they want to retain the ownership of any large amount for capital in their business or profession. Some small amount of legal tender we should be disposed to count as part of the ' fixed ' capital of most business firms, required as petty cash and for certain other ready money purposes. Though most even of this small amount is kept for them by banks, it may be regarded as continuously owned by the businesses, and as forming a small fraction of their fixed capital. Apart from these purposes no one wants to have the continued ownership of any quantity of legal tender, or indeed of any other currency, except banks and money lenders. What the ordinary person wants of money is not to own it but to get the temporary use of it as purchasing-power When he receives legal tender from the government or from some person who got it from the government, he does not want to keep it, but to get out of it a single use in an act of exchange, a single pull upon its power as a medium. In order to get this use he must straightway part with his ownership, passing it on to someone else. His attitude towards a coin, which for the time being is his property, is thus seen to be different from that adopted by him towards any other sort of property; he neither wants to consume it nor to keep it to assist him in his business. He wants not the coin or bank note but the single use of it as a conveyance or commercial cart, but instead of hiring the use of this conveyance for the single act he buys it and sells it again when he has done with it. Just so in certain countries, where horses are plentiful and cheap, and commerce simple, travellers will do with horses, buying a horse for a single journey and selling him at the journey's end. This is evidently only a mode of hiring, the difference between what they give for the horse and what they get constituting the price of hire. In substance, that is what is done in the case of legal tender ; although, as it does its work in currency, it is always the legal property of its temporary owner, it really passes along on a hire system, each person who gets it paying a trifle towards the hire to the person who parts with it, i.e. contributing a trifle towards the expense of the government in producing and keeping in currency the legal tender.

If we prefer, we may regard the first recipient of this legal tender from government as paying the whole hire for a long series of its uses in currency before it is called in, and getting back all but a fraction of this hire from the next person to whom he passes it, the latter passing it on once more on the same terms, and so on throughout its currency Though no such fractional payments for hire can be traced, it is difficult to deny, first, that government is paid by the users of legal tender for its use, secondly, that each user getting an equal use with every other must pay the same price, thirdly, that there is no other way in which these little payments for the use of legal tender can be made except in the way above described.

That this is the real nature of the part played by money and of the relation of the ordinary individual towards money becomes quite evident when we turn from legal tender money to the non-governmental sort which, as we see, plays so much the larger part in the industry. This sort of money, with limited currency, is quite evidently hired, and though the full price of its hire, the discount, is paid at the beginning of its currency by the person who gets it from the banker or broker or other money-lender, if it is used by other persons as purchasing-power before it returns to the bank or otherwise is cancelled, it will hardly be denied that each such user pays something in kind for the use he gets of it.

But though this seems to us the most reasonable way of representing the method in which the services of money as a medium of exchange are remunerated in the course of currency, the essential thing is to recognise that governments and banks are the true owners of the vast bulk of money, and that other persons only hire and pay for the use of it. Exactly how they pay is a matter of quite secondary importance.

For until we recognise the fundamental difference in the relation of governments and banks on the one hand, and ordinary business persons on the other, towards currency, we can have no clear grasp upon the relation between gold, general currency, and prices of commodities.

If this fundamental position is correct, the only persons who can be rightly said to buy gold apart from its use in the arts are governments and banks. These persons want to convert it into currency or into guarantees of currency which it is their business to produce and to put into circulation ; ordinary persons cannot be regarded as buying gold, but only as buying its use from the real buyers of gold, governments, and banks—its direct use from governments, as issuers of coins or gold covered notes, its indirect and subsidiary use from banks as issuers of bank money partly supported by a gold reserve.

§ 2.—The acceptance of this distinction enables us easily to dispose of the crude theory that every increase in the quantity of gold available for currency must necessarily be attended by a proportionate rise of prices, other things equal. No such result occurs or tends to occur, either directly or indirectly.

Even if all the increased output of gold was conceived to pass into the possession of individuals who used it to buy increased quantities of goods, its direct effect on prices would be far smaller than is commonly supposed. For it would increase demand for goods, not by the percentage it added to the amount of gold in actual circulation, but by the percentage it added to the total currency, the vast bulk of which, as we saw, was credit money, but which, within the limits of its currency, has just the same effect upon prices through demand as gold itself. Its indirect effect in stimulating output of credit money we will consider shortly, but its direct effect is not proportionate to its increase of the supply of gold, but to its increase of the supply of currency in general.

Even in admitting this quantitative effect some caution is needed. If capital and labour, employed last year in producing £10,000,000 worth of cotton, iron, or other goods, were directed into gold mining and produced £10,000,000 more gold instead of other wealth of the same value, it is untrue that any considerable addition would have been made to the purchasing-power of the community or any considerable effect produced on aggregate prices. For, as we have seen, the cotton and iron capitals, cancelled by this change, were able to support credit currency, if not to their full value, to a large proportion of it ; and the loss of this currency must be set against the gain from increased gold.

If, however, the increased productivity of gold mining without any such diversion from other industries produced the extra £10,000,000, and its owners were to apply it directly as additional purchasing-power in increased demand for commodities, there would be produced a rise in general prices equivalent to the ratio which this £10,000,000 bears, not to the amount of gold in currency, but to the total purchasing-power of the community including all forms of credit money. Now the total purchasing-power of the community during the year is equivalent to its total income during that period. If, therefore, £10,000,000 were added to the dividends of gold mines paid to British subjects in income, and the whole of it were expended so as to produce its full effect on prices, the latter would not amount to more than a rise of $\frac{10}{2000}$, assuming that the income of this country be estimated, as it is approximately, at £2,000,000,000. This will suffice to exhibit the absurdity of imputing any large fluctuation of modern general prices to the direct influence of an increase or decrease in output of gold, due to some new discovery of mines, or to some special drain upon the output in order to put some country on a gold basis.

For the whole amount of gold in the bank reserve and in currency in Great Britain does not exceed some £50,000,000.

If the increase of £10,000,000 entering our national income were all expended directly in demand for commodities, it is manifest that its effect on prices would not exceed our estimate. The very common notion that it would is based upon a quite illicit line of reasoning to the effect that the trades producing the goods first bought with the £10,000,000 would use this increased income in demanding a corresponding increase of commodities on their part, and so on with other trades supplying these commodities, until the original increased demand and its effect on prices are multiplied many times over. This argument is utterly fallacious ; the effect of the £10,000,000 upon the aggregate demand and so on prices is completely exhausted on the first application, all that is added to the total income and so to the total purchasing-power of the community for the year is £10,000,000.

But it is also true that there is another indirect effect on prices in the event of the £10,000,000 passing, as most of it would, into the gold reserve of government and banks. It would there go to increase the supports and guarantees of credit currency, the banks would be enabled and disposed to give discounts and loans on easier terms; ' money ' (i.e. the hire of money) would be cheap. Now when ' money ' is cheap more of it is likely to be taken by business men who use credit currency ; it will be a favourable opportunity to set on foot new productive enterprises and to extend existing ones. Business men will, therefore, be disposed to take bank money more freely at the low price which the influx of gold has occasioned. The really large and important first effect of the £10,000,000 on prices would be not upon prices of commodities but upon the price of money, i.e. the rate of discount. It is through this latter that we may trace the larger effect the new gold may exercise on general prices. For if business men take from the banks a largely increased supply of cheap money, they apply it, as all money is applied, in demand for goods, mostly for plant and raw materials in order to create or enlarge a business. This demand of theirs may far exceed the amount of new gold that has come into the banks, because the money thus taken out is only floated on this gold as a guarantee. In this way the gold coming into the banking system may stimulate a far larger demand than is represented by its amount, and so produce a far larger rise of general prices than it would if it were directly applied in demand for commodities instead of passing into the control of banks.

Those, however, who insist that in this way, at any rate, the quantity theory of the influence of gold on prices is justified, because it must produce its full natural effect through stimulating bank credit, are quite mistaken.

For no constant power can be attributed to a given flow of gold, or to a given fall in rate of discount, to induce the creation of new credit. The effect of a given increase of gold and of a given fall in discount will differ widely in different conditions of trade. Sometimes it will stimulate a large, at other times a small, increase in actual credit money. For, though money may be cheap, business men will not set on foot new businesses or extend old ones unless they see a reasonable chance of selling the increased output of goods at a profit.   Now, though cheap money is an obvious economy and keeps down expenses of production, this economy may be no sufficient offset against other rises of expense or against a depression of price due to slackness of demand.   This is only to say that the elasticity of credit varies enormously with other industrial conditions and the calculations and expectations based upon them.

For we have seen that the primary basis of credit is property of various kinds reckoned at its probable vendible value, based, where it is business capital, upon its estimated earnings.   The mere fact that the gold guarantee of such credit is strengthened will not in itself suffice to produce a great enlargement of credit money and so of actual demand for capital goods, unless there is a healthy state of production of commodities which are bought by consumers at profitable prices.   An increased influx of gold at a time when, from bad crops or from some slackness of demand following some national extravagance of war, a bad condition of industry existed, would not have much effect in stimulating credit or in raising prices.   Before traders or manufacturers take advantage of cheap money they must see their way to selling at a profitable price the increased output, which cheap money would assist them to supply.

For when trade is bad and prices both of goods and of securities low, it does not follow that an influx of gold, lowering further a rate of discount probably already low, will have any appreciable effect in stimulating business enterprise and raising prices.   On the other hand, when trade is sound and prices of goods and securities are firm or rising, a small influx of gold and a slight fall of rate of discount may have a greatly disproportionate effect in stimulating the creation of credit money and in raising general prices.

§ 3.—The quantity of valid currency depends primarily not upon the quantity of gold but upon the rate of production and consumption of concrete wealth, i.e. upon the amount of conveyance to be done by the medium of exchange.

If it is true that most forms of vendible property can be made to support credit money in some fairly constant ratio to their value, then the quantity of 'money' in a country will evidently depend upon the quantity of such forms of property and the scale of its values.

When production is large and, owing to healthy consumption, demand is also high, there is a great deal of 'conveyance' to be done, and the amount of valid credit currency to do it is correspondingly large   The business to be done by means of money makes its own medium of exchange, so to speak. Gold bars are needed to shore up falling confidence, they do not constitute the real basis of the monetary system, which is wealth of every kind, nor do they determine how much valid credit shall exist.

There is no inherent or eternal necessity that gold or any other expensively produced commodity should be required as a guarantee of currency. If government could be trusted not to abuse the right of issue, uncovered inconvertible notes might form the sole legal tender, and bank reserves might be kept in terms of this tender. Or, if the state were competent to do the banking and the money-lending business, resuming the sole function of issuing all forms of money which it once possessed, there would be no necessity, perhaps no utility, served in keeping a store of gold, at any rate so far as internal trade was concerned. What people want in the ' money ' for which they part with their superfluous commodities is, as we have seen, the full assurance of being able to get, now or when they want, a fair equivalent in any other sort of commodities they wish. This assurance a strong government could give without the trouble and cost of keeping a store of gold to back its word. If our present banking system can support upon its very narrow gold basis so large a credit currency, possessing as it does no power to make good its failure to redeem its pledges by drawing on the general wealth of the nation, it is tolerably clear that the state, possessing full power by taxation to draw to an unlimited extent upon the national wealth, could support as large a credit currency without the need of keeping any gold reserve. Under a private banking system, such as we have, a gold reserve is necessary in order to provide against the collapse of excessive or improper credit. Under a state banking system the whole national resources of the nation would furnish that reserve. In point of fact, this reserve does already stand behind our gold reserve whenever, as has several times occurred, it shows signs of inadequacy. The legal right to demand gold, and the reserve of gold, are not the real final supports of our currency. For, not to speak of the Bank of England notes to the amount of some £18,000,000 covered not by gold but by government securities, there is the power to suspend the Bank Charter Act, thus enabling a further unlimited issue of uncovered notes to be authorised by government in order to relieve a banking crisis. The authorisation of this suspension has several times sufficed to stop a run upon the banks, i.e. a demand for gold, for though this suspension, followed by an uncovered issue, would give no increased stock of gold and no increased power to get gold, it would give power to get a form of legal tender which for practical purposes, within this realm and even elsewhere, is ' as good as gold.'

It is ' confidence ' in the government, not gold, which is clearly the support of this issue, and ' confidence ' means a belief in the will and the ability to secure for the uncovered legal tender a stable purchasing-power equal to that possessed by gold. This ' confidence ' is so much greater than that of even the strongest banking business, inasmuch as it rests not on a reserve of gold limited to a small proportion of its assets, but upon the whole financial resources of the state, including its full power of taxation. The mere knowledge that the state possesses this power to support the credit system, and the belief that it would in an emergency use this power, stands to-day behind the credit of the banking system of this country, relieving it to some extent of the necessity of careful banking and of keeping a fully adequate reserve.

The case of the banking system, worked for private profit, and earning extraordinary high dividends by a highly restricted competition, is peculiar in its relation to the state. The obligation of the state to preserve the public from the disastrous effects of a financial collapse actually operates as an obligation to preserve the banks from the natural consequences of bad banking, thereby assisting them to economise their resources, to keep a smaller reserve than they must otherwise, and so to earn higher profits on their capital than they could if they had not this potential state support. However defensible on grounds of social necessity, this actual or potential reliance of a profit-making industry upon state aid is the most illicit form of socialism imaginable ; it is a public premium upon carelessness and extravagance. Nor is that all. *Ne Deus intersit nisi nodus vindice dignus.* A small bank may suffer the natural consequences of its indiscretion and be allowed to bear the full penalty, but a great bank, likely in its fall to bring about a collapse of general credit, must be sustained, if the support of its fellow banks does not suffice, by government. The knowledge of this discriminative support tends to give an advantage to large banks as compared with small, and driving a larger and larger proportion of banking into a few huge businesses, in great measure non-competing, helps to build up the strongest and most lucrative of limited monopolies in this and other countries.

The worst results of this illogical union and equally illogical division of the currency business between governments and profit-making companies have not been realised in this country, but in the United States, where during the recent financial crisis the national treasury was compelled in the public interest to relieve the great financial corporations from the natural penalties of their sins, they furnish a striking example of the instability of the present system.

It is hardly possible that the present anomalous position of our credit money system can continue long. Either governments must tend more and more to take over from private industry the banking and money-lending industries : or if the inherent delicacy of these financial acts be such that the more mechanical methods of bureaucratic management are incompetent to cope with them, the informal state support or guarantee which exists now must be regularised, accompanied by measures of public supervision and by adequate taxation of the monopoly profits of a valuable publicly created business. If money-lending, like liquor dealing, is left in private hands, it should be licensed, supervised, and made to yield its proper special quota to the public revenue.

If a universal provider in whose present and future stability I had complete confidence gave me orders payable in goods, these orders would be to me as good as gold. But if I had not complete confidence I should prefer gold. If a state such as ours either undertook the issue of all credit money or guaranteed it, the degree of confidence within the nation would doubtless be adequate to support an uncovered and inconvertible paper currency. It might, however, still be necessary to keep a gold reserve for purposes of foreign exchange, though even here it is at least arguable that, if England were known to keep no gold, her notes would possess sufficient confidence, at any rate in all civilised countries, to perform the functions in international balance which her gold now performs, i.e. that they would be generally accepted on a par with gold at their face value.

Gold is only necessary ' because of their unbelief ' : just as the ground and the reality of that unbelief diminish the gold guarantee of credit money grows smaller. So long as most money is issued by private enterprise some gold must help to make it pass. Even if governments were sole issuers or gave full guarantees, many governments do not command such confidence even among their own subjects, much less among foreigners, as to secure their paper a free currency at par. Not until, if ever, such a political society of nations is formed as can provide an international guarantee of national credits does it seem feasible to dispense entirely with a gold or other intrinsically valuable support for international currency. But it remains true that as our industrial and commercial civilisation advances gold has a constantly diminishing influence in the determination either of aggregate quantity of currency or of prices.

CHAPTER XVII

INSURANCE

§ 1. Insurance produces four utilities—(1) reducing the pain or subjective injury of an accident, (2) producing a sense of security, (3) evoking productive energy, (4) preventing objective waste.—§ 2. Economy of provision against risks drives insurance into very large business forms. The state tends to displace private enterprise so far as the chief working-class risks are concerned. The investment side of the insurance business constitutes a formidable barrier against full nationalisation.

§ 1.—No description of the outlines of modern industry would be complete without reference to the business of Insurance, which is so intimately associated with finance. It is not, however, from the standpoint of its place in general finance that we must first approach it. We have first to ascertain what part, if any, insurance plays in the industrial system so far as the latter is regarded as an instrument for producing and distributing goods and services. What does insurance produce? We can best formulate our answer by first putting another question, viz. What damage would be done if there were no insurance? The life of a producer often comes to a sudden end; if no provision were made for securing to those dependent on him a continuance of at least a part of the income he earned when alive, they must sink suddenly into a lower standard of living, perhaps into penury, and both their happiness and their present or future efficiency as producers might be greatly impaired. By paying a comparatively small sum over a long term of years, which involves the habitual deprivation of what, if expended otherwise, would constitute the least useful and pleasurable part of his whole expenditure, he is enabled to avert a certain damage of a serious kind affecting the comforts, conveniences, or even the necessaries in the standard of life of his family. What insurance here produces is evidently the difference in disutility between the sum of the small losses involved in the payment of the yearly premiums and the great loss involved in the sudden total withdrawal of the whole or a large part of a family income. The substitution of the former small disutility or cost for the latter large one is in effect the production of so much utility, not merely from the standpoint of the individual but from that of the society to which he belongs. It causes, directly, no increase of concrete goods or services, but by assisting a more equable distribution over time of the aggregate of such objective wealth, it causes more to be got out of it in satisfaction and in subjective utility. In averting a damage to the productive power of industry by a sudden loss of family income insurance may also be considered as directly productive of industrial energy.

Insurance against fire, shipwreck, and other risks of destruction to property fulfils a similar purpose in the industrial economy. Except in a quite secondary way it does not aim at preventing the destruction of such property, but it prevents the loss from falling suddenly in its full force on any owner, by distributing it over a large number of owners and over a large period of time. If I live long enough, the chances are that my house will be burnt down. If I have not insured, I shall suddenly find myself without a roof over my head and with no ability to get one. If I insure, I must content myself with a very slightly inferior house, but I have absolute security against the former terrible predicament. So it is with every sort of business insurance: the sudden total destruction of some important part of my material capital may destroy the whole efficiency of what remains and may suddenly cancel the value of my business ability.

We may then clearly distinguish four utilities produced by insurance, two subjective, two objective. In the actual working of the industrial system a number of separate sudden accidents occur, involving damage to the individuals whose lives or property are concerned ; insurance spreads the loss over a large number of persons and makes it continuous instead of irregularly recurrent. This 'socialisation' and equalisation in time greatly reduce the net amount of pain or subjective injury caused by any single accident. This is the first subjective utility.

Again, the higher nervous organisation which human life under modern conditions of civilisation evolves, makes men more anxious about the future, while at the same time the complexity of modern industry and life makes it more difficult to foresee and make special adequate provision against the various accidents. Without insurance the worry caused by conscious inability to provide against an increasing number of more highly-appreciated risks would become an almost intolerable strain, enhancing the subjective or human cost of production throughout the business world. As the spread of education and the stir of modern city life cause larger and larger numbers of the workers to have more feeling for the future of themselves and their families, this extensive and intensive growth of anxiety is exhibited in an immense expansion of private and public insurance. The main direct object of such insurance is the production of a sense of security. With these two subjective goods two objective goods are associated. Anxiety or fear depresses the spirit, weakens the intellect and will of man, thus damaging the faculties which are most important in the best processes of production. A reasonable measure of security is essential to evoke the best productive powers ; without such security man cannot, and will not, do his best. The production of security is therefore a direct enhancement of productive energy.

Finally, as we have seen, a sudden damage to the standard of living of a family by loss of life or injury to the means of livelihood may cause a further loss of productive power. The death of the uninsured father may cause a physically injurious or a demoralising reduction of income, a removal to a less healthy neighbourhood, or the withdrawal from school of the children at a too early age to put them to work. The destruction of an uninsured mill or workshop may involve much further loss by waste of other capital and prolonged unemployment of labour, through financial inability to replace the property destroyed.

§ 2.—Thus objectively regarded, the industrial function of insurance is to supplement the ordinary provision for wear and tear of the industrial fabric, which we saw was the first charge upon the product, by an extraordinary wear-and-tear fund to meet the irregular and unforeseen injuries to the human or non-human factors of production.

To this end a great and elaborate system of insurance finance springs up, adjusted to meet the different sorts of risks involved in various industrial processes. Although the chances of death may not be precisely equal in any two cases, though the risks of fire may not be precisely equal for any two houses, the law of averages enables trifling and often incalculable differences to be safely disregarded, the innumerable little pluses in some cases being balanced by corresponding minuses in others. This system of provision against risks, of course, works out more accurately the larger the number of cases involved. If ten persons formed a company paying yearly premiums for mutual life insurance, the death of one of them in the first year would wreck the company ; if a thousand formed a similar company the policies paid would still vary considerably, taking one year with another, and a grave epidemic might cause financial difficulties ; but if ten million lives were so insured, the fluctuations in the yearly liabilities would be very small, especially if the insured persons were drawn from a wide local area with great varieties of occupations. It is this consideration which drives all insurance business into larger and larger companies for safety and economy, and impels even large companies, though competing for business, to pool their risks by re-insurance or by systematic distribution. The recognition of the dangers involved in the private monopoly of insurance, together with a perception of the fact that for certain common risks the entire nation constitutes a better business basis for insurance than any smaller group within the nation, is driving a larger and larger quantity of insurance business into the hands of the state. This is particularly the case with regard to the graver accidents or other injuries to the lives of the workers, whose narrow means, ignorance, or insufficient appreciation of the future preclude them from making adequate provision. Old age, poverty, accidents, sickness, burials, maternity, unemployment, are coming more and more to be recognised as a proper sphere of state insurance. The normal wage-system does not enable individual wage-earners by private combination to make any sufficient or secure provision against any or most of these contingencies. If, as is acknowledged, it is not merely the interest of the individuals concerned, but of society, that proper provision shall be made, the state will be the instrument employed. Germany among the older states, New Zealand among the new, have gone far in their experimental legislation along this road ; other nations follow.

The question of the mode of raising this public insurance fund, whether by special contributions from workers and employers, supplemented by state subsidies, or by payments from the general national revenue raised by ordinary processes of taxation, will mainly depend for its answer upon the view of the incidence of taxation taken by statesmen. Those who hold that a contribution can be stopped out of wages without impairing the supply or the efficiency of labour, and that it is socially desirable to employ the intricate and expensive method of retail collection, so as to enable each man to realise his public duties and rights, will prefer the German method, or some modification of it. Those who hold that a compulsory contribution, however small, out of wages, must either injure the efficiency of labour, or else be transferred on to employers' profits or other ' surplus,' will tend to reject the retail method of contribution as wasteful and clumsy, and to prefer the simpler method of providing these funds of social insurance out of the general revenue of society.

How far or how fast the state socialisation of the insurance business will go it is difficult to prognosticate. At present the manifest interest of society in the life, health, and physical well-being of the working classes, and the equally manifest inability of those classes to provide for these essentials on their own account, are the driving forces towards state insurance, which at present does not transcend these limits. Insurance against mere losses of property and life insurance of the richer classes are generally left to private enterprise, partly because such losses are considered to be of individual rather than of social consequence, partly because private enterprise still seems better adapted to cope with their special requirements.

It appears, however, unlikely that this somewhat arbitrary distinction between the public and the private spheres of insurance will be permanently maintained. If, as is admitted, the larger the area of insurance the better the security, this fact would seem of necessity to turn the scale in favour of state as compared with private insurance, not merely for the working classes, but for the rest of the community.

There is, however, an important qualifying circumstance which needs here to be taken into account. All insurance companies, especially life companies, combine with the function of insurance that of investment. The productive disposal of the premiums which they receive implies the direction and application to industrial purposes of a large quantity of 'savings.' But the chief life companies not merely thus invest their insurance premiums but are a general medium for investments which are combined almost inextricably with insurance. For this purpose a great variety of policies are devised, some with annual dividends, others with reversionary additions which go to swell the amount of the insurance, others again with deferred dividends to be paid at certain intervals, or to go as reductions of the insurance premium. An almost endless variety of methods exists of paying the premium and of receiving the bonus and the sum insured, most of them combining in some degree participatory profits with insurance.

A continually increasing quantity of investment is thus placed in the hands of insurance companies, which have become in most developed industrial nations main conduits of finance, dividing with the great joint-stock banks the function of directing the flow of available new capital into the different channels of productive employment.

Though governmental regulation tends to tighten round the administration of these companies, regarded either as general repositories of the people's savings or as insurance instruments, with the especial object of insisting upon adequate reserves and of checking misapplication of funds, no government has yet felt strong enough to contemplate the nationalisation of this great department of finance. Indeed, it seems difficult to conceive a government department entering the general business of investment. If, as is quite conceivable, a state should extend its insurance business so as to cover the whole range of life policies, it might probably decide to invest the premiums in purchasing consols or in financing public works, rather than by employing them as capital in outside trade, paying the policies as they fell due out of the general·current revenue, even as the Post Office insurance is in effect administered to-day.

Indeed, the future attitude of the modern state towards the new structure of finance, whose control over industry and politics is rapidly being concentrated in a few virtually non-competing groups, opens some of the most momentous issues of the new state-craft.

CHAPTER XVIII

UNEMPLOYMENT

§ 1, Cyclical unemployment cannot be attributed to failure of wheat harvests, for (1) statistics show no correspondence between changes in world production of wheat and fluctuation of employment, (2) the effect of a shortage of wheat upon the aggregate employment could not be large. A simultaneous shortage of several important raw materials may appreciably affect employment, but statistical evidence does not indicate such shortage as a chief cause of cyclical unemployment.—§ 2. Machinery or other improvements in an industry may cause an increase or decrease of employment in that trade or related trades, according to 'elasticity of demand,' but cannot account at any given time for any large proportion of displacement.—§ 3. For the main cause of unemployment we must look to the action of the 'unproductive surplus' in stimulating automatic saving at a higher rate than is needed and can be used to assist in making provision against future consumption. Economic checks on over-saving only operate where much mischief is done. The unemployed problem is that of the existence of a simultaneous excess of all factors of production.—§ 4. Analysis of the course of actual depressions confirms this interpretation. The psychological or 'credit' explanation turns ultimately on the known inability of business men to dispose of goods at profitable prices, i.e. the failure of consumption to keep pace with power of production.—§ 5. The existence and amount of over-saving is concealed by the mechanism of investment. In depressed trade over-savings need not stand in a growing pool of idle capital: their owners may invest them, not in setting up new capital forms, but in acquiring property from impoverished owners.—§ 6. This analysis furnishes a test of the efficacy of all remedies or palliatives of unemployment. The validity of remedies depends upon their power to stimulate consumption by increasing the proportion of spending power vested in the workers or in public bodies.

§ 1.—SOME waste of productive energy in the working of an industrial system is inevitable. Even in an industrial society where all the arts of production and all the standards of consumption were either stationary or else changed with slow and calculable regularity, climatic and other natural influences affecting crops and other raw materials must have some considerable effect in determining the volume and the regularity of the employment of the factors of production engaged in working up such raw material into vendible commodities.

Where each little locality is for most ordinary purposes self-dependent, using its own agricultural and other natural resources to supply the needs of its own inhabitants by its own industry, such natural happenings as droughts, storms, floods, diseases of crops and cattle, must involve great irregularity of employment. Where millers only grind the wheat grown within a few miles of the mill, where spinners and weavers are entirely dependent for their wool upon a single country-side, employment even in the staple manufactures must remain very uneven and precarious. Every expansion in the area of the market for raw materials and for products evidently diminishes the aggregate waste of industrial energy from these natural causes. For it is less likely that crops will fail over an entire county than in a single parish, in the whole country than in a single county ; and when there is a world-market for wheat the aggregate waste will be reduced to a minimum. Every improvement in transport, in storage, and in markets, equalises both in space and time the uses of raw materials for production and for consumption, and tends correspondingly to regularise the working of the whole industrial system.

Now that a relatively free exchange enables each country to make up any natural failure in its own resources from a larger number of other countries in most important sorts of perishable materials, the irregularity of national employment due to such causes has greatly diminished.

The notion, therefore, widely prevalent in earlier economic interpretations, and still entertained in some quarters, that the great periodic depressions of industry and employment in such a country as England are even now directly attributable to failures of harvests, will not stand investigation.

The statistics of wheat production and of unemployment show no such coincidence of fluctuation, either in duration or in intensity, as to support the view that a failure of harvests is the main cause of cyclical unemployment.

The statistical bureau of the Agricultural Department at Washington has published since 1890 an annual computation of the wheat harvests of the world, which, though not possessing any high degree of exactitude, is the best available evidence. Since Great Britain draws more freely than any other country on the world supply of wheat, it is reasonable to suppose that the extent of the causation of unemployment due to short harvests will be indicated clearly, if not closely, in the relation between the fluctuations of the Washington figure for wheat and the average percentage of trade-union members out of employment in Great Britain. The following table presents the material of the comparison :—

Year.			Wheat Harvest in Bushels.			Percentage Unemployed.
1891	..	..	2,432,322,000	..	..	3·00
1892	..	..	2,481,805,000	..	..	6·20
1893	..	..	2,562,913,000	..	..	7·70
1894	..	..	2,672,341,000	..	..	7·70
1895	..	..	2,552,677,000	..	..	6·05
1896	..	..	2,506,320,000	..	..	3·50
1897	..	..	2,333,637,000	..	..	3·65
1898	..	..	2,921,005,000	..	..	3·15
1899	..	..	2,725,407,000	..	..	2·40
1900	..	..	2,627,971,000	..	..	2·85
1901	..	..	2,929,333,000	..	..	3·80
1902	..	..	3,103,710,000	..	..	4·60
1903	..	..	3,189,813,000	..	..	5·30
1904	..	..	3,152,127,000	..	..	6·85
1905	..	..	3,200,959,000	..	..	5·60
1906	..	..	3,435,401,000	..	..	4·10
1907	..	..	3,108,526,000	..	..	4·20

Now, making due allowance for the gradual increase in the wheat supply required to meet the needs of a growing world population of wheat consumers, and bearing in mind that the effect on the wheat supply should be related rather to the unemployment of the following year than to that of the same year, this table clearly shows that no considerable causal influence is exerted by the wheat harvest upon the state of employment in this country.

This inductive testimony accords with a sound theoretic interpretation. Important as is the wheat harvest in its bearing upon human welfare, its direct effect on volume of employment is commonly misunderstood. The statistics indicate that a shortage of the wheat harvest, making allowance for the normal increase, seldom exceeds one-tenth. Now, the direct result of such a shortage would be upon the employment in the set of industries engaged in preparing, carrying, and distributing this important article of food : robbed of one-tenth of their usual supply of raw material, these industries would find that one-tenth of their plant and labour was superfluous. Now, even if we place so high an estimate on the proportion of employment engaged in handling wheat as to impute to them one-eighth of the whole volume of industry, a shortage of one-tenth in the wheat harvest would seem only to imply as a direct effect a reduction of one-eightieth in aggregate employment.

A shortage of wheat, however, it is urged, will reduce the general value of employment by diminishing the demand for other sorts of commodities. There are two ways in which this argument is worked. Though the price of wheat will rise, some argue, it will not rise enough to give the cultivators and the handlers of wheat for transport, manufacture, or distribution, as large an income as they normally possess. They must, therefore, reduce their demand for the various commodities upon which they expend their income, and unemployment in the trades producing these commodities must ensue. Others argue, on the contrary, that the shorter supply of wheat will cause a rise of price so great that a larger aggregate amount of money will be paid for the short supply than for a fuller harvest. For the elasticity in demand for wheat, it is contended, is very slight. The well-to-do will not consume less bread because the price is high, while the effect of dear bread upon the workers is to make them curtail their expenditure in meat and other foods so that they tend even to increase their consumption of wheat.[1] Thus a larger share than usual of the general income will go in buying wheat, and a smaller share will be available for buying other goods. Unemployment, therefore, ensues in all these other trades.

Now, in the first place, it is evident that these two arguments cut one another's throat, one implying that a larger spending power is given to the producers and handlers of wheat, the other a smaller spending power. It is evident that each of the contentions can be reversed. If the spending power of the wheat producers and handlers is reduced because a smaller aggregate sum is paid for a short harvest, the spending power of the rest of the community upon other articles is *pro tanto* increased. If, on the other hand, a larger aggregate of money were paid for the short harvest, its recipients have their spending power increased by just as much as the general consuming public find theirs reduced. There is a change in the distribution of spending power and of consequent demand for employment, but no net diminution. Some dislocation of trade may be fairly attributed to the change of distribution of income, but there is no reason to assume that the aggregate of spending or of employment will be less.

There is, however, another way in which it can be urged that a short harvest will cause general unemployment. The producers of metal, textile or other goods produce them in order to exchange them for all other commodities, including wheat. The shortage of wheat, with a rise in its value per bushel, will signify that the value of a unit of steel, cotton, or other goods, in terms of general commodities (inclusive of wheat), has somewhat shrunk. So far, then, as the quantity of wheat obtainable in exchange is in part a motive to all other producers to employ their capital and labour, this motive is now weakened. Some capital and labour in other trades will, therefore, pass out of employment because the potential owners of what they could produce find the real wealth they can

---

[1] The validity of this assumption, however, cannot be maintained. Since there is an actual shortage of wheat the well-to-do or the workers, or both, must consent to consume less.

get for them reduced in quantity. There will be in various industries employers who will find that their ' real ' profits will be reduced, first, by the fact that they must raise wages in order to enable their employees to pay the higher food-prices without which they cannot consume enough to maintain their working efficiency ; secondly, by the fact that their profits expressed in money are diminished in purchasing-power so far as their own consumption is concerned.

Now this contention is valid. So far as the competition of employers for profits governs production and employment, a fall in real profits, due to a reduction in the exchange rate of other goods against wheat, must be considered to have some influence in reducing employment. If a number of other foods and raw materials besides wheat suffered simultaneously from a shortage, which was continued over a series of years, it is undeniable that the shrinkage in the amount and the purchasing-power of interest and profit would have a considerable effect in reducing the employment of capital and labour in all sorts of industry. Though the failure of even so important a supply as that of the wheat harvest, mitigated as it is by the unconsumed part of last year's supply, could not of itself suffice so to affect prospective profits as materially to influence employment, it may reasonably be held that a simultaneous reduction of output of several important foods and materials, lasting for one or several years, might have a considerable joint effect, operating in two ways : first, by direct effect on the trades handling the ' short ' supplies ; secondly, by the indirect influence through exchange upon the real interest and profit of *entrepreneurs* and investors. *Entrepreneurs* and investors are essentially speculators producing goods in the expectation that they will sell at prices which will yield as good profits as they did formerly. If they come to recognise that as the result of failures of important supplies their goods can only effect sales on terms which will reduce their real profits, they will slacken production in their trades, and this conduct, reacting upon other trades, will get a cumulative effect.

This, I think, must be recognised as one important contributory cause of cyclical employment. A simultaneous shortage in two such important commodities for England as wheat and cotton, accompanied by other minor shortages, may have exercised an appreciable influence in precipitating the depression of 1908.

But such evidence as is available does not justify the view that the only or the chief industrial cause of cyclical employment lies here.

We have already seen that the size of the wheat harvest, so far as it is measurable, does not appear by itself to exercise any appreciable effect upon employment.   No sufficient or reliable computation of the world supply of foods and materials in general exists to enable us to ascertain by direct comparison how far their fluctuations agree with the fluctuations of employment.   But so far as rise in price is indicative of shortness of supply [1] the statistical evidence does not afford much support to those who would explain general trade depression by failures of harvests or of other supplies of materials.   The following Table, which compares our trade union employment with Sauerbeck's Index Numbers recording price changes in foods and materials during the last twenty years, discloses no appreciable effect of changing prices either of foods or material upon employment.

Sauerbeck Index Numbers.

Year.	Percentage Unemployed.	Food Prices.	Material Prices.	Total Prices.
1888	4·15	72	69	70
1889	2·05	75	70	72
1890	2·10	73	71	72
1891	3·40	77	68	72
1892	6·20	73	65	68
1893	7·70	72	65	68
1894	7·70	66	60	63
1895	6·05	64	60	62
1896	3·50	62	60	61
1897	3·65	65	59	62
1898	3·15	68	61	64
1899	2·40	65	70	68
1900	2·85	69	80	75
1901	3·80	67	72	70
1902	4·60	67	71	69
1903	5·30	66	72	69
1904	6·85	68	72	70
1905	5·60	69	75	72
1906	4·10	69	77	77
1907	4·20	72	80	80

While, then, the irregularities of world harvests and other supplies must be considered likely to exercise some influence upon the aggregate volume of employment of industrial energy, even in a country which, like Great Britain, utilises most fully the world market, these irregularities furnish no adequate explanation of cyclical trade depressions.

§ 2.—Nor can we trace these major wastes of employment to the changes either of methods of production or of consumption which are continually taking place in progressive communities.

[1] Of course it must be remembered that a rise of prices may be directly due to increase of demand as well as to decrease of supply, a consideration that must greatly weaken such statistics as evidence of causality.

The introduction of new machines and other labour-saving processes, the substitution of one material for another, steel for timber, electricity for gas, cotton for wool, &c., is constantly throwing out of employment specialised capital and labour in particular trades ; changes in the *locale* of industries, the decline and eclipse of local or even national industries by changes of taste or fashion among consumers, are constantly taking place.

Where such changes are gradual and foreseen no considerable amount of waste either of capital or labour need be involved : a suspension of the flow of new forms of capital and labour into a trade will enable it to die a natural death without any appreciable quantity of positive unemployment ; a labour-saving economy may be adopted in an expanding trade so as to cause no absolute displacement of labour. Except in the rare cases of a rapid application of new industrial power to large industrial industries, such as took place in the early decades of the nineteenth century in England, changes arising from new industrial processes are seldom so rapid and simultaneous as to cause great displacement of labour.

Where it is not a case of displacing hand labour by machinery, but of displacing inferior by superior machinery, it usually pays the employer to make the change slowly, and though there have been some recent exceptions to this rule, this law tends to secure a more gradual movement in the further development of machine economy.

That the introduction of labour-saving machinery is directly responsible for a certain not inconsiderable amount of unemployment of labour is, however, undeniable. It is true that, on the whole and in the long run, machinery does not of itself tend to reduce the quantity of employment. Indeed, it is urged with some reason that machinery ought to make for increased employment, inasmuch as by increasing the absolute productivity of labour, it enables a less efficient worker to work and earn a livelihood than could do so when hand labour called for greater physical capacity. In any case, there is no reason in the nature of things why improvements in other instruments of production should cause less labour to be employed. The first obvious effect of machinery is to cheapen expenses of production and lower selling prices. This will stimulate demand for the product, and that stimulation may be so great as to afford employment in the trade for as large or even a larger number of workers than before. The assumption, however, that machinery must increase the aggregate employment, either in this particular trade itself, or in that trade *plus* the machine-making and subsidiary trades, is, of course, unwarranted. All depends upon the effect of the machine in lowering the selling price, and the effect of the lower selling price upon effective demand. In no two cases will these effects be quite the same. There will always be some effect in stimulating demand, but the effect may be so great as to cause an increase of employment, or so slight as to mitigate to a trifling extent the displacement of labour which it is the first object of machinery to compass. The introduction of spinning and weaving machinery into Lancashire and Yorkshire afforded a considerable increase of employment, and a number of successive inventions and improvements during the second and third quarters of the last century had a similar result, but later increments of machinery have not been attended by similar results; on the contrary there has been a decline in the number of persons employed in some of the staple textile processes. The introduction of type-setting machines into printing works has been followed by a large increase of employment; the introduction of clicking machinery into the shoe trade has been followed by a net reduction of employment.

These instances will serve to illustrate the truth, obvious from general reflexion, that the net effect of machinery upon employment in a trade will vary with the ' elasticity of demand ' for the particular product of that trade.

When the fall of prices due to introduction of machinery has not caused such an increase of demand for the product as to give employment to as large a number of workers as before in this trade and the trades making the machinery, there is still no reason to impute a net reduction of employment to the machine. For the consumers of this lower-priced product will now have to spend a smaller portion of their income in buying it, and will have a larger portion free to demand increased quantities of other sorts of commodities ; the effect of their increased purchases of these latter will be to stimulate the industries and the employment of labour engaged in making these commodities, and the labour saved in the first industry will be absorbed in the latter.

This theory of the effect of machinery on volume of employment, is, with a certain qualification which will appear later, quite correct.

But while there is no reason to regard machinery as responsible for any large proportion of the unemployment which shows itself during periods of depressed trade, it is idle to ignore the fact that the progress of machine economy implies a continual displacement of bodies of workers in trades where such changes are rapid or unforeseen, and that these displaced workers may undergo a considerable period of unemployment before they are absorbed in other trades. Many of them, especially those no longer young, are not able to find other work which they can get and keep, or if they can it is lower grade, lower paid and less reliable employment than that from which they were displaced.

A large number of little wastes of labour-power, amounting to a small percentage of the total labour-power in a progressive nation, is constantly in evidence, constituting an amount of unemployment, which, though essential to the present working of the industrial system, is directly attributable to machinery, and is naturally resented by the workers called upon to bear it.

Such displacement, however, together with other detailed unemployment due to special trade causes, is always occurring, and the multiplicity of its causes makes it likely that it forms a fairly constant factor in the unemployed problem.

It is no more possible to explain the deep depressions of employment marked in Great Britain by the years 1868, 1879, 1886, 1893, 1904, as due to the introduction of machinery, than to regard them as the products of bad harvests. In one or two of these depressions, one or other or both of these causes played some appreciable, though a minor, part.

§ 3.—Neither is it possible to explain the large depressions of employment by misapplication of capital and labour as between trade and trade, too much being put into some trades, too little into others—the miscalculation of investors. For the characteristic feature of a full trade depression is its general character ; all the staple industries are seen to be congested with productive-power either simultaneously or in close causal order, a general fall of selling prices being accompanied by a slackening of all the main processes of production in the manufacturing, transport and distributive trades ; abundance of 'free' capital exists, seeking, but unable to find, any profitable investment, while mines, mills, foundries, factories, warehouses, shipping and railways are all working short time.

These are the periods when the engineering, shipbuilding and metal trades show unemployment in their trade union members reaching as high as fifteen per cent. and when many other trades better able to distribute the slackness reach ten per cent. of unemployment.

The actual drop of the rate of production in such periods, as compared with years of active trade, is far larger than even such percentages would indicate. For the slowing down of the whole industrial system is not at all adequately represented in the actual closing of works or the reduction in number of hands. Though no even approximate measure of the reduction in the pace of the output of production during depressed years is yet attainable, it will probably be found largely to exceed the trade union figure for unemployment.

It is not unnatural that, for the chief underlying cause of those trade depressions which exhibit large under-employment of the several factors of production over the whole field of industry, we should look to the operation of that 'surplus' of rents and other 'unearned' income which lies heavy upon the economic system. In order, however, to understand how the existence and size of the 'surplus' affect the magnitude and regularity of production and employment, it is necessary to revert to the preliminary analysis of the quantitative relations between production and consumption in Chapter III.

In our investigation of the processes of spending and saving we pointed out that for any industrial society the proportion of its income which in any given year could be saved for conversion into new forms of capital must depend upon the state of the industrial arts upon the one hand, and the standards of consumption upon the other, and that, though these arts of production and consumption were not fixed, their changes were comparatively slow and regular, and could not be forced to respond to any increase in the proportion of spending or of saving. In other words, if the aggregate income of Great Britain were taken as £2,000,000,000 per annum, this representing the payments made to all the owners of factors of production, it could not be a matter of indifference for the future volume of production whether £300,000,000 or £400,000,000, were saved. For if £300,000,000, saved and invested in new forms of capital, provided adequately for the increased demand for final commodities which the rising consumption of the growing population will create in the calculable future, maintaining full employment for the factors of production, an attempt to save and apply to productive purposes £400,000,000 out of the same aggregate income would be an excess of saving that would defeat its purpose, creating more forms of capital than were wanted and than would actually be used.

The test of an extreme hypothesis will make this evident. If some great spiritual or hygienic preacher could impose the gospel of a 'simple life' so effectively upon an entire industrial community as to induce an abandonment of the consumption of all luxuries and comforts, leaving only the use of bare physical necessaries of life, it is obvious that these could be supplied by about one-half of the existing capital and labour of the community, and that the other half would remain unemployed. The appearance of unemployment might be averted, either by reverting to more primitive methods of production, or by putting all forms of capital and labour on half time, but the waste would be inevitable. A community capable of turning out £2,000,000,000 worth of commodities which sought to consume only half this quantity and to put the other half of its income into new forms of capital, would be evidently guilty of insane conduct. The impracticability of such an economy would be obvious.

But if in a community where the right present adjustment between spending and saving were 17 to 3, there operated forces tending to shift the proportion to 16 to 4, i.e. to save £400,000,000 instead of £300,000,000 out of a general income of £2,000,000,000, the social waste might not be so easily detected or so quickly checked.

Now my proposition is that the existence of a ' surplus ' income, not earned by its recipients and not applying any normal stimulus to industry, has the effect of disturbing the economical adjustment between spending and saving, and of bringing about those periodical congestions and stoppages of industry with which we are familiar. In a single-man, or ' Crusoe ' economy, the proportion between consumption and saving, i.e. between the amount of energy given to making consumables and that given to making new tools and breaking new ground, would be determined by a close comparison between present and future pleasures and pains. Crusoe would find himself willing to give so much extra energy to making provision for increased consumption next year, but no more. So with a completely communistic society, if it could be got into proper working order ; it would regulate the proportion of its saving to its spending by a careful calculus of present and future human satisfaction. The rightness of such calculations would be based upon the fact that all saving required a proportionate effort on the part of the individual or the community that made it. If in a society that was not communistic but individualistic this prime condition were present, and all saving involved a corresponding effort or sacrifice, the right adjustment between saving and spending would be equally secure. But if, as regards any large proportion of the saving, this condition is not present, there is no automatic guarantee for the maintenance of the right proportion between spending and saving. Now that ' saving ' which is made out of unproductive surplus income is not amenable to this calculus ; unearned in origin, such ' surplus ' is not allocated to the supply of any particular human needs, as is the case with that income required to maintain or stimulate human efficiency of production. It may, indeed, be said that human craving for expenditure upon luxuries is insatiable, and that wealthy owners of ' surplus ' income must be conceived as balancing present against future satisfactions, and so making painful sacrifices when they save. But such balancing will be far looser and will yield very different results from the balancing of working men who are called upon to save. Even if the cases are rare where complete satiety of satisfaction for present expenditure is attained, there are many cases where this condition is approached, and where all further ' surplus ' accumulates automatically. There is reason also to believe that even among the merely well-to-do a large proportion of the more fortuitous ' surplus ' which comes from successful investments, not being wanted to support the current standard of consumption, is reinvested. This phenomenon naturally arises from the fact that the arts of individual consumption are more conservative than the arts of organised industry. The standards of life are for most people more conventional and more stable than the standards of work. The result is that where the command of the new wealth due to industrial progress passes largely into the hands of a small class, much of it is accumulated and reapplied to industry from sheer inability to make consumption keep pace with rising income. The visible and considerable rise in the luxurious expenditure of all the rich and well-to-do classes is only an inadequate attempt to keep pace with the modern increased power of production.

Though we fear inductive evidence upon such a point is not available, it will hardly be disputed that the proportion of saving is generally in direct ratio to the sizes of incomes, the richest saving the largest percentage of their income, the poorest the smallest. If this be so, any tendency towards greater equalisation of incomes, either by the successful pressure of the workers for a larger share of wealth or by the taxation of ' surplus ' for purposes of public expenditure, will involve a reduction in the proportion of saving to spending in the aggregate income.

Now, is it seriously maintained by anyone that a readjustment of incomes so equitable and so socially expedient would check industrial progress by unduly restricting the quantity of saving and investment ? Would the endeavour of the workers to raise their standard of consumption and of the state to raise the public standard be checked and thwarted by the lack of the requisite capital and labour to meet the new demand for commodities ?

Is it not rather obvious that this increased demand, due to a readjustment of income, providing and requiring, as it would, increased employment alike of capital and labour, would so stimulate the operation of industry as to validate at least as large an absolute quantity of saving as before, though a smaller proportion of saving to spending has been effected ?

If there were two communities upon the same industrial level, each with an aggregate income of £2,000,000,000, but one of these distributed this income so that the wage-earners took only £600,000,000, while in the other they took £1,000,000,000, is it contended that the general volume of consumption would not be larger in the latter or that there would not be enough capital and labour to maintain the larger volume ? Not merely would the volume of consumption be enlarged by diverting 'surplus' into wages of efficiency, but the character of the consumption would be steadier, depending, as it would, upon the rising standard of consumption of the workers, than the same amount of consumption expended upon the luxuries of the rich. Indeed, one of the most important results of this reform would be that the more stable character of national consumption would react upon industry, making the employment of capital and labour more regular and calculable, and reducing the relative importance of the fluctuating trades engaged in satisfying shallow tastes and trivial needs.

If this *à priori* reasoning be sound, it establishes at least a *prima facie* case for regarding 'surplus' income as an important cause of restricted and irregular employment. There is no natural limit set upon the proportion of 'saving' out of surplus income. The two normal economical checks usually adduced as preventives of excessive saving are thrown out of gear. The first, the falling rate of interest, though not wholly inoperative, will be less effective in its action upon this sort of saving than upon any other. Indeed, the inadequacy of changes in the rate of interest as regulator of the amount of saving is very generally admitted by economists. The second check, the effect of falling prices, due to increased production, in stimulating spending and so checking saving, has no true efficiency. For the first direct effect of falling prices is a corresponding fall of money incomes, which, as we have seen, are derived from retail prices by distribution at the various stages of production : and if money incomes fall *pari passu* with prices, there is no reason to expect that a fall of prices will stimulate demand for commodities. If it be alleged that, though prices fall, incomes will not fall correspondingly, because a larger number of purchases will be made at the lower prices, we can only reply that this begs the very question at issue. The play of elasticity of demand is here inhibited by falling incomes.

In point of fact, trade depressions, with falls in profits, interest and prices, are not thus easily or automatically checked.

It is not, of course, denied that the industrial system does apply checks for the adjustment of the relations between production and consumption. What is here contended is that these checks are made less effective by the existence of an improperly digested surplus in the economic system, and only operate after much waste of productive power has taken place.

The natural effect of such a surplus will be to put into the industrial system a larger quantity of new forms of capital than are economically needed to maintain the future supply of commodities at the pace at which they will be withdrawn for consumption. The endeavour to use this excessive capital to produce commodities results in that congestion of the system which is the immediate cause of trade depression and of unemployment. It is not merely a case of unequal production, an excess followed by a deficiency. If in an industrial community, where the right adjustment of spending to saving is 15 to 3, there should be a disturbing force tending to force the proportion to 14 to 4, the aggregate of production over the whole period of boom and depression will be less than if the right proportion had been maintained throughout.

The ' unemployed ' question is not distinctively or peculiarly a labour question : it is the problem of the simultaneous excess of all the factors of production. In a full depression all the forms of capital and of labour requisite to produce wealth are there, but they cannot produce. This is sometimes denied. It is admitted that plant and fixed capital exist in superfluity and are unemployed along with labour, but it is maintained that the circulating capital required to pay wages and so employ labour is wanting. So there is a reversion to an exploded wage-fund doctrine to explain depression. A formal refutation of this doctrine fortunately is not necessary here. For the fact of a deficiency of the means to employ labour is denied. Whether wages be taken as the money which must be advanced to labour before its product is sold, or as the food and other commodities which are needed to support labour, there is no necessary deficiency of either. So far as the money is concerned, when a depression is set in money is usually cheap, and any employer can get credit on easier terms than usual, provided he can give security, i.e. can show that there is a probability of his selling at profitable prices the goods he could produce by setting at work his idle plant and labour. So far as the real wages or commodities are concerned, it is manifest that, if the capital and labour which stand idle at all the different points in the processes of industry used their actual producing power, the required commodities would be produced as fast as they were needed for consumption by the wage-earners who now had money to spend in buying them.

So far we have set our argument to show that there is an *a priori* necessity for an unproductive ' surplus ' to disturb the quantitative relation between production and consumption, and so to lead to periods of depression.

Let us, however, now approach the problem from the other end, examining the nature of a periodic trade depression. The simplest diagnosis of a depression is that it shows all the factors of production simultaneously existing in excess of the actual industrial requirements. Not in this trade or in that, but throughout the whole industrial field are found mines, mills, foundries, railways, factories, warehouses, shops, with the labour that belongs to them, working short time or lying idle. There is more productive power of every sort than is wanted for actual production. Why cannot these productive factors co-operate to produce commodities as heretofore when trade was active ? Because the organisers of production have reason to believe that, if they set the available productive power fully to work, they could not sell the product at a price which would cover the expenses of production.

There is only one rational explanation of why they cannot do this year what they did last year. If there is operative in the system any force tending to increase the producing power faster than the rate of consumption, as we see there is in the over-saving of the surplus, it will produce just the result which we see. A trade depression is a condition of general under-production directly connected with a condition of under-consumption. This is an undeniable statement of the facts. We think it will also be generally admitted that under-production, or unemployment, is directly due to inability to sell all that could be produced at profitable prices.

§ 4.—It is, however, often urged that the direct cause of the slackening or stoppage of production is the refusal of bankers and other credit makers to furnish credit to would-be producers at a reasonable or at any price, and it is quite evident that this phenomenon must be taken into account in explaining a depression. But why do bankers at the beginning of a depression refuse producers or would-be producers credit upon the terms they furnished it formerly ? It is not because they have not the ' money ' to advance ; on the contrary, at such times loanable capital lies in their hands in larger quantities than usual. They do not furnish money as formerly, because they have lost ' confidence ' in the ability of customers to repay the loans, and because the collateral security that is offered has shrunk in value. But why have they lost 'confidence'? and why have securities (usually ' shares ') sunk in value ? Their ' confidence ' and the value of securities have shrunk for the same reason, because of a belief that the products which the borrowers design to produce will not find a profitable market. Now this belief, this lack of confidence, this shrinkage of securities, are not mere psychological phenomena: they have their ground in actual facts relating to the sale of goods. The lack of confidence which leads bankers to refuse credit is attributable to their knowledge that sales of commodities have already been effected at a shrinking margin, that the actual markets are becoming congested with unsaleable commodities, and that the bottom is not yet reached. In other words, the psychological explanation of depressions is an interpretation through finance of the actual maladjustment of productive power and rate of consumption in the industrial system.

The financial system, with its instruments of credit, has the effect of postponing and concealing for a time the effects of this maladjustment and of making the crises more violent when they actually occur. It is not difficult to understand how this must be

Let us start from a period of prosperous trade with high, firm prices. Every manufacturer and merchant at such a time wants to do as much business as possible : he wants to extend his premises, put in new plant, buy larger stocks of materials and employ more labour, so as to earn a higher margin of profit on the largest possible output. He therefore seeks to use his credit to the full : he can get a large supply of money, comparatively cheap, because bankers and other furnishers of money believe that the investment will fructify in profitable sales affording a certainty of repayment, and the ' collateral ' for the same reason ranks high in value, for the value of stocks and shares is directly dependent upon profitable sales of the product of the company. In prosperous trade, then, bankers create the maximum of ' money,' supporting the ' boom,' and helping the business men to increase to the utmost the actual productive power and the actual rate of output. Now, if this rate of actual output never became excessive, i.e. if there were an adequate provision that the rate of consumption should rise *pari passu* with every increase in rate of production, there is no reason why any lack of ' confidence ' should enter the mind of bankers and financiers.

But suppose that from the cause we here adduce, some comparatively slight deficiency of spending and corresponding excess of saving, there has been put into productive operations a little more capital and labour than is wanted to maintain the supply of commodities at former prices, what will happen ? A weakening of prices will be the first symptom, and as prices begin to fall the margin of profit diminishes, and with this diminution of the earning power of capital the repayment of loans, the meeting of bills, become less certain, while the collateral securities also shrink. At the first signs of a weakening of markets the banks, not believing the check to trade is serious, may probably buttress with further credit firms in whose success they are already strongly interested, enabling the firms to tide over difficulties for a time, and to go on producing full blast.　But if there exists some real excess of producing power, this further use of credit can only make things worse, helping to continue loading the markets with unsaleable goods, bringing down selling prices, converting former profits into losses, and causing a shrinkage of values of securities.

As soon as this state of things becomes pretty evident, the so-called ' want of confidence,' which seems to many economists the *fons et origo malorum*, comes into operation.　Banks begin suddenly to raise the price of money, and to refuse advances to businesses which they had fed up with credit ; the money which passes into their control from the saving and investing public is no longer invested productively.

Weak businesses, now dependent on credit, not in order to earn profits but to prevent collapse, find greater and greater difficulty in getting it on any terms, and they begin to break.　For a time ' money ' may be procurable for stronger firms, though at such high price as diminishes their profits already hit by low prices, and so lowers the value of their stock, reacting once more upon their credit.　Businesses which can conceal their real condition in the earlier stages of depression may still utilise the credit system to enable them to continue producing in a falling market, which they thus help further to congest.　Every art is used to procure credit to tide them over what is believed to be, and actually may be, only a temporary crisis.　But if a real prolonged depression is on its way, it is easy to see that such abuse of credit must aggravate its effect. When want of confidence is fully set in, and it is practically impossible to obtain ' money ' from bankers, while no one will look at any new investment, the ' stoppage ' of production and the consequent unemployment of capital and labour assume large dimensions.

Sometimes the ' want of confidence ' is precipitated by a dramatic collapse, which suddenly exhibits the growing rottenness of trade.　Some bank or investment company, whose securities have run down or have become unsaleable, is unable to avert suspicion, or to tide over a depression, or to meet its obligations, and is obliged to close its doors.　Suspicion is directed, rightly or wrongly, on other financial houses believed to be directly involved in the failure or to have been engaging in similar bad trading ; depositors and investors, seeking to clear out, convert suspicion into panic, and the panic may spread until otherwise substantial and conservative houses are involved, unless the rotten businesses are cut adrift and a solid organised stand is made by corporate action of the strong financial houses.

So absorbing is the distinctively financial aspect of these crises which often herald a widespread depression, and so clearly traceable is the financial collapse to psychological conditions, that not only financiers but commercial men and manufacturers are often led to treat booms and depressions of trade primarily as tidal movements in the minds of men. Out of a normal state of quiet confidence somehow men grow sanguine, and a state of excessive confidence supervenes which breeds speculation and risk-taking; this over-confidence is maintained, and grows until some incident, small in itself, calls a halt, the tide begins to turn, and the irrational excess of confidence becomes an irrational defect, causing a contraction of the springs of credit corresponding to the former expansion, and so bringing to a stoppage the wheels of industry !

Now, our analysis of the relations between finance and industry leads us to focus our attention upon price-changes as the index and the governor of industrial operations. Booms and depressions are traced to those actual movements in the relations between supply and demand for commodities which are admittedly the sole immediate causes of rises and falls of prices of commodities. A general fall of prices is simply a failure of demand to keep pace with rate of supply, implying a condition of over-supply and, until further production is checked, of over-production. Such fall of prices, with growing over-supply, lowers present and prospective profits, thus bringing down the price of shares, and thereby causing the high rate of discount and the stringency of credit, which are the direct agents in checking production and in bringing about unemployment of real capital and labour. The whole financial system is based upon actual industry : reflects, anticipates, and frequently exaggerates its forces and tendencies. Depressions, with their accompanying unemployment, must therefore be traced through their operations in the delicate mechanism of finance to the failure of consumption to keep full pace with the increase of productive power so as to furnish a full and equable employment for this power.

§ 5.—Those who deny the existence of any actual tendency towards under-consumption or over-saving, commonly adduce the fact that even in a deep depression no very large amount of money-savings remain idle, as loanable capital, in the hands of bankers and other investment agencies. This fact is not denied, but furnishes no refutation of the hypothesis of over-saving. For there is no need to suppose that excessive saving is accumulated to an indefinite extent in idle loanable capital. There is another outlet which serves to conceal the extent of the excess. Though the amount of new saving which can take shape in new forms of capital is limited, a further amount may find employment in acquiring for its owners possession of properties already in existence, the possessors of which are compelled by the very pressure of a trade depression to part with them. The importance of this aspect of investment during trade depressions is generally overlooked and deserves special attention.[1]

Take the case of an economic community of a progressive type with an income of twenty units, spending seventeen, and saving three for regular investment in new productive capital, which finds full, regular employment in meeting the growing demand for commodities. Now suppose, owing to some change in distribution of incomes, some return to simplicity of living or some increased appreciation of future as compared with present satisfactions, spending is reduced to sixteen, saving raised to four, what must happen ? The increased savings cannot take shape in productive capital, for, as the increase of current and prospective consumption of commodities is reduced, a smaller amount of new productive capital can be put into operation, and any attempt to put into operation as much as before must speedily be checked by the obvious glut. Instead of three units of saving taking shape in productive capital, there is now only room for two and a half. But owing to increased saving four are available. What happens to the extra one and a half ? There will be some hoarding, i.e. some lingering of loanable funds in hands of financiers, from slowness in finding any sort of investment.

Let us say that this disposes of half a unit—an excessive estimate. What becomes of the remaining one ?

In order to answer this question, we must look to the effect of the diminished spending of the saving classes upon the general income from industry. Since there is a reduced demand both for commodities and for new capital goods, there will be a shrinkage of money income and real income among all industrial classes. Those among these classes whose income is reduced very low will be disposed to part with any property, land, houses, factories, etc., they may possess, in order to keep living and to pay their way. This means that a large amount of such properties will at such a time become a new field of investment for the savings which cannot take shape in new productive capital. The surplus unit of saving will find this form of investment, consisting in the acquisition of productive capital already existing and belonging to classes

---

[1] The first clear exposition of this process of investment in trade depressions is contained in a recently published American work, *A Neglected Point in connexion with Crises*, by N. Johannsen.

impoverished by the very increase of saving which has glutted the investment market. Saved by the saving class, it will be spent by the non-saving class. From the standpoint of the community it represents no saving at all, but simply a transfer of spending from one class to another. But the class which gets it only maintains its former spending, while the class which parts with it has reduced its total spending. So there remains as a net effect of the operation a reduction of total demand for commodities and new forms of capital. This means reduced employment for capital and labour, diminished rate of production, and shrinkage of the general real income. This is the condition known as depression. Why does it not continue indefinitely and grow ever worse ? Because from the very beginning of the maladjustment between spending and saving a process of readjustment gradually comes into play. Directly a shrinkage in demand for commodities and new productive capital occurs, the lessened rate of production begins to reduce all incomes, including those of the saving class. Aggregate income no longer stands at twenty, but falls to eighteen, or even seventeen. The saving class who were trying to save four out of a total twenty, leaving sixteen for spending, are not willing to save four or even three out of an aggregate income reduced to eighteen or seventeen. Their permanent standard of comfort stands in the way. When the shrinkage of production and of income has gone far enough, not merely is the actual amount of saving reduced, but the *proportion* of saving to spending is brought back towards the normal rate which preceded the attempt to over-save, or even below that rate. When the depression has reached its lowest, there is for a time a state of actual under-saving, i.e. an insufficient provision of new productive capital to meet the reasonable calculations of future demand for commodities. This condition even checks the recovery of trade. But it is only transitory. Another automatic check on over-saving is associated with this. When the investment of surplus saving in the acquisition of existing properties has gone a certain way, all the safer investments of this order will have been made, and the prevailing depression will have brought down the less safe ones to so low a value that they will no longer find buyers. So far, then, as saving is motived by a desire of the savers to make profitable investments, the depression must weaken this motive, imparting precariousness to all new productive capital, and reducing the quantity of sound investment in the acquisition of existing productive capital.

These checks prevent the maladjustment from going beyond a certain point. But they do not become operative until there is actual waste of productive resources, and an actual condition of unemployment and under-employment of capital and labour, due to the attempt to save a larger proportion of the general income than the present state and prospects of the industrial arts render feasible.

The operation of these checks, then, requires a correction of our original hypothesis, which was that a community, when the right proportion of spending to saving was seventeen to three, might alter that proportion to sixteen to four. The latter proportion, as we now see, will not be actually attained, for with the attempt to move towards it, the total income twenty will at once begin to shrink, and, as we see, this shrinkage will prevent the establishment of sixteen to four. In a word, any attempt at over-saving will be checked when it has gone a certain way, by means of the under-production and shrinkage of income it inevitably produces.

Thus far we have treated employment as issuing from a demand operative through the application of money. But the argument is fortified if, ignoring for the moment the use of money, we reduce commerce to its simplest terms, that of production and exchange of goods. Let A, producing *a* goods, which are necessaries, for exchange against *b* goods, luxuries produced by B, represent the increased saving class. Formerly each *a* as it was produced went to B, causing a *b* to come to A for A's consumption. Now A wishes to save more instead of consuming *b*. He therefore refuses to make the former exchange of *a* against *b*. But B wants *a* just as before. In order to get it he has to offer to A not *b*, but something A will consent to take in exchange for *a*. This something is a house or some other ' property ' he owns. A in this case can go on producing *a* and exchanging it with B as before, except that, instead of receiving bits of *b*, he receives bits of house or other property that belonged to B. B consumes as before, but he stops producing *b*, having lost the market for it, and the aggregate employment of labour and capital for the community is thus reduced.

If, however, as is likely, the whole supply of *a* which B formerly consumed is not ' necessary ' to him, he will economise his use of *a* when he finds that his market for *b* is reduced by the new saving policy of A. He will take bits of *a* at a slower rate than before, exchanging his house or other property against them. This will force A to produce *a* at a slower rate, and will saddle his trade with some unemployment, i.e. A will be partially frustrated in his attempt at increased saving by an inability to exchange his product as freely as before, an inability directly due to his attempt to over-save, or, in other words, to his refusal to consume *b* as formerly. In this event there will be more unemployment than if B had insisted on consuming *a* at the former rate, for to the unemployment in B's trade, due to a complete stoppage in producing b, is added some unemployment in A's trade due to a smaller production of a in a given time.

If A be taken as representative of all the 'over-saving' class, and B of the rest of the community, the validity of this argument cannot be impaired by suggesting that B can find any other market for the b he formerly exchanged against a by lowering the price and exchanging it against c or d made by other parties C and D. The first act of the 'over-saving' group, in refusing to exchange their products as formerly against products simultaneously produced by the non-saving group, will inhibit the latter from demanding more goods than before, however much the price were lowered.

An increased rate of saving on the part of a community must either take shape in the continuous increase of new forms of capital produced in expectation of an increase in the rate of growth of future consumption, or in a compulsory substitution of present for past saving, effected by enabling present over-savers to get possession of properties already in existence which represent past savings. In the latter case, since the acts of saving stimulate no new production of capital-forms, they involve a corresponding volume of unemployment.

The following brief summary of the argument attributing cyclical unemployment mainly to under-consumption may here be conveniently appended :—

1. The 'demand' for labour is directly measured by the amount of money which employers offer for the purchase of labour-power, or by the amount of commodities available for purchase by this amount of money.

2. This amount of direct monetary demand for labour is not, however, fixed, but varies with, depends upon, and is derived from the purchases of actual goods (productive or consumptive) at current prices. The money paid in weekly wages in the normal condition of trade is derived from the money paid for actual goods, which flows back through the several processes of production, stimulating the factors to replace in supply the goods which have been purchased.[1]

3. The immediate effect upon demand for labour of demanding capital goods (the application of savings) is the same as that of demanding consumptive goods.

4. But if any economic force incites saving to rise above a certain definite proportion to spending, the futility of applying such saving

---

[1] Only in the case of an increase of demand for labour in order to work an increase of plant for new industry, it is requisite to assume that some stock of food, &c., some wage-fund the result of *previous* saving, has been provided. The continuance of current production, all that is requisite to stop depression, requires no such provision.

to demand more capital goods is made apparent by the fact that some existing capital goods cannot function in production.

5. While, then, the first effect of such over-saving (under-consumption) is to employ labour to produce more forms of capital than are economically requisite to supply consumptive goods at the rate at which they are demanded, the secondary effects are (a) a congestion of the industrial system with goods, productive and consumptive, which are not bought as fast as they are produced ; (b) a diversion of new individual savings from investment in new forms of capital to investment in the acquisition of previously existing properties forced into the market by the shrinking incomes of their owners.

6. When both spending and real saving (creation of new forms of capital) are reduced, the aggregate rate of demand for labour and capital is reduced and production runs at low pressure.

7. This means a general fall in income, for income is nothing else than the annual product of industry. When the rate of reduction has reached a certain point, the proportion of saving to spending is cut down below the normal rate, and a process of recuperation begins, no large further increase of capital taking place while the consumption of a growing population increases, though at a slower pace than usual.

8. The cancelment of large quantities of existing capital, representing over-saving, and the retardation of new saving for investment, restore for a time the right adjustment between real capital and rate of consumption, and a spell of good trade with full employment for capital and labour ensues. This continues until the chronic impulse towards over-saving due to surplus income again becomes fully operative, preparing a new period of depression.

If this analysis be accepted, it explains not merely the necessity of trade depressions but their periodicity, and the tidal movements in volume of production and employment which occasion so much perplexity and so much distress. For it is not necessary to assume that some sudden change in the proportion of saving to spending leads to a trade depression and its unemployment. If there exists a normal tendency towards over-saving or under-consumption, such as appears to be involved in the existence of an unproductive surplus of unearned income, the regular pressure of that excess will express itself in some such rhythmic order as that of the booms and depressions which actually occur.

§ 6.—No remedies for ' unemployment ' can be effective, so far as the whole industrial system is concerned, which do not correct the normal tendency of production to outrun consumption, evidenced to the ordinary business man by the greater difficulty in selling than in buying. Local or even national remedies such as technical instruction, improved machinery of manufacture or of transport, enabling a particular district, trade, or nation, to out-compete others, by better or cheaper production, may secure a larger share of the volume of employment, shifting more unemployment on to less efficient trades, localities or nations. But, treating the industrial system as a whole, it is evident that improvements of productive power cannot remedy a generally prevalent unemployment which attests an existing excess of productive power.

Indeed, we may go further and affirm that the most real and injurious check upon the progressive efficiency of industry, whether in the shape of inventions, investment, and the education of labour, is furnished by the recurrence of long periods of trade in which ability, capital and labour-power stand idle or half employed.

Though in a progressive system of industry a certain margin of waste, tolerably constant, must be incurred through misapplication of industrial power and miscalculations of future demand, there is no reason in the nature of industry why these great oscillations of the volume of production and employment should recur. To say that the modern system of industry will not work without a margin is merely to assert that whatever is is inevitable. No other adequate explanation is given than that of a normal failure of consumption to keep pace with productive power, and a consequent periodic accumulation of materials and goods in the productive system which congest that system and cause injurious stoppages. The financial machinery of adjustment thrown out of gear fails to act with rapidity and precision, and the equilibrium between the rate of production and of consumption which is eventually brought about is always effected upon an unstable basis which underestimates the increasing power of production shortly disclosed when business has resumed a normal course.

No remedy for unemployment is valid unless it is seen to stimulate the current of consumption by converting surplus income, either into wages spent in raising the standard of comfort of the workers, or into public revenue spent in raising the standard of public life. Surplus income, by its excessive saving and by its irregular spending, impairs the volume and the regularity of employment : its diversion either directly into wages or into public expenditure for steady purposes of popular support and progress is the only method of securing full and regular employment.

It is only by the application of this principle that we can test the utility of concrete palliatives for unemployment which modern governments devise. Proposals which, for educational or other purposes, aim at removing from the labour market certain classes of superabundant labourers are genuine correctives of the over-supply of current productive power. If the large employment of young boys and girls can be curtailed by the abolition of half-time and compulsory attendance at continuation and technical schools, their removal from the labour market will furnish some increased employment of adults at higher wages, and will generally strengthen the power of low-skilled adult labour to organise and to obtain higher pay. The same result will attend any removal from the competitive labour market of inefficients and weaklings, and semi-invalids incapable of any sort of hard, regular work. If they can be placed in hospitals or training colonies, fuller and more regular employment and some rise of wages will ensue in the trades in which they were casual hangers-on. Not only would the labour market by such measures be relieved of the less effective portion of its own supply, but the increased cost of keeping and educating these classes devolving on the public purse would, following the line of our analysis, cause some net increase of consumption and thus involve increased employment for capital and labour.

Since large numbers of efficient and skilled workers suffer both from seasonal and cyclical unemployment, it is not obvious that improved teaching, general or technical, will increase the volume of employment. Though individuals, by training, will get a better chance of obtaining work, they will do so at the expense of other individuals, unless at times when, and in trades where, the demand for trained labour exceeds the current supply. During periods of general depression there are no considerable trades prepared to take on more trained workers, so that the training of unemployed persons cannot at such times be deemed an efficacious remedy. Taking a more general view of the effects of improved general and technical education upon the volume of employment, I should be disposed to distinguish the direct from the indirect consequences. So far as such education enables workers to increase the quantity, as distinguished from the skill or quality, of their output it cannot contribute to alleviate unemployment : on the contrary, it would appear to increase the sum of the excess of the supply of labour at such times. Any improvement in the skill of individual workers, or even of the nation as a whole, resulting from better training, would enable these individuals or this nation to keep a better hold upon employment than other individuals or other nations in world industry at times of general trade depression. But since large numbers of workers whose efficiency is adequate to secure them regular employment in good times are unemployed when times are bad, it cannot be argued that any raising of the general level of efficiency, or any increase of the numbers of efficient workers would in itself secure an increase in the aggregate demand for skilled labour. As a local, or even as a national policy, such technical training might of course be efficacious in procuring for one town or one nation a larger share of employment at the expense of another town or another nation. But when a cyclical depression in the industrial world exhibits an excess of competent workers in the various trades, to furnish a larger supply of equally or more competent workers is no remedy. This rigorous application of a quantitative doctrine of supply requires, however, this not unimportant qualification. A general rise in education and technical training among the workers will stimulate among them an increased desire and capacity for organisation, economic and political, and may thus incidentally produce a considerable effect upon wages and the standard of consumption. Just in proportion as it conduces thus to increase the share of the product which comes to labour, and to reduce the unproductive surplus, does it enlarge the total volume of employment.

By no other economic reasoning is it possible to defend the policy of public expenditure upon unemployed relief works or unemployed insurance, to which most modern states have committed themselves. If the hypothesis of under-consumption or over-saving as the chief cause of cyclical unemployment be rejected, how can it be contended that to take money from taxpayers in order to furnish materials, tools, and wages for unemployed workmen has any other effect than merely to shift the personnel of unemployment ? If the money taken in taxation must either have been spent upon commodities or have been saved and invested, i.e. spent upon new forms of capital, the labour that would have been expended in making these commodities or these forms of capital will now be unemployed. There will be no addition whatever to the volume of employment as a whole. Instead of a number of men being employed in the ordinary course of trade to make goods for consumption, or to make more mills and machines, a number of other men will be employed by public departments to make a road or an artificial lake; the aggregate amount of employment will be just the same, though the product will be a good deal smaller.

The plausibility of this argument, however, disappears before closer inspection, in the light afforded by our analysis of income. The money income of a man represents, as we have recognised, some product actually made by the factor of production which he owns, it is nothing else than a demand note enabling him to obtain possession of consumptive goods or capital goods already in existence, equivalent to the product which procured for him

his money income.   He can, without doing any other productive
act, withdraw some food or clothing from the existing stock for
his own consumption, paying this money for them, or he can
withdraw from the existing stock some machine or some materials
and apply them to his business.   By this act of purchase, whether
of consumptive goods or capital goods, he stimulates a large
number of producers engaged in various processes to make another
product similar to that which he has bought and withdrawn.

But his own act of spending, whether upon consumptive or
on capital goods, is not conditioned by any act of employment or
production on his part ; he has already performed this act before
he has got possession of the money he expends.   Now suppose,
instead of allowing him to spend this ' income ' in buying consumptive or capital goods, the state seizes some of it and applies it to
unemployed relief works, is the state spending it under the same
conditions as regards employment as if the man had spent it himself ?

The real issue depends upon the pace of the application of
spending-power.   If the taxpayer would have paid away his money
in ' demand ' as quickly as the state would have paid it in relief
works, no increase in volume of employment is produced by taxing
him.   If, on the other hand, the effect of taxing him is to apply
the money in demand for labour *more quickly* than it would have
been applied, the aggregate of employment within a given period
is increased by this acceleration of demand.   The entire economic
case for state relief insurance seems to turn upon the question of
the acceleration or retardation of demand.   Now, assuming that
my hypothesis, that the largest proportion of saving proceeds
from the upper portions of high incomes not required to satisfy
any keen or constant pressure of need, be correct, the normal effect
of taxing or rating such incomes for unemployed relief will be to
accelerate the application of such income in demand for labour.
For, during a time of depressed trade, saved income cannot be applied
in furnishing new forms of capital as easily or quickly as during
good trade ; large quantities of savings will be kept waiting for
investment or will be applied in acquiring the existing properties of
weak owners.   While, therefore, saving which is immediately applied
as a demand for labour to produce new plant and other concrete
capital employs as much labour as the same income if it were spent
in buying commodities, this is not the case when the condition of
trade retards the rate of effective investment.   Taxation, therefore,
properly directed to fall upon the unearned incomes of the wealthier
classes, will have the effect of accelerating the use of such income
in demand for labour.

This argument of the effects of transferring private income by means of taxation into expenditure on public relief cannot be dismissed as a vague hypothesis. Every financier and business man is aware that, during a prolonged depression, quantities of loanable capital stand out of all new industrial uses awaiting an opportunity to operate productively. It is hardly disputable that a process of taxation which should arrest some of these stagnant savings, and apply them to production through public expenditure, would secure an earlier demand for labour than would otherwise have occurred. Workers would have in their hands wages which they would apply in consumption at an earlier date than if they had to wait until some bank felt justified in making an investment in a loan which some business man should employ for paying wages. During a depression there is no motive to apply savings in demand for labour because such application implies the further congestion of a market already congested. Therefore, there is a reasonable presumption that a taxing process which intercepts such savings and converts them into immediate employment of unemployed labour will have the effect of increasing the aggregate volume of employment within a given time, and not merely of changing the personnel of the unemployed.[1]

[1] The Minority Report of the Poor Law Commission points out that without any considerable amount of taxation the Government can, in times of trade depression, borrow at low rates large quantities of unemployed floating capital and idle plant, operating it by unemployed labour so as to produce wealth (p. 1198). The only new taxation involved in this process would be that required to pay the interest on the borrowed capital, and to meet any deficit due to the inferior quality of the plant and labour got into employment by governmental action.

CHAPTER XIX

THE HUMAN INTERPRETATION OF INDUSTRY

§ 1. The industrial system, here treated objectively, can be interpreted in terms of human will and satisfaction. The operation of each factor of labour, capital, ability, involves expenditure of human energy consciously directed to some definite end. The thought and will comprised in these activities differ widely in quality, some acts being more creative, others more imitative.—§ 2. Industrial progress consists largely in the better economy of will and intellect throughout the industrial system. Criticism of the competitive system rests ultimately on the waste of social or co-operative energy involved in a clash of wills and a crossing of purposes. This waste differs widely according as the technique of a profession or trade gives prominence to direct self-seeking. The growth of combination brings a fuller consciousness of common purpose, though this is offset by diminished regard for the consumer's interests. The diminishing sense of social utility of labour due to the complexity of modern industry is its greatest injury.—§ 3. From a subjective economy the land factor must be eliminated, nature being given. A ' Crusoe ' or a socialistic system is easily realised as a calculus of human ' costs ' and ' utilities.' In order to apply such a calculus to our system, so as to make commercial values correspond with human values, it will be necessary to consider (1) the technical conditions of the work, (2) the nature of the workers, (3) the distribution of the labour-cost, upon the cost side; and similarly (1) the technique of the consumption, (2) the sort of consumers, (3) the distribution of the commodities, upon the utility side.—§ 4. An art of social progress will further require the calculus of current hedonism to be reduced to terms of social good as tested by some ideal standard. The conscious control of industry will thus be realised as a contribution towards the wider art of politics. Social economy in industry aims at securing a natural relation between production and consumption among classes and individuals in accordance with the maxim, ' from each according to his powers: to each according to his needs.' This is a general law of distribution in the organic world admitted by Individualism as by Socialism.—§ 5. A subjective interpretation of the ' surplus ' would express it in waste of life and of work. An economical use of the surplus for health, education, and security would develop and enrich individual personality, substituting a more qualitative for a quantitative economy. Individuation of needs will react on the character of work, imparting new elements of skill and art ; each gain is twofold, reducing some vital cost while raising some vital utility of consumption. Thus reformed distribution would issue in (1) enlarged production of objective wealth, (2) diminished vital cost and increased vital utility per unit of production.

§ 1.—OUR treatment of the industrial system has been essentially objective. Its structure we have regarded as consisting of concrete factors of production, men, land, plant, machinery, &c., giving forth physical and mental powers which make products, partly commodities, material or non-material, for consumption, partly capital goods, these products being continuously distributed to the owners of the various factors of production in payment for the use of these factors. Although, in our description of the working of this system, we were compelled to take account of certain motives which directed human conduct in giving out productive energy in the shape of labour, ability, and saving, and in dividing the product among the owners of the factors of production, these motives were treated not as possessing any interest of themselves but merely as affecting the working of the industrial system.

Even in our analysis of the part played by the 'surplus,' we concerned ourselves exclusively with its reactions upon the productive efficiency of the industrial system. We saw that it impaired this efficiency in three ways : first, by depriving some factor of production, usually labour, of a payment necessary as a physical and moral stimulus of increasing efficiency ; secondly, by relieving the recipients of 'surplus' of the necessity of productive exertion and thus atrophying their productive powers ; thirdly, by weakening the life and growth of the state in denying it the public income it requires. In a brief consideration of the labour movement, state socialism, and taxation, as methods of diverting surplus from injurious waste into economic energy, as well as in the discussion of the malady of unemployment due to the unhealthy operation of the surplus in the system, we were concerned exclusively with the bearing of these policies upon the working of the system objectively regarded. In considering the forces or tendencies to displace competition by combination in various industries, to strengthen the position of skilled labour by collective bargaining, to erect a new power of finance, or to evoke legislative interference with private enterprises, we have confined ourselves to a narrowly economic interpretation of these movements, making no attempt at tracing their bearing upon social progress conceived in any broader sense.

But while the treatment of production, consumption, and wealth taken here has been directed to secure a comprehensive view of the objective system of industry, it is evident that a subjective interpretation of this system, in which human energies of production and consumption are reduced to terms of human satisfaction or well-being, is essential to an art of political economy, regarded as a part of the wider art of politics.

For a system of industry which we have regarded objectively as an operation of productive forces is also an operation of human wills, and the product which we have regarded as material good

or services is also a complex of various modes and amounts of
human satisfaction.   At every point in the elaborate structure of
industry each business cell is a complex psychical structure in which
the intelligent will of the employer or manager applies stimulus
and direction to the wills of workmen and owners of capital, planning their co-operative activity so as to meet the anticipated demands
of groups of consumers, which demands themselves are acts of will
responding to the pressure of conscious wants.   Each regular
detailed application of labour-power in the manipulation of material
or the guidance of tools, or the tending of machinery, involves
some conscious effort of mind, often very complex in the elements
of pleasure and of pain which it contains, varying infinitely in the
nature and the amount of these subjective contents, from the
almost pure and elevated pleasure of the artist, working freely at
his best, to the almost unmixed and degrading pain of the manual
or mental routine worker in the last hour of his daily toil.   Equally
fine and diverse, could we distinguish them, are the sorts and degrees
of moral and intellectual energy represented in the ' saving ' which
places, sustains and enlarges the fabric of capital throughout the
industrial system.   Take for example the road beds, rails, rolling
stock and stations constituting most of the real capital of the
Canadian Pacific Railroad, and resolve it, by imagination, into the
innumerable acts of saving done by the thousands of men and
women who caused these quantities of unconsumable productive
goods to be made and kept where they stand as organic parts of
this great road, the faith and far-sighted intelligence of those who
found the first capital for an investment which seemed to most
men so unpromising, qualities of will and intellect which, in lessening
degrees, must be accredited to those who later took up shares or
purchased them.   In all these myriad acts of saving, the play of
will and intelligence, the moral significance, the subjective cost,
will be different.   No two rails represent precisely the same amount
or sort of abstinence.   The subjective import of this organisation
of capital will vary as regards each unit, from ' saving ' that involves
no pain at all but a pleasure from the realisation of a growing fund
of abiding wealth and the power and personal glory attached to its
possession, to a ' saving ' that implies painful denial of some much-
desired convenience or comfort in order to make provision against
a dreaded breakdown or a destitute old age.   When it is borne in
mind how that the actual fabric of capital implies not merely that
a number of persons have been willing to forgo an amount of
present satisfaction for a larger anticipated amount of future satisfaction, but that this ' willingness ' breaks up into an infinite number
of separate acts of will, each different from the other in its psychical

composition, and that each of these acts, rightly and fully interpreted, would be seen to be causally related to a special bit of concrete capital, some idea of the subjective complexity of capital begins to dawn upon the mind. It is, of course, true that each person who has saved a sum of money and bought a share in the C.P.R. has not personally willed and caused to be made any particular rail or engine, but it is owing to his act of saving that some particular rail or engine is there, his energy of mind co-operating with the directive will of some engineer who converted it from a general into a specific act of investment. The factor of ability, whether in the inventor or the organiser and director of industry, is of course more easily recognised in its subjective character. In fact, there has sometimes been manifested a tendency to concentrate the psychical interpretation of industry on the functions of the *entrepreneur*, treating him as the sole repository of a will and intellect which uses labour and capital, as it uses natural resources, as mere instruments for its creative energy to work with. It is necessary to protest against the exaggeration of this ' heroic ' view of industry by insisting that the entire fabric of industry is alive with a power of will and intelligence which does not emanate merely from a few directive centres, but proceeds with various degrees of freedom and initiative from every cell in the system. But while the abrupt distinction sometimes made between the ' creative' energy of ' ability ' and the ' imitative ' energy of ordinary labour has no validity, since no work in which the will of man functions is purely imitative or repetitive, there are wide differences of degree between the sorts of productive energy classed as ability and those classed as labour which require full recognition. The elaborate operation of thought and will involved in a delicate ·act of invention, or in some fine calculation of the play of forces in a market, or in a single critical act of organising judgment, carries us into the most intricate region of psychology, for we have to trace the consequences of this determinant act of ' ability' in innumerable changes which it brings about in the wills and minds of the multitudes of owners of labour-power and capital that co-operate with its owner.

§ 2.—In the structural changes of modern industry and in the social changes which accompany them an ever-growing importance attaches to the discovery, selection, training and economical application of these finer sorts of psychical forces which are the chief direct instruments of progress in the arts of industry. Such equalisation of intellectual and other opportunities as enables an industrial society to select those individual forces from the entire population, instead of from a small class, and so to apply them as most fully to utilise their creative qualities, is the prime condition of industrial progress. When any radical alteration in the structure of a business is contemplated, such as the change from a private business into a joint-stock company, or the adoption of some co-operative or profit-sharing basis ; when it is proposed to organise into a single trust or cartel the competing businesses in a trade, or to transfer some trade from company control to municipal or state enterprise, or when the substitution of some general scheme of socialism for the existing business system is under consideration, the most crucial issue will be the effect which the proposed change is likely to exercise in stimulating or depressing, in economising or in wasting, the use of these finer creative and directive capacities of the human mind. But in estimating properly the socially productive worth of these superior qualities of mind, it will also be remembered that they do not operate in the void, that their productive efficacy, however great, is strictly dependent on and limited by the psychical quality of the entire co-operative business structure through which they play, and that an improvement in the intelligence or goodwill of this human structure may be as large a source of progress as any heightening of the capacity of inventors or of *entrepreneurs*. This larger interpretation of the spiritual structure of the business is sometimes ignored by a shallow analysis which treats the ordinary labour and capital in the business as a merely inert mass vitalised entirely by the intellect and will of the directing and organising person.

Not merely is each business thus to be regarded as an organic co-operation of intelligent wills functioning more or less harmoni-ously towards a common purpose, but the relations of businesses in a common trade, and the relations between the general trades in the industrial system, must also be similarly expressible in terms of purpose. The identity and diversity of interests which cause the businesses in a trade to compete with one another for some objects, to combine for others, involve active and complex plays of intelligent will. Though, regarded from the standpoint of the individual business, the structure of the trade seems rather an equilibrium of opposed forces than a harmonious co-operation, a higher industrial standpoint may recognise the detailed warfare of busi-nesses in a trade as a truly co-operative economy which enables the industrial energy of the whole trade to function most productively. Such, at any rate, has been the consistent interpretation of the individualist defender of the competitive system, to whom the so-called waste of competition is only the friction involved in an essentially co-operative system driven by an enlightened self-interest operating from a number of individual business centres. The play of this self-interest from many opposing intelligent wills is subjected to a regulative and compensative treatment which brings them into co-operative harmony for the good of the consumer, who represents the goal of industry.

On the other hand, the criticism of the competitive system, though sometimes directed to the objective wastefulness involved and to denial of the net utility to the consumer, really rests for its validity upon a psychological interpretation of the business struggle. Enlightened self-interest does not, it is contended, evoke those individual energies which are most socially productive so well as those which are competitively successful, while it tends, by throwing the control of businesses into the hands of hard, pushful men, to keep out quieter and more essentially creative minds : moreover, by keeping each improvement of industrial method in the hands of a single firm which has just discovered or adopted it, it retards the advance of the general trade. But the real gravamen of the charge rests on a distinctively moral assumption. If, as the defenders of the competitive trade system assert, the system is in essence and in result co-operative, and designed to serve industrial society as a whole, can that end be satisfactorily attained by a procedure which concentrates the will of each human unit not upon that end, not even upon a clearly recognised means to that end, but upon a purely selfish consideration which entirely eliminates the social service ?

The moral economy of the business consists in the more or less conscious co-operation of all the wills engaged in it towards a common end ; the moral economy of the trade is supposed to consist in the conscious opposition of the wills engaged in it. Surely there must here be involved a huge waste of moral force, involving some corresponding waste of objective productive energy.

But this, it will rightly be urged, is not a full or general interpretation of the competitive system. It is primarily a question of conscious motive in individual production. Now the consciousness of social service as a stimulus to work is not inconsistent with competition. The artist who labours to express himself to others can only succeed on condition that he keeps before his mind these others : mere self-expression is not art at all. Though, therefore, the artist may be working for gain, and may be conscious of his competitors, the interest in his work and his capacity to do it involve some regard for the public. The same applies also to the artisan so far as his manipulation of material involves conscious regard for its utility, and therefore consideration of the needs of the consumers. So, too, with the professions; however keen the rivalry of professional men to get employment may be, the nature of the work they do involves the detailed operation of disinterested motives leading them to value their work for its real social utility rather than for the gain it brings

them.   This is the well-recognised difference between a profession
and a trade, which has always underlain the lower esteem in which
tradesmen and the trading spirit have been held.   It is, indeed, in
commerce, and primarily in retail trade, rather than in manufacture
or any branch of production, that the ethics of competition appears
to do most damage, the reason, of course, being that in the dealing
processes antagonism of human interests is sharpest, and the conscious energy of dealers is most confined to the pursuit of personal
profit.   In most manufactures, though the employer is not in
business ' for his health,' but primarily to make profits, the skill
and intricacy of the practical operations which he conducts absorb
much of his attention, and pride in the character of his business and
the quality of its products dignifies his conduct.   Just in proportion
as he is not forced to concentrate his thought and feeling upon the
art of getting business away from other firms and pushing his claims
against theirs in the market does his work take conscious shape
in his mind as the social function which it really is.   Just in proportion as the competitive activities assume prominence is he compelled
to sink this social feeling, to push his goods in conscious rivalry with
those of other firms, and to cultivate those arts of sweating, adultera-
tion and deceit which seem necessary to enable him to sell goods
at a profit.

Such considerations indicate that the moral economy of competition is not simple or uniform : where it takes shape in the rivalry
of Euripides, Æschylus and Sophocles to win the favour of an
Athenian public for their respective dramas it may act as a direct
incentive of the highest form of social wealth : where it operates
among struggling grocers in the same street it may mean starved
assistants, short weights and doctored goods.   So far as our system
of industry has recently been more competitive, it is likely that the
worse influences of competition have gained ground ; for the growth
of great sub-divided businesses with mechanical methods of production have tended to weaken for the great mass of workers engaged
in them all adequate realisation of the social utility of the work they
do, while the development of modern markets has tended on the
whole to sharpen the rivalry between competing firms, by loosening
their old relations to ' customers ' and bringing them into more
detailed rivalry at a larger number of points.   On the other hand, it
must be borne in mind that our analysis has shown that it is not
generally true of the industrial system to say that it is becoming
more competitive : on the contrary, combination is displacing, or
at any rate is modifying, competition in many departments.   Here
it must be recognised that an improved moral harmony is established
in the trade, by removing or abating the hostility of businesses and

substituting unity of operation and solidarity of interest. Viewed in this aspect, a trust or other close trade combination is a higher moral structure than the cluster of competing businesses it has displaced ; even if some loss of incentive to efficiency has been sustained by stopping the struggle for orders, the saving of competitive skill and effort may bring more concentration upon improvements of productive processes, and a single large trade, working with conscious co-operation of all its parts, is an advance in social organisation upon the conditions of a competitive trade. So, likewise, the lateral and horizontal extensions by which a trust or trade combination may spread its control over other processes, earlier or later, in the line of industry to which it belongs, getting control of raw materials, transport or distribution, or attaching to itself other related and subsidiary trades, make for a superior solidarity of industrial activity which implies a more harmonious co-operation of individual wills and a direct stoppage of conscious antagonisms.

Since, however, the dominant motive in all such combinations is considerations of personal profit on the part of their organisers, there is no security that any public utility in the wider sense is served. Indeed, while enlightened self-interest under competition does seem to impose on rival producers some direct consideration of the public good, a trust or other monopoly may come consciously to regard the consuming public as a prey, merely calculating what is the highest price it can extort without checking its sales.

It is thus conceivable and not improbable that an industrial system where internal co-operation had been advanced in many trades by the substitution of combination for competition might present a definitely more anti-social character in its wider aspect, numerous trusts and combines tyrannising over the consumer and engaging in a rival policy of plundering his purse. But wherever the danger clearly presents itself, as for instance in certain transport industries, in banking and insurance, and in undertakings which from their dependence upon land or other limitation of supply tend to become strong monopolies, measures of industrial control tend to be evolved by the state or municipality to secure some consistency between the interests of the public and those of the monopoly. Where such reconcilement seems too difficult, the tendency is for public bodies to take over the industry, securing that direct and complete harmony of interests between a trade and the social good which, theoretically at any rate, attends socialisation of industries.

The moral and ultimately the economic case for complete state socialism is sometimes based upon the argument that until the true and full social significance of every industrial act is enforced upon the intelligent will of all participants, by stamping upon every productive operation the hall-mark of direct social service, there must necessarily be a waste of human incentive and a deficiency of co-operative will.   But, if we may apply an analogy, this would be equivalent to insisting that full health and orderly co-operation was not attainable for the bodily organism unless every cell and every organ of the body were functioning directly and consciously for the good of the whole organism instead of for the good of itself or of some small local nucleus of corporate action, as is commonly the case.   Decentralisation of ends and motives must be a psychical equivalent and implication of that growing specialisation of parts which belongs to advancing complexity of organisation.   When each village was a virtually self-sufficing economic unit, some sense that he was helping to feed his neighbour must have accompanied the work of the husbandman who tilled the soil; but the Dakota farmer, whose wheat will pass into an elevator in Chicago and after long travel will go to feed some unknown family in Glasgow or in Hamburg, can hardly be expected to have the same feeling for the social end which his tilling serves.   Education and a more vivid imagination may do something to extend the range of his sympathetic vision, but the intricacies of a world-wide system will preclude a grasp of the full social meaning of his industrial operations.   This seems to involve a certain dehumanising influence in the great staple industries so far as direct appreciation of the social utility or human purpose of the work is concerned, though some compensation should be found in the enlarged sense of comradeship provided by the larger co-operation in which each worker feels himself engaged.   Moreover, as we have seen, it is not true that great businesses are absorbing the workers and that small businesses with a closer and more direct utility in their work are disappearing.

Indeed, it is not certain that the gravest of indictments directed against modern industry, that it tends to make the work of most men more uninteresting and unattractive in itself, is valid.

But it is deplorably true that a very large proportion of industrial work is in itself distasteful to those who do it, and that this distaste is not to any appreciable degree mitigated by any sense that the toil of performing it conduces to the happiness of mankind.   The bulk of the hard routine manual and mental labour probably falls in this category; it carries with it no interest or goodwill, nor does any glimmer of its social value brighten the vision of the toilers who perform it.   Such toil, destitute of noble purpose, demoralises and derationalises the workers, and, through its reactions upon individual and social character, constitutes the heaviest drag upon the car of human progress. If we seek to interpret the industrial system as a system of human wills in co-operation for the social good, this forced consent of so many of the human units to perform their part is its worst defect.

§ 3.—So far we have confined ourselves to an endeavour to translate the operation of actual industry into its simplest psychical terms. In doing so we are of course obliged to omit one set of industrial forces, viz. those which proceed from Nature as a factor of production. In the objective treatment this factor was put on an equal footing with the human factors, labour, capital, ability, for in this way was it best possible to set the problems of production and of the distribution of the product. But, when we take the subjective or psychical view of industry, we find no facts to correspond with the productive powers of nature or with the rent paid for them, save the reaction of rent as an element of surplus in its operation on human incentive, a point to which we shall revert presently.

If, now, our industrial system, expressed in terms of human feeling, is to be brought into relation to any art of social progress for criticism or judgment, this can only be accomplished by a closer method of psychical calculus than is usually applied. It would be necessary to resolve the productive energy which constitutes the life of the industrial system into the human ‘costs’ which it involves, the amount of painful or injurious human effort, upon the one hand, and into the human utilities attending its consumption in the commodities it vitalised, the amount of pleasurable or beneficial satisfaction, on the other hand ; a comparison or balance of these psychical quantities would express the net subjective ‘ value ’ of the industrial operations, and industrial progress would receive its human interpretation in the art of minimising ‘ costs ’ and maximising utilities. Although it would be beyond the possible scope of this book to carry out this subjective interpretation of industry and of industrial progress, it is possible to indicate the method of such analysis and some of the fruitful results it might be expected to yield.

Where an individual was a self-sufficing economic system, as Robinson Crusoe on his island, the psychical determination of industry would be evident. Experience would work out a very accurate calculus of the disabilities of production and the utilities of consumption for different sorts of products. Given on the one hand the known material resources of the island, tools saved from the wreck and the kinds and degrees of productive skill possessed by Crusoe, and on the other hand the needs of different sorts of articles for food, clothing and shelter, protection against enemies, physical enjoyment and mental entertainment, he would plan a disposal of his time and energy so as to yield a maximum surplus of satisfaction over cost. Each new proposed undertaking would be subjected to a careful estimate in order to find out whether it was 'worth while.' This estimate would not merely balance the time and trouble involved in producing a given amount of some particular supply, say a crop of corn, against the utility or the separate satisfaction of consuming it : on each side of the equation, the cost and the satisfaction would have to be regarded as items in a general economy of effort and of satisfaction affecting in various subtle and important ways the value of the other items and so of the entire standard of work on the one hand and of life upon the other. The proposal to cultivate a new piece of land so as to raise a new crop, adding a new burden of physical effort, or displacing some other form of work already undertaken, would alter the disposal of Crusoe's working time, and much would depend on how the new work involved could be distributed so as to fit in with or relieve other sorts of work ; whether it involved stretches of long continuous toil, or whether it incapacitated him from doing any other necessary work as efficiently as heretofore, or from enjoying any leisure which he now enjoyed. Again, the 'worth' of the crop would be considered, not merely with reference to its amount and the satisfaction of its consumption, but as to whether it would displace some other article of food got on easier terms, whether it supplied some important defect of his existing diet, and so enhanced the worth of the other constituents, or was merely supplementary. Every new piece of productive work, it will be seen, must have many and subtle effects on Crusoe's standard of work, the disutility of his production, and his standard of life, the utility of his consumption. The problems of industrial progress in such an economy will be very elaborate. ' Shall he give thirty days to cutting and hollowing a tree to make a boat which enables him to procure an easier and larger supply of fish ? ' becomes a question of great delicacy, depending for its answer on minute calculations of chances, and of physical and psychical reactions.

But, assuming a clear knowledge of all the conditions involved, Crusoe would solve each practical problem by application of a subjective calculus of costs and satisfactions. Progress would be measured by him in a reduction of costs and an increase of satisfactions.

A communistic or socialistic society, so far as it was capable of operating effectively, would evidently be a mere enlargement of this Crusoe economy, the close economy of the powers and needs of a collective person. Energies of each individual and each group would be so utilised that the aggregate product would represent, in the distribution of the various sorts of effort it involved, a minimum ' cost ' of production, and, in the distribution of the utility it contained, a maximum satisfaction of consumption. The current criticism of communism and a completely socialistic state is directed, not against the ideal of such an economy, but against the feasibility of realising it by the application of effective stimuli to the individual wills of its members. The defence either of a completely individualistic economic system or of the existing mixed economic system is based on the claim that the play of enlightened self-interest does, in fact, procure a nearer approximation to the economy of minimal costs and maximal utilities, as subjectively interpreted, than any other presently possible system.

Though we are not here concerned to discuss the feasibility or desirability of ' abolishing the competitive system ' and of substituting a non-competitive or socialistic system of industry, we are bound to indicate the ways in which and the extent to which the present analysis of expenses and surplus invalidates the claim of *laissez faire* economists that the existing system is an economical one for the production of subjective wealth or human satisfaction.

If it were accurately economical, commercial values would correspond with human or subjective values, that is to say, a stock of one sort of goods worth £1000 would contain the same net balance of satisfaction of consumption over pains of production as £1000 worth of any other sort of goods. If investigation of all relevant facts convinced us that £1000 worth of bread, of coal, and of motor cars, and of any other assortment of goods, contained the same balance of human satisfaction over human cost, each estimated by the existing valuations of the average member of society, this equality would furnish a very strong presumption in favour of the existing economy as making for the minimisation of human costs and the maximisation of human utilities. But actual comparison of the ' natural history ' of £1000 worth of different classes of goods will soon expel any such notion, by showing that this same monetary value may represent the widest divergence of human disutility of production and human utility of consumption, and that in many instances the greater cost is accompanied by the smaller utility. So far as pleasure and pain are comparable and measurable (and an industrial system rests on the assumption that they are), can it be pretended that £1000 worth of four such diverse articles as wheat, diamonds, surgical operations, and pictures express or even tend to express the same net balance of satisfaction over cost ? The human cost of producing £1000 worth of diamonds is probably greater than that of producing £1000 worth of wheat, its utility in human satisfaction is certainly much less; £1000 worth of pictures will represent a smaller sum alike of cost and of utility than the same value of wheat, while the high utility of the surgical operations, attended by a relatively low cost, will immensely outweigh the picture value. Be it remembered that we are not immediately concerned with the ' real ' human values as determined by the good of humanity or any other ideal standard, but with the actual valuations of the existing average man. Why these variations in the human or subjective value of the same quantities of commercial value should exist becomes evident when we remember the differences in the bargaining power of the owners of factors of production at different points in the processes of production, and the consequent emergence of pieces of ' surplus ' which accumulate and are represented in price. It is this inequality of bargain and the rents, surplus profits, &c., based on it, that are seen to be responsible for the unequal distribution of work and of income which exists in industrial society. With the amount of surplus or loaded cost contained in the £1000 the amount of human value will vary inversely, the smaller the surplus the greater the human value, either in ease of production or pleasure of consumption.

In our analysis of the objective structure of industry we have regarded the process of production as the operation of units of productive energy whose embodiment in goods, as expenses of production, measures their value. A steam-engine or a bale of cotton, regarded from this standpoint, is worth so many pounds, because the prices of the various units of productive energy in the different processes mount up to this sum.

If we preferred to take the standpoint of the consumer, as do many economists, and to measure the value of goods according to the number of units of various sorts of utility which they can furnish in the processes of consumption, still measuring the utility objectively, the logic of this method is impregnable. A steam-engine worth £1000 is thus resolved into a number of units of traction, reckoned in horse-power or car miles or otherwise, the price of which mounts up to the £1000 ; similarly the bale of cotton goods is resolved into the utility for wear or ornament furnished by the articles of clothing which are made out of it, this utility being reckoned objectively and without direct reference to the satisfaction of the feelings of consumers. So far as the distinction between the objective and subjective utility of goods can be maintained, the consumer's standpoint is equally valid with the producer's in the interpretation of the industrial system. It was the greater facility of measurement from the cost side which the structure of industry affords that made us prefer to interpret the industrial system as a stream of productive energy rather than a stream of consumptive utility.

But now that we come to an endeavour to express goods in terms of social or psychical value it becomes evident that equal, simultaneous and related attention must be given to the productive and consumptive aspects.

If we are shown a stock of goods valued at £1000, this price index throws no light whatever upon the amount of painful effort which went to its production or upon the amount of pleasurable satisfaction which will attend its consumption. Nor will any objective analysis of expense or utility give the knowledge which we require for the human interpretation of the phenomenon.

It is of supreme importance to make this clear. Let us suppose we have a supply of 1000 tons of coal, worth £1000, or £1 per ton. Our objective analysis of productive energy resolves this supply into so many units of mining energy, say 1500 hours' hewing, &c. But this analysis gives no knowledge of the amount of subjective cost, or painful effort, involved. In order to get that knowledge, we must know exactly (1) the technical conditions under which the work is done; (2) the physical and other conditions of the workers actually engaged; (3) the distribution of the 1500 hours among the workers. (1) will include such matters as the thickness, hardness, &c., of the seam, the atmospheric and other conditions of the mine affecting the ease or safety of the work. (2) will refer to the age, race, strength, diet, skill and experience of the particular workers, as for instance, the employment of immature youths or old men, or the food habits of the workers. (3) will refer to the length of shifts, night work, overtime, the relative length of shifts for men and boys, the number of days per week, or other factors in the continuity or condensation of the labour. As regards the distribution of the units of productive energy, considerations of economic stimulus by bonuses and other modes of premium wages, individual or gang labour, &c., will enter in. A detailed knowledge of all these conditions of working, involving an investigation of the physical and technical efficiency of each individual worker, would be requisite in order to translate with any accuracy the 1500 units of mining energy into units of subjective effort.

So, again, turning to the objective utility of the 1000 tons of coal, let us say that as it represented 1500 units of mining energy for production, so it represents 1500 units of heating energy for consumption, i.e. if used with normal care it will give out so many units of heat. Does this afford any knowledge of the subjective utility, the human satisfaction, attending its consumption ? No.

For that we must pursue an investigation closely analogous to that indicated on the side of production. We must learn (1) the technical conditions of its actual consumption, e.g. whether it will be used in some central heating furnace, in slow combustion stoves, or in wasteful open fires, whether directly for furnishing warmth to human beings or conferring some indirect benefit by forwarding some industrial process ; (2) the sort of consumers who will use the heat, whether children, or adults, weak or strong, active or sedentary persons. Here, again, exact subjective analysis would require separate investigation of each user analogous to that demanded in the case of workers ; (3) the distribution of the utility among a large or small number of consumers, for longer or shorter times, more or less continuously, will evidently affect the quantity of subjective utility afforded by its consumption.

This is, of course, nothing but an application of certain quite obvious criticisms upon the formal measurements of wealth. The human worth of any given stock of material or immaterial wealth must evidently vary, and vary indefinitely, according to the good or bad conditions of its production, according to the good or bad conditions of its consumption. Where it is made by vigorous workers, on short hours, under good hygienic and technical conditions, it will involve a minimum of painful or distasteful effort, human disutility ; where it is made by feeble women and children, working long hours in some insanitary workshop or home, it will involve a maximum of this disutility. Where it passes into the consumption of consumers who need it most, and is distributed among them according to the urgency of their needs, as measured by the satisfaction it affords, and is so consumed as to give them all they are capable of getting from it, it affords the maximum of subjective utility. Where it goes into the possession of a few who already have enough to satisfy their felt wants, and so is applied extravagantly to supply some routine purpose of luxurious order, its subjective utility may be reduced to zero.

The development of this subjective analysis is, of course, essential to the human interpretation of the wealth of nations. It opens the practical problem of the distribution of economic work and economic enjoyment which is the contribution of the art of industry to the wider art of society. The crude customary method of assessing the industrial well-being of a nation in terms of the quantity or the value of its marketable products, or of their quantity or value per head of the population, is seen in the light of such analysis to be destitute of all real significance. For of two nations possessing the same average wealth per head, one might, by a more human and equitable apportionment of the work and of the product, get out of this product double or treble the human utility or satisfaction which the other got.

§ 4.—Nor have we thus far touched the most important link between industry and the art of social progress. For in our subjective interpretation of cost and utility we have taken as the standard of our estimate the actual feelings or appreciations of workers and consumers, thus translating production and product into terms of current pleasure and pain.

Now, an art of social progress cannot acknowledge the validity or sufficiency of such a calculus. The good of society which it seeks cannot be adequately expressed in current terms of hedonism. The order and progress of a happy and prosperous society involve a constant correction of current individual valuations of work, and of enjoyment ; some work, involving painful effort and ' disutility ' from the present standpoint of the feelings of the worker, may be fraught with gain to himself or to others which will ultimately rank as social well-being ; some consumption, highly esteemed by individual consumers for the pleasure it affords, will be recognised to involve individual and social waste and injury. Thus the objective industrial standard of wealth requires a double process of rectification before it is brought into accord with the art of social progress. The objective product of industry must be translated first into a net balance of pain over pleasure in the processes of production and consumption, taken on the current valuation of producers and consumers ; secondly, into a balance of social welfare as indicated by the ideal standard which every society must set before itself. The rational justification of any such social ideal belongs to philosophy and does not concern us here. It is enough for our purpose that every nation or other social being has some conception of its good and of social progress according to which it claims to assess and to direct social conduct. Industry as a branch of social conduct will be amenable to this rule. Society will, therefore, in proportion as it comes to realise its good, insist more urgently that the industrial system shall, in its structure and working, be brought into conformity with the wider material and moral conditions of social growth.

Industrial progress, thus socially interpreted and directed, will consist not merely, as now, in the technical improvements of the industrial arts so as to increase the supply of products, but also in the continuous redistribution of the burdens of production and the benefits of consumption of products so as to minimise the social cost of the former, and to maximise the social gain of the latter process. In this process of adjustment the standard of current individual estimates of the disutility of production and of the utility of consumption will be taken as important indices of social gain or waste, but will have no final authority assigned to them, for these indices will themselves be subject to adjustment in accordance with a far-sighted and collective instead of a short-sighted and individual standard of welfare.

Such is the broad rationale of the social interpretation of an industrial system. Its realisation in practice is through a social economy of productive powers brought into organic relation to a social economy of consumption. The social art of production will aim at such applications of productive energy as form the required products with the minimum of human pain and injury or vital cost. The efficiency of this economy will depend upon (a) what are the sorts and quantities of the required products; (b) what industrial methods are employed to produce them; (c) how the 'vital cost' involved is distributed among the different producers.

The social art of consumption will aim at such application of consuming power as bestows upon the commodities the maximum of human pleasure and benefit, or vital utility, in their consumption. The efficiency of this economy will also depend upon (a) what are the sorts and quantities of the commodities; (b) what are the methods of consuming them; (s) how the vital utility is distributed among different consumers.

The organic relation between the arts of production and consumption clearly discernible in the individual may be extended to the social economy. A self-sufficing individual, if such may be conceived, with an intelligent comprehension of his real interests, would utilise all his different faculties of body and mind in proportion to their strength for the series of productive processes which he found necessary to sustain and improve these faculties, and so to realise himself in work and in enjoyment. This proportionate distribution of work would imply the minimum of strain and waste ; the proportionate variety of products it would yield would in amount and kind be naturally fitted to yield the appropriate economy of satisfaction through consumption. A large portion of his working time and energy must be devoted to manual work, partly of a routine sort, partly involving various sorts of manual and mental skill ; in the higher portions of such work the mental and moral faculties will get more exercise, and various definitely intellectual work of planning and invention and of scientific investigation will emerge. The material or immaterial products of such labours would be in kind and quality such as to sustain and stimulate the faculties employed in producing them, the enjoyment attending their consumption being a reflection of the harmony in consciousness. Both the utility got by such a man out of the food he grew, and the enjoyment of it, would be dependent on the work of producing it. 'Whosoever will not work neither shall he eat,' is not merely a moral but a physical law ; some corresponding output of physical energy in work (or some work substitute, exercise in sport) is physically necessary to the digestion of food. The development of this doctrine to the larger individual economy is obvious ; there is a natural economy of efforts and satisfactions which every intelligent man works out for himself.

In an individual living in society the distinctively individual economy must be qualified by recognition of the social aspect of each person which imposes a special contribution of energy towards the maintenance of society, a contribution which comes back to him as a member of society in social benefits. Now a social economy does not differ at all in essence from the individual economy. In both cases the art consists in distributing the productive energy of work so as to minimise the strain or waste, and in a corresponding apportionment of the product so as to sustain and stimulate the powers of work. Incidentally, though not accidentally, the maximum of enjoyment is afforded by this harmonious apportionment of products. Where the existing operation of industry imposes upon large classes of workers a continuous monotony of narrow manual toil, involving a constant strain upon certain muscular functions and atrophying all other productive activities, it not only evokes this productive energy in the most vitally expensive way, but it imposes upon them a corresponding narrowness of consumption and enjoyment, thus minimising the vital value of their wages. Similarly with the over-specialised and over-driven mental workers in our competitive machine, the excessive narrow cerebration and the neuro-asthenic condition it evokes cause a corresponding double vital loss on the producing and consuming side. As for the non-productive classes in our society, the idle upper class who need not work because others are legally compelled to work for them, the idle lower class who either cannot get work, are incapable of doing it, or prefer to live as scavengers upon society, the vital injury and loss involved in their existence belong to the natural history of parasitism.

The art of social economy in industry aims at the thorough application to the industrial system of this natural relation between production and consumption. It is, perhaps, most compactly and accurately expressed in the formula, ' From each according to his powers, to each according to his needs.' This is the organic law of distribution as applicable to the industrial system as to the animal organism. But its applicability to industry is less obvious

That the bodily organs must be fed by the alimentary system with close relation to the nature and amount of the work they severally do and the waste of tissue and output of energy involved, is self-evident, and the economy must be carried out in such detail that each cell must have its food apportioned to its waste. In the bodily organism it is evident that under normal conditions a direct and proportionate relation exists between power and needs, the greater output of energy in work constituting a greater need. This, however, must be qualified in the case of injury or disease to any organ ; there a wider organic economy displaces the narrower one and requires that the disabled part, though capable of doing no present work, shall have a larger supply of food and other organic defence placed at its disposal.

Why is it not evident that this same organic law with the same ' exception ' is applicable strictly to the industrial system regarded as part of a social organism ? The chief reason, I think, consists in the loose thinking which has been brought to bear on the application of the formula, 'From each according to his powers, to each according to his needs.' It is commonly treated not as the natural law it is, not even as a mandate of economic justice, but as a philanthropic counsel of perfection. It is supposed that normally some contradiction lies between powers and needs, and that the application of the rule would involve that those who did most work would not get most pay, or at any rate that equal pay would be given for unequal work on the ground that common humanity meant equality of needs. Yet a little reflection will show this criticism to be quite unwarranted. As our analysis of individual economy disclosed, there is a natural harmony between output of work and intake of food for the several faculties of man. The social-economic economy is the same. Normally the kind of work which takes most out of a man requires that most shall be put into him : the worker who does most work usually requires most food. In the analysis of individual and class wages we plainly recognised this harmony of production and consumption. Clearly discerned in rough muscular work, it remains applicable to all the higher forms of work : the skilled mechanic has a more complex standard of needs than the unskilled labourer, and the maintenance of his economic efficiency requires their satisfaction. Professional men and other brain-workers may have a still more complex standard of needs, corresponding to the greater delicacy of their work : their income must furnish more seclusion in the home, books and other private apparatus, opportunities for travel and wide intercourse, Though no defence of the gulf which divides the incomes of most members of the professional and employing classes from the manual workers can be based upon this natural law, it furnishes a rational justification for the maintenance both of class and individual distinctions of income. As in the physical so in the industrial organism the wider application of this natural law involves a suspension of immediate reciprocity between work and sustentation in the case of infirmity, disease, or accident. The organic economy of society requires a special provision for the needs of weak or disabled members, children, the old, the sick, the mentally or morally defective, and the unemployed; their needs are to be met not with reference to any current powers they exercise, but by an educative, curative, or preventive policy, directed, either to secure for society the use of their future powers, or to enable society to bear more easily a burden which it cannot shed.

Although the formula is usually repudiated as either a revolutionary or a perfectionist humanitarian doctrine, it is worthy of observation that the theory of individualistic distribution conforms to it. The operation of the *laissez faire* competitive economy rests on the assumption that economic stimuli are applied so as to evoke productive energy from each according to his powers ; while it is claimed that the apportionment of the product which ensues is ' according to needs;' including under needs the economic stimuli to production. Moreover the *laissez faire* economy usually admits the legitimate operation of ' charity ' to supply exceptional needs which are either temporarily or permanently divorced from any corresponding powers,

§ 5.—Our criticism of the operation of the present industrial system as an instrument of social economy is that it works too wastefully: it does not evoke productive energy ' according to powers;' nor does it distribute the product ' according to needs.' The ' surplus ' is at once the measure and the instrument of this waste. Its injury is three-fold. First, as unearned individual income not merely does it fail to support or stimulate productive effort, but it diverts individual energies into non-productive channels, atrophies socially serviceable activities, and substitutes either a life of idleness or one of frivolous and socially injurious activity. Surplus acts on its recipients as an inhibition upon labour.

Secondly, so far as it represents the result of sweating, rack-renting, or other processes of oppressive bargaining, it injures the productivity of labour by robbing the labouring classes of their natural stimulus to progressive efficiency.

Thirdly, by enabling individuals to take for their private income what is produced by society and is required to satisfy the needs of social life, it damages the efficiency of the state and of the public services it is called upon to render.

The subjective interpretation of the surplus would furnish a complete analysis of the waste of life involved in the defective working of the industrial system, both in respect of the distribution of work and of its product.

For wherever an inequality of bargaining-power yielded to the stronger some unearned gain, it would be seen that this involved the imposition of a wasteful or excessive vital cost upon some producer, while at the same time it damaged the vital efficiency of its recipient by enabling and so inducing him to consume without producing, thus injuring both his powers of work and of enjoyment.

Through the injurious operation of the surplus, again, we can best comprehend the degraded and degrading character of so large a proportion of the work and of the enjoyment in modern industrial society.   Sweating and luxury, the opposed aspects of the surplus, are directly responsible for large masses of debased demand whose evil character is stamped upon the processes of production.   From the under-pay of the poorer grades of workers issues the demand for bad materials, clumsy manual or cheap machine work, which evoke and sustain many of the worst conditions of labour both in factories and workshops, while the capricious nature, the foolish, frivolous, and often directly noxious character of the luxuries, to the demand for which so much ' surplus ' necessarily goes, are reflected in the industries which produce them, and in the character and tastes of those employed in these industries.

The significance of the direct interaction of production and consumption in determining the quality and so the vital worth of work, the quality and so the vital worth of wealth, can only be understood by watching these injurious results of the 'surplus,' and by considering how the absorption of this ' surplus ' and its better application to personal efficiency and social service might improve the character of work and of enjoyment.   Health, education, security, these three great departments of the ' public good,' adequately administered by society, would, by their reaction upon the standard of life in all classes of the community, so change the relative valuations of wealth, and so operate through changed demands upon industry, as to produce an incalculably great increase of subjective or real wealth.

The operation would be through human interests and tastes upon the arts of industry.   For health, education, and security will individualise the character, develop a varied personality in each, and give free play to all the faculties to seek the activities and enjoyments which belong to them.   This individuation and variety of needs will create a corresponding character in the productive work required for their satisfaction.   Thus a coarse quantitative economy, favouring the excessive dominion of monotony and mechanism, yields to a more qualitative economy of adaptive variety and human art. As the surplus, rightly utilised in improved conditions of labour and in improved social services, expands and elevates the character of the individual citizen, custom and routine will lose force as regulative influences in his life, personal tastes and particularity of wants will find expression through an ampler and securer income. This will mean an increased operation of art in industry, for every satisfaction of an individual want involves some conscious skill of adaptation in the productive processes. When a sense of personal dignity requires well-fitting clothes, it demands a skilled fitter and cutter, and so it is with every other element, material or non-material, in a standard of comfort. From each improvement in the personal standard of life due to a better utilisation of the surplus will come some related improvement in the standard of work. Mechanical routine will not disappear from industry, but upon the several mechanical processes a superstructure of skilled work will be imposed. This lightening of the mechanical burden of toil, and the corresponding increase of skilled and interesting work, means a reduction in the vital cost of production as well as an increased enjoyment of the product. Nor is that all. Every improvement of industry in the form of new elements of skill and human interest reacts again upon the worker in his capacity of consumer, stimulating his intelligence and taste, and so helping once more to improve industry. There is no limit to this interaction in the arts of production and consumption : each gain is a double gain, reducing some vital cost of work while it increases some vital utility of enjoyment.

The ideal of this progressive economy is an industrial system in which the intrinsically interesting work shall be at a maximum and the burden of routine toil at a minimum. The improved distribution of work and income attendant on an equitable disposal of the surplus would, as we see, reduce the proportion and the absolute amount of purely mechanical or unskilled toil. But in any industrial system a great deal of monotonous and uninteresting labour must remain. The notion that all or nearly all the burden of toil can either be displaced by interesting labour or can be shifted on to the shoulders of machinery is quite chimerical. Some 'costs' of production in the shape of hard, uninteresting, and even repulsive work cannot be evaded. But in as far as such work is distributed 'according to the powers' of the workers, not falling with excessive burden upon certain individuals and classes, the pain or subjective cost will be minimised. Translating industry into terms of true individual and social welfare, we may even go further and recognise that some amount of dull mechanical labour, both of hand and brain, is a useful discipline and exercise for man and plays a serviceable part in the progress of society. But, in general, every rise in the standard of consumption and production will signify an increasing individuation, personal skill, intelligence and interest in productive work. The final meaning of this progress is a transformation not merely of the character but of the conception of the industrial system. If every man had no more work to do than ' was good for him,' if most of his work was interesting to him and was not prolonged unduly or performed under stress, and if such work as was uninteresting was safe and served as exercise or discipline to muscles, brain, and will, the product of industry might be got at a vital cost trifling when compared with that actually paid even in the best-ordered industrial society of to-day.

The supreme significance of such a reformed economy would consist in the practical assimilation or identification of production and consumption, work and enjoyment. This identification is actually achieved in what we term the fine arts, where the satisfaction and interest of creative achievement is at its maximum. The final harmony of industry is reached when we see a worker who lives in and for his work, who expresses himself freely and joyfully in it, and who is at one and the same time producer and consumer. Though only a small proportion of total industry can be raised into harmony upon this level, it is by an increasing measure of this transfusion of values that the qualitative as distinct from the quantitative progress of industry can be estimated.

There is, however, no reason for eliminating quantitative growth from our conception of economic progress. The proper absorption of the surplus for its right purpose as the food of industrial efficiency would not only bring a better application, but an enlarged volume of productive power. Improved distribution of income with enhanced security of life would establish a full and regular demand for the employment of all productive powers, so that the quantity of the product of industry would be increased as well as the quality improved. Expressed in economic formula the social progress thus achieved would mean (1) a larger production of objective wealth, (2) a smaller vital cost per unit of the increased product, (3) a larger vital utility per unit.

INDEX

335

THE END